Pulling the Devil's Kingdom Down

Pulling the Devil's Kingdom Down

The Salvation Army in Victorian Britain

Pamela J. Walker

UNIVERSITY OF CALIFORNIA PRESS
Berkeley · Los Angeles · London

University of California Press
Berkeley and Los Angeles, California

University of California Press, Ltd.

London, England

Library of Congress Cataloging-in-Publication Data

Walker, Pamela J., 1960–.
    Pulling the devil's kingdom down : the Salvation
Army in Victorian Britain / Pamela J. Walker.
        p.   cm.
    Includes bibliographical references and index.
    ISBN 0-520-22591-0 (alk. paper).
    1. Salvation Army—Great Britain—History.
2. Great Britain—Church history—19th century.
I. Title.
BX9719.G7 W35   2001
287.9'6'094109034—dc21   00-055166

Manufactured in Canada

9 8 7 6 5 4 3 2 1
10 9 8 7 6 5 4 3 2 1

The paper used in this publication is both acid-free
and totally chlorine-free. It meets the minimum
requirements of ANSI / NISO Z39 0.48-1992
(R 1997) (*Permanence of Paper*).

For my mother,
Elizabeth Walker

Contents

Illustrations

Acknowledgments

This book began as a doctoral dissertation at Rutgers University, where I had the good fortune to be a graduate student. I would like to thank all my fellow students and the faculty for providing me with an intellectual environment that was at once challenging and nurturing. My Ph.D. supervisor, Judith R. Walkowitz, was an outstanding teacher, and she continued to read my work long after I ceased to be her student. Her advice, insights, and criticism improved this book in countless ways. For all of this help she deserves a tambourine of her own. The other members of my dissertation committee, Leonore Davidoff, John R. Gillis, Phyllis Mack, and Peter Mandler, were generous with their time and advice, and they greatly enriched this book. A fellowship from the Charlotte Newcombe Foundation supported the last year of my graduate studies; I am immensely grateful for the freedom it allowed me and also for the foundation's confidence in my work.

Major Jenty Fairbank, Mr. Gordon Taylor, and the staff at the Salvation Army Heritage Centre, London, were always kind, generous, and efficient. They made research pleasant as well as productive. Because I am not a Salvationist, Salvationists will not always share my view of their organization, but I hope this book will make a contribution to a wider understanding and appreciation of the Salvation Army's history. I am also grateful to the staff of the British Library, in particular Mr. R. Smith of the Manuscripts Collection, and to the members of the staff at Lambeth Palace Library, London; Churchill College, Cambridge University;

Queen Mary and Westfield College, the University of London; the Public Records Office, London; and the John Rylands University Library, Manchester. Mr. Michael Diamond and Mr. Max Tyler are the holders of two extraordinary collections of music-hall material. They both generously allowed me to look through their collections of Salvation Army songs and illustrations and answered my many questions. Their kindness made this a better, and funnier, book.

I am thankful for the research support from the dean of arts and from the dean of graduate studies and research, Carleton University, over several years. During 1993–94, I was a visiting research associate with the Women's Studies in Religion Program at the Divinity School, Harvard University. Thanks to Constance Buchanan and everyone associated with the program for providing such a stimulating intellectual environment. In particular, Beverly Mayne Kienzle, who asked me to co-edit a book on women's preaching, greatly enhanced my understanding of the wider historical context of my research, made collaboration a pleasure, and encouraged me at key moments.

The enthusiasm and expertise of my editor at the University of California Press, Stan Holwitz, have made this project a pleasure. Laura Pasquale and Rose Anne White guided the book through production efficiently and with good humor. Pamela Fischer provided excellent copy editing.

Many friends read and discussed chapters with me, and I am so grateful for their time and invaluable criticism. They are Polly Beals, Ian Christopher Fletcher, Michael Anthon Budd, Scott Cook, David Dean, Andrew Davies, Joy Dixon, Gretchen Galbraith, Deborah Gorham, Janet Larson, Mary Catherine Moran, Barbara Robinson, Tori Smith, David Scrimshaw, Lillian Taiz, Susan Tananbaum, Deborah Valenze, Rachel Weil, and Susan Whitney. In addition, three anonymous readers from the University of California gave excellent advice. Frank Hardy guided me through the British census returns and offered me important advice on the use of other sources. He, and the late Noelle Hardy, did much to make my time in London happy. Ellen Ross, Dorothy Thompson, and Peter Bailey each helped with difficult research problems and shared their extensive knowledge of British history with me. When I telephoned Jerry White with only a vague introduction and many questions about nineteenth-century occupations, he invited me over for dinner and proceeded to classify all the occupational data in Chapter 3. Many thanks for his kindness. Allison Bennett helped me understand many puzzling features of English life and made me feel at home in London. Brenda Clarke enabled me to begin this project, and she always made the process fun. Jonathan Burston's friendship has sustained me throughout. Jayne Mitchell gave me the beautiful pen I used to write the entire book. Her love and the company of Ron, Laura, Benjamin, and Owen Mitchell have been indispensable. My extended family has taken a great interest in this book, and I have always appreciated their enthusiasm. I look forward to the time the newest members of my family, Emily and Ethan Miller, learn to read so they can enjoy this book. My friends at The Living Room at the AIDS Committee of Ottawa allowed me to witness the power of faith and struggle, enriching my life and deepening my appreciation of the issues raised in this book. Historian and archivist Peter Dervis shared many an hour enlightening me about Salvation Army uniforms as well as lifting my spirits. Donald Dervis provided many delightful diversions from writing, and I am thankful for his generosity and affection. My partner, Paul Dervis, contributed to this book in so many ways. His practical advice on writing allowed me to overcome many difficulties, and his unwavering confidence in this project enabled me to finish it. Introducing me to the Red Sox, late-twentieth-century theater, and Garci Mac-Charles made life altogether better, and his love has enriched everything. Our daughter, Esmé Charlotte Dervis, was born on Catherine Booth's 171st birthday, just as I completed this book. Her sparkling smile made proofreading much easier, and I look forward to sharing the next research project with her. My mother, Elizabeth Walker, instilled in us a love of books and ideas and always encouraged us to think and act independently. Her example of service and activism is an inspiration. This book is dedicated to her, with love and gratitude.

Introduction

Salvation Soldiers live to fight,
Oh yes! oh yes!
Against the Devil with all their might,
Fight in Jesus' name!
"Down with wrong" our Soldiers cry,
Oh, yes! oh, yes!
To lift up Christ we live or die,
Glory to His Name![1]

Marching in scarlet sweaters emblazoned with the words *Salvation Army*, crowds sang these words to the tune of "Camptown Races" as they passed through the bustling streets of England's working-class neighborhoods. With brass instruments blaring and tambourines shaking, they preached holiness in front of pubs and on street corners, calling on all to come and be saved. Today, the Salvation Army is widely known as a charitable organization, and its red kettles are a familiar sight to holiday shoppers. *Major Barbara* and *Guys and Dolls* supply the prevailing images of its past. But the Salvation Army's origins and its contribution to the changing religious and social culture of Victorian Britain are seldom known or appreciated.

This movement, founded by William and Catherine Booth, began as the East London Christian Mission in 1865. The Booths, along with a small group of associates, preached in the streets of the East End and in rented halls. In 1878, its mission stations were found not only in London but along the south coast, in the Midlands, and in the north, with 127 paid evangelists and 700 voluntary workers. That same year, it adopted the name *Salvation Army*. Its distinctive uniforms, ranks, and military vocabulary; its tracts, called *Hallelujah Torpedoes;* and its prayer services, known as knee drill, followed. In 1884, the Salvation Army employed 1,644 officers to run its 637 corps, as its missions stations were then called, and it engaged other officers in its growing mission to the Empire.[2] Its members were overwhelmingly working class.[3]

The Salvation Army was a neighborhood religion. It invented a battle plan that was especially suited to urban working-class geography and cultural life. Religious words were sung to music-hall tunes; circus posters and theater announcements were copied so closely that observers often failed to distinguish them; preachers imitated the idiom of street vendors; and congregations were encouraged to shout out responses to the preacher, much as they might in the music halls. Salvationists culled techniques from contemporary advertising and revivalism. Their military language aptly expressed Salvationists' command to do battle with the enemy. The Army regarded pubs, music halls, sports, and betting as its principal rivals, yet its ability to use popular leisure activities as its inspiration was a major facet in its success. Equally important was Salvationists' ability to mine an older Nonconformist radicalism through which they were able to express their spiritual vision and respond to their opponents.

The Salvation Army disrupted and refashioned gender relations in many facets of its work. The Hallelujah Lasses, as Salvationist women were known, embraced the opportunity the Army provided to challenge and resist the conventions of femininity and enhance women's spiritual authority. Their claiming the "right to preach" disrupted a powerful source of masculine privilege and authority. The Hallelujah Lasses preached, gave communion, and handled all the spiritual and practical demands of a corps. Virtually no other secular or religious organization in this period offered working-class women such extensive authority. Salvationist men, in turn, testified that the Army offered them a new way of conducting themselves as men. Before, they had spent all their time and money on beer and betting, thinking it was the "manly" thing. The words of the preachers transformed them. The Holy Spirit moved them to claim a new masculinity that eschewed drinking and betting in favor of being part of a community of women and men devoted to evangelizing others. This activity, they testified, was truly manly.

By the 1880s, Salvationists were a common sight in working-class neighborhoods, and other Christians began to comment on this dynamic organization. Many regarded the Army as a serious threat to wider Christian efforts to evangelize and civilize the working class. They argued that using music-hall tunes destroyed reverence for the sacred and that female preachers excited the humble to self-importance and thereby wreaked havoc in the church and the family. Sermons condemned Salvationist belief and practice, while newspaper and journal articles debated how Christians ought best to contain this movement. At times, Salvationists also met with sustained opposition from the communities they hoped to convert. Men declared their masculine culture of pubs and sports to be threatened, and others objected to women's preaching or the Army's ecstatic worship. When Salvationists preached in the streets, gangs pelted them with food and old shoes, drowned out the voices of the preachers, and attacked the processions. Salvationists became stock figures of fun in music halls, popular theater, and comic magazines. These battles are critical to an understanding of working-class religiosity and culture more broadly.[4] The Salvation Army is a significant example of a movement formed expressly to oppose the staid complacency of other Christians and nonbelievers. While it certainly did not succeed in converting the "heathen masses," it did spread its message to women and men who rarely were found in the churches or chapels.[5]

The Salvation Army has received scant attention from scholars. Its place in Victorian working-class communities, its relationship to the women's movement, its innovative use of popular and commercial culture, and its integration of Methodism, revivalism, and holiness have not been explored. This neglect is, in no small part, due to the preeminence of two issues in the literature on religion in Victorian England: secularization and the relationship between religion and working-class politics. Debates about secularization have a long history. The 1851 religious census linked urbanization and working-class irreligion, shaping the way the Church and chapels attempted to reach out to the working class. Most clergy believed their efforts to be in vain. They despaired over the souls of England's urban working class and the consequences of their irreligion for the well being of the nation. Their perspective was well documented in sermons, the periodical press, and the organizational records of the many agencies established to evangelize the working class. Charles Booth's London surveys also found that religious observance was uncommon among the working class.[6] One school of historians that has attended to that perspective has chronicled the failure of the churches to reach the working class and has proposed a number of explanations to account for its alienation. Equally influential, a large sociological literature has theorized a general relationship among urbanization, modernization, and secularization.[7] These accounts would therefore view religious organizations like the Salvation Army as archaic and its evangelists as struggling to revitalize what was already moribund.

A second approach to Victorian religion proceeded from the influential work of social historians E. P. Thompson and E. J. Hobsbawm. Thompson, in his now-famous words, sought "to rescue the poor stockinger, the Luddite cropper, the 'obsolete' hand-loom weaver, the 'utopian' artisan, and even the deluded follower of Joanna Southcott, from the enormous condescension of posterity." Despite Thompson's ground-breaking celebration of the dreams and achievements of laboring people, which had long been dismissed, he accuses Methodists of remaking working people through "indoctrination, the Methodist community sense, and the psychic consequences of counter revolution." Methodism was the "chiliasm of despair," taken up by workers defeated by the onslaught of industrial capitalism.[8] . Hobsbawm had a more positive evaluation of Methodism's effect, arguing that it stimulated an independent workers' political consciousness and helped to build trade unionism and labor politics.[9]

Thompson's and Hobsbawm's studies raised provocative questions and inspired decades of historical scholarship that examined the relationship between working-class religion and politics. Their work continues to influence historical scholarship, including this book.[10] Still, this perspective leaves many questions unasked. When religion is assumed to be politically quietist, historians of working-class culture and politics regard it as external to working-class community life. If religious institutions contribute to the growth of working-class consciousness, then religion is merely a steppingstone to more significant political organizing. As Deborah Valenze has argued, "Political consciousness is often seen as the enlightened heir to religion, finally enabling the less powerful to shake off the control of hegemonic classes."[11] From this point of view, Salvationists could be seen as deluded fanatics or socially ambitious individuals who hoped to gain a veneer of respectability from a religious affiliation.[12] At best, the Salvation Army might provide laboring people with organizational skills and self-confidence that could be harnessed for more socially valuable ends. The Salvation Army as a movement; its theology, rituals, and beliefs; and its response to the struggles of working-class men and women in the neighborhoods it evangelized remain unexamined.

Much of the literature on the Salvation Army has been written by members of the organization and published by it. The six-volume *History of the Salvation Army* contains a wealth of detail. But it is an institutional history, and it lacks a critical perspective or a sense of the wider historical context.[13] Biographies of leading Salvationists are plentiful. They are rich in detail but tend to justify rather than analyze the Booths' work.[14] Two scholarly histories of the Salvation Army—Glenn Horridge, *The Salvation Army, Origins and Early Days: 1865–1900*, and Norman Murdoch, *Origins of the Salvation Army*—offer a more critical and analytical perspective than the Salvation Army's own publications, but both are based on a narrow body of sources and are thus limited in the questions they address.[15] Scholars of Victorian religion, notably K. S. Inglis and Hugh McLeod, have considered the Salvation Army as one movement within the wider context of Victorian religious culture.[16] John Kent, *Holding the Fort: Studies in Victorian Revivalism*, by examining the revivalist and holiness movements in England, provides the historical context for the Booths' theology.[17] Victor Bailey has explored the anti-Salvation Army riots and the Salvation Army's relationship to the labor movement.[18] Dean Rapp has documented that the Salvation Army was among the first religious organizations to make its own films and to use film as an attraction at its meetings.[19]

This book proposes a new approach to the Salvation Army. Studies of working-class urban religion, gender, and popular culture and previously unexamined archival sources shed a different light on the Salvation Army's history, suggesting new questions that earlier studies neglected. Scholars have now challenged the link between urbanization and secularization, for cities were, in some instances, replete with successful missionary opportunities.[20] McLeod, in his *Piety and Poverty*, reveals the immense complexity of the relationship between urbanization and religiosity, particularly when three cities are compared. McLeod notes that while an "extensive historical literature" has explored the alienation of the working class from the churches, "the picture presented in this literature has often been exaggerated and over-simplified. In particular, too little account has been taken of gender differences. It has also been too readily assumed that non-churchgoers were irreligious."[21]

Like McLeod, Callum Brown argues that historians have relied too much on limited sources and too readily accepted the secularization thesis. He argues, "The industrial worker, as often as not, is the silent player whose story of alienation from religion the cleric berates, the intellectual applauds and the historian sympathetically chronicles."[22] Brown argues against the notion that the nineteenth century was a period of religious decline. He asserts that "as the British working class evolved in the nineteenth century, religion became a major element in its culture and values." Historian Sarah Williams has proposed that "the time has come to historize the concept of secularisation like the notion of social class and to see it as a part of the discourse which we are engaged in studying rather than as an objective historical process."[23]

This scholarship is particularly important because the Salvation Army was a creation of urban life. Salvationists eagerly seized on the particular opportunities for evangelizing that cities offered. Their theology and practice were deeply influenced by urban culture and social relations. The Salvation Army never succeeded in converting the majority of working-class women and men, but it was neither marginal nor archaic but rather an expression of wider cultural trends. Salvationists did convince upward of three thousand people to crowd into London halls on weeknights in the 1880s, and twenty thousand people met at Alexandra Palace in 1887 to celebrate its anniversary. Its notoriety and success were a result of an ability to utilize urban working-class culture for its own ends. The Salvation Army offers a particularly rich body of conversion stories, theological disputes, and battle plans from these working-class Christians engaged in a dynamic, growing movement.

Faith was at the center of the Salvationist experience. Every aspect of Salvationists' activity and belief—including the ecstatic conversions that Salvationists strived for, the conviction that women had a right to preach, and the willingness to face attacks from clergy or street gangs—expressed deeply felt religious convictions. Yet so much of the history of working-class religiosity fails to explore belief and faith. Historians of other periods have written rich, nuanced studies of popular religious belief; the conviction that these societies were religious ones justifies such close attention to questions of belief.[24] But scholars have assumed just the opposite about Victorian working-class culture. Salvationists, however, were religious, and to understand the movement we must attend to the sources and meaning of that faith.

The persistence of older religious traditions can be discerned in the Salvation Army.[25] Salvationists also drew on urban, commercial culture, militarism, and holiness to articulate their religious vision. The Army converts participated in a religious experience that cannot be reduced to denominational membership. That experience, or belief, was shaped by the exchange between Salvationist theology and the cultural world in which Salvationists evangelized. Understanding how Salvationists fashioned a religious organization and created meaning within its boundaries and practices sheds light on this one organization and also more widely on the question of working-class belief and moral subjectivity.

Salvationists provide a rich opportunity to explore working-class perceptions of gender, spirituality, community, and social change. They were a part of diverse working-class communities, and their activities and concerns reflected that participation. Salvationists addressed domestic violence and marital relations; they worked with "fallen women" and agitated the government about laws concerning prostitution. Work in the Army offered new professional opportunities to thousands of women, and the Army was widely recognized as an innovator in women's employment. Salvationists were concerned with literacy, education, and oral fluency. They reviled popular leisure pursuits and fashioned their own alternatives. Salvationists' perspective on all these issues was particular, and it could be a vexed one. Salvationists believed that prayer and the presence of the Holy Spirit were powerful, effective means to create personal and social change. On the one hand, elites agreed with Salvationists' Christian faith, but, on the other hand, they despaired of the effect these ardent evangelists might have on the nation's religious life. While Salvationists' intense evangelicalism distinguished them from many working-class people, their language and theology were consistent with commonly held beliefs about nature and the spiritual world, beliefs that many middle-class evangelicals did not share. Neither fully part of nor estranged from either world-view, Salvationists strived to ignite a revival in the hearts of all. The Salvation Army never included more than a small percentage of overall church members, but its strategies and faith were an authentic and complicated expression of religiosity in an urban working-class context.[26]

ONE

The Roots of the Salvation Army

The Booths, Methodism, and Female Ministry

William and Catherine Booth yearned to rescue all the souls rushing to hell. Their encounter with holiness and revivalism convinced them that staid formality would crush any attempt to save souls and that the silence imposed on women could only harm their cause. The Booths' impatience with conferences and committees disposed them to fashion the Army with a strict order of command. The tambourines, music-hall tunes, uniformed preachers, and ecstatic services of the Salvation Army caused a sensation among believers and nonbelievers alike. The Army quickly grew to include thousands of officers and soldiers, but its origins may be traced to William and Catherine Booth, whose influence and power remained decisive well into the twentieth century.

The movement the Booths founded was shaped by their own religious and personal concerns. Their commitment to Methodism and their disenchantment with its rules and restrictions shaped the theology and practice of the Christian Mission and the Salvation Army. Their encounter with revivalism and holiness theology influenced how they evangelized. Equally important were William's and Catherine's family backgrounds, class position, and the evangelical partnership they forged in their marriage.

Among the most significant and groundbreaking features of the Salvation Army was the unusual prominence and authority of women. Catherine Booth was the decisive intellectual and practical influence on this unique status Salvationist women enjoyed. She exemplified a new model of Christian womanhood, articulating a new approach to female ministry and creating an influential career as an evangelist. As well as formulating the Salvation Army's egalitarian policies, she served as an inspiration to thousands of young women who preached under the aegis of the organization. She built on a foundation laid by radical, plebeian Methodist women early in the century and demonstrated the continued significance of that tradition for women's rights advocates even until the last decades of the nineteenth century. Her assertion of women's *right* to preach the gospel disrupted a powerful sphere of masculine privilege while opening a reconsideration of women's spiritual and practical authority. Her theology and her own preaching had a profound effect on the beliefs and practices that were to distinguish the Salvation Army from its contemporaries and that would gain it a large following as well as sustained criticism. The Salvation Army's history must begin with the religious culture, theological concerns, and individual lives of William and Catherine Booth.

CATHERINE'S METHODIST CHILDHOOD

Catherine Mumford Booth was born in 1829 at Ashbourne, Derbyshire. Her father, John Mumford, was a coach builder, a skilled artisan. He and his wife, Sarah Milward Mumford, were members of a Wesleyan Methodist chapel where John was a lay preacher. Religion was at the center of young Catherine's life, and she shared this intense faith with her mother. Mrs. Mumford, wishing to shield her daughter from worldly influences, allowed few friends and no frivolous pastimes. She carefully oversaw her daughter's education. Catherine attended school briefly, but in 1843 she was confined to bed with curvature of the spine and fell ill soon after with consumption. During those years of enforced solitude, Catherine read widely, especially theologians like Charles Finney and John Wesley as well as spiritual biographies. By age twelve she had read the Bible cover to cover eight times.[1] She was a serious, devout child. Her cousin asked her one Sunday to guess the price of her new boots, and Catherine was mortified by her own failure to refuse her cousin's game.[2]

In her 1847–48 diary, written when she went to Brighton in an attempt to recover her health, Catherine recorded her moments of despair crossed with feelings of faith. A letter from her mother "made me weep tears of joy as soon as I had read it; . . . she is the dearest earthly idol of my heart but now she is dearer still."[3] She longed for her mother and knew her mother missed her; still she hoped God would enable her mother "to lay her child upon the altar of thy cross and say thy will be done."

She also reflected that her loneliness provided an important discipline. Since their separation, "I draw more from the Fountain."[4] Later, she wrote, "I have felt much cast down at the thought of being from home when I so much need its comforts and away from my Dear Mother; . . . we shall soon meet again and after all our meetings and parting on earth we shall meet to part no more in Glory."[5]

The firm and enduring faith that infused Catherine's and Mrs. Mumford's lives set them apart from the men in their lives. Mrs. Mumford expressly chose a husband who shared her religious convictions, and his skill should have promised her a secure place in a community of respectable artisans. But John Mumford lost his faith in the early 1840s. He began to drink heavily, and his subsequent irregular employment caused his family considerable economic difficulty. His wife and daughter, moreover, worried about the state of his soul. In February 1848, Catherine wrote in her diary, "My dear father is a great trial to us."[6] Over the following decades, he stopped drinking for short periods, but sobriety never lasted. On her 1869 death certificate, Sarah Mumford was listed as a widow, although John Mumford lived another twelve years; this entry on her death certificate suggests that they did not live together during the later years of their lives.[7] Catherine's only sibling, John, born in 1833, emigrated to the United States in 1849. She never mentioned him in her diary and only rarely in her correspondence. Her infrequent comments make it clear she counted him among the unsaved. He signed the pledge and declared himself saved several times, but he always fell away again and took to drink.[8] Catherine's ardent belief in the faithfulness and righteousness of women, which she expressed so frequently in her later writings, was first apprehended in her own family.

The emotional tenor of this mother-daughter relationship corresponded to nineteenth-century evangelical expectations. Mid-nineteenth-century evangelicals elevated motherhood and intensified the importance of the mother in a child's spiritual life. Mothers were often regarded as the most powerful guides to piety. One evangelical in the United States, writing in 1836, proclaimed that of all those who bring souls to Christ "none have higher claims than mother."[9] Similarly, Susan Warner's *Wide, Wide World* (1850), a bestselling novel of its day, articulates a "feminine theology" in which the mother's love is the earthly example of God's love and heaven is imagined as the place of the final reunion of mother and daughter.[10] This novel, the only one Catherine ever mentioned in her extensive correspondence, expressed a theology and an emotional universe similar to the one young Catherine described in her journal. That theology not only encouraged a particular emotional relationship to one's mother but made motherhood singularly important, a power that could potentially displace patriarchal authority. Although the church's doctrine and regulations excluded women from office and determined what a mother could teach, it did allow mothers a unique and instrumental role in the creation of a community of the faithful. Sectarian Methodist women preachers were often called "Mothers in Israel," a name that linked the domestic and spiritual while celebrating pious mothers as nurturers, protectors, and guides. The absence of a masculine equivalent emphasizes that this was a role only women could fill.[11]

In the Mumford family piety and righteousness were female virtues. Methodism offered women an unusual opportunity to exercise these virtues in institutional ways. All Methodists joined classes, where members prayed aloud and spoke of their spiritual experiences. Members could advise each other on spiritual difficulties and benefit from hearing the testimony of others. The Wesleyans encouraged women to sing, pray, testify to their experiences, and eventually to lead classes.[12] The class meeting was an important starting point for Catherine. When she was seventeen, her class leader insisted that she overcome her excessive timidity and begin to pray aloud in class meetings. Methodists not only spoke to believers but sought out the unregenerate. When she was still in her teens, Catherine began to speak and to correspond with her cousins and friends, trying to lead them to religious conviction.[13] The high degree of women's participation in Methodism's formal structure, the importance of individual testimony, and the emphasis on converting others gave Catherine confidence in her own ability to speak in public and in the general efficacy of women's prayers and testimonies.

Methodist women provided Catherine with examples of female preaching and public ministry. John Wesley, the founder of Methodism, argued that women were forbidden to preach as a rule but exceptions could be made for women with an extraordinary calling. A number of Methodist women, notably Mary Bousanquet Fletcher, Sarah Crosby, Mary Barritt Taft, and Ann Cutler, preached to female and mixed audiences with great effect during the later decades of the eighteenth century and the early decades of the nineteenth century. Ann Cutler (1759–1794) was from a poor Lancashire family engaged in cottage industry. Her biographer wrote that "as she laboured with her hands, she would retire twelve or fourteen times a day for a few minutes of scripture reading and prayer."[14] Her preaching, sharp, loud, and direct, was credited with bringing many souls to salvation.[15] Mary Barritt (1772–1851) received encouragement from Ann Cutler and began itinerant preaching in the Yorkshire Revival of 1792. She married Zachariah Taft in 1802 and preached with him at his Dover Circuit. The Dover Methodists were appalled by her activities and her husband's unwavering support of her work.

This controversy foreshadowed what was to come. The Wesleyan Connexion, the organizational body of this branch of Methodism, forbade preaching by women in 1803. This decision hastened the creation of the Methodist sects, including the Primitive Methodists and Bible Christians and others that supported women's ministry. These sectarians promoted apocalyptic fervor and emotional revivals over the orderly practices of institutional religion. They organized all-day gatherings where, instead of listening to sermons, participants spoke of their spiritual experiences each in turn. Female preaching was associated with these revivals. To the elite leadership of the Wesleyan Connexion these women, drawn almost exclusively from the laboring classes, were deeply offensive. Their direct, unadorned vernacular speech, emotional fervor, and independence were hardly examples of appropriate feminine decorum and submission. And their activities were outside the control of the male chapel administration.[16] Nevertheless, many were drawn to the sectarian Methodists. At least six women preached in Derbyshire, where the Mumfords lived during the 1820s.[17] The particular religious culture in which Catherine was raised helped to shape her intellectual and social life by providing examples of laboring people creating their own religious language and practice. Because Methodist women enjoyed an unusual degree of spiritual authority within both domestic and public realms, Catherine had an important foundation for her own work. She strived to revitalize that legacy throughout her life.

CREATING AN EVANGELICAL PARTNERSHIP

In 1851, a controversy broke out among the Wesleyans that was to have a profound effect on the subsequent careers of Catherine Mumford and William Booth (see Figures 1 and 2). The debate concerned the exercise of Connexional authority and discipline. Jabez Bunting, president of the Connexion, said, "Methodism hates democracy as it hates sin."[18] Yet many doubted that the Connexion's regulations and structure worked in the best interests of the members. This problem became acutely evident in 1842, when Methodist James Caughey arrived in England from

the United States and commenced work as an itinerant preacher. Many
were impressed with his ability to effect conversions with his revivalist
preaching, and he was soon a household name among English Methodists.[19] The Wesleyans' governing body, however, disliked his irregular
methods and asked the Americans to call him home. Two days later, superintendents were forbidden to hire Caughey or any other itinerant who
worked outside the Connexion's discipline.[20] Many Methodists believed
these decisions meant that the desire for rules and orders had surpassed
the hunger for souls. Discontent lingered. Finally in 1849, an anonymous
author published the "Fly Sheets," a series of pamphlets denouncing the
leadership as slothful, tyrannical, and indifferent to what the Connexion required in order to grow and prosper. When investigators failed to
discover the authors, the leaders expelled three prominent men believed
to be responsible. Many laypeople thought to be sympathetic to the authors were also expelled.[21]

Catherine was living in Brixton, a suburb of London where the Mumfords had moved in 1845. She was dissatisfied with the Wesleyans at Brixton, finding them cold and formal, unlike the ardent believers she once
knew. She later recalled, "I can remember often leaving chapel burdened
at heart that more had not been achieved of a practical character."[22] Instead of using prayer meetings to help people on the verge of a decision,
Brixton Wesleyans conducted meetings in an orderly, half-hearted fashion, and people were left to find their own way. Not surprisingly, her
sympathies lay with Caughey and his associates. Her quarterly ticket of
membership was denied in 1852.[23] She soon joined the Reformers, a loose
body of men and women who had also left the Wesleyans because of
this controversy and who wanted a more democratic structure with more
zealous members. This move occasioned her first meeting with William
Booth.

William Booth was born in 1829 at Snenton, a suburb of Nottingham. Less is known about William's early life than about Catherine's because no diaries or letters from that period of his life have been found.
His mother, Mary Moss, was the daughter of a laborer and hawker. She
worked as a domestic servant until she married Samuel Booth in 1824.
He made a living at a variety of trades, including work as a nailer and
builder. Samuel Booth apprenticed his son William to a pawnbroker in
1843. This apprenticeship represented a certain move up the class lad-
der for the family. In 1843, Samuel Booth died leaving his widow dependent on her son for support.[24] Little is known of the family's religious life. William joined a Wesleyan chapel and was fully saved at age

fifteen. He began to preach in the streets of Nottingham soon after. Like
Catherine, William found ample opportunity among the Methodists to
develop his considerable preaching skills.

In 1849, William moved to London, where he again worked for a
pawnbroker. In a letter to a friend in Nottingham written shortly after
his arrival in London, he wrote:

> Our shop is uncommonly pleasantly situated no shop in Nottingham the equal
> to it; . . . we have prayers every evening. We gather round the table and sing
> a hymn. Master then reads a chapter and afterwards prays, all this is to me
> very agreeable. . . . Far away am I removed from the Society in which I was
> so delighted with never a friend with whom to hold sweet communion yet my
> trust is in the bleeding Lamb both now and evermore I am determined to stand
> by the cross.[25]

William soon became active in a London Wesleyan chapel. Influential
Methodists began to notice this energetic and devout young man. The
Reformers required preachers for their new chapels and offered to engage William as a full-time preacher for 20 shillings a week. William
agreed.

William and Catherine were serious Christians, their religious convictions informing every aspect of their lives. Their sense of religious purpose is revealed in a letter Catherine wrote to William just before their
engagement in 1852. "If you feel satisfied on these two points, first that
the step is not opposed to the will of God and secondly that I am calculated to make you happy come on Saturday evening and on our knees
before God let us give ourselves afresh to Him and to each other for His
sake, consecrate our whole selves to His service, *for Him to live and to
die.*"[26] The relationship was a romantic one, and they wrote long, detailed, and loving letters during their frequent separations. In 1855
Catherine wrote, "I dreamt about you last night. I thought I was reading to you sitting on your knee, and you looked into my eyes with a look
of unutterable affection and drew me tightly to your bosom. The book
of course was quickly lain aside and with a full heart I returned the loving clasp most warmly."[27] William expressed similar sentiments. He wrote
to her, "I was dreaming in the night that you came into my room before
I was out of bed, etc."[28]

The years of William and Catherine's engagement, 1852–55, were
times of constant struggle. During these years they formed a partnership,
based on a shared commitment to evangelization, that would characterize
their relationship for the rest of their lives. Together, they debated theological questions, strived to find a place for William where his preach-

ing could flourish, and considered the position women ought to occupy in the church. William wished to find a religious body where he could train for the ministry and establish himself as a preacher. His arrangement to preach for the Reformers at Walworth Chapel soon proved unsatisfactory. The Reform leadership retained too strong a hold on the chapel for William to be able to exercise what he saw as his proper authority.[29] Catherine approached the Rev. Dr. David Thomas of Stockwell New Chapel where she had begun to attend services. He suggested that William study for the Independent (Congregational) ministry under the Rev. John Campbell. William strongly objected at first, protesting that he was too strongly attached to the Methodists to consider such a change. He also objected to the Independents' Calvinist doctrine of election.[30] Catherine convinced him to consult with several Independent ministers; they convinced William that many of their clergy did not endorse a Calvinist theology. Yet once he began to study with the Rev. John Campbell, he discovered that these disagreements were in fact too significant to ignore, and he broke off his studies.[31]

William was then invited to take the Spalding, Lincolnshire, circuit by a group of Reformers.[32] The position was difficult; the circuit required that he sometimes give eight sermons a week at several chapels scattered over a twenty-seven-mile area.[33] The leaders offered him a salary of £52 a year, informing him that another man gladly offered to serve the circuit for less. William eventually managed to settle for £70 a year. He still thought that insufficient to support a wife, and he despaired of ever being able to marry Catherine.[34]

Leaving that Connexion in February 1854, he entered a small class of students studying for the Methodist New Connexion ministry under the Rev. Dr. Cooke. Little study was required, and William was left free to preach in London chapels and even to travel to other circuits. Very successful tours in such places as the Potteries and Newcastle-upon-Tyne enhanced William's reputation as a revivalist.[35] Catherine rejoiced in his successes, yet she was equally sharp in her criticism when she believed his revivals were improperly managed. "What a wretched policy, to leave Newcastle just when the work is at its height and yet I presume it will be so, and after all this trying *you* must abandon at least half the results to chance, or somebody little better as far as human instrumentality goes."[36]

During these years, Catherine lived in Brixton with her mother. She continued to read avidly, to teach Sunday School, and occasionally to write for Methodist periodicals. She took up the study of the piano, which she detested, because William wished that his future wife could play.[37] She also shared in the running of the household, which was no small task when her father brought in no income. She and her mother struggled to make ends meet, renting out rooms and practicing every economy they could.[38] Catherine considered going out as a domestic servant when their troubles were particularly pressing.[39]

Her letters to William are full of ideas and comments on his difficulties and achievements. She initiated his brief period of study with the Independents, and she continued to offer counsel on his career.[40] One thing she urged consistently and energetically was study. When he decided to begin with the Methodist New Connexion, she wrote, "I am pleased you are trying to arrange with Mr. Cook [sic], *nothing* could give me greater satisfaction than for you to *study* under the direction of such a man."[41] A few months later she wrote, "I am sorry to hear you talk of '*trying* to be a student once more and if you fail giving it up forever' don't say I will *try* but "I *will* be one." . . . So far from my regretting that you will have your days under your own control I *am glad* because I trust it will help you to gain application."[42] When this advice did not generate the desired result, Catherine responded with more specific suggestions:

> You generally enjoy a room to yourself; could you not rise say by 6 o'clock every morning and convert your bedroom into a *study;* . . . after breakfast and family devotion could you not again retire to your room and determinedly apply yourself to it till dinner; . . . don't let little difficulties prevent its adoption; . . . everything depends upon it in the future, you could not sustain your position in that circuit without it, much less rise to a better, which I have no doubt you will, *if you study.*[43]

Catherine began to develop an interest in writing sermons. She took notes for William on sermons she heard and sent them to him. She marked up books she was reading, sermons by Finney or works on teetotalism, and sent them to guide him in his studies.[44] She also suggested sermon topics and appropriate scriptural passages. William responded enthusiastically. "I want a sermon on the Flood, one on Jonah, and one on the Judgement. Send me some bare thoughts; some clear startling outlines. Nothing moves people like the terrific."[45] For the rest of her life, Catherine advised William and not always gently. In 1856 she wrote her mother describing a service where William "excelled himself and electrified the people." William added, "I have just come in the room where my dear little wife is writing this precious document and snatching the paper have read the above eulogistic sentiments. I just want to say that the very same night . . . she gave me a certain lecture on 'blockheadism', stupidity etc and lo' she writes to you after this fashion. However she is precious . . . with all her eccentricities and oddities."[46]

While she read theology, learned to write sermons, advised her future husband, and managed her household, Catherine began to reconsider the position of women in the church. She started to articulate a theology that she would continue to develop and refine for the rest of her life. Catherine faced significant restrictions. Despite her evident skill and knowledge, Catherine, like her husband, had little formal education. The heavy demands of her household always precluded any sustained, formal study. Moreover, autodidacticism was increasingly devalued as Methodism grew and established new standards for the ministry. The title of *Reverend* distinguished the ministers from the lay preachers and evangelists, and only those who had received a formal education could hold the highest positions of authority. Catherine encouraged William to study knowing that the enhanced value placed on such credentials made it necessary as well as knowing that it excluded those without such opportunities, like herself.[47] By mid-century most Methodists accepted that scripture forbade women's preaching, and the female preachers who were so important in early sectarian Methodism were rarely seen.[48] Yet in the face of formidable restrictions placed on Methodist women and the pressing claims of her domestic life, Catherine began to reconsider the significance of female ministry.

RETHINKING THE POSITION
OF WOMEN IN THE CHURCH

In 1852, shortly after her engagement, Catherine wrote William, "I only desire to be (if God spares me) your 'helpmate' and *companion,* in fact *One* with you. My remarks on the position and character of my sex were not in the *least personal,* I fear nothing for myself, but my heart often aches and weeps over 'hurt of the daughters of my people' and I often make their cause a matter of supplication to the 'God of Heaven.'"[49] Nevertheless, Catherine was convinced that the church had wrongly denied woman her rightful place, and she began to expand and clarify her interpretation of the position of women.

The Rev. Dr. David Thomas, the minister Catherine had asked to help William gain admission to study for the Congregational ministry, preached a sermon on women on April 22, 1855. He suggested that woman's moral and spiritual nature was weaker than or inferior to that of man. Catherine wrote a letter of protest.[50] The letter displayed both the limits of her formal education and Catherine's potential as a writer and a polemicist. Her grammar was inconsistent, and she made many spelling errors but her argument was clear and forceful.[51] There is no recorded mention of a reply to her letter. She began with an apology and an assertion of the rightness of her own views.

> Dear sir, you will doubtless be surprised at the receipt of this communication and I assure you it is with great reluctance and a feeling of profound respect that I make it. Were not for the high estimate I entertain of both your intelect and your heart, I would spare myself the sacrifice it cost me, but because I believe you love *truth* of whatever kind and would not willingly countenance or propagate erroneous views on any subject I venture to address you.

She argued that no one could speak of women's natural capacities because they have yet to be seen. A woman's education, "even in this highly favoured land," has been "such as to cramp and paralize rather than to develope and strengthen her energies and calculated to crush and wither her aspirations after mental greatness. . . . [It] has been more calculated to render her a serf, a toy, a plaything, than a self-dependent reflecting intellectual being. Christianity offered women equality. Women and men suffer the same penalties and enjoy the same hopes for eternity. "In Christ Jesus there is neither male nor female but they are both *one* and the promise of the outpouring of the Spirit is no less to the handmaidens than to the servants of the Lord." Catherine did not comment on how this reasoning might affect women's work in the church but instead proposed that devaluing women made them inferior mothers. Women, she wrote, would influence the next generation. Only when they were no longer "indoctrinated from the school room, the press, the platform and the *Pulpit,* with self-degrading feelings and servile notions" would "the fountain of human influence become pure."

That same month, Catherine also wrote to William, sending him a copy of the letter to the Rev. Dr. Thomas with a request for his thoughts. William replied,

> From the first reading I cannot see anything in them to lead for one moment to think of altering my opinion. You combat a great deal that I hold as firmly as you do—viz. her [woman's] equality, her perfect equality, as a whole, as a being. But as to concede that she is a man's equal, or capable of becoming man's equal, in intellectual attainments or prowess—I must say that is contradicted by experience in the world and my honest conviction. . . .

I would not stop a woman from preaching on any account. I would not encourage one to begin. You should preach if you felt moved thereto: felt equal to the task. I would not stay you if I had the power to do so. Altho' I should not like it. It is easy for you to say my views are the result of prejudice; perhaps they are. I am for the world's salvation; I will quarrel with no means that promises help.[52]

He had just completed his first year of service with the Methodist New Connexion, and a few weeks later he would attend the annual Conference to receive his assignment for the following year and, he hoped, permission to marry.[53] Yet, Catherine would not simply acquiesce in his views.

She wrote an impassioned response to William's letter. In this letter she never fully articulated what she envisioned for Christian women, yet she clearly wanted women to enjoy a wider sphere of action even if its precise outline were indistinct. Catherine argued that scripture contained no clear injunction against women holding positions of public, religious authority. She brought forward women like Miriam and Deborah to show that God had chosen women to prophesy and to lead. And, Catherine argued, women's position was enhanced in the New Testament. In Christ, "there is neither male nor female and while outward resemblance of the curse remains, in *him* it is nullified by *love* being made the law of marriage. . . . Who shall call subjection to such a husband a curse?"[54] She cited the work of Adam Clarke, the Wesleyan preacher and several times president of the Wesleyan Conference, in whose biblical scholarship she found an important source of support for women's preaching and prophesying in the church.[55] With more such men, Catherine wrote, "we should not hear very *pigmies* in Christianity reasoning against holy and intelligent women opening their mouths for the Lord in the presence of the Church."[56]

Still, Catherine remained concerned primarily with women as wives and mothers, just as in her letter to the Rev. Dr. Thomas. The church's restrictions on women were especially pernicious, she argued, because women became less able mothers. "If what the writers on physiology say be *true* and experience seems to render it unquestionable, what must [be] the effects of neglected mental culture, of the inculcation of frivolous *servile* and self-degrading notions into the minds of the Mothers of Humanity?"[57]

Catherine believed the necessary change would come from women themselves. "I believe woman is destined to assume her true position, and exert her proper influence by the special exertions and attainments of her *own sex;* she is to struggle through *mighty* difficulties too obvious to need mentioning, but they eventually dwindle before the spell of her developed and cultivated mind."[58] She declared, "Who shall dare thrust women out of the Church's operation or presume to put *my* candle which *God* has lighted under a bushel?"[59] And she noted, "I solemnly assert that the more I think and read on the subject, the more satisfied I am of the true and scriptural character of my own views."[60] Yet such confidence and self-assertion remained difficult to balance with the subjection she believed was also her duty. She wrote to William, "Perhaps sometime with thy permission (for I am going to promise to *obey* thee before I have any intention of entering such work) I may write something more extensive on the subject."[61] The uneasy balance of self-assertion and subjection remained a difficult one, but for the next few years Catherine's efforts were focused on managing William's religious career, not her own.

In June 1855 Catherine and William married, and for the next two years, the couple traveled. The Methodist New Connexion had assigned William to work as an itinerant evangelist. This was a highly unusual step. His salary of £100 exceeded the usual £68 paid a to circuit preacher, but, more important, his work was outside the usual Connexional practice.[62] Typically, men in his position were assigned to a circuit and were not expected to preach outside it. A substantial number of Connexional leaders regarded his success as justification enough for his unusual assignment.[63]

William's theology and preaching were deeply influenced by revivalists in the United States, particularly James Caughey and Charles G. Finney. These preachers proclaimed in dramatic, emotional language that sinners must find salvation or expect to suffer the eternal torments of hell. They stressed the need for holiness, which was the presence of the Holy Spirit in the heart, mind, and will of the penitent.[64] The revivalists incited preachers to implore congregations to seek salvation immediately. William was such a preacher, and his labors were counted a great success. The *Methodist New Connexion Magazine* described his work at Hull. "In the evening the chapel was filled, and the extraordinary ministry of the preacher produced an effect which we trust will not soon be effaced. . . . Appropriate and vivid illustrations, and the appeals for an immediate decision were heart-searching. . . . Many signs, groans, and heartfelt responses were heard throughout the congregation."[65]

Catherine traveled with William when she could. She eagerly reported their triumphs to her parents. From Sheffield in October 1855, she wrote, "The work progresses with mighty power—everybody who knows anything of this society are astonished and the months of gainsaying are stopped. God's son is glorified and precious souls are being saved by scores. 440 names have been taken and tomorrow is expected to be a mighty day."[66] Although she rejoiced in the conversions achieved through William's preaching, moving from place to place and living in rented rooms was not easy, especially with a growing family. Her first child, Bramwell, was born in 1856. Anticipating the birth of their second child, Catherine wrote to her mother, "I have shed many tears about it, I can assure you, perhaps it is wrong. I will try to be more resigned. If we had a home it would not be so bad but these lodgings are such a bore. We are not very comfortable here besides getting twenty six shillings a week out of us."[67] In 1857, the evangelistic tours ended when the Conference assigned William to preach in a regular circuit. Although many members of the Conference supported William's evangelistic work, others found the large, enthusiastic crowds who attended his services, professing conversion, an unwelcome deviation from the usual, orderly Methodist practice.[68] Debates between those who favored orderly services that would build a stable congregation and those who yearned for zealous preaching that sought the lost wherever they might be had long divided Methodists. This debate contributed to the schism among Wesleyans in 1851 as well as to the earlier development of the plebeian Methodist Connexions. Revivals, including William Booth's, were associated with a loss of respectability. To some, revivals brought disorder, even licentiousness, as well as the unscriptural presence of female preachers. The Booths regarded the formal practices and regulations, including the restrictions placed on women, as worldly brakes on the full exercise of the Holy Spirit.

But William dutifully went to his assigned circuit at Brighouse, a small town near Bradford in Yorkshire. The Booths found it cold and unwelcoming. "The people don't seem to take to us, the services don't succeed as we expected and many things seem to indicate that Wm is out of his place," Catherine wrote. She continued to hope that William would soon be assigned to full-time evangelistic work, despite the practical difficulties presented by such a life. She wrote to her mother that while Brighouse "is unquestionably much easier, it is far less congenial."[69] Catherine gave birth to their second son, Ballington, at Brighouse. The baby was baptized by Caughey, who continued to preach independently in England. The birth was difficult and aggravated Catherine's chronic spinal problem.[70]

In 1858, his four-year probation complete, William was called to the Methodist New Connexion Conference to be ordained. He hoped to find a new sphere of labor for his preaching, but again he was assigned to a circuit. He was sent to Gateshead, a town of about fifty thousand inhabitants near Newcastle-upon-Tyne. Catherine wrote her mother, "The chapel is a beauty—seats they say a thousand. . . . They [are] such nice folks. I feel just like anyone liberated from prison getting from that hated Brighouse."[71] The Booths remained at Gateshead until 1860.[72] They were a great success. In 1858, 92 members were listed on the chapel register. By January 1860, 224 names were listed.[73]

WOMEN'S RIGHT TO PREACH

The years in Gateshead were especially important for Catherine. She gave birth to two daughters, Catherine in 1858 and Emma in 1860. Her domestic responsibilities were heavy. William's salary allowed Catherine to engage one general servant, but she found herself plagued by the difficulty of finding a trustworthy and diligent girl who could meet her exacting standards. One servant, in any case, could relieve her of only a certain amount of domestic labor and the care of four small children.[74] Catherine found motherhood difficult and demanding. She wrote her mother in 1858 that her two sons got "into more trouble every day." "I feel so unfit to struggle with [Bramwell]. . . . You know how nervous and impatient I am. I feel sometimes ready to lie down and die with dissatisfaction with myself. I fear I am not doing my duty to him as I ought."[75]

The Booths believed in a strict discipline, which included corporal punishment. William whipped Ballington at age two when he awakened in the night crying.[76] When William was away on one preaching tour, he told Catherine to inform Bramwell "that if he does not obey and set his brothers and sisters an example in this matter he must be prepared not only to lose his dog but to live in the attic when I am at home, for I will not see him."[77] The Booths' strict discipline was typical of nineteenth-century evangelicals, but it also occasioned considerable anxiety for William and Catherine, who regarded the success of their child-rearing practices as essential to their children's salvation.

During these years, Catherine first publicly articulated her position on female ministry and commenced her own preaching career. These two important steps were occasioned by the evangelistic tour of Mrs. Phoebe Palmer. In 1835, Mrs. Palmer (1807–1874) began a women's meeting in her home in New York City; it was called the Tuesday Meeting for the Promotion of Holiness. This meeting grew to include men and became a center for holiness advocates. Soon she began to address larger audiences. Mrs. Palmer's preaching followed a style considered to be modest and respectable in a woman: she never appeared without her husband, and, rather than speaking from behind the pulpit, she came forward and often walked down the steps of the platform before addressing her audience. The dramatic conversions effected by her preaching convinced many in the holiness movement that female preaching was part of God's plan.[78] The *Wesleyan Times* reported on one 1859 service in Newcastle: "Mrs. Palmer now modestly walks within the rail of the communion, not to preach according to the modern acceptation of the term, but simply to talk to the people, which she does with all the gracefulness of an intelligent and well-educated Christian lady."[79]

Mrs. Palmer's writings, including *The Way of Holiness* (1843) and *Faith and Its Effects* (1849), made her well known to a wide audience, including the Booths. Catherine told her mother Mrs. Palmer's books "have done me more good than anything else I have ever met with."[80] In 1859, when Mrs. Palmer began a four-year preaching tour of England with her husband, Catherine enthusiastically followed her progress.[81]

Both the revivalist and the holiness movements originated in the United States. These two movements were intertwined, drawing on similar theological sources, and they developed within a transatlantic context. British and U.S. evangelists read each other's literature; toured both countries; adopted each other's music, preaching techniques, and strategies; and influenced the direction of theology and practice in Britain and the United States. Catherine wrote William, "In America (that birthplace of so much that is great and *noble*) tho' throwing up as all such movements do, much that is absurd and extravagant and which *I* no more approve than you, yet it shows that principles are working and inquiry awakening."[82] The Booths' place in this transatlantic evangelical culture engaged them with ideas and practices that were outside the mainstream of English Nonconformity at mid-century. It opened up a whole range of new possibilities for evangelical work.[83]

This theology formed a fundamental part of the movement the Booths would found, as we will see in Chapter 2. But in the late 1850s, the reappraisal of the role of women created by holiness theology was critical to Catherine Booth's understanding of female ministry. Revivalists like Finney and Caughey encouraged women to speak at meetings and to pray before mixed audiences. Women in the United States took up these opportunities in a number of ways. Mrs. Palmer's ministry remained within a tradition that the revivalists deemed highly acceptable for a woman.

Others, including Amanda Berry Smith and Antoinette Brown, established independent preaching careers and created a new model for female ministry.[84] These innovative women were important to Catherine's growing conviction that the restrictions placed on women were unscriptural and damaged women as well as the church.

As Nancy Hardesty has shown, this theology admitted a reconsideration of the injunctions against female preaching that went unquestioned in other denominations. First, the shift away from original sin as the permanent and principal state of the human condition lessened the burden of Eve's sin. Original sin had long been used by theologians to justify women's subjection. Second, this interpretation of conversion relied heavily on a reading of the Acts of the Apostles, where women figured prominently, particularly at Pentecost, where women as well as men received the gifts of prophesy. Third, holiness theologians justified deviating from a literal reading of the Bible when a greater good was served. As ardent temperance advocates, for example, they did not use communion wine. This willingness to reinterpret scripture opened the way for reconsidering women's position. Lastly, the presence of the Holy Spirit could be used to justify unconventional behavior. Advocates of holiness found they could not refuse the prompting of the Holy Spirit even when it moved a woman to kneel and pray for the souls of drunkards in the middle of a saloon or to speak and preach in church.[85]

Not everyone shared Catherine's enthusiasm for the holiness and revivalist movements. Shortly after Mrs. Palmer's arrival in England, several pamphlets were published condemning her ministry. The Rev. Arthur Augustus Rees, a former clergyman of the Church of England, was in 1859 the minister of the Bethesda Free Church in Sunderland, an independent congregation of about one thousand members.[86] He published his pamphlet, *Reasons for Not Co-operating in the Alleged "Sunderland Revivals,"* in order to explain to his congregants why he had shunned this woman's preaching and to warn them against her meetings. The pamphlet opened with quotations from the poets, beginning with these sentiments from Milton's well-known passage:

> For contemplation he, and valour formed,
> For softness she, and sweet attractive grace.
> He for God only, she for God in him

Rees continued with Lord Lyttleton:

> Seek to be good, but aim not to be great,
> A woman's noblest station is—Retreat;

> Her fairest virtues fly from public sight,
> Domestic worth,—that shuns too strong a light.

Finally, Rees called on Shakespeare.

> 'Tis beauty, that doth oft make a woman proud;
> 'Tis virtue that doth make them most admired;
> 'Tis modesty that makes them seem divine.
> A woman impudent and mannish grown,
> Is not more loathed than an effeminate man.
> Women are as roses, whose fair flower
> Being once displayed, doth fall that very hour.[87]

These poetic citations and a barb written in Latin illuminated the vast differences between the culture of Rees and that of the revivalists.[88] Rees was an educated man; his clerical authority was derived from his familiarity with elite literary culture as well as scripture. The revivalists, while they studied the Bible and evangelical biblical commentary, believed their fervor and faith to be the origin of their spiritual power. Neither Catherine nor William had any interest in or knowledge of the kinds of literature that Rees regarded as eminently suitable to buttress his arguments.

The injunctions of St. Paul against female preaching formed the substance of Rees's argument. He insisted that these were explicit and universal. "It does not refer to those only who claim to be inspired, but to all; it does not refer merely to acts of public preaching, but to all speaking."[89] Underlying his interpretation of St. Paul, however, was a desire to uphold the distinction between a masculine public sphere and a feminine private sphere, which characterized mid-Victorian gender relations. Women must not speak publicly, Rees argued, because "their station in life demands modesty and humility, and they should be free of the ostentation of appearing so much in public as to take part in the public services of teaching and praying."[90]

Christ's charge to Mary Magdalene could not be used to justify women's preaching because that was a private message. Women could teach their children at home or even address groups of women because such activities did not take women out of their rightful, feminine sphere. For women to act in the public sphere would be to usurp the authority of men, which they were forbidden to do. That prohibition was grounded in nature, according to Rees, because Adam was formed first. Women's subjection was extended by God because woman was "the door through which 'sin came into our world and all our woe.'" Thus, women were "under a denser cloud of suffering and humiliation."[91]

Even if good were to come of women's preaching, Rees contended, female preaching was wrong in principle and generated much evil during revivals. The second half of his pamphlet detailed the adverse effects of revival meetings. He criticized the noise and excitement generated by the emotional preaching, and he questioned the conversions that occurred in such a setting. How, he asked, could true and false conversions be distinguished when the only evidence came from those who admitted to being so recently unregenerate and would mistake any emotional experience for assurance of salvation? Rees's criticism of revivals buttressed his denunciation of women's preaching because it occurred within this disorderly, emotional setting.[92] The association of revivals with female preaching and the consequent disorder was not new, and it continued to plague the Booths for the rest of their lives.

Catherine, enraged, wrote to her mother, "I am determined that fellow shall not go unthrashed," and she then realized her earlier ambition of writing something more extensive on the position of women in the church.[93] Her pamphlet, *Female Teaching: or, the Rev. A. A. Rees versus Mrs. Palmer, Being a Reply to a Pamphlet by the Above Gentleman on the Sunderland Revival* was published in December 1859, just a few days before the birth of Emma, her fourth child.[94] The pamphlet was a far more ambitious project than her earlier, personal writing on the subject had been. For the first time she distinctly advocated women's preaching.[95]

Catherine's defense of women's preaching rested on two lines of argument. She considered Christian women's place in the order of things and closely examined specific scriptural texts that addressed women's prophesy. She began with a consideration of creation. She cited the first creation story, Genesis 1:27–31, in which God created male and female together and gave them dominion over the earth. The subordination of women occurred later, as a punishment for her transgressions. Thus women's subjection was neither natural nor eternal. "If woman had been in a state of subjection from her creation, in consequence of natural inferiority, where is the force of the words, 'he shall rule over thee', as a part of her curse?"[96]

Like Rees, she believed women's nature was different from men's. Unlike the reverend, Catherine maintained that such differences especially fitted women for preaching.

Making allowance for the novelty of the thing, we cannot discover anything either unnatural or immodest in a Christian woman, becomingly attired, appearing on a platform or a pulpit. By *nature* she seems fitted to grace either. God has given to women a graceful form and attitude, winning manners, persuasive speech, and, above all, a finely-tuned emotional nature, all of which appear to us eminent *natural* qualifications for public speaking.[97]

Women, Catherine recognized, were also bound by a social order put in place after the Fall. God had decreed distinct spheres of labor for men and women and had subjugated women to their husbands. But, Catherine maintained, these injunctions did not preclude female ministry.

> Will [Mr. Rees] inform us why women should be confined exclusively to the kitchen and the distaff, any more than man to the field and the workshop? Did not God, and has not nature, assigned to man *his* sphere of labor, "to till the ground, and to dress it?" And, if Mr. Rees claims exemption from this kind of toil for one portion of his sex, on the ground of their possessing ability for intellectual pursuits, he must allow us the same privilege for women.[98]

Catherine attested that the curse did not place women in subjection to men as beings but only to their husbands. Neither an unmarried woman nor a widow "is subject to man in any sense in which one man is not subject to another; both the law of God and man recognize her as an independent being."[99] Even for wives, their subjection was mitigated by Christ. Although woman and man shared in the Fall, woman had brought Christ into the world with the aid of no man. The resurrected Christ first appeared to a woman, Mary Magdalene, and charged her to spread the news. This public duty was given to her because her faith was so much greater than that of the men. "One was probably contemplating suicide, goaded to madness by a conscience of reeking with the blood of his betrayed and crucified Master; another was occupied in reflecting on certain conversations with a servant maid; and the rest were trembling in various holes and corners, having all forsaken their Master, and fled."[100] The resurrection did not remove the curse. Rather, it redeemed women "in a moral sense" and ought to have dispelled any belief in the spiritual superiority of men.[101]

Catherine devoted the body of her pamphlet to examining the Biblical passages that Rees and others used to justify excluding women from the pulpit. For Catherine, this was undoubtedly the core of the debate. If female preaching were forbidden in scripture, she could offer no possible justification for the practice. Catherine used what she termed a "common sense" interpretation of scripture. On the one hand she considered passages in relation to the whole Bible, and on the other hand she considered the historical context of each passage.

She first considered two passages from Corinthians, frequently cited to justify prohibitions on women's preaching.

> Every man praying or prophesying, having his head covered, dishonoureth his head. But every woman that prayeth or prophesieth with her head uncovered dishonoureth her head. (1 Cor. 9:4–5)

> Let your women keep silence in the churches; for it is not permitted unto them to speak; but they are commanded to be under obedience, as also saith the law. And if they will learn anything, let them ask their husbands at home; for it is a shame for women to speak in the church.(1 Cor. 14:34–35)

The first passage, she argued, was intended to instruct women in how they must dress when they were preaching. It did not forbid the activity itself but only inappropriate behavior for men or women. The second passage must harmonize with the first, and therefore it could not forbid the practice. Drawing on several theologians, Catherine asserted that the Greek word translated as "to speak" was more precisely translated as to chatter or to prattle. The passage could not refer to women's preaching because the women were asking questions, albeit in a disorderly manner, seeking to learn, while preachers were themselves the teachers. Lastly, the passage did not refer to all women generally but to the women of Corinth only.

She also discussed a third passage.

> But I suffer not a woman to teach, nor to usurp authority over the man, but to be in silence. For Adam was formed first then Eve. (I Tim. 2:12–13)

Catherine argued that the passage could not possibly mean that a mother could not teach her children or even a wife instruct her husband if he were unregenerate. This passage was not intended to prohibit all teaching but only the usurpation of authority from men. She supported her position by citing the prophecy of Joel, "I will pour out my spirit upon all flesh, and your sons and your daughters will prophecy" (Joel 2:28), which was echoed in Acts 2:17. The Old and New Testaments told of women prophets and preachers whose work must have been in harmony with divine injunction. Priscilla, Junia, Phoebe, Persis were all, she noted, described as helpers, prophets, and fellow laborers in the gospel. Just like the men, they were recognized as leaders in the early church by the very theologians who silenced women.[102] Christian women had long followed the example of these Biblical women and, Catherine asserted, with significant results. She closed her pamphlet with a warning: on the day of account the misinterpretation of scripture may be found to have resulted in "loss to the church, evil to the world and dishonour to God." [103]

Catherine's pamphlet was not hermeneutically original. She relied heavily on other Biblical scholars and quoted them at length, particularly the work of Adam Clarke. Clarke had converted to Methodism under the influence of John Wesley. His formal education was not extensive; he worked first as a local and later as a regular preacher. He always exhorted his congregations to seek conversion and sanctification. He rose to be president of the Wesleyans three times, in 1806, 1814, and 1822. He was also an assiduous scholar, publishing translations from the classics and other languages and highly regarded Biblical commentaries.[104] As a Methodist, Catherine would certainly have valued Clarke's work, and his scholarship added an important weight to her argument. Much of her argument was similar to that in the existing literature on women's ministry. Hugh Bourne's *Remarks on the Ministry of Women* (1808) and Luther Lee's *Women's Right to Preach the Gospel* (1853) employed arguments similar to Catherine's.[105] Another Methodist, the Rev. Robert Young, wrote *North of England Revivals: The Prophesying of Women* (1859) to defend Mrs. Palmer against her critics. His Biblical argument was similar, although, like Mrs. Palmer, he advocated a limited sphere for women.[106]

Yet Catherine's pamphlet was exceptional, and her argument had significant consequences for the position of women. The mere fact that it was written by a woman was unusual. Catherine wrote her parents, "It is pretty well-known that a *Lady* has tackled him [Rees] and there is much speculation and curiosity abroad it seems. . . . I should like to have given him more *pepper* but being a Lady I felt I must preserve a becoming dignity! I suppose his pamphlet is deemed unanswerable by some. Bah! I could answer a dozen *such* in my way."[107]

The most innovative and ultimately significant aspect of Catherine's thinking was her assertion that women's preaching was a part of the natural order. Women in various Protestant traditions had justified their public preaching by limiting the kinds of authority women could acquire through their activities. Mrs. Palmer published *The Promise of the Father; or a Neglected Spirituality of the Last Days* in 1859 to defend her own work. She put forth a different justification of her own activities.[108] Her book began, "Do not be startled, dear reader. We do not intend to discuss the question of 'Women's Rights' or of 'Women's Preaching', technically so called. . . . We believe woman has her legitimate sphere of action, which differs in most cases materially from that of man; and in this legitimate sphere she is both happy and useful."[109] Women, in her interpretation, did not possess any particular right to preach but could only prophesy under the prompting of the Holy Spirit. "Women who speak in assemblies for worship under the influence of the Holy Spirit assume thereby no *personal authority* over others. They are instruments through which divine instruction is communicated to the people."[110] Only when God spoke through them, when they were vessels of the Holy Spirit, might women preach. It would seem, however, that the Holy Spirit never prompted women to take positions of leadership in the church or in society as a whole. Female preaching would not threaten the social order or imbue women with an undue sense of personal authority. Mrs. Palmer's argument was by no means unique; similar arguments had been used by many women since the Reformation.[111]

Catherine certainly agreed that the Holy Spirit must call women to preach. However, this call was not, in her view, any different than a man's call. A Christian was one who was filled with the Holy Spirit and acted in accordance with God's will. Preaching, in Catherine's view, could be both the rational and systematic exegesis of scripture and the outpouring of the Holy Spirit; it was both institutional and spontaneous. Preaching that was both inside and beyond the institutional church was a radical claim for a woman, and it had complex consequences for the women who took up Catherine's call.

Unlike Mrs. Palmer, Catherine harmonized women's social subordination with spiritual authority albeit in ambiguous ways. She clearly stated that any qualified woman had *the right* to preach "independent of any man-made restrictions."[112] Yet women must preach as women, remaining bound by obedience to their husbands, who could refuse to allow them to preach. She did not regard the Holy Spirit as a force that would enable women to transcend the limitations of gender. This understanding of the work of the Holy Spirit differed from that of members of other prophetic movements, including the Quakers. Quaker women, especially during the movement's early years, believed that they ceased being limited by worldly restrictions when filled with the light of God. Phyllis Mack argues that when a Quaker woman preached, "this light or voice or conscience, was catapulted from the depths of her soul, through layers of temperament, appetite and habit, finally bursting through the individual's outer layer—her social status, her physical shape, her gender—to unite with other Friends in prayer, to enlighten strangers in the public arena."[113] Catherine, however, believed that gender could not be transcended in this life, or perhaps even in the next.[114]

Catherine refused to justify women's preaching by claiming that women were the weak, the foolish, or the low who would confound the wise. Deborah Valenze has demonstrated that many sectarian Methodist women preachers embraced these images and used them to buttress their claim to preach. Catherine, however, was proud that she was more widely read than many Christians, and she gladly used her knowledge and eloquence in her own defense.[115] She reported to William that after preaching one evening, "I had a very good test afforded me to try my humility, by a good brother who could scarcely put *three words* together praying very earnestly that God would crown my labours seeing that He could bless the *weakest* instruments to his service. You will smile and so do I but it did me good. Why should I not be willing for the weakest and most illiterate to count me among the weak things of the world."[116] Catherine cherished her dignity and eloquence. She rejected the disorderly, loud style that she believed did not depend on clear, theological reasoning and an appropriate feminine demeanor. One woman she heard preach "is a regular Primitive Female preacher, she puts off her bonnet and shawl and goes at it like a *ranter;* says some good things but without order or arrangement and shouts til the people jump again."[117]

Although the style of that Primitive Methodist woman was less common by the 1860s, by which time the sectarians had distanced themselves from revivals and "sensationalism," Catherine's objection was not simply about preaching style.[118] The difference lay in Catherine's justification of women's preaching. She always insisted that Christian women possessed the right to preach and that this right was based on their natural capacities and qualities. Therefore, she did not justify her claim by placing herself outside of social convention and order but rather proclaimed her right to preach as a part of the contract between God and humanity as expressed in the Bible. In one letter to William, she noted that Deborah "seems to have been supreme as well in *civil* and in spiritual" matters.[119] Similarly, she never employed the prophetic language of Revelation as did many nineteenth-century visionary women, including Joanna Southcott, leader of a millenarian movement between 1801 and 1814, and Mother Ann Lee, founder of the Shakers. She did not regard herself as a singular prophetic figure but as a dutiful Christian wife and mother. Women's preaching, Catherine argued, could be sustained within a conventional gendered social order in an institutional church committed to vigorous soul saving.

HER MINISTRY BEGINS

When Catherine wrote her pamphlet proclaiming women's right to preach the gospel, she had not yet taken up preaching. She was still a

shy woman who spoke and prayed aloud only with difficulty. Her domestic responsibilities were heavy, and William's career was not yet established. Her health was never strong, and her back gave her pain
throughout her life. When she did begin to preach, it was occasioned by
the mundane struggles of her life. Her struggles and her response to them
reveal that her particular class and social status were exceedingly important to her interpretation of women's preaching as well as providing
opportunities for her to establish a preaching career. In 1857, she and
William went to see a "popular female preacher," and she was encouraged by William's enthusiasm and buoyed by the possibility of earning
10 shillings per lecture. She wrote her parents, "I only wish I had begun
years ago if I had only been fortunate enough to have been brought up
amongst the Primitives I believe I should be preaching now, you laugh!
but I believe it the cares of a family and the bother of a house and *servants* now preclude any kind of labor that requires much study but I don't
think lecturing on temperance would require much."[120]

A few weeks later, she reported to her mother that she had addressed
a meeting of the Band of Hope, a children's group promoting temperance and Christian living, and would shortly address both a female audience and a mixed audience. She was eager for success: "*First* to do good,
2ly to gain something towards meeting the extra expenses my delicate
health occasions to my husband 3ly to be able to do something towards
educating my children and 4ly tho' not least to be able to make some little return for all your kindness past and present, are these not worthy
motives?"[121] These financial considerations were part of the daily reality of Catherine's life. Both Catherine and William were children of artisans unable to maintain even a tenuous place in that community. Her
letters frequently mentioned both her mother and her mother-in-law's
financial worries. Like most daughters of the artisanal class, Catherine
was educated to support herself and to contribute to the household. While
her father's inability to support the family made her contribution a pressing necessity, she was keenly aware that a woman's labor was essential
to the survival of a household. Hence, the financial struggles that led to
her preaching career were very much a part of the ordinary course of
life.[122] In contrast, a middle-class woman of her generation could not
have engaged in waged labor without the loss of her gendered class status. It was therefore possible for Catherine to regard preaching as an eminently suitable course of action, practically as well as theologically, in
ways that a middle-class woman like Mrs. Palmer did not. She relished

her work, writing to her parents, "I felt quite at home on the *platform*—far more than I do in the *kitchen*."[123]

She began to preach on occasional Sundays after William had spoken. In August 1860, she wrote her parents,

> I had a splendid congregation on Sunday night, I took the pulpit very much against my own desire but in compliance with the general wish, Wm opened the service for me and I spoke exactly an hour from the Prodigal Son, I was very much agitated and did not get a moment's liberty the whole service in fact *I* felt very much discouraged but I have heard nothing but the greatest satisfaction expressed by the people.[124]

She enjoyed the novelty of her work, writing her mother, "I have never seen my name in print except on bills on the walls, and then I have had some difficulty to believe that it really meant *me* however I suppose it did and now I never shall deem anything impossible anymore."[125]

Her independent career began in earnest in the autumn of 1860, when William fell ill and left the circuit to recover at a hydropathy clinic. She took his place. She wrote him, "Last night my preaching went well. It was by far the best effort I have made. I spoke an hour and a quarter with unwavering confidence, liberty and pleasure to myself, and if I may judge, with blessing to the people."[126] She needed to succeed for financial reasons. She reassured her husband, "If money fails, I will try and get some more. I will get up some lectures and charge so much to come in, and with such an object in mind, I could do far beyond anything I have done and the people would come to hear me I know."[127]

Her situation was made worse when, just after William left, all the children fell ill with whooping cough. The nursing and general household work were trying. Her problems were not always recognized by the Connexion. "But I cannot give my time to preparation unless I can afford to put my sewing out. It never seems to occur to any of them that I cannot do two things at once, or that I want *means* to relieve me of the one while I do the other! . . . What I do, I do to the Lord. Still I am conscious they are the partakers of the benefit and ought not to forget our temporalities as they do!"[128] She summed up her situation when she wrote to William, "I must try to posses my soul in patience and do *all* in the kitchen as well as in the Pulpit to the glory of God—the Lord help me. I will attend to the Jacksons' accn't as soon as I get some money."[129]

The Booths' remarkable arrangement met with little resistance. The Bethesda chapel Leaders Meeting minutes recorded "its cordial thanks to Mrs. Booth for the addresses delivered in the chapel Sunday last which it has no doubt will be productive to good and earnestly hopes that she may continue in the course thus begun in which we unitedly pray that the blessing of God may attend her and crown her labours with success."[130] The Methodist New Connexion Conference minutes contain no reference to Mrs. Booth's activities. The press, however, did note this unusual arrangement. A *Wesleyan Times* article titled "A Minister's Wife Preaching for Him!" described one service. "Mrs. Booth officiated for him on Sunday evening last, in Bethesda Chapel. The lady grounded her discourse on 'strive to enter in the strait gate' etc. and the large audience which had congregated to hear sat with evident interest listening to her chaste and fervid eloquence for upwards of one hour."[131] Catherine's preaching was also described in the secular press. She was amused by one description. "I am represented as having my husband's clothes on! they would require to be considerably *shortened* before such a phenomenon could occur would they not?"[132]

As Catherine commenced her preaching career, she attained entire sanctification. Catherine was converted at age sixteen and joined the Wesleyan chapel, but she became convinced that she had not reached the spiritual state God required of her.[133] She was filled with a sense of her own unworthiness, writing in February 1861, "Oh I cannot describe I have no words to set forth the sense of my own utter vileness, the rebellion of my heart against God has been awful in the extreme, it is because His mercy endureth forever that I am not in hell."[134]

She was guided in her struggle by Mrs. Palmer's writings and that "precious book," *The Higher Life*.[135] She wrote her mother that "I struggled through the day until a little after six in the evening," when she and William began to pray together. After a long prayer, William said,

> "Don't you lay your all on the altar?" I replied, "I am sure I do." And he said, "Isn't the altar holy?" I replied in the language of the Holy Ghost, "the altar is most holy, and whatsoever toucheth it is holy." Then said he, "Are you not holy?" I replied with my heart full of emotion and some faith, "Oh I think I am." Immediately, the word was given to confirm my faith. "Now ye are clean through with the word I have spoken unto you." And I took hold, true with a trembling hand, and not unmolested by the tempter, but I held fast the beginning of my confidence, and it grew stronger, and from that moment I have dared to reckon myself dead indeed unto sin, and alive unto God through Jesus Christ, my Lord.[136]

This experience provided her with a newfound confidence in the righteousness of her work, and the doctrine itself became an important part of the theology of the movement the Booths would found.

LEAVING THE METHODISTS

The Booths' work in Gateshead was a success. The congregation grew substantially, William's reputation was enhanced, and Catherine commenced her own successful career. The Booths were, nevertheless, discontented. Both fervently believed William's talents were being squandered because the Methodist New Connexion Conference was reluctant to allow work beyond the conventional labor of a circuit preacher. Catherine had been highly critical of the Conference for some time. In 1856, while on a revivalist tour, she had commented to her parents, "The cold, apathetic money-grubbing spirit of some preachers and leading men are a constant thorn in [William's] side, oh for a church of earnest, consistent, and soul-saving men but alas! such is *not* the Methodist New Connexion!"[137] In 1857, William consulted Caughey, who was traveling through England on a revivalist tour, about how best to proceed in the face of the Conference's limitations and regulations. Caughey advised him to wait until he was ordained and then to consider working outside a denomination. Caughey believed there was ample opportunity for him in both England and the United States. Catherine compared Caughey's situation with William's. "[Caughey] is not handcuffed or shackled by conferences or annual committees he can go where he likes and stop as *long* as he likes and I know some one else who will do so bye and bye unless those who oppose get out of the way."[138]

The Methodist New Connexion, of course, did not regard its practices as shackles but rather as necessary discipline and order. The Conference had allowed William to work as an itinerant revivalist for several years. Clearly a substantial body of Connexional leaders were not satisfied with that arrangement. When the Conference assigned William to a regular circuit, it was following the usual practice.[139]

In 1861, his assignment at Gateshead complete, William was sent to the Newcastle circuit. He reached an agreement with the people that allowed him to continue as a circuit preacher as well as to work as an itinerant evangelist. He was to be the superintendent of the circuit, giving a portion of his labor to the circuit and the rest elsewhere. He would be paid according to the time he spent with the circuit.[140] Members of the Newcastle circuit, however, became disillusioned with the practical realities of this arrangement and complained to the president of the Conference. The president wrote to William in July, noting that these complaints "revealed the astounding fact that he had not preached once in the Circuit and had no appointment on the plan extending to October

27th." The president promptly instructed William to "take your circuit according to our rules and usages" and added that the situation would be laid before the Annual Committee for their consideration.[141]

The Committee resolved that when William had "entered the ministry of the Methodist New Connexion he engaged to conform to its rules and regulations and on these terms alone he was received into its ministry. . . . The Committee decrees Mr. Booth guilty of a strange dereliction of duty."[142] He was instructed to begin his duties in Newcastle immediately. If he failed to do so, he would be replaced. William protested. He wrote to the Committee,

> The arrangement was agreed to unanimously by a Special circuit meeting and at the last Quarterly Meeting after working it for some time. I informed friends that if they were dissatisfied I was perfectly willing to retire but they preferred to abide by it for the year and I can only account for your letter the supposition that some officious person had unofficially written to you on the subject. . . . You asked me to tell you frankly what I intend to do. . . . But once again I say that I intend to be an Evangelist if that be possible. . . . My first impulse was to resign but I cling to the idea that my connexion with the Conference might be retained. Another year without sacrificing my convictions, and I thought the arrangement made with the Circuit secured. In this hope I find from our letter that I am mistaken, and that no place is open to me by which I can work out those convictions and retain that Connexion. One or the other I must give up. The former duty to God and souls I cannot forego, and therefore painful, intensely painful is the act I must adopt the latter, and place my resignation in your hands.
>
> I do this after much prayerful deliberation. I know I am sacrificing and I know that I am exposing myself and those I love to loss and difficulties but I am impelled to it by a sense of duty to souls to the church and to God. Were I to quail and give up the fear of the difficulties that appear just now to be in my path, I feel sure that I should in future reproach myself with cowardice in the cause of my Master, and that even those who differ with me in opinion would say that I was not true to the professions made in the Conference when I said, "I had offered myself to the Lord for this work if I went forth without a friend and without a farthing."[143]

With a fervent conviction of their singular commitment to God's service, the Booths left the Methodist New Connexion. They never again worked under any human authority except their own. Catherine expressed no regrets. She wrote her parents,

> I am sick of the Methodist New Connexion from *top* to *bottom*, I have lost all faith in its ministry and I see nothing in it but a slow consumption. . . . I cannot believe that it is right for my husband to spend another year plodding round this wreck of a circuit preaching to 20 or 30 or 40 people when the

same amount of cost to himself he might be preaching to thousands and bringing hundreds of wanderers into the fold of Christ. Wm is *afraid* he thinks of me and the children and I appreciate his love and care but I tell him God will *provide* if he will only go straight on the path of duty.[144]

The Booths had already established a strong reputation as revivalists. The broad community of evangelicals welcomed their labor. They commenced a series of revivals across England. Over the next four years, they preached in Cornwall, Wales, the Midlands, and the north.[145] They preached together. Catherine reported to her mother from St. Ives in October 1861, "We had the chapel packed and hundreds went away."[146] Their preaching provoked opposition that Catherine seemed to relish.

> When [the Wesleyans] come to invite Mr. Booth, he will politely tell them that he cannot come if his wife is forbidden to help him! or else accept their invitation and announce me just as usual as a matter of course, and then what will become of the rules and usages and what a predicament for the chairman of the district. Next to the glory of God and the salvation of souls I rejoice to be a thorn in the side of *such* persons.[147]

She also took pleasure in the warm reception she often received, despite official condemnation of her work. "The common people in their simplicity used to ask, 'why can't we have Mrs. Booth too?' Poor things, it is their ignorance you know!"[148] In 1864, William again fell ill. Catherine began to preach on her own, a practice she continued for the rest of her life.

The years of itinerant preaching were difficult. The Booths' income was small and irregular, and by 1864 they were £85 in debt.[149] The birth of Herbert in 1862 and Marian in 1864 only added to their difficulties. William and Catherine were frequently ill. In January 1862 Catherine wrote her mother,

> I don't know what is the matter with me but I am sick and ill all day just as tho' it was the first three months with me. Sometimes I think that I miscarried when I was so ill and that I am now beginning again and sometimes I think the child is dead and that is what is making me so poorly. . . . I hope all will be well, what I feel most is the useless life I am living, I do hope it is not a fresh beginning, I am ready to die at the prospect of another nine months as the past. Pray for me I need patience.[150]

To make matters more difficult, the Wesleyans, the Primitive Methodists, and the Methodist New Connexion barred itinerant revivalists from their pulpits; these regulations severely restricted where the Booths could preach.[151] They took to holding services in rented buildings, including circuses, a dancing academy, and various halls. Still, their expenses often exceeded their income.[152] Finally, in 1865 both Catherine and William received invitations to preach in London. It quickly became clear that London's vast population offered ample opportunities for evangelical work and their efforts would be welcomed by London's evangelical community. They could settle their six children in a stable home. Catherine quickly established a strong reputation in London, and speaking invitations fully occupied her time. Many women later recalled the importance of her example as they began their own careers. The Booths had settled on the path that would lead them to establish the Christian Mission and subsequently the Salvation Army.

Catherine's later description of the decisions that prompted her to begin her preaching career, however, emphasized her passivity and reluctance. The tensions and ambiguities her preaching caused remained the focus of the two stories she recounted about how she first began to preach. In the first, she described how she eagerly anticipated hearing a "much-honoured minister" preach, but on her way to chapel she looked up "at thick rows of small windows above me, where numbers of women were sitting, peering through at the passers-by or listlessly gossiping with each other." It was "suggested to my mind with great power" that she would be acting more like her redeemer if she spoke with these women instead of enjoying the service herself. "I knew I had never thus laboured to bring lost sinners to Christ, and trembling with a sense of my utter weakness, I stood for a moment, looked up to heaven, and said, 'Lord, if thou wilt help me, I will try,' and without stopping longer to confer with flesh and blood, turned back and commenced my work."[153] After speaking to several of the women, she convinced a forlorn woman to admit her into her home so that she could speak with the woman's drunken husband. The woman told Catherine that despite her best efforts, the deathbed pleas of their daughter, and the misery and poverty it created, her husband would not give up drink. Catherine read him the parable of the prodigal son. He wept and prayed with her and soon promised to sign the pledge. In this story, Catherine emphasized both her reluctance and fear and the enormous power she could assume when she acted according to God's will. She assisted the wife and daughter's quest to stop the husband's drinking, and thus she implicitly aligned women's interests with God's will.

In her second story, Catherine recounted how she sat in the minister's pew listening to William preach, "not expecting anything in particular." She suddenly felt the presence of the Holy Spirit compelling her to go forward and speak. She resisted.

And then the devil said, "Besides you are not prepared. You will look like a fool and will have nothing to say." He made a mistake. He overreached himself for once. It was this word that settled it. "Ah!" I said, "this is just the point. I have never yet been willing to be a fool for Christ. Now I will be one!"

Without stopping for another moment I rose from my seat and walked down the aisle. My dear husband was just going to conclude. He thought something had happened to me and so did the people. We had been there two years and they knew my timid bashful nature. He stepped down and asked me, "What is the matter, my dear?" I replied, "I want to say a word." He was so taken by surprise that he could only say, "My dear wife wishes to speak," and he sat down. . . . But oh, how little did I realise how much was then involved! I never imagined the life of publicity and trial that it would lead me to, for I was never allowed to have a quiet Sabbath when I was well enough to stand and speak.[154]

She told the congregation she had willfully refused God's prompting her to speak, but she would no longer do so. Her story turned the suppression of women into an evil act; instead of doing God's will those who silenced women were in league with the devil. Still, only her desire to obey God's will could bring her forward to speak. Her defiant claim of women's right to preach did not translate into confidence in her own abilities. She emphasized the pain and loss she endured and the disruptive consequences of her following the dictates of the Holy Spirit.

Her two accounts of the inception of her preaching career describe neither the financial difficulties that were so pressing when she began to preach nor the scriptural passages that inspired her. Instead, she emphasized that obedience was a struggle and that her spiritual assertion came at great cost. The tension between authority and obedience characterized the movement she and her husband would found. Salvationists assumed their place within a strict hierarchy and expected the prompting of the Holy Spirit to guide their soul-saving work no matter how unconventional it might be. Order and discipline were intertwined with spontaneous preaching and ecstatic bodily conversions. The resulting tension had particular consequences for women. But in 1865, Catherine and William Booth were simply evangelical partners, intent on settling in East London to preach to the heathen masses.

The Salvation Army was the creation of two individuals whose life experiences and beliefs shaped the movement's theology and practices. Catherine Booth's class background and her ardent belief in holiness and revivalism gave her a unique perspective on women's preaching and a career that made her a prominent and influential public figure. William Booth's experience with the Methodist New Connexion convinced him to work independently, free of the restrictions imposed by governing bodies and settled congregations. Their evangelical partnership offered many advantages. They shared a commitment to revivalism. The unusual sight of a husband and wife sharing a platform drew audiences during their itinerant years and helped them to meet many other evangelicals. Later, when William Booth struggled to find financial support for the Christian Mission, Catherine's preaching helped fund the Mission and support the Booth family. Of course, the Salvation Army was not simply the Booths' creation. The larger social and religious context would also shape the direction of this new movement, which began in the streets of London.

Creating the Salvation Army

In July 1865, William Booth began preaching in the crowded streets of East London. He was engaged by the publishers of the evangelical weekly the *Revival* for three weeks of preaching in Whitechapel. William preached in the streets to gather a crowd, then held services in a tent pitched in the Quaker Burial Ground in Whitechapel Road.[1] The *Revival* reported that four to five hundred people attended his services in the first two weeks alone.[2] On 27 July, the *Revival* eagerly reported that "searching questions, loud warnings, hearty exhortations, Jesus the Saviour from all guilt, the penalty and power of sin, Mr. Booth is this sort of preacher." The writer warned, however, that "we should be glad to know if Mr. Booth saw his way to give himself to the perishing tens of thousands of the East of London but this cannot be accomplished without increased funds."[3]

When the three weeks of services were complete, the Booths determined they must stay in London. It offered both preaching opportunities and the possibility of a more settled life than they had. William wanted to reach the unsaved, those who ignored the regular work of the church and chapels. London offered ample opportunity for such work. As well, it gave a respite from the constant travel of the past four years. In the first issue of the Christian Mission's magazine he described his reasons for settling in East London.

> In every direction were multitudes totally ignorant of the gospel, and given up to all kinds of wickedness—infidels, drunkards, thieves, harlots, gamblers,

blasphemers, and pleasure seekers without number. Out of a population of nearly a million souls, it was confidently asserted that some eight hundred thousand never crossed the threshold of a church or chapel. . . . The strangest and falsest notions of God, religion and the future state prevailed; and, thus consequently, misery and vice were rampant everywhere. To meet and stem this flood of iniquity, some few were laboring arduously and effectively; but around them was this vast and troubled ocean of depravity, foaming and dashing still.

A voice seemed to sound in my ears, "Why go . . . anywhere else, to find souls that need the Gospel? Here they are, tens and thousands at your very door. Preach to them, the unsearchable riches of Christ. I will help you—your need shall be supplied."[4]

William rented the Assembly Rooms, New Road, Whitechapel, for Sunday services as he continued to preach in the streets. He called his society the East London Christian Revival Society but soon after renamed it the East London Christian Mission.

The Christian Mission was part of a broad evangelical missionary effort to reach the urban working class. Its theology drew on Methodism, American revivalism, and the holiness movement. William Booth's openair preaching was similar to the work that had been done by evangelicals for decades. The Mission, however, differed from other home missions. The authority it granted women, its emphasis on holiness theology and revivalist methods, its growing independence, and its strict hierarchical structure were all features that sharply distinguished it from its contemporaries. The Christian Mission was created in the midst of the working-class communities it aimed to transform. It fashioned an evangelical practice from the geography and culture of the working-class communities it strived to convert. It was a neighborhood religion.

Its growth was quick and dramatic. In 1865, it was a local, East London organization that rented out rooms for Sunday services. By 1879, it had 72 stations in London, the Midlands, the North, and the Northeast. A year later, it had 172 stations and 363 officers. By December 1886, it had 1,749 congregations, known as corps, with 4,192 officers in Great Britain, and 743 corps and 1,932 officers abroad.[5] As the movement grew, William Booth determined that the democratic system borrowed from the Methodists for the first fourteen years had to be abandoned in favor of an autocratic and hierarchical structure. Under the banner of the Salvation Army, disciplined and faithful soldiers and officers fought the enemy in the streets, music halls, and gin palaces of England's urban working-class communities. Thousands of working-class men and women flocked to the rented halls, while others chased the preachers from the streets, hurling old boots at them. Christians from the established denominations who had cautiously supported the Christian Mission soon recoiled from this noisy, ecstatic, and spectacular Army.

CREATING THE CHRISTIAN MISSION

William's work initially received enthusiastic support from many evangelicals. After the Religious Census of 1851, Christians were convinced that the urban working class was less likely to attend worship services than any other group, and Nonconformists and Anglicans sought innovative means to reach that class.[6] In particular, East London posed a new challenge for Christian evangelicals and social reformers. In the earlier Victorian period, evangelical effort had focused on older impoverished areas like Seven Dials and Drury Lane, the same neighborhoods in which Charles Dickens placed his fictional underworld of crime.[7] But by the 1850s, the population of East London had grown dramatically, and by 1861 it was home to many of London's 178,000 Irish immigrants, and after 1880, the majority of its Jewish immigrants.[8] These immigrants were not English, and their religious affiliations made them doubly foreign in the eyes of England's Protestants. In the 1850s and 1860s, immigrants and the English-born came seeking employment in East London's docks, shipbuilding, needle trades, and various industries that located there because of the low rent and minimal regulation. This employment was frequently poorly paid, casual, and disrupted by the vicissitudes of the world economy. In the winter months, the demand for relief was high.[9] The East End appeared to many social reformers and evangelicals to be a looming, impoverished district populated by the residuum.

The vision of the East End as a pressing social threat did not dominate social commentary until the 1880s, but already in the 1860s London's evangelicals were alarmed by the spiritual state of the East End's inhabitants. An 1862 article in the *Revival* called on Christians to act. "The East End of London claims more attention than any other part of London and until it is raised from its fallen condition, the mission of the Revival movement in this modern Babylon will be far from complete. . . . Ragged, filthy, dissolute and corrupt as the people are, the blessed Jesus died even for them. . . . Dog-fanciers, bird-fanciers, drunkards, gamblers, thieves, will be your audience, but many of them are eager to listen to you."[10] East London seemed to require special means because it was so vast and uniformly poor. The 1860s marked the beginning of a vision of the "slums" that were no longer "scattered and containable pockets" but "vast teeming wildernesses."[11] Evangelicals early identified the East End as a pressing threat because its population grew quickly and was not well served by the existing parish structure. It appeared to offer an opportunity that, if missed, would have serious consequences for its inhabitants and perhaps the nation as a whole. William Booth wrote in 1867, "In other parts of the Metropolis, and of the great cities of our land, there are quarters, of limited extent, as dark and wicked, but they are as islands in a surrounding sea of wealth and intelligence, while here is a vast continent of vice, crime and misery."[12] By the 1860s, many Christians had set out to evangelize London with methods designed to address its particular problems. William Booth was among them.

The Booths' work was deeply influenced by the revivalist movement in the United States, particularly two of its leaders, Charles Finney and James Caughey. The Booths regarded both men as innovators, but equally significant both men worked within the Booths' own Methodist tradition. Finney and Caughey revived some practices the Methodists had ceased to use by mid-century, and they enhanced and systematized others. They relied heavily on the writing of prominent Methodists including John Wesley, John Fletcher, and Adam Clarke. Finney's principal methods included the protracted meeting and the anxious meeting, which were two kinds of services designed to attract the undecided and to utilize particular techniques that would induce individuals to seek conversion before the service was through. These meetings would, on occasion, last through the night, and they were carefully crafted to bring individuals forward. Finney also made extensive use of the anxious seat, a special pew or seat set aside from the others where individuals could be counseled by a trained evangelist and prayed over by the congregation. Finney told his congregations that Christ died to remove their sins but they must yearn and strive for salvation. Those who ignored the need for salvation would suffer for all eternity.[13] This theology encouraged individuals to seek salvation actively and preachers to devise means to encourage them. Conversion, Finney believed, came in two stages. Initially, sinners were awakened, willing to listen with attention. Then, sinners were "convicted of sin," aware of their sinful nature and anxious for the required remedy. Finney asserted that each stage required a different style of preaching. In the first stage, the revivalist must excite sinners' emotions, and in the second, address the spiritual affections.[14] He wrote, "The object of the ministry is to get all the people to feel that the devil has no right to rule this world but they ought to give themselves to God and vote in the Lord Jesus Christ as governor of the Universe."[15]

Finney toured England in the 1850s, and the Booths followed his progress with interest. His book, *Lectures on Revivals of Religion* (1835), was a handbook for organizing revivals, and it made his methods widely available for study. The Booths read his work and followed his career closely. Many, including some evangelicals, disapproved of these techniques. For some, this theology overemphasized the role of individual will at the expense of the Holy Spirit or the sacraments of the Church. Others deplored the dramatic preaching that Finney regarded as necessary to convince sinners to seek salvation.

Caughey was also an important influence on the Booths. The controversy surrounding his English tour led the Booths to join the Reform movement in 1852. In 1857, the Booths met Caughey, and his advice encouraged them to persevere.[16] William and Catherine's years of itinerant preaching were modeled on Caughey's work; they drew on his published work as well as his preaching style. Caughey was admired for his eloquent preaching, and he did not hesitate to use fear to move the undecided. After preaching, Caughey would go to the pews and bring people forward to pray at the anxious seat while the congregation sang hymns and prayed.[17] These methods were highly effective, and he was credited with thousands of conversions during his years in England. Although a Methodist, Caughey worked outside the denominational structure, traveling extensively to accept invitations from congregations.

While these methods were not unknown in England, they were not commonly used by Nonconformist clergy. Indeed, William's use of such techniques furthered his estrangement from and eventual break with the Methodists. William later wrote,

> [Seeing Caughey preach] had a powerful effect on my young heart. The straightforward conversational way of putting truth, and the common sense method of pushing people to a decision, and the corresponding results that followed, in the conversion and sanctification of hundreds of people, made an ineffaceable impression on my mind, filling me with confidence in the power and willingness of God to save all those who come unto Him, but with an assurance of the absolute certainty with which soul-saving results can be calculated upon when proper means are used for their accomplishment.[18]

The Booths preached in a dramatic revivalist style, filling their sermons with strong language, gripping incidents, warnings of God's wrath, and the assurance of full pardon. They also used the anxious meeting and the anxious seat, or penitent form, in their meetings.

Their revivalist preaching was just one aspect of their work that distinguished them from the broader evangelical community. Catherine's preaching was also a controversial and dramatic deviation from usual evangelical practice. Catherine was, by 1865, a well-known preacher, and in fact an invitation to her first brought the Booths to London. Catherine arrived in London in February 1865 to conduct a revival for the Free Methodists in Rotherhithe, a suburb. The Booths rented a house in Hammersmith and settled the children there while William continued to work in the North and Midlands until his work began in Whitechapel in July.[19] When the Rotherhithe revival was completed, she conducted another series of services at a Free Methodist chapel in Bermondsey.[20] In October, when she was seven months pregnant, she began to preach at the Horns Assembly Room, Kennington.[21] Catherine's preaching was highly esteemed. Her earnings were an important source of income for the family, and when William established his mission in East London, Catherine raised needed funds from her audiences.[22]

Yet many of the evangelicals whose support was crucial to William's efforts deplored female ministry. The *Revival* condemned women preachers in a November 1862 lead article. "The first woman taught her husband with the tree of the knowledge of good and evil; and with a righteous wisdom the Holy Ghost forbids her ever to teach the man again." The Apostle Paul, furthermore, enjoined women to silence and subjugation. "For woman to assume the place of teachers would be something like an assertion that God was the author of confusion instead of peace."[23] The *Revival* published other articles criticizing women's ministry, including one that criticized Mrs. Booth and Jessie Mcfarlane for their immodesty and argued that the conversions that might result from their preaching were not signs that such practices were endorsed by God.[24]

In August 1865 the *Revival* began to shift its position. The editors, Samuel Morgan and Richard Chase, were also members of the East London Special Services Committee that engaged William in 1865 to preach for three weeks in the East End. They took that opportunity to voice their suspicions of Catherine's activities. They wrote to the Booths, inquiring "whether it be right for mothers of families to be away from their home duties on any account, not excepting this most important work. Furthermore, besides the particular instances of harm done to which we refer, it appears questionable on Scriptural grounds (see St. Paul to Timothy, I Ephesians and Titus). We are only anxious that the Lord's will in the matter should be done."[25]

The Booth's reply did not survive, but Morgan and Chase's position did begin to shift. In August 1865, just as William's term in Whitechapel was coming to a close, the *Revival*'s lead article cautioned against too hasty a denunciation of women's preaching. "While the people of God are crying . . . it behooves us to be very watchful, lest we reject the blessing because it comes (as it often does) in an unexpected way, and in a fashion distasteful to our pride and prejudice."[26] This cautious endorsement acknowledged that while women's preaching was peculiar, it was also effective. The author added that he recently had occasion to hear Catherine Booth preach. "We had never before seen this lady, nor had the caustic tone of her pamphlet on Female Teaching prepossessed us to her favour. It is long since man or woman made in our hearing a more searching and experimental, though winning, declaration of the truth of the Gospel."[27] Other articles followed in 1865 and 1866; they argued forcefully in favor of women's ability to save souls.[28] This shift in the *Revival*'s position may well have been occasioned by the publisher's association with the Booths.

The editors of the *Revival* were not alone in their belief that female ministry went against scripture and nature. While it was not unusual for home missions to engage women to run mothers' meetings, do house-to-house visiting, or teach children, preaching was nearly always a masculine preserve. Women's presence may well have disturbed some of the Mission's supporters. For example, when William Booth published *How to Reach the Masses with Gospel* (1872) to gather support for the Mission, he described "workers of the Mission as "a blacksmith, a navvy, another a policeman, another a sailor."[29] He added that "we must not omit to mention three ladies, who have given up their whole time in the work of the Mission without being chargeable to its funds."[30] The charwomen and needlewomen whose names appeared on the Mission circuit plans were most likely omitted because this pamphlet was essentially written to gather support for the Mission's work. William Booth knew that many potential middle-class supporters might take offense at the enhanced position of women. This conflict was to continue to divide the Booths from much of the broader evangelical movement and to distinguish their work from that of many other home-mission movements.

Female preaching was not the only source of conflict among the Mission's supporters. The Booths unfaltering willingness to act on principle, even in the face of fervent opposition and harsh criticism, frequently resulted in conflict. Moreover, the Booths had no interest in working under the direction of others. In the early years of the Christian Mission, however, the movement required money and the endorsement of prominent evangelicals who would lend credibility to the organization.

William secured substantial financial support from Samuel Morley, a wealthy industrialist and Member of Parliament (MP) from Nottingham. In addition, the *Revival* published regular requests for contributions.[31] In 1867, the Committee of the Evangelisation Society granted the Mission £14 weekly to continue its work. Funds were also raised from the congregations.[32]

In 1868, William established a Council of ten prominent philanthropists to assist him in the work and to lend their names to the Mission.[33] Men like Samuel Morley, MP., the Rev. J. H. Wilson of the Home Mission Society, and W. E. Smith of the Evangelisation Society secured the Mission's reputation and helped to raise its public profile. And yet this arrangement was never entirely satisfactory. Neither the Council nor the Mission's financial supporters ever fully supported the Booths' expansive plans. In 1868, the Council considered purchasing a Whitechapel building known as the People's Market. It was a commercial failure and seemed well-suited to the needs of the Mission. Negotiations failed to bring agreement on a price, and the Council decided to seek other premises.

Henry Reed, a wealthy Christian and a supporter of the Mission, had invited the Booths to preach at services he organized and offered to build William a substantial hall. But the offer came with two conditions. William would preach nowhere else, and if Reed disapproved of William's work, he could withdraw the hall at any time. Despite the appeal of stability and security, William declined his offer.[34] William continued to consider the People's Market, however, even if the Council did not, and in October 1869 the Mission purchased the building and arranged with an architect to make the necessary renovations.[35] The project did not proceed as William had planned, and the cost of the renovations exceeded his funds by £500. Because William alone had made arrangements with the architects, the Council regarded his decisions with dismay, and the architects threatened to sue William if payment was not forthcoming.[36] William's expansive plans and his desire to work without the burden of committees had resulted in a serious financial crisis.

Moreover, the Booths' own income was precarious during these years. Catherine's preaching brought in an income, but in December 1866 she gave birth to Eva, and in April 1868 to her eighth child, Lucy. She was ill for a considerable time after each birth and was unable to work. William took no salary from the Mission, relying only on various unreliable sources, including income from lodgers and the donations of supporters. William decided to appeal to Reed. Reed's reply, dated April 10, 1870, is important because it reveals how strongly the Mission's supporters disapproved of the unconventional aspects of the work and regarded the Booths' ambitious plans as a weakness. Like most serious Christians of his day, Reed believed debt was sinful. "Your note confounded me. To find you owed £500 upon the hall was sad—but to tell me you are also £500 more in debt, to this I know not what to say. . . . O the dishonour you are bringing on the cause of Christ; . . . but I forbear, my soul is troubled."[37] He advised William to sell off the building as quickly as possible along with all the fittings and to sell his house.

> I would then go into a small house. . . . Your wife and daughters must keep the house and do everything. . . . Your wife would have to give up taking halls and leaving home (I never saw this to be the path of duty); . . . all this is retrenchment . . . . My great fear is your wife; if she will honestly and humbly join you and encourage you to what is right, I believe you will, for you are much influenced by her—but for her to give up all and come down to a plain, loving wife and mother, willing to stop at home . . . I know this practically will need to be hard.[38]

The Booths did not follow his advice. The debt was met by small contributions, and William purchased the Mission's soup kitchen, located at 188 Whitechapel Road, thereby relieving the Mission of a part of its debts and acquiring a stable income for the family. He set up "Food-for-the-Millions" shops, where hot soup could be purchased all day and a three course dinner could be had for sixpence. By 1872, there were five shops, all managed by the Booth's eldest child, Bramwell, then sixteen. The shops failed in 1874, but they served their purpose for five years.[39] Moreover, the Booths' solution to the crisis enhanced their independence and decreased their reliance on the goodwill of others.

STRUCTURE AND DOCTRINE

The Mission continued to seek support from benefactors. Extant records reveal little about the precise sources of Mission funds, but it is clear that the Evangelisation Society continued to support the Mission into the early 1870s.[40] Individual contributions were also an important source of income. William Booth's report of the Mission's work, *How to Reach the Masses with Gospel* (1872), contained a list of the Mission's contributors; donations ranged from £500 from "an old disciple" to £2 from the Misses Charrington and 3s. from Mrs. Bagster for a total of £2,000.[41] Other benefactors continued to make large contributions. William Booth recalled that one benefactor, Frank Crossley, gave between £60,000 and £70,000 during his lifetime.[42] Reed, before his death in 1880, created a

£5,000 fund to provide a means of support for the Booth family that would not deplete the Mission's funds.[43] The Mission, however, relied increasingly on its members, and by the late 1870s preachers were expected to meet all expenses and their own salaries with funds supplied by those who attended their services.

This support allowed the Mission to grow. In 1868, the Mission began to publish its own magazine, the *East London Evangelist*. The journal was a small, monthly publication resembling the *Revival* and other Nonconformist magazines. It contained reports of the Mission's work and requests for donations, short theological and practical religious essays, and biographies of exemplary Christians. In 1870, the publication was renamed the *Christian Mission Magazine*.

In 1868, the Mission held Sunday services in the New East London Theatre, where attendance averaged twenty-five hundred souls. In addition, services were held elsewhere in London: at the City of London Theatre, Shoreditch; the Oriental Theatre, Poplar; the Eastern Alhambra, Limehouse; and in rooms in Whitechapel, Poplar, Spitalfields, Hackney, Millwall, Stratford, Mile-End, and Bishopgate Street. The halls were not prepossessing by the standards of most churches.

> In rushes the little crowd, down a dark, narrow, confined passage, leading to one of the dingiest and gloomiest places of amusement to be found, perhaps in all of London. There is nothing very elevated or refined here. The walls are black with dirt, the gaudy tinselled ornaments half-hidden with layers of dust, gaslights so few in number as to give an extremely cheerless and dispiriting look to the whole place. The stage—not a very large one—is fitted up with scenery and wings representing the interior of some impossible mansion; while for the use of the preacher and his colleagues, a white and green property table . . . has been placed in front of the footlights. A series of rickety steps . . . furnishes a ready means of communication between the stage and the audience.[44]

The crowd, observers agreed, was "composed of the lowest class, as may be supposed, with a sprinkling of the higher grade, such as maids and sempstresses."[45] Few of the shopkeeping class were present; "the place was far too vulgar for them."[46] These were the people "who reject every invitation to public worship, and who, (to use the expression of one of their number) make a practice of going nowhere."[47] In 1868, the East London newspapers estimated that between seven and fourteen thousand people attended the Mission's 140 weekly services. And the number continued to grow.[48] The 1873 Christian Mission Conference reported a total of 901 members at four London stations. It reported that the Whitechapel station, for example, had 300 members and a weekly attendance of 2,151 at its twelve meetings.[49] In 1872, it had established twelve London stations—in Whitechapel, Bethnal Green, Poplar, Millwall, Stratford, Limehouse, Shoreditch, Bow Common, Stoke Newington, and Hackney—and had set up stations outside London in Hastings, Croydon, Carshelton, Bromley, Ninley, Ramsey, Battle, and Edinburgh.[50]

Furthermore, as the Mission became more established, it depended less on committees of prominent men who were not members. William disbanded the Council between 1872 and 1874; no record has been found that establishes the exact circumstances of this move. Governance of the Mission was taken up by William Booth, Bramwell Booth, and several close associates, most notably George Scott Railton (see Figure 3). Born in 1849, Railton was the son of a Methodist preacher. His parents met when both were in Antigua working as missionaries. At age sixteen, while employed by a firm of merchants, he began to work with missionaries in the London docks. At age nineteen, he felt called to be a missionary in a region of Africa that had not previously seen Christian evangelists. He embarked alone but ran out of money in North Africa. When he returned to England, he learned of the Christian Mission from his brother, who became acquainted with William Booth when the two men were at a hydropathy clinic. He applied for work in 1873and was immediately engaged as the Mission secretary. He also lived in the Booth household for the subsequent eleven years. Salvationists said he was a "radical of radicals" who despised religious sham and hypocrisy. He believed ecclesiasticism was among the worst aspects of Christian churches.[51] Until his death in 1913, Railton was an ardent supporter of the Mission and the Salvation Army; the author of many of the Mission's tracts, biographies, and public statements; a close advisor to the Booths; and a critical voice in many influential decisions.

In addition, the Mission created a system of committees and offices modeled on Methodist practice; this system grew and changed with the Mission. As Railton explained in his history of the movement's first twenty-one years, "A number of more or less harmonious but differing elements were at work together, and it would have puzzled anyone to say at any given moment which of these elements would eventually prevail."[52] Consequently, the Mission's course of action was shaped by its members, and its prosperity depended on their participation in the conferences, meetings, and daily work of each station. The Mission's structure encouraged the working-class men and women who joined to acquire the skills necessary to carry out the work and to influence the

decisions that would govern that work.[53] At its first annual Conference
in 1870, twenty-eight men and five women were in attendance.

At that Conference, the Mission established its doctrines, objectives,
and rules.[54] Each mission station was administered by an elders' meeting, which was to be composed of itinerant preachers, leaders of believers' meetings, hall stewards, poor stewards, and representatives from
the children's mission, Sunday School, and temperance societies. Mission stations were grouped together into circuits. The officers of the circuit were to meet quarterly to establish a circuit plan, pay expenses, receive local preachers on trial, and renew memberships. An annual
Conference would meet each year, and it would include the general superintendent, the superintendents of each circuit, and two laypersons
from each circuit.

The daily work of each station was shared among various offices. Leaders ran believers' meetings. The leader was to "meet his class weekly,
opening and closing the meeting with singing and prayer. He shall relate
his own experience first and then inquire into the experience of his members, one by one, and administer such encouragement, instruction and
reproof as their state requires." Society and hall stewards kept the account books and paid the rent and other expenses. A local preacher
"preaches the Gospel as he has opportunity, while at the same time following his trade or calling." The itinerant preachers "are those who are
wholly engaged in the Mission and who are supported by the voluntary
offerings of friends and the societies." The Conference detailed the ob-
ligations of each office. Open-air services were to precede all indoor services and were to include short addresses with short prayers and hymns
in between. Public, indoor services were also to include "lively singing
and short praying," and sermons were not to exceed forty minutes. In
addition, each station was to hold prayer meetings following public service for those "who are seeking pardon, purity of heart, the witness of
the Spirit, or to have their backslidings healed." Weekly bible classes and
meetings for promoting holiness were held for members, and a public
watch night was held on the last evening of every year. The Mission did
not offer baptism. It was a controversial practice among evangelicals,
and the Mission wished to avoid the conflict that might ensue. Members
could arrange to have it administered elsewhere, but they were to refrain
from discussion of the issue. The Lord's Supper was administered
monthly to those with members' tickets, but if a two-thirds majority was
in favor, it could be administered more frequently. This system demanded
participation and engagement. The Christian Mission was not for the

fainthearted. The principal task of the Mission was to evangelize the "neglected crowds of people who are living without hope and to gather those
converted into Christian fellowship in order that they may be instructed
in scriptural truth, trained in the habits of holiness and usefulness, and
watched over and cared for in their religious course."

The Mission's doctrines were essentially Methodist. In fact, many of
its doctrines were stated in the exact language of the Methodist New Connexion's doctrines.[55] The doctrines adopted at the 1870 Conference were,

1. We believe that the scriptures of the Old and New Testaments were given
by inspiration of God, and that they only constitute the divine rule of Christian faith and practice.

2. We believe that there is only one God who is infinitely perfect, the Cre-
ator, Preserver, and Governor of all things.

3. We believe that there are three persons in the Godhead—The Father, The
Son and the Holy Ghost, undivided in essence, co-equal in power and glory,
and the only proper object of religious worship.

4. We believe that in the person of Jesus Christ the divine and human natures
are united, so that He is truly and properly God and truly and properly man.

5. We believe that our first parents were created in a state of innocency, but
by their disobedience they lost their purity and happiness; and that, in consequence of their fall, all men have become sinners totally depraved, and as
such are justly exposed to the wrath of God.

6. We believe that Lord Jesus Christ has by His suffering and death, made an
atonement for the whole world, so whosoever will, may be saved.

7. We believe that repentance towards God, faith in our Lord Jesus Christ,
and regeneration by the Holy Spirit are necessary to salvation.

8. We believe that we are justified by grace through faith in our Lord Jesus
Christ, and that he that believeth hath the witness in himself.

9. We believe that it is the privilege of all believers to be "wholly sanctified"
and that "their whole spirit and soul and body" may "be preserved blame-
less unto the coming of our Lord Jesus Christ". (I Thess. V.23)

10. We believe in the immortality of the soul; in the resurrection of the body;
in the general judgement of the end of the world; in the eternal happiness of
the righteous; and in the endless punishment of the wicked.

In addition, members were required to abstain entirely from alcohol and
tobacco and to renounce fashionable dress. They could not work in any
aspect of the drink trade or in the publication or sale of irreligious publications nor could they post bills for theaters, concerts, or balls in their
windows. These rules required serious commitment. Few Anglicans or
Nonconformists, for example, advocated abstinence from alcohol, and
most would have regarded the Mission's insistence that women remove

decorative feathers from their hats as an unduly strict reading of 1 Timothy 2:9–10.[56]

Holiness, the ninth doctrine, was a distinguishing feature of the movement and a central element in Salvationist conversion narratives, as we will see in Chapter 3. The doctrine was reemphasized in an 1876 Conference resolution and was among the beliefs most frequently explained and advocated in Christian Mission and later Salvation Army publications.[57] The theology had its roots in England, but it was given a different inflection as it was taken up by Americans and eventually brought back to England. John Wesley in *A Plain Account of Christian Perfection* (1770) argued that Christian perfection might be attained in this life and, while desirable, was not required for salvation. In the 1820s and 1830s, some theologians in the United States reinterpreted the doctrine, asserting that it was the duty and privilege of all Christians to attain entire sanctification. This theology was especially important to Charles Finney and his associates. U.S. Congregationalist and Presbyterian clergy criticized these theologians and declared their heresy comparable to John Noyes's Oneida perfectionism. Others embraced holiness theology. Oberlin College became a center for holiness after Finney joined its faculty in 1835. Holiness theology returned to England with this sharper focus in the 1850s and 1860s through the published works of these theologians and the evangelical tours of Caughey, Finney, Palmer, Robert Pearsall, Hannah Whitall Smith, and others.[58]

Holiness theology taught that Christians could be fully delivered from sin, "and all the powers, faculties, possessions, and influences of the soul are given up to the service and glory of God."[59] To attain holiness, a believer must first be convinced that sin is hateful and must desire holiness. The believer must then renounce evil and consecrate herself and all that she possesses to God, having faith that Christ's blood cleanses her from all sin. The Booths believed that entire sanctification was an absolute necessity for a Christian life and the only assurance of heaven.[60] Men and women had to be entirely sanctified to join the Mission or, later, the Salvation Army. This doctrine was an exceedingly important influence on the Mission's practice. Because holiness was a condition of religious office, worldly and bodily distinctions could be regarded as insignificant. Thus this theology provided the possibility of reconsidering the cultural, sexual, and racial hierarchies that structured authority in Christian churches. Black and white women on both sides of the Atlantic argued that entire sanctification qualified women to preach.[61]

Holiness theology was particularly important for women. They enjoyed a range of possibilities for work and spiritual authority equaled in virtually no other contemporary English denomination or virtually any voluntary organization. The Christian Mission was created at a moment when other evangelicals had begun to support a cautious widening of women's sphere. A number of women in the 1860s, including Jessie Mc-farlane and Geraldine Hooper, worked as independent evangelists like Catherine Booth, accepting invitations from congregations to speak in chapels or from local societies who rented out halls or theaters.[62] All these women remained outside the formal organization of the denominations; they had no voice in denominational decisions, they were never assigned a congregation or circuit, and they enjoyed no regular salary. Their ministry never included communion or baptism. Their services aimed to ignite the hearts of sinners and return them to their churches.[63] The respectable, dignified demeanor of these middle-class women and the absence of any organizational or sacramental authority made them acceptable to a broad range of Christians. Their credibility as Christian women was enhanced by their modest attainments.

New opportunities created for working-class women again extended the reach of the churches but without disrupting the established division of authority. Mrs. Ellen Ranyard (1810–1879) founded the Biblewomen in 1857. She believed the Christian message was not reaching the urban poor and that new methods of spreading the gospel were desperately needed. Ranyard recruited working-class women to perform such duties as making house-to-house visitations, organizing mother's meetings, and selling Bibles door to door on an installment plan. Ranyard engaged middle-class women to supervise the Biblewomen and to organize support for their efforts. They would find their "own desolate homes and weary life had become brightened and cheered by the power of a new effort."[64] The monthly report of their work, the *Missing Link,* rejoiced in the "revived female ministry" of "Sunday school teachers, district visitors, hospital nurses, missionary collectors, conductors of mother's meetings, writers of Gospel tracts, essays and articles in religious serials, and books abounding in Gospel truth."[65] The Biblewomen combined opportunities for working-class women with the larger church and chapel effort to save the "heathen masses."[66]

Both the independent female preachers and the Biblewomen enhanced women's religious work at mid-century. Nevertheless, their activities were carefully constrained and included no pastoral or organizational authority. The working-class women Mrs. Ranyard engaged were carefully supervised by middle-class women. The Christian Mission was part of

this expansion of evangelical women's work, but it was far more extensive. The Christian Mission authorized women not only to speak but also
to hold office, vote, and participate in the creation and adoption of policy. The 1870 annual Conference declared, "As it is manifest from the
Scriptures of the Old and especially the New Testament that God has
sanctioned the labours of Godly women in His church; godly women
possessing the necessary gifts and qualifications shall be employed as
preachers itinerant or otherwise and class leaders and as such shall have
appointments given to them on the preachers plan; and they shall be eligible for any office, and to speak and vote at all official meetings."[67]

The Mission's 1870 policy on women was enacted immediately; it may
have simply codified existing practice as many women were already listed
on the circuit plans.[68] Women were present at the annual conferences
from 1870, and in 1875 Annie Davis was the first woman to take charge
of a mission station.[69] These were not measures born of crisis, nor did
the work require an extraordinary call. The Mission believed women had
gifts and talents that they should exercise freely. Women's authority was
thus sanctioned and institutionalized.

A NEIGHBORHOOD RELIGION

The Christian Mission's relationship to the working-class communities
it strived to convert was as pragmatic and equivocal as its relationship
to evangelical Christianity. That which helped the Mission prosper was
eagerly seized and expanded, and that which served only to hinder it
was discarded. In many respects, the Christian Mission's approach to
working-class communities resembled the work of other evangelicals.[70]
From the second half of the nineteenth century, social commentators often claimed that the crowding, filth, and disorder of urban life made city
dwellers more subject to disease and immorality than were those living
in rural areas.[71] Likewise, William Booth argued that much of urban
working-class life served no purpose but to nurture sin. "The public house
rules supreme, with beer and gin for its inflexible hierophants. No wonder that drunkenness, licentiousness, and crime abound in all directions;
no wonder that the reeking streets are filled with lost and miserable
women, or that the narrow courts should form so many nests for
thieves."[72] Nevertheless, the Christian Mission, and later the Salvation
Army, were at once a part of and a challenge to working-class communities. It was a neighborhood religion. It created a battle plan that was
especially suited to urban geography and the culture of working-class

neighborhoods. The stations and circuits, for example, corresponded to the neighborhoods they evangelized. In contrast, the Church worked on a parish system that bore little relationship to the newer working-class neighborhoods. Moreover, the Christian Mission strived to transform whole neighborhoods. At the 1876 annual Conference, William Booth told the crowd that a mission station "is not a building or a chapel or a hall; it is not even a society but a band of people united together to mission, to attack, to Christianize a whole neighborhood or town."[73]

This organizational approach was an especially appropriate response to working-class religiosity. Historian Jeffrey Cox has called the beliefs of the urban working-class "diffusive Christianity." Few residents of Stepney or Bethnal Green attended church or chapel services, but most were involved with church life in some way. Most children were baptized and attended Sunday School, and the majority of marriages were solemnized in the church. The clergy dispensed various kinds of relief, often tied to a visit from a district visitor. In addition, churches and chapels organized clubs and societies to appeal to a range of interests. Although the clergy despaired over the low attendance rates at church and chapel services, nonattendance did not hamper the variety of ways the working class utilized the churches.[74] The Christian Mission did not foster such instrumental, distant relations between itself and the larger community. It demanded ardent, engaged commitments from its followers, and it constantly strived to extend its reach.

The streets of working-class neighborhoods provided the Mission with the opportunity for open-air preaching, its first and often most successful form of recruitment. Mission evangelists preached and sang in the open air because people would stop in the streets and listen. The streets were always full of people. Journeys to and from work, marketing, and visiting brought people of all classes into the street, especially in the densely populated East End. London housing was notoriously crowded. In 1887, one survey found that over half the families of dock laborers lived in one room, and even the better-off families of policemen occupied only two.[75] Each house contained many residents, and the houses were built close together. In the older areas, the courtyards and lands surrounding the houses were part of the communal, public space shared by neighbors. In newer dwellings, the cellular, enclosed areas were replaced with wider streets that opened on both ends.[76] Both residential patterns meant that just by marching down a street preachers had easy access to an abundance of potential converts. One middle-class observer of East London life said, "So many of our people, young and old, passed their time leaning out of windows, sitting on the steps, or swarming at play in the middle of the road, that the slightest provocation collected a crowd."[77] Once a crowd gathered, converts spoke of their experience, sang hymns, and prayed. They implored the crowd to think of their souls and urged them to come to a meeting at the hall. The Christian Mission also held tea meetings, where tea and cake were offered for a small sum; afterward the crowd listened to speakers, sang, and prayed. Members were also taken on occasional excursions. In July 1870, fourteen hundred members were taken for a Sunday outing to Reed's estate.[78]

The Christian Mission did not confine itself to the conversion of individual souls. It strived to transform urban culture, particularly working-class leisure. Working-class leisure activities were a combination of casual, local entertainment and well-organized, capitalist business ventures. The gin palace, the penny gaff, and the music hall were all distinctly urban institutions that relied on a large population with just enough spare cash to pay for admission or a drink or two.[79] After 1870, shorter work hours, bank holidays, and the small rise in real income made leisure an increasingly diverse and significant element of working-class communities. By 1870, London had thirty-one large music halls, the largest ones having a seating capacity of over three thousand. The public houses were also important local sites for sharing drinks and gossip with work mates and neighbors. Finally, pugilism and keeping birds were popular sports, and even those who did not actively participate could still enjoy the spectacle and the betting.[80] Altogether this was a cultural world the Christian Mission deplored. Plebeian Methodists of the early nineteenth century had already struggled to suppress village festivals, drinking, and blood sports because of the brutality, drunkenness, and waste of time they associated with such pursuits.[81] The Christian Mission's campaigns were not dissimilar; they tried to shame and frighten revelers and to provide appropriate alternatives to mass culture.

Most middle-class Christians demonstrated their distaste for the sinful world of commercial leisure by keeping their distance from it. The Christian Mission, in contrast, held services in music halls, sang hymns in front of public houses, and appropriated the language and much of the style of commercial entertainment. The Effingham Theatre, White-chapel Road, was one of the buildings used in the early years. It was originally a public house, and in the 1860s the proprietor initiated variety concerts called "free and easies," where the crowd sang along.[82] The Mission borrowed the name "free and easy" as well as some of its dramatic style. "Numerous audiences have been drawn to listen to his exordiums by the somewhat plagiaristic announcement of a 'Change of Performance: the Rev. William Booth will preach in this theatre Sunday next.'"[83] The services were lively, and the audience was encouraged to participate.

> The "free and easy" then began. "Christ He Sits on Zion's hill" was the hymn that began it. . . . One man was rocking himself backward and forward, shouting words at the top of his voice, and occasionally relieving his pent-up feelings by shouts of "Glory", "Hallelujah" &c. A female might be seen whose emotion took the form of tears, whilst a third might be noticed in ecstatic agony, beating the air with clenched fists. . . . At last, several Gipsies were put up. . . . When the devil told him he was not converted he asserted he was . . . and read him the first two lines of the hymn . . . which was more than he could stand, and so "Mr. Devil tucks his tail under his arm, and off he bolts." Of course this signal failure was the occasion of jubilant cheers, and the people were not slow to acknowledge it in the customary fashion.[84]

These services and the posters that advertised them so closely resembled music-hall performances and notices that observers sometimes failed to distinguish them. Thus, they drew large, enthusiastic crowds.

Seaside towns provided another venue for the Mission to reach a large working-class population and attack commercial leisure. Brighton and Margate were among the first towns the Christian Mission established itself in outside London. The railway opened these towns to the working class, and by the 1850s over five thousand day visitors arrived in Brighton by train on holidays. When bank holidays were established in the 1870s, thousands used the day to visit the seaside. Seaside towns grew more quickly than any other type of English town. Besides sea bathing, visitors enjoyed the theaters, music halls, pleasure gardens, brass bands, and zoos.[85] Filled with festive visitors looking for amusement and lured by pleasure, these towns offered rich opportunities to save souls. Because visitors were free from the bustle of everyday life, they were likely to stop and listen to a preacher and reflect on the message. Catherine Booth "opened" many of the seaside towns in the late 1860s and early 1870s. She worked in partnership with the Mission. She used her services to save souls and to establish a base for the Mission and raise funds for the work. In addition to seeing seaside towns as appropriate sites for the Mission's work, she thought it would be less exhausting to work at the seaside than elsewhere, and she hoped the climate would help her always precarious health.

The Christian Mission, and the Salvation Army in turn, made use of the web of relationships that made up working-class communities. As soon as people were saved, the Mission asked them to stand before a

crowd and relate their experience of conversion. There were several reasons, both practical and theological, for this strategy. First, as holiness
was the most important criterion for religious office, any man or woman
who was entirely sanctified was ready to speak. Second, the Christian
Mission was little more than its converts. They built the movement as
well as filled its halls. Third, while the clergy found it difficult to bridge
the chasm of class and culture that divided them from their flock, the
Mission's converts could not help but address family, friends, and work
mates when they preached in the streets. Indeed, the Mission urged converts to speak to everyone they knew about salvation. Speaking before
friends and family ensured that an individual's commitment to a new life
was well known, and it also made them an example for others.

CHANGING TO A MILITARY STRUCTURE

The Christian Mission was effective. It grew dramatically in the 1870s.
It expanded from twenty-one stations in 1872 to seventy-two in 1879.
They were established along the south coast at Hastings, Portsmouth,
and Plymouth, in the Midlands at Coventry and Wolverhampton, in the
north at Sheffield, Manchester, Bradford, Leeds, and surrounding towns,
and in communities in the Northeast including Whitby, Middlesbrough,
Hartlepool, Bishop Auckland, Sunderland, South Shields, Consett, and
Newcastle-upon-Tyne. Four Welsh stations were established in Cardiff
and the Rhondda Valley. In 1878, 127 evangelists were employed by the
Mission and another 700 voluntary workers were engaged in Mission
work.[86] The Mission had ceased to be a small, London home mission. It
was now a national movement with a large staff that attracted the attention of the press and other denominations. At this point, the Christian Mission transformed its structure. It moved from a democratic, participatory system to an autocratic and strictly hierarchical one.

There is little evidence to account for this change. No doubt the leaders and members debated the problem of organization extensively, but
these discussions were not recorded and so we have only the limited and
partial accounts of those who instituted the changes Railton, in a history of the movement written in 1889, asserted that the old system was
unwieldy and led to division. He argued that it was nearly impossible to
wait to submit decisions to the annual Conference when the organization was growing so rapidly and continually requiring new procedures
and solutions to pressing problems. Railton claimed that often a man
was appointed to a place for twelve months but was instead sent to be-

gin work in a new town. When he informed the annual Conference of this new arrangement, "everybody's mouths were too full of Hallelujahs to make any other remark."[87] Railton observed that several buildings hired out for the Mission had been abandoned, contrary to William Booth's wishes, and "the spirit, as well as the wishes of the Conference, were being threatened by individual interference."[88]

The report of the 1878 Conference published in the *Christian Mission Magazine* merely announces the changes without detailing either the events that led to the reorganization or how the leadership arrived at this particular organizational structure. William Booth told the gathering that the reorganization was a necessity because they were engaged in war. "Now this is war. We are sent to war. We are not sent to minister to a congregation and be content if we keep things going. We are sent to make war against the bulk of the people, against any number, and stop short of nothing but the subjugation of the world to the sway of the Lord Jesus."[89]

A new Deed Poll had been drawn up, and the Conference was asked to approve it. This was, however, approval of a particular sort. Those who could not abide by it were asked to withdraw, and William Booth promised to assist them in finding new positions. The 1878 Deed Poll had three important provisions. First, as the general superintendent, William Booth was responsible for the "oversight, direction, and control" of the Christian Mission for the rest of his life. Second, the general superintendent could appoint his successor. Third, the general superintendent "should have power to expend all monies contributed, but should annually publish a balance sheet. That he should have the power to acquire or dispose of property and to set up or revoke trusts."[90] The Deed Poll could not be altered without an act of Parliament.[91] William Booth was now the autocratic head of the Christian Mission, and his power was broader and more comprehensive than that of the leader of any other Protestant denomination. He was assisted by Bramwell Booth as chief of staff and a small number of advisors. While these men and women might manage particular aspects of the work, the ultimate authority rested with William Booth.

This system consolidated authority in the Booth family. Bramwell Booth was chief of staff until he was appointed general in 1912. The other children all preached while still in their teens and assumed leadership positions from a young age. Ballington directed the first training program for Army officers in 1879 at age twenty-two, then went on to command the Army's work in the United States. Catherine, at age twenty-three, opened the Army's work in France in 1881. In 1880, twenty-year-old Emma was placed in charge of training women officers and commanded the Army's work in India in 1889. In 1884, Herbert succeeded Ballington as the principal of the men's training home, and in 1892 he was placed in charge of the Army's work in Canada. Eva assisted Emma in the training home beginning in 1884 and later commanded the Army in the United States; she was appointed general in 1934. Lucy worked in Ceylon beginning in 1889. Only Marian, who was disabled in childhood, never assumed a leadership position. The Army thus became a Booth family dynasty and many of its harshest critics denounced the Army on this ground.[92] But William and Catherine raised their children to devote their lives to evangelical labor and had absolute confidence in the faith and conviction of their children.

The name Salvation Army was adopted in 1879. It aptly described the movement's aims as well as the dedication, faith, and obedience required of its members. Elijah Cadman was the first to call himself a captain.

> I wrote out a bill—it was just when people were half expecting to go to war—and I said, "War in Whitby! 2,000 men and women wanted to join the Army!"
> They thought it must be something wonderful when the women as well the men had to fight, and I signed at the foot, "Captain Cadman" so that's how I got my title.[93]

Like much else in the Salvation Army, Cadman's innovation spread and was soon institutionalized. In 1878, the Army adopted its flag and the motto "Blood and Fire."[94] The first brass band began to accompany the outdoor meetings in Salisbury.[95] In 1880, the officers and soldiers were dressed in red guernseys and uniforms. A series of ranks, each with its own duties and responsibilities, evolved. Field officers were men and women entirely employed in work for the Army. A captain, usually assisted by a lieutenant, was in charge of a corps. Each corps was made up of soldiers and local officers, including a sergeant major, color sergeant, and corporal, who assisted the field officers in their work on a voluntary basis.[96] The *Orders and Regulations for Field Officers* noted that "in the Army men and women alike are eligible for all ranks, authorities and duties, all positions being open to each alike."[97]

A corps covered a town, a portion of a town, or several villages grouped together, and it included all the soldiers of the Salvation Army who lived in that area. Corps were grouped into districts under the command of a major, and several districts formed a division under the command of a colonel. As the Army moved outside England, it created territories, which were a country or group of countries, with a marshal in command and a commissioner in charge of all the officers and soldiers in that territory.[98] This structure provided a clear, unequivocal chain of command and division of responsibility

From 1882, all who wished to join the Salvation Army were required to sign the Articles of War. The Articles began with a statement of belief.

> Having received with all my heart the Salvation offered to me by the tender mercy of Jehovah, I do here and now publicly acknowledge God to be my Father and King, Jesus Christ to be my Saviour, and the Holy Ghost to be my Guide, Comforter and Strength, and that I will, by His help, love, serve, worship and obey this glorious God through all time and through all eternity.
>
> Believing solemnly that The Salvation Army has been raised up by God, and is sustained and directed by Him, I do here declare my full determination by God's help, to be a true soldier of the Army till I die.

The Articles continued with a summary of the Army's doctrines. It also included an extensive code of conduct. Members promised to abstain from alcohol and baneful drugs; never to use profane language; not to allow in themselves any falsehood or deceit in business or the home; never to treat "any woman, child or other person whose life or happiness may be placed within my power, in an oppressive, cruel or cowardly manner"; to spend "all the time, strength, money and influence I can" in carrying on the war and leading family, friends, and neighbors to God; and to obey all the lawful orders of the officers and to uphold the orders and regulations.[99]

The notion of a war against sin not only explained the need for strict discipline and a hierarchical structure but also expressed the ardent, inspired obedience that pervaded the members of the organization and their belief that sin was their enemy and surrounded them. Sin was the music halls, gin palaces, and public houses. It was the crowds who gathered to taunt Salvationists, pouring beer over them and drowning out the preaching with shouts and whistles. It was the spirit that made men drunken and brutal, women degraded and wild. It was policemen and magistrates who jailed Salvationists when disruptive crowds gathered around their outdoor services. In order to defeat evil, Salvationists believed they must create soldiers and officers fully committed to the struggle, whose discipline, faith, and fortitude were unquestionable. This discipline was achieved through and within a religious practice. Conversion brought Salvationists to a knowledge of their own sinfulness and, in releasing them from it, enlisted them in the war.

THREE

Conversion

Theology and Narratives

John Allen was a London navvy, an unskilled laborer, and almost every-one regarded him as a good fellow. "If oaths and curses and foul lan-guage poured from his mouth as freely as tobacco smoke, they were no more objectionable in the eyes of most of his mates than the incense of his favorite weed."[1] He was raised by loving parents in a small village. Although his mother had prayed on her deathbed that he would meet her in heaven, he took little notice of her prayers and set off to London in search of work as soon as he was old enough. One afternoon in the late 1860s, he came upon a Salvationist preaching in East India Road. "With dirty unlaced boots and short black pipe in his mouth, he looked as tough a six foot morsel as ever an open air preacher had to face. But anybody who hoped he would disturb the meeting was disappointed. The meeting disturbed him."[2] A group of twenty "converted roughs" sur-rounded him and prayed fervently for his soul. "He began to groan and bellow like a bullock, for mercy himself, and this continued for about twenty minutes. He then sprang to his feet, and stretching out his long arms, he cried with glaring eyes, 'I do believe. I do believe.' The tears had made two clear alleys down his face. He then jumped and shouted again and again. 'The blood of Jesus cleanses me from all sin.'[3] John Allen soon after joined the Salvation Army. He was "every inch a navvy still," and he "came down with irresistible force upon all the sinners he could get at."[4]

This biography was not intended merely to relate Allen's experience.

His biographer hoped readers would consider the state of their own souls
and learn from Allen's story what they must do to be saved. His life was
to serve as an example and a call. Moreover, his biographer strived to
turn converts into evangelists. He implored readers to think of the "laughing, drinking, laboring jostling throng" of thousands of English people
who were all rushing to hell.

> Shut your eyes and ask God to help you to look at it, till you see the laugh-
> ing faces turn white and pinched in the grasp of death, till you see the fiery
> eye-balls gaze with horror on the fiend companions who come to require the
> soul. Look till you see the gay forms that sported about two hours ago writhe
> in the agonies of a torture you cannot possibly exaggerate, and hear the bit-
> ter ceaseless wailings of the very voices you just heard shouting with laugh-
> ter! Look till the little wreathes and puffs of smoke you saw come from them
> just now swell out into dense black firelit clouds, that roll and roll and twist
> and swell again till they cover the whole scene with dense darkness—the smoke
> of your neighbours' torment ascending up for ever and ever! . . . Oh, that is
> it. That is it. That is what I want every converted man in England to feel. If
> you believe in hell, look at it. Look at it until your heart throbs again to keep
> somebody from perishing there, aye, till you are ready to lay down your life
> to save them from it.[5]

Allen's biography articulated several essential doctrines and practices
at once. It described how the conversion of a sinner might occur and what
the dire consequences would be should one fail to heed the warnings. It
also demonstrated the impact of conversion on Allen and verified the
depth of the change by describing his subsequent career as an evangelist. Moreover, it called readers to action, pressing them to take these lessons into the world. It thus combined biography, theology, and a call.

INTERPRETING CONVERSION

The Salvation Army's approach to conversion was among its most
significant doctrinal and practical issues, and it sparked intense controversy among Victorian Christians. Some critics of the Salvation Army,
for example, disputed the ability of reprobates to judge and know the
Spirit's working in their hearts. Others disagreed with the Army's disin-
clination to teach theology in any depth before declaring someone to be
fully saved. Many believed the Army's failure to celebrate baptism or
communion deprived Salvationists of two crucial ways to know the Holy
Spirit. Others dismissed the Army's dramatic transformations as pure con-
ceit with no more substance than the ravings of a drunkard. These criticisms reflect profound differences among Victorian Protestants about

the nature of the church, the sources of religious authority, the ways God
works in the world, the nature of sin and atonement, and the relationship between the body and the soul. Salvationists approached conversion with a theology of salvation as well as notions about gender, the
body, and spirit that infused their encounters with the Holy Spirit with
particular meaning. Indeed, these questions suggest that we must consider "the soul as a category of historical analysis."[6]

Historians, however, have often considered how the religious convictions of a man like John Allen are related to class consciousness,
with little attention to the religious problems that are at the heart of
Allen's biography.[7] This emphasis is especially evident in discussions
of evangelicalism, which is regarded as one part of a bourgeois effort
to subdue laboring people. Gareth Stedman Jones, in his influential article "Working-Class Culture and Working-Class Politics in London,
1870–1914," argues that while "Salvationists paraded up and down the
main streets" of every poor borough in London, by the end of the century it was "inescapably clear that middle-class evangelism had failed to
recreate a working class in its own image."[8] Stephen Humphries in his
Hooligans or Rebels? likewise regards the resistance of working-class
youth to religious education as one aspect of their refusal to conform to
middle-class ideals.[9] Regina Gagnier in *Subjectivities: A History of Self-
Representation in Britain, 1832–1920* makes a similar argument regarding the nineteenth-century conversion narrative when she asserts that
it worked in two "contradictory" ways.

> First it reproduced the official ideology of the middle-class religious societies
> that published—and occasionally forged—such tracts; hardship in this life was
> necessary for redemption in the next. Second, it permitted the dream of a pil-
> grim's progress to people whose life-events were doomed to endless repeti-
> tion—a dream that empowered the religious radicals, typically Methodist,
> whose ideology generated working-class movements.[10]

All these scholars begin with the notion that religion worked in the
interests of the middle class, which energetically, and unsuccessfully, attempted to indoctrinate working-class people. Religion, therefore, was
an alien presence in working-class life. "Religious ideology" was undif-
ferentiated and always quietest, counseling patience and forbearance for
laboring people.

This framework, however, cannot account for or even describe Allen's
narrative. Allen's biography was written by George Scott Railton, a leading Salvationist, with the explicit purpose of furthering the Army's evangelical mission. Allen, a laboring man, spent his life refining and spread-

ing Salvationist theology and furthering the organization's goals within his own community. His biography did not suggest that Christianity will make a convert acquiesce to the hardships of working-class life. Rather it preached an active, militant engagement with the sinful world to forge a community of believers. These conversion narratives demonstrated a complicated relationship to urban working-class culture, organized politics both bourgeois and proletarian, and the wider community of evangelicals. Certainly the Army's analysis of the causes and consequences of working-class struggle would not have corresponded with the views of labor activists, publicans, socialists, or prostitutes. But neither was it entirely at odds with other such working-class voices. The Salvation Army was as authentic, complicated, and mediated an expression of working-class belief and desire as any other movement of working-class people. To dismiss Allen, and thousands of other Salvationists, as deluded or duped denies the creativity of those men and women as well as the particularity of their vision.

A second scholarly approach emphasizes the psychological aspects of conversion. For example, Chana Ullman in *The Transformed Self: The Psychology of Religious Conversion,* argues that a large percentage of the converts he studied had a strong mother and an absent or passive father. Ullman argues that religion provides a need left unfulfilled by the father. He asserts, moreover, that "a dramatic conversion seems to depend on a suspension of intellectual scrutiny." [11] Historian Philip Greven in *The Protestant Temperament* relies on psychoanalytic theory to argue that child-rearing practices were critical to the formation of adult piety.[12] The work of such scholars is possible only when subjects can be interviewed or, as in the case of Greven's Puritans, when they left a minutely detailed record of their spiritual progress.[13]

It is not possible to investigate Salvationists in this way for reasons that are both practical and theological. Limited literacy; the lack of leisure time, adequate light, paper, and ink; and perhaps the belief that no one was interested in the lives of ordinary people meant few Victorian working-class women or men wrote about themselves. Salvationists were exceptional in writing anything at all, and their narratives were typically short, lacked intimate personal details, and culminated in the writer's conversion. Moreover, crucial theological principles distinguished Salvationists from many other Protestants. Salvationists believed entire sanctification was a decisive event that could occur in a moment. The saved soul should then immediately turn to saving others. Intense self-contemplation was discouraged, and there was no need for extensive spiritual writing. Thus, Salvationists simply did not produce a literature that would enable historians to engage in detailed psychological study.

Such an individualized, psychological approach to religious conversion also has methodological limitations. It is not possible to predict adult beliefs or actions based on childhood experiences except in the broadest sense, and it is therefore questionable to account for conversion through a convert's description of his or her childhood. An adult may despair or grieve, but how those emotions are experienced and interpreted depends on the social and cultural context. Individuals will not seek solace in Jesus unless they already know and accept Christian theology. It would be exceedingly unlikely, for example, for Allen to have become a Buddhist. It is never possible to glimpse the convert's past except as it is told in the present. As Paula Fredricksen has noted in her study of conversion in the life of Paul and Augustine, "It is from the vantage point in the present that the convert constructs a narrative that renders past and present continuous, intelligible and coherent." The conversion narrative thus can reveal only the retrospective self.[14]

Salvationist conversion narratives were never intended to give a full biography. These were highly formulaic tales that, while focused on an individual life, followed a set of conventions in both style and content. Each event was retold to demonstrate a theological point, often drawing on a scriptural text that revealed its truest meaning.[15] A convert's father might be mentioned or not, and yet this absence or presence tells nothing significant about the convert's early family life. Converts reconstructed their life stories into narrative. The ambiguities and differences between the story and the narrative were hermeneutics.[16] Salvationist narratives require attention to different levels of meaning that operated at once. Converts did relate a straightforward autobiography that included details about parents, childhood, marriage, work, and spiritual life and that culminated in an encounter with God that forever changed their lives. In this sense, a narrative is an important source of information about a Salvationist's age, marital status, work history, and the like. But these details were not presented in order to simply place the convert. Each narrative shaped and supplied an interpretation of an individual life.

Conversion stories often drew one phrase or image from a scriptural passage to suggest a meaning beyond the actual event described. Many conversion narratives referred to Paul, whose cataclysmic encounter with Jesus turned him from persecutor of Christians to an evangelical for Christ. Other biblical stories describe a turn that was far less dramatic.

Jesus saw Matthew, and "he saith unto him, Follow me. And he arose, and followed him." (Matt. 9:9). The Bible speaks of moving from darkness to light (1 Pet. 2:9) and from death to life (John 5:24) and of dying and rising again in Christ (Rom. 6:2–8), and all these passages are found in Salvationist narratives. Salvationists frequently combined these biblical passages with references drawn from some aspect of their local culture. Familiar writers like John Bunyan were important. As well, other less obvious sources that were particularly familiar to Victorian working-class readers, such as music-hall songs, broadsides, and references to work life, helped to shape these narratives and to link them with the daily lives of laboring people.

Conversion narratives were the most common form of Salvationist writing. Soon after they were saved, converts were asked to stand and testify to their experience before the saved and unsaved. Thus, the initial version of the narrative was often a public, spoken performance. These oral testimonies were then developed and soon would form the basis for further testimony, sermons, hymns, and theological discussion. Salvationists firmly believed that any sanctified person had knowledge that was more precious and more meaningful than that of the most learned theologian.[17]

THE CONVERTS

It is difficult to acquire a full picture of the women and men who joined the Salvation Army and produced these conversion narratives. The Army's headquarters were bombed during the Second World War, and only one Christian Mission membership book survived. The Army never publicly published membership statistics in any regular fashion. It is difficult to determine whether the individuals who produced these narratives were officers or soldiers, and that distinction is obviously important in discerning the level of commitment as well as the individual's experience in giving public testimony.

It is also difficult to determine with any precision how many men and women joined the Salvation Army before 1900 or were members at any given time. A few sources give a general picture however. The *War Cry,* first published in 1879, had an initial weekly circulation of 20,000, which grew to 110,000 in 1880. The Salvation Army did not distribute the paper free because it was thought that free copies would be discarded unread. These circulation figures may be compared to that for the *Christian World,* the most widely read religious newspaper, which was 120,000 in the same period. The *British Weekly,* a penny newspaper for the "advocacy of social and religious progress," had a circulation of 20,000 in 1886. The *Daily News* had a circulation of 150,000 in 1870.[18] The London religious censuses of 1886–87 and 1902–3 also provide valuable information despite the well-known limitations. In 1886–87, 29,395 individuals were present at one Salvation Army Sunday service out of 1,167,312 total attenders in London. In 1902–3, a total of 22,402 individuals were present one day at 149 Salvation Army halls out of a total of 1,003,361 religious attenders in London.[19] No comparable figures were gathered for the rest of the country. In 1886, 2,260 officers ran 1,006 corps in the United Kingdom, but the number of members in any corps is unknown.

These figures may be assessed in a number of ways. On the one hand, only 0.72 percent of London's population in 1886 and 0.49 percent in 1902 attended Salvation Army services. Historian Norman Murdoch concludes the Army was a failure in London. Hugh McLeod notes that the Army was less successful in London than in provincial towns like Scarborough, Hull, Barnsley, and Bristol.[20] On the other hand, one writer noted in that in 1902 the Salvation Army included nearly 18 percent of London's 416,977 Nonconformist attenders. Given the reluctance of working-class women and men, the Army's principal constituency, to attend religious services anywhere, this number appears more significant. The Salvation Army was not organized like other denominations. Its concern extended beyond its own members to include those who attended its services, read its publications, or just stopped to listen to the street preaching. Most Army services were widely advertised, and in the 1880s crowds of over three thousand regularly filled the Army's London halls for weekday meetings, and enormous crowds attended day-long summer meetings at Alexandra Palace. Many of these people never joined the Salvation Army, and they might have come to escape a dreary evening at home, to jeer at the odd proceedings, to witness a woman preach, or as a step on a religious quest. Other denominations recognized the appeal of the Salvation Army's meetings. In Sunderland, for example, the Primitive Methodist chapel postponed its own revival services when the leaders learned William Booth would be preaching there for one week.[21]

The Salvation Army was a revivalist sect that aimed to ignite the hearts of believers and to bring sinners to a full realization of the horror of their condition. Ellen Chase, a Deptford rent collector, for example, recalled one woman who was a "tough customer" before the "Salvation Army and domestic trials" brought her around, but the woman did not necessarily continue to attend Salvation Army services.[22] Counting attenders at Sunday service misses all those who stopped to listen on a street corner and fails to capture the spirit of the Army's mission. Nevertheless, it is clear that the Salvation Army never included more than a small percentage of British people by whatever standard it is measured.

Biographical details for 529 women and 624 men have been drawn from conversion narratives, the 1871 and 1881 censuses, institutional records, and printed and manuscript autobiographies and biographies.[23] Wherever possible, the information has been cross-referenced, but still few of these sources provide a complete portrait of any one individual. This information, moreover, was not gathered for any statistical purpose and must be read with caution. For example, one man's prior religious affiliation may be known but nothing else, while for another man both his work history and marital status were recorded but not his age or religious background. It is also difficult to interpret existing information. A woman, for example, might be listed as a laundress; that could mean she had her own mangle and took in a little laundry or that she worked full-time for wages in a well-established West End laundry.[24] Moreover, it is essential to remember that the evidence is fragmentary. If one woman was a laundress and another was twenty-one and unmarried, it cannot be said that young, unmarried, unskilled women joined the Army for the laundress might have been forty-seven and the young woman highly skilled. It is possible, nevertheless, to discern a general composite portrait of Salvationists that places their conversion narratives in a social context.

Salvationist women were overwhelmingly single (65 percent) when they joined the Army, and few (3 percent) were listed as married, although the status of many remains unknown. Men were more often single (39 percent) than married (22 percent), but the difference was not so marked as for women. There are several possible reasons for this difference. The men might have been older when they joined; their conversion narratives certainly suggest a long period of resistance and struggle before they were converted. Unfortunately, there is little information on the age of converts so this reason must remain speculative. Men's testimonies also suggest that their wives were often critical in their decision for salvation. Women virtually never assigned an equivalent role to their husbands. Therefore, married men were possibly more likely to receive needed encouragement.

Over three-quarters of the women were employed in unskilled or semiskilled work. Another 17 percent were employed in skilled occupations. Men were more frequently employed in skilled occupations. Nearly half the men were artisans or skilled laborers, and another 14 percent were small employers, retailers, wholesalers, or clerical workers. Only 24 percent were semiskilled workers and 13 percent were general or unskilled laborers. This difference in occupational status could be the result of several factors. First, compared with women, men as a group were more likely to be employed in better-paid occupations that were considered skilled. Second, the Salvation Army might have attracted the poorest women, but it did not similarly appeal to the least-skilled and poorest men.

The religious background of Salvationists is striking, but, again, this analysis is speculative because the religious background of only a small number of converts was recorded (19 percent of men and 21 percent of women). Nevertheless, some broad patterns emerge. The majority of men (92 percent) and women (88 percent) were Nonconformists prior to joining the Army, and most of the Nonconformists were Methodists. About half the former Methodists were Wesleyans, and a third were Primitive Methodists. The remainder were divided among the Bible Christians, the Methodist New Connexion, and other smaller connections. Still, the distinctions between Methodists must also be tempered. Many Salvationists recalled changing connections because of a crisis in the connection, because they were dissatisfied, or because they moved to a new town and a different chapel was closer or more agreeable. Many attended both church and chapel as children so even that distinction was not necessarily sharp. George Lansbury recalled that his mother believed the Church of England was fine for ordinary life, but if her children misbehaved, she sent them to the Primitive Methodists, who preached about a vengeful, punishing God.[25] Similarly, a woman brought up in Elswick recalled that although she and her friends attended chapel, they also enjoyed the Salvation Army. "Everyone followed the Salvation Army."[26] Nevertheless, the Nonconformist, especially Methodist, background of the Salvationists is striking because the majority of English people were Anglicans, with Methodists making up only 5 percent of the population at mid-century.

It is exceedingly difficult to make strong arguments about the relationship between gender or class status and religious belief. But this portrait does suggest several important points despite its limitations. Salvationists were, without question, overwhelming working class, and the movement appealed to men and women across distinctions of skill and status that were exceedingly meaningful to Victorian working-class people. The Army drew in far more Nonconformists, suggesting it was most successful when its theology and religious practice were already familiar. The Army's Methodist roots were no doubt most appealing to other Methodists. This appeal underscores that Christianity was not exclusively a middle-class concern, but, as we will see, the Army's theology and practice were different from those of many of the other Nonconformist bodies. Finally, Salvationist conversion narratives express a theology that was shaped by a particular cultural context.

THE THEOLOGY OF CONVERSION

The Army was part of a broad evangelical community, and much of its theology was shared with other revivalists and evangelicals. Finney and Caughey's work continued to be influential. U.S. evangelists Robert and Hannah Pearsall Smith toured Britain in the mid-1870s and revitalized interest in holiness. Dwight Moody's preaching and the sacred songs of Ira Sanky were immensely popular. Like its contemporaries, the Army emphasized Biblicism, conversion, and activism, and it placed Christ's redeeming work at the heart of its Christianity.[27]

Salvationists laid particular emphasis on the theology of conversion. Conversion delivered people from sin, allowing them to observe God's commandments on earth and assuring them a place in heaven. Since the fall, as *Doctrines and Disciplines* explained, all people were "depraved—that is deprived of God's presence and power in our souls, and not only so but actually wicked in disposition." Thus, all people come "under the curse and condemnation of the divine law and are therefore exposed to its penalty, which is everlasting death." The only hope was to "come to Christ and be converted." Jesus Christ made known God's will, was a perfect example, and atoned for humanity's sins in his death. No one could do or suffer anything to merit salvation. Through Christ's sacrifice, "He obtained for us the presence and operation of the Holy Spirit." The Holy Spirit brings about humanity's salvation "by raising up men and women to fight for God. By qualifying them with wisdom, love and zeal; by giving them thoughts and messages direct from himself and by sustaining them and comforting them in conflict." In order to achieve this salvation, a person has to first repent, be convinced that he or she is a sinner in danger of going to hell, and be willing to give up all sin. And the penitent must say, "I repent and come unto Him, trusting only to the blood of Jesus Christ for mercy and I believe that He does now receive and forgive me." When God pardoned the sinner, he then "turns him round to love God, holiness and holy people. It is like being made over again." Still, in this state, "there is still left hanging about the soul, and dwelling in it, many of the old evil tendencies which, although brought under subjection by Divine grace, still often arise, overcome and drag him into sin."[28]

Salvationists asserted, however, that Christians need not remain in this state but must seek entire sanctification. "Entire sanctification supposes complete deliverance. Sin is destroyed out of the soul and all the powers, faculties, possessions, and influences of the soul are given up to the service and glory of God." This state should not be understood as "sinless perfection" because an entirely sanctified person could still be tempted, err in judgment, and suffer infirmities of mind and body. But it did enable the convert to "enjoy the direct guidance of the Holy Spirit."[29]

In order to achieve entire sanctification, or holiness, a person had to have conviction, renunciation, consecration, and faith. For conviction, people had to feel themselves to be sinners and to acknowledge the need to be holy. Renunciation meant giving up all sin. Consecration required that a person "lay himself at Jehovah's feet, and offer to live wholly to please and profit Him." When a person was fully consecrated, "all is laid on the altar—body, soul, spirit, goods, reputation, all, all, all,—then the fire descends and burns all the dross and defilement and fills the soul with burning zeal and love and power." Finally, faith meant believing "the blood of Jesus Christ does now cleanse me from all inward sin and makes me pure in heart before Him. I do here and now commit myself to Him; believing that He receives me, and that He will evermore keep me holy while I trust Him."[30] Thus, a sinner became sanctified and was enabled to live a new life. This experience was direct and could not be mistaken. As one Salvationist said, "Some people say, 'how do you know you are saved?' 'I was there when it was done,' I tell them."[31]

Holiness advocates, as historian Timothy Smith notes, have often been viewed by scholars as representatives of an "eccentric, if not lunatic strain" in evangelicalism.[32] Historians of Victorian culture have argued that holiness theology was a religious version of the Victorian cult of self-help.[33] Thus, it is not surprising that Salvationist theology has been regarded as a slightly deluded expression of self-help for those whose material circumstances did not allow for much advancement in this world. Roland Robertson, for example, argues that membership in the Salvation Army was "a status-aspiration for those of the destitute or working class who embraced the principles of Salvationism; it was also a means of status-protection for those who were already lower middle class."[34]

This argument is unsatisfactory. Salvationism offered less prestige or status than membership in virtually any other denomination. Until the early twentieth century, Salvationists were regularly pelted with rotting food, arrested for disturbing the peace, and made the objects of vituperative sermons and pamphlets by clergy. Men in skilled occupations who decided to become officers frequently accepted a loss in pay, especially if they were sent to new corps. Moreover, this argument reduces faith to a rational calculation based on self-advancement.

Historian D. W. Bebbington approaches holiness differently, arguing that holiness theology was in fact a reaction against self-help. Self-help required struggle, steady effort, and deferred rewards. "The holiness movement, in total contrast, encouraged its adherents to turn aside from struggle as a futile assertion of the self in order to discover the rest of faith." Holiness did not require steady effort but could be attained immediately and would be followed by the gratification of an elevated spiritual life.[35] Bebbington regards holiness as a part of the romantic movement. His interpretation, however, is based largely on an examination of its upper-middle-class advocates.[36] While Bebbington's interpretation may capture the spirit of those holiness advocates, when this doctrine took root and flourished in the urban working-class context of the Salvation Army, its meaning changed. For Salvationists, holiness required intense struggle with their own sinful nature and against the powerful enticements to sin that surrounded them. That encounter with the Holy Spirit did not end in peace and repose. It made the convert into an evangelist ready to do battle with evil.

GENDER AND CONVERSION

Conversion was a change in position, direction, and destination. Narratives usually began with a chronicle of the convert's early life that suggested how this change came about. Because conversion required a remaking of the self, it had different implications for working-class men than for working-class women. In particular, the gendering of labor, wages, leisure, and authority deeply affected the Salvationist understanding of sin and conversion. Sin was regarded as a distinctly masculine dilemma, and religiosity was strongly associated with women, specifically mothers. The social relations of urban working-class households provided the context in which these struggles were enacted.

Working-class men lived in a world in which masculine dominance was expected and upheld, and yet their position was always fragile and open to contest. Men's wages were typically the mainstay of the family. The most stable and well-paid work was reserved for men, and even when women were employed, men were always paid more. Yet men could never be sure of their status as principal wage earner.[37] In London, for example, many trades were seasonal. An 1887 survey found that over 70 percent of men in certain trades were unemployed during part of the year and most were out of work for two months or more.[38] Married women had to earn money to supplement the household income. Their ability to do so varied by region. In many areas they found only seasonal, casual work, while in other regions, such as Lancashire, married women could secure well-paid regular work in textile mills. Children's wages were also crucial. Moreover, a wife's ability to labor, to bargain, to borrow, and to stretch small sums of money ensured her family's survival. Charles Booth, in his survey of London, found that in poor families "the comfort of the house depends even more than in other classes, on a good wife."[39] This meant working-class men could not claim to be the unquestionable head of household whose word was law. Women held considerable authority, and their domestic position enabled them to challenge men in all kinds of ways.

A working-class man expected to have money for beer, tobacco, and gambling, but the precise amount of his pay packet that was set aside for his use was open to question. A "good husband" provided for his family, but many husbands chose to ignore their wives' struggle to make ends meet on what they brought home. Ellen Ross's study of working-class mothers in London demonstrates that women frequently fought with their husbands to secure adequate support. Even a moderate beer drinker could easily spend a sum each week equal to the amount required for meals for a family of five to six for two or three days.[40] One working man recalled that a fellow factory worker who did not provide for his family found his wife had given him the rent book between two slices of bread for lunch. Another woman fought more directly. When her husband was spending money she needed, she told a social investigator, "I've gone into the public house and tipped up the table where he was drinking, and once he struck me, I gave him a black eye, then and there, and he's never touched me since."[41] While women did spend money on drink and other leisure activities, there was no expectation that money would be set aside for them to spend on their own. Andrew Davies, in his study of working-class leisure, concluded that "the predominance of men was the single most important factor that shaped the character of pub life."[42]

Salvationist men frequently recounted how their fathers brought them into a world of manhood represented by earning wages, drinking, and male camaraderie. "Sunderland Bob" recalled his father handing him a beer can and saying, "Sup, Bob, I shall make a mon o' thee yet."[43] A bricklayer testified that his foreman told him "I should never be a good tradesman unless I could drink and smoke along with the other men."[44] John Allen recalled,

> I could average twenty-eight shillings a week, and quite thought myself a man at eighteen, of course, getting a man's wages, and began to think if I earned the money I ought to spend it to enjoy myself. Being partly led by those who were older than myself, and partly by my own inclinations, at the end of three years I became strong in sin. The Oriental Music Hall used to be my favourite resort. I became an experienced, noted swearer, and not particular about a fight if put upon.[45]

Although drink was an important element in working men's lives, Salvationists strived to convince men that drinking made them dependent and foolish and that it was one of their burdens. The Army criticized not only drink itself but also the wider culture of leisure that gloried in drink and gambling. Keeping dogs and pigeons for racing, pugilism, and betting were all popular pleasures. Men could be found on Sundays in the streets, buying and selling their birds, placing a bet, or watching a fight. The leisure activities working-class men favored had particular meaning in their context. Pugilism was a performance of bodily strength and mastery that could provide an opportunity to display a masculinity based on prowess and valor. Betting on pugilism or on animal fights and races held the promise of making money in a way not totally dissimilar to that provided by much available work: it required skill, but it also depended on a certain element of chance.[46] These activities, furthermore, offered a masculine camaraderie that defined itself through the explicit exclusion of women. Leisure was, therefore, an important way to establish and display masculine privilege and community.

The Salvation Army condemned all these activities. Drink, it said, made men violent, and betting wasted money that could be better spent on food or boots. All these pursuits distracted men with empty pleasure. Thus, when men came to speak of their sins, they rarely described sins of the mind—heretical beliefs, anger toward God, or pride. Rather theirs were sins of the body, which were often the leisure activities common to working-class urban men. Drinking, attending theaters and music halls, pugilism, and gambling were the sins that led these men to penitence and caused them to weep in remorse. Hence, when the Salvation Army urged men to forgo sin, it inevitably induced a shift in gender relations, particularly men's relationship to competing notions of masculinity.

The way conversion intensified or resolved tensions over money, leisure, and the gendered division of authority within working-class urban households was an important element in many narratives. Men's conversion marked their decision to reconsider common masculine prerogatives. Women's ability to convince men to seek salvation was rooted in both their domestic position and men's confidence in women's greater religiosity. Again and again, men's stories present women's call as the compelling force. Men heard women's voices, literally and figuratively, pleading with them to relinquish sin and seek salvation. Salvationist men described how their loving, Christian mothers struggled to keep the home together and bring the children to salvation despite their fathers' careless drunkenness. Men cast their conversion as a rejection of the manly activities they once enjoyed and the embracing of their mother's heartfelt desires for them. Charles Fry remembered how his mother prayed "constantly, earnestly, and believingly" for her drunken husband and prodigal sons. He testified that her "holy life and fervent prayers were as a wall of fire around her boy, guarding him in the hour when the devil *must* otherwise have been victorious until her faith obtained its reward and the mother's God became the God of her son."[47] "Drunken Will" rushed to his mother's side when he was converted, telling her, "Mother, your boy is saved."[48] John Trenhail was convicted of sin when he remembered his dead mother, who "could still look down and see her wayward boy."[49] In all these narratives, mothers were cast as the ones with the authority to name sin, to castigate sinners, and ultimately to induce men to answer the call.

Wives were also critical figures in men's conversion narratives, and it was clear that women benefited from men's change of heart. When a slaughterer spent his wages on "beer and bacca," his wife went out to char. "I fisted her wuss than ever when I found out that she used to come on the quiet to the Hall here. I was mad jealous of her doing it that I used to feel like killing her sometimes. It used to seem to me that she did it on purpose to show me up, and make me feel ashamed of myself." His wife told him, "I can wait Jack. It is not you and me that is rustling, lad; it is in the devil in you fighting the Lord in me. The victory may be far off, but I can wait, for it is certain." One drunken night he beat her badly and she implored him, "'Let me hear you say, God forgive me, and I shall die happy.' . . . It wasn't until morning light I found a voice to say what she had asked me hours before . . . and that's how I came to join the Salvationists."[50] Her desire for his conversion was based on a concern for his spiritual condition, but equally her success signaled an end to his drunkenness, his violence, and perhaps even her charring. The concrete, material improvement in a wife's lot was a common theme in women's descriptions of men's conversion. Another woman told a butcher who ridiculed the Army, "It used to be starvation before they came . . . now he brings his wages home to me instead of taking them to the public house."[51] In all these narratives, women were the bearers of religiosity and righteousness, just as Catherine Booth argued in her defense of women's right to preach. Their words had the power to draw sons, fathers, and husbands forward.

Women's conversion stories were unlike men's in two distinct ways: sin figured in women's narratives differently, and the turn toward God was therefore also different. A small number of women remembered their youth as a time of reckless sin. Nancy Cunningham's mother was a pious, God-fearing woman. Her father drank hardly at all. But he introduced his strong-willed daughter to drink when she won a village sport competition. She became a real drinker when she went to work in a factory where all the other girls drank.[52] "Fish Pollie" left home early to marry a drunken man. "She became the most fearfully desperate woman. In the midst of such a life a large family was reared, all of whom were taught the art of sin and plunged headlong into a life of iniquity."[53] Both women's lives became utterly taken up with drink. But unlike the men, who eagerly sought the companionship of other men and adult masculine status through drink, women described drink as an obstacle to attaining womanliness by any standard. Their conversion narratives depict their drunkenness as fundamentally at odds with family life or a place in the community. But these women were exceptional. Few women described such a sinful past. Though such sins were a pivotal part of part of men's stories, bodily transgressions rarely played the same part in women's narratives.

Typically women's stories described childhood and youth as a time of seeking. Harriet Lawrence's conversion story told of her pious and loving mother, who took her to the Primitive Methodist chapel. Harriet always wanted to "do something to make people good." When she became a Salvationist, she would slip the *War Cry* into the hands of passersby and say, "Read it! Perhaps it will make you think of your mother."[54] Ada Watts "early learned to love God," and she never strayed from that path.[55] Some men also found faith early and never lost it. Colonel Taylor, for example, was trained to love God from babyhood

and always thought of God.[56] Still, a conversion narrative that lacked a
sharp turn from sin to salvation was a distinctly female form.[57]

The continuity in Salvationist women's stories was related to the
broader context of their lives. Working-class women simply could not
raise their fists or abandon their children to the streets while indulging
a taste for beer without relinquishing a claim to womanliness. Such behavior might result in their exclusion from neighborhood networks of
mutual aid and sharing or decrease the likelihood that neighbors would
intervene in domestic quarrels or family crises. Thus, a woman's stories
of drunkenness, violence, or gambling would be read differently than a
similar story from a man. Salvation Army advertising often highlighted
a man's sinful past. For example, a poster announcing the arrival of Billy
McLeod promised he would recount his "youthful days, crooked pals,
early scrapes, booze and swagger" and describe his thirteen fights in the
prize ring.[58] Women's authority rarely rested on a sinful past. Although
Rebecca Jarrett was among the Army's most prominent reformed prostitutes, the biography published by the Army was written to conceal her
participation and that of her mother in her "fall." A few women, like
Nancy "Dickybird" Cunningham and Jane Johnson, "Champion Drunkard of the World," were already renowned in their own communities and
built on that reputation as preachers.[59] But the Army usually presented
women as examples of faith in the face of suffering and as possessors of
a righteousness that triumphed over sin.

Working-class communities also affirmed women's greater religiosity
in various ways. The title "Mother in Israel" was given by plebeian
Methodists earlier in the century to exemplary women. Women who were
credited with many conversions, who were particularly gifted evangelists, or who were especially generous in assisting others received this title. All men were known as "brothers," indicating the particular power
ascribed to women.[60] Salvationists also used "Mother in Israel" in addition to the more formal ranks. Borrowed from plebeian Methodist language, this title expressed the distinct spiritual power attributed to Army
women. Not dissimilar notions were shared more broadly. Richard Free,
a Church of England clergyman, was posted to the Isle of Dogs in the
1890s. He recalled that religious affiliation was so strongly associated
with women that any man who wished to remain active in the Church
beyond adolescence "must be prepared to tred in the footsteps of the martyrs. Henceforth, he will be a marked boy, a marked man; the brand of
Christ will be upon him."[61] Margaret Loane, a district nurse who
worked in London's East End, recounted an incident when she was nurs-

ing a woman who was obviously disturbed by a persistent knock at the door. Loane determined that the vicar's wife was at the door and went to tell the husband. "Lerrer knock," he replied valiantly. "I'm not a tome. When the Missus is about, she can do's she like."[62] These anecdotes correspond to the Salvation Army narratives' depiction of religion as women's domain, resisted by men.

PAST AND PRESENT

Conversion narratives frequently included events that could not be fully understood until conversion revealed their true meaning. This form of understanding parallels a belief that the events and characters of the Hebrew Bible could be fully understood by Christians only when they were fulfilled by Christ. Many nineteenth-century spiritual autobiographers applied this same hermeneutic to their own lives in the sense of likening themselves to a biblical figure or, as was typical of Salvationists, reinterpreting past events that prefigured their eventual encounter with the Holy Spirit.

Men, in particular, used narrow escapes from death to dramatize their desperate state and God's mercy. Frank Smith learned early to "choose the devilish and the bad," and his ignorance of God left him unable to see that God "was speaking to me in various ways, by several narrow escapes of life."[63] These events seemed random until religious conviction revealed their true meaning. Captain Sutton "went into deep, deepest sin and had some narrow escapes of my life. Once, while in drink, I fell from a waggon, my clothes catching on the prongs of a pitchfork, if it had not been for the mercy of God, they must have gone straight through me, and my poor soul in hell."[64]

Because working conditions and domestic arrangements were so dangerous, it is not surprising that "narrow escapes" figure prominently in men's testimonies; they were in fact far more likely than women to die violently.[65] The description of these events also shifts the point of view in the narrative. These accounts are meaningful only because they are retrospective. When they occurred, the men had not yet come to a conviction of sin, and so these frightening and painful episodes appeared to be random accidents. But once these men were saved, they were able to look back and see the events as God's warning. These stories also served to warn listeners that they too might be liable to God's wrath. That lesson was made abundantly clear by a story related by Major James Dowdle. When he refused beer from a work mate, the man eagerly drank it himself. Later that day the man was found dead; "his body was picked up by a guard of the train who was running on the down line as we were running on the up line."[66]

Men also described the violent abuse of their wives as another kind of warning they failed to heed. Captain Wilson was a "drink fiend" who threatened to kill his wife. His children fled from him.[67] William Beatty would fly into rages, kicking his wife and dragging her about the room.[68] Another man testified that his young daughter's prayers had brought him to the Army hall to be saved. "I used to give my wife black eyes, but we are both here tonight and happy."[69] These stories illustrate both how far these men had fallen away and the depth of their transformation. Their behavior was relentlessly bad, but they could not see it. A man admitted that his wife had a husband who was "as hard and as cruel a beast as a poor soul was ever tethered to. . . . I was the curse of her life. . . . I used to fist her. It is to the glory of the Lord I confess it. He could wash white as snow the heart of such a wretch as I used to be."[70] Another man said, "Instead of being a brute, I intend to be a man."[71]

Women's narratives rarely described harsh warnings, troubled wandering, or degraded behavior that preceded conversion. Indeed, women typically struggled with a deep longing for God's presence and their own sense of fear and disability. Sarah Hugill, "when quite young, felt a desire springing up within her that she would like to serve God and she longed for someone to point her to Jesus." When a series of revival meetings were held in her town, she became alarmed. "I have gone home from meeting many a time with a face swollen from crying, and tried to hide it from my parents, and gone to my bedroom, and wept for hours as if my heart would break, feeling that if I had got into bed and closed my eyes, I should possibly wake up in hell before the morning."[72] Women described the sense of sin as the force that filled them with a desire for change. Captain Lockwood remembered that, as a child, "I always felt I was a hell-deserving sinner and never gave any thought during my childhood of going to bed without asking God to take care of me during the night and wash away all my sins, that I might go to Heaven when He would call me away."[73] While these women counted themselves sinners, it was not because they thoughtlessly disregarded God but because they were painfully aware of their inability to do what they knew was required of them.

Many women's narratives, in fact, describe the decision to join the Salvation Army as the happy result of a religious life. Elizabeth Churchill was born in 1863 and raised in London; her father worked in the Customs House. Two brothers, a sister, and her beloved mother all died before she was seven years old. When she was thirteen, her stepmother and another brother died. In the midst of all these sorrows, Churchill described her childhood as a contented time. Her father was "a *real true*, Christian, having been fully saved and surrendered to God when he was sixteen years of age." When Moody and Sanky visited England, Churchill's aunt gave her their hymn books and taught her to sing the sacred songs. When the family moved, it was to a house closer to the London Tabernacle so they could hear the Rev. Archibald Gilkie Brown preach. Churchill saw the Salvation Army working in the streets and she "joined that organization in July 1884." Churchill's narrative contained no dramatic changes in her behavior or her beliefs that might account for her decision to join the Salvation Army. Her membership in the Army is presented as almost the inevitable fulfillment of her spiritual life.[74]

Many women claimed, in fact, that conversion satisfied a yearning they had long felt. Jenny Wright was an active Sunday School scholar who hoarded her savings to give to the missionaries. But when the Christian Mission came to town, she began to wonder about her religious life. "I felt there was something lacking in my own experience, but did not know what it was; I got into such a state of mind about it, that I wondered if I had ever been saved. . . . A whisper seemed to come, 'it is a clean heart that you want.' . . . I fell upon my knees, and cried unto the Lord for a clean heart, and He gave it to me."[75] Miriam Smith "fell in" with the Salvation Army. "After seeking the Savior with her whole heart, her burden rolled away, and she realised the peace of God, which passeth all understanding."[76]

None of this was to suggest, however, that a woman's path was easy. Much Salvationist literature presented women with the responsibility not only for their own souls but also for those of their families. This sentiment was expressed in its strongest form in an 1880 *War Cry* article, "Mother, It's All Through You!," which was a conversion narrative in reverse. It told of a young girl who attended an Army meeting with a companion. She was urged to seek salvation immediately but declared she would wait until the next week. She was struck by a vehicle before the week was out. She had only few hours to live, and her heartbroken mother came to say good-bye. The girl pushed her mother away, saying, "Don't come to kiss me! I might have been saved but for you; it's all through you I am going to hell; you never taught me to pray, never taught me about my soul, and now I'm dying and going to hell—and It's All Through YOU!" The mother soon after became an imbecile, and her only son was killed in a pub while playing billiards. The *War Cry* advised, "Oh, mothers and fathers, take warning, lest you find yourselves at the last day amongst the unhappy crowd, who, while waiting to hear the awful sentence pronounced upon themselves, will see the children they loved writhing with agony and pointing their hell-scorched fingers at you saying, 'It's all your fault; it's all through you.'"[77] The warning was addressed to both mothers and fathers, but as there was no father in the story, the child called only her mother to account. Women could hardly spend their youth wallowing in drink and sin as a man might for they bore responsibility for their own souls as well as the spiritual welfare of their children. Thus, women's stories rarely included the same dramatic movement between past and present, instead remaining one continuous narrative.

JOURNEYS

Journeys figure prominently in women's and men's conversion narratives. Losing their childhood faith, coming to realize their own sinfulness, and finally seeking and finding salvation were often cast as a journey from place to place. Tom Payne was born at Coombe Hill near Chepstow. He found work when he was young chasing birds away from potato fields. At age twelve, he found work on a farm some distance from home. During the next few years, he moved from place to place working at a variety of unskilled jobs. In Wales, he was convicted of sin, but drink proved too strong a temptation and he fell away. He finally met John Allen in Cardiff and began to consider the state of his soul again.[78]

George Taberer was born in small village in Warwickshire to God-fearing parents. As soon as he went to Liverpool to work on a ship, he lost all religious feelings and began to drink and blaspheme.[79] Nellie Seymour's mother abandoned her when she was a baby, and she was raised by her pious and loving grandmother, who died when Nellie was fifteen. With no one to take her, Nellie went to London alone. She soon lost all the good her grandmother had instilled in her.[80] William Baugh was born in a village near Salisbury. From age nine, he worked in the fields. He had no particular religious ideas. He moved to Barnsley as a young man to find work. There, he met some Methodists and finally learned of the Army.[81] Emmanuel Rolfe's conversion narrative underscored the meaning of a journey. He was born to poor parents in a Wiltshire village, and from an early age he labored in the fields with his father. He decided to move to Middlesbrough. A companion asked to accompany him to hear

William Booth preach on Lot's escape from Sodom and Gomorrah. Rolfe realized he too must flee if he would escape from hell.[82]

The existence of journeys in these narratives built on several conventions as well as the common lived experience of working-class men and women. Bunyan and his successors wrote autobiographies with two assumptions: the Exodus of the Israelites prefigures the journey of Christians, and the Hebrew Bible's record of the Exodus "approves and even necessitates . . . a history that demonstrates a providential design in human history."[83] The image of a journey reminded readers of the forty years Israelites wandered and of the pilgrim's flight from the wrath to come. It also evoked the convert's move from sin to salvation. For Salvationists, a journey had implications both practical and providential. In Salvationist narratives, the journeys were frequently taken from the village to the city, where drink, theaters, and music halls enticed men and women, causing them to forget the lessons so carefully instilled by their mothers. But the city also provided opportunities to hear God's word. The Salvation Army was founded to save the urban working class. It eagerly integrated neighborhood culture into its evangelizing wherever it served to build the movement. Urban life made the Salvation Army necessary, and it provided Salvationists with bountiful opportunities to evangelize.

Journeys from place to place typified the experience of the very people the Army strived to reach. In the second half of the nineteenth century, many laboring people moved from place to place seeking work in a turbulent economy. Like the sectarian Methodists of the early nineteenth century, who articulated a spiritual response to the erosion of plebeian village communities, the Salvationists took the experience of urbanization and migration and invested it with spiritual significance, making it more than an economic necessity.[84]

Salvationists also described a lengthy and troubling search for a religious experience that could satisfy their spiritual hunger. Many struggled to bring their lives into accord with the theological principles they already believed. George Taberer was a member of the Anglican Church and sang in the choir. Nevertheless, he remained a drunkard.[85] Alf Reynolds was apprenticed to a ropemaker, but when he struck his employer during a dispute, he was dismissed. He could find work only as a navvy. He was miserable with the state of his life and knew he needed to find salvation. He spoke to his clergyman, who told him to wait three months and get confirmed by the bishop.[86] Similarly, Captain Richardson was the daughter of respectable laboring people. They sent her to

Sunday School, where she was confirmed by the bishop of Durham. Yet she found no peace and longed for something more.[87] Captain Kilby was confirmed, but "instead of making me any better, this seems to have been a starting point for evil in a more determined way."[88]

Not only the Church failed to meet spiritual needs. Charles Rich was brought up a strict Calvinist Baptist. He was taught that conversion would happen without any action on his part. "In spite of this teaching I was very early impressed with my need of a Saviour, longed to know that God for Christ's sake had forgiven me but 'wait' said my Pastor Sunday after Sunday, 'God in his own time will reveal Himself to you.'"[89] John Addie heard the Army preaching in the street, and he longed to attend their meetings. "The step was very strongly opposed by my Scots-Presbyterian parents." They could not comprehend his desire to join such a sect and lose all his chances of worldly success.[90] Kate Watts was brought up Congregationalist, but she wanted something more. When she tried to attend a revival meeting, the gatekeeper pushed her away because she was only eleven years old.[91] These stories work not only to describe individual experience but compare the Army's approach to conversion with the theology of other churches. The Church as well as the Nonconformists relied on external forces to bring souls to God. Both counseled patience and waiting on the rituals or some distinct sign from God that would bring a penitent to salvation. These stories insist that waiting was futile. Rather than helping, these churches erected obstacles. The Salvation Army's theology stood in sharp contrast. The Army, they asserted, provided a path to seekers.

Salvationists also detailed their journeys from one denomination to another as they sought the kind of religious life that would satisfy their yearning. Captain Wilson was born in a Yorkshire village and raised without religion. He moved to Manchester at age seventeen and eventually went to jail. He told the prison chaplain that he was miserable. The chaplain slammed the door in his face, saying, "It's your sins!" When Wilson finally realized his sins could be forgiven, "the light came into my soul and the burden rolled away." Upon his release from jail, he went to a Methodist New Connexion chapel. The minister preached "such a flowery sermon that I did not understand him." When Wilson said that he was recently released from jail, the minister looked away. "I looked at him with his gold ring and gold guard, and thought, is this religion?" When his old mates started to taunt him, he moved to Leeds to begin a new life. There he met an elderly woman who decided to pay him a salary to evangelize among "poor despised drunkards." He soon met with some

Salvationists who taught about holiness, and he decided to join them. His wife initially opposed the move to London, but her objections were overcome and he commenced work in Marylebone.[92] William Fawcett was the son of a Primitive Methodist preacher. His father died, and his mother married a man who drank heavily. Fawcett left home and worked in several places. He started smoking and drinking, but he was saved when he walked by a Primitive Methodist chapel. At age nineteen, he hoped to be called to full-time work as a preacher, but he was refused for reasons he never learned. He became an independent evangelist for a time and finally joined the Salvation Army.[93]

William Ridsdel was brought up in a "state of semi-heathenism" until his parents were saved. He mother prayed for him until at last "he ventured his all on the Atoning Blood." He immediately bought a Bible and a dictionary and taught himself to read for "his thirst now for education became intense." He became a Primitive Methodist preacher but was cold and "a backslider at heart." He read about the Christian Mission in a magazine, and after some consideration he moved to London to join the Salvationists.[94] James Bale was sent to a Wesleyan day school and a Brethren Sunday School. He moved to London in search of work and began to attend the Hall of Science and espouse secularist views. Some time later, he decided to attend a Moody and Sanky meeting, where he was saved. He joined a chapel. When he decided to move to Barnstaple to run a pub, his chapel had no reservations about his work even when he began to drink heavily. Finally, the Army came to town, and he determined that if he did not go to a meeting, he was bound for hell. His wife was reluctant to attend until he promised he would drink all night if she did not accompany him. They were both saved at that meeting and soon after entered the Army's work full-time along with their eldest daughter.[95]

These stories indicate denominational distinctions that in some instances might matter deeply, but they did not disturb a man sent to a Wesleyan day school and a Brethren Sunday School who joined the Army. What mattered was not prior affiliation or tradition but individual experience. James Bale, as we have seen, was a chapel member, but he felt he was going to hell before he sought out the Salvation Army. Joining the Army harmonized his beliefs with his life. Thus, conversion was both a turn toward a new life and a deeper engagement with a system of values he already embraced. These converts clearly came to the Army with a Christian theology that they sought to have confirmed and developed. Salvationists frequently lamented the plight of Britain's "heathen masses," but these writers rarely suggested that they were secular or lacking a fundamentally Christian perspective. Converts were troubled not because they did not know they were sinners but because they believed themselves bound for hell. Indeed, they believed themselves to be sinners precisely because of their religious beliefs. James Dowdle was brought up by pious parents, but he recalled he "sought evil associates, attended theaters, music halls, singing saloons, and other places of amusement, to stifle and drown my own convictions and to keep me from thinking how deeply I had fallen."[96]

These stories emphasized that these men and women were pilgrims, seeking only to know God. Salvationists sang, "This world is not my home, this world is not my resting place." And they sang, "I'm a pilgrim bound for glory, I'm a pilgrim going home. I'm bound to go where Jesus is, I'm bound to go."[97] These hymns reminded listeners that they must attach themselves not to this world but only to the Spirit. The journey in search of meaningful religious life meant worldly displacement mattered little in the face of eternal life. These narratives urged readers to apply this theological lesson to their own lives, to loosen the ties to place and tradition, and to turn their thoughts to God in order that they might be saved.

CONVERSION THROUGH THE BODY

Conversion was an encounter with God. For Salvationist men, that encounter was often a cataclysmic, bodily engagement with the Holy Spirit. In particular, men's stories drew on biblical images to convey their arduous struggle to accept the Holy Spirit. Cornelius Smith yearned for salvation. "I often groaned before the Lord, and hated myself after every defeat."[98] Finally, he went to a mission hall.

> It seemed as if I were bound in a chain and they were drawing me up to the ceiling. I was unconscious until I fell on the floor, and they told me afterwards that I lay there wallowing and foaming for half an hour, like the son the father brought to Jesus. (Mark ix.17) When I came to myself, I seemed to hear the voice of Jesus saying, "Thou dumb and deaf spirit, come out of him, and enter him no more." And the spirit rent me sore, and came out of me that same hour. . . . The bands fell off, my tongue was loosened and I immediately rose and told the people that Christ had saved me. . . . The change was so great that I walked about the hall, looking at my flesh. To me it did not seem the same colour. My burden was gone, and I told the people I felt so light that if the room had been full of eggs, I could have walked through and not broken one of them[99]

Smith's narrative adopted the language, structure, and events of the story in Mark 9:17–27. By using the biblical story, Smith gave his own story the weight of scripture. But more important, he demonstrated that Jesus could intervene in his life just as he did when he was on earth. Smith's faith had immediacy, a sense of God's presence acting in this world. There was nothing between Smith and Jesus, no ritual, no clergy, no church. Jesus spoke, and Smith was freed of his burden. Smith chose to express this transformation in physical terms. He foamed, wallowed, and fell into unconsciousness. When the Spirit left him, it rent him. Finally, he experienced salvation as a physical change. His flesh appeared to be another color, and his body was so light, he could walk on eggs. He had indeed become a new creature.

These bodily images were common to men's narratives. Sam Rees's biographer said, "Nothing but his present joys will blot out the remembrance of the agony of soul he endured; he could neither work, eat, drink, nor sit still but he felt he must either have his soul right or perish everlastingly."[100] The night Valentine Case sat up praying and seeking God, "my whole body seemed to be melting under the influence that was upon me; . . . the perspiration ran off me, the sheets were quite wet." He prayed, "Lord, you see how soft I am, it's your Spirit that is doing it, I will never live in sin any longer, if you will but stamp your image on my heart."[101] Frank Smith heard Bramwell Booth preach on the thirty-sixth chapter of Ezekiel. "Oh, how I was moved by the Spirit of God that night, and when the invitation was given both my wife and I went to the fountain, and oh! the blessed ten thousand times blessed, hallowed, melting, feeling that took entire possession of my being, the moment I surrendered all to God, only those who have been blessed in like manner can know, words fail.[102]

When Charles Fry was saved, "I walked about the room and sometimes fairly danced and that was the only time I did dance. I felt as though the arms of the Saviour were literally around me."[103] Captain Hansen recalled, "I was impressed to get on my knees and while in prayer my faith rose higher and higher until I could believe the Lord was ready to give all He had promised. I asked Him to give me the blessing of a clean heart, and that moment the Lord filled my soul to overflowing so that the glory ran out of my eyes like a stream. Many a time the Lord has flooded my soul since."[104] Two men who went to a meeting together recalled how after "praying and a lot of believing, we swung ourselves right into the arms of Jesus. Up we got, hugged each other, kissed each other, shook hands with all in the room, and then parted until the early morning love feast."[105]

Many men spoke of smelling, tasting, hearing, or seeing evidence of God, building on Hebrews 6:5 and 1 John 1:1. One man left his wife on her knees praying for him as he set out to find work. "In a moment, the road seemed to open in front of him and the smoke of the bottomless pit to ascend and he could seem to smell the brimstone of Hell."[106] George Taberer was in a state of utter despair. He earned only 6d a day, his wife was confined to her bed, and he drank all the time. He heard a voice say, "Cut your wife's throat and then cut your own. It will end all the difficulties." A second voice said, "Do thyself no harm." He heeded the second voice because he knew it was God speaking.[107] Captain Glover was in the country one day when he clearly heard God ask, "Where art thou?" just as he spoke to Adam in the garden.[108]

Others described themselves falling at the feet of Jesus and losing their burdens. James Bennett "threw down his burden and found himself free, praising his Saviour. . . . He fell at the feet of Jesus, weary, worn and sad but he soon found in Him a resting place and Jesus made him glad."[109] When Captain Kilby went to an Army meeting, "I threw myself at God's feet, and cried, 'I'll do anything for Thee, Lord! and go anywhere for Thee!' It was a hard struggle, dying for me was hard work; but when I was willing to let go, God gave me His smile and His favour."[110] These stories drew on several scriptural texts, including John 11:32, in which Mary fell at the feet of Jesus just before he raised her brother Lazarus from the dead, and Revelation 1:17, in which John fell at the feet of Jesus as if dead. But these converts were not simply using scriptural text to describe an event. The very physicality of these narratives powerfully evoked images of falling and rising, death and resurrection, sin and salvation, which are central to Christianity. Jesus was both fully human and fully divine, and his death brought eternal life. These conversion narratives built on these themes and images.[111] That physical struggle could release these men from the bounds of the body and the physical limitations of ordinary life was a powerful reading of Christian imagery.

The stories often contrasted size and strength with spiritual weakness. One Salvationist recalled, "One night a six foot navvy, with tears streaming down his face, took hold of my hand, saying 'You are right and I am wrong, what shall I do?'" Another officer said, "We shall never forget one occasion when a gipsy had come in and found salvation. To see five big men hugging and kissing one another, while the tears poured down their faces did us all good."[112] The physicality of these conversions conveyed the depth of the transformation Christ had wrought. Images of falling and of death also conveyed how dramatic a change was required.

If Christ could raise Lazarus from the dead, then why could he not lift any man's burden of sin? It was not merely a change in behavior or accepting membership in a new organization. This change demanded that the convert's old self die and a new self emerge. A new self required a disciplined body that was forged in an intense bodily struggle with sin and in the embrace of the Holy Spirit. Because Salvationists defined men's sins in physical, bodily terms, so too was conversion bodily. Conversion required that men use their bodies as disciplined vehicles of the Holy Spirit. In order to move from a body dedicated to sin to a body infused with the Holy Spirit, men had to undergo a profound struggle. Men could then say, "I live but yet not I for Christ liveth in me."

Scholars have sometimes regarded this kind of ecstatic religious practice as evidence of some kind of psychological disturbance, often associated with a repressed or perverted eroticism.[113] These narratives do describe conversion in language that could be read as sexual. But as literary critic Michael Warner has argued, "You can reduce religion to sex only if you don't especially believe in either."[114] Salvationists embraced a theology and lived within a cultural context that gave these bodily experiences particular meaning. Salvationists did not regard these bodily experiences as self-expressive or physically pleasurable. They were moved by God, often against their wills. Bramwell Booth, for example, thought that those who resisted conversion were most likely to be struck by physical manifestations of the Holy Spirit.[115] One Salvationist claimed that "I should have died had it lasted. Flesh and blood couldn't have borne it."[116]

This kind of encounter emerged out of a specific understanding of the body as well as a distinctive theology. Salvationist men regarded the body as porous and God as an ever-present force. To dissolve the body's boundaries was desirable and indeed necessary if a man wished to transform himself. The goal was not to seek bodily pleasure as such but to find God. These men described that encounter as a pleasure that struck more deeply and profoundly than any merely physical experience. It expressed Salvationists' understanding of God as a present power in their lives that could be felt and seen in the moment of conversion. It also corresponded to Salvationists' deep conviction that experience was more significant that mere rational, intellectual knowledge. To encounter the Holy Spirit, to hear God's voice, to smell the fires of hell, or to fall to the floor was a far more meaningful way of knowing God than merely assenting to a creed or knowing a set of doctrines. This understanding of conversion was an expression of both a theology and beliefs about experience, knowledge, and the body.

THE EFFECTS OF CONVERSION

Conversion made men and women anew, but it was never imagined as a force to turn the world upside down. This vision was not apocalyptic; the requirements of daily life—work, and family— remained. The Holy Spirit's presence did not permit men and women to transcend gender, nor did it render masculinity and femininity meaningless.[117] Salvationist theology imagined gender as a part of ultimate reality that would follow each soul to heaven. Salvationists often insisted that faith could inscribe gender divisions that were unattainable without God's power. When, for example, Salvationist men gave up drinking, they claimed they were more manly for "it takes a man, with God's help, to sign the pledge and keep it, any fool or donkey can drink."[118]

This masculine authority was linked to other kinds of social authority. The *War Cry* declared,

> How many have been straining every nerve to get into Parliament; they are ambitious of power and position. We can't all get there. Some of us don't want to. But we may all have the power of a higher order and further reaching; and that is the power to "open men's eyes" to "turn them from darkness to light, and from the power of Satan unto God". And this is the power offered to all God's children, even the humblest. In fact the humblest have the most of it.[119]

The righteousness that drew on the political disenfranchisement of the working class was implicitly directed at men, as political representation was an exclusively male privilege. This appeal worked both to link social and political power with salvation and to suggest that religion more than compensated those men who were excluded from the exercise of political rights. Drawing on a long tradition of English Nonconformity, it insisted that the poor and disenfranchised enjoyed a special righteousness based on their exclusion from other kinds of power. But the Army was not offering compensation for the discontented. This rhetoric was intended to mobilize men for a campaign Salvationists believed was of far greater significance than any act of Parliament.

Similarly, if femininity was closely associated with religiosity in Salvationist theology, then a woman's conversion would reconcile her with her truest self. Women's narratives frequently rejoiced that the convert could be a true mother. Rosie Banister had a drunken mother and spent her youth in pubs and prisons. "She was always trying to teach her children true womanliness although she was being dragged down and falling herself." Pamela Shepard prayed, just after her conversion, "Lord, help

me now to be a mother. I have never been worthy of the name mother."[120]
Again, these narratives seem to insist that conversion will not unmake
the conventions of femininity but rather will enable women to withstand
the struggles of urban working-class life.

Conversion was not an end point but the start of a new struggle between sin and a Christian armed to do battle and prevail. Just as soon
as converts were able they were to begin evangelizing others in the street,
at home, and at work. If all conversion narratives combined a biography, theology, and a call, then conversion was only the first step into a
life of evangelizing all those sinners who had not yet found God.

Saving Souls

Salvationists at Work

When Elijah Cadman, chimney sweep and pugilist, heard a street preacher speaking of sin and salvation, his life changed course (see Figure 4). He knocked down the seats at his boxing school and gave the rope to an old woman for a clothesline; he gave up his pipe, the pubs, and his old companions. In 1876 he joined the Salvation Army. The first time he preached at the Mission, he stood on a platform rail to show how the spiritually undecided wobbled. He was so effective, William Booth engaged him as an evangelist immediately.[1] His salary was 33 shillings a week, but he was warned that "even this we do not usually offer to candidates till they have proved that they can get that amount from the congregations and societies our aim being to make the mission entirely self-supporting as soon as possible."[2] He was first sent to Hackney, a notoriously difficult station, which nevertheless succeeded under his leadership. He became a respected evangelist, well known for his energetic preaching in a direct, plain style. Two years later, Cadman was asked to train Brother Gouldbourne as an evangelist. Headquarters wrote, "He cannot read but must learn at once. . . . I understand he can do any amount of work. You must show him how, and teach him to read as quickly as may be."[3] Cadman was among the first to adopt military titles, and his success in drawing a crowd with a poster proclaiming "War in Whitby" encouraged others to follow his lead.

Adalaide Cox was also a well-known, innovative Salvationist (see Figure 5). She was the daughter of a clergyman, and from an early age, she sought salvation. When she was thirteen, she heard God speak to her and henceforth she knew she was saved. She soon began work with several mission organizations that visited the poor and the sick. But when she brought some poor people to her father's respectable North London church, her parents brought her mission work to an abrupt end. She first caught sight of the Salvation Army when she was nineteen. "The Hallelujah Lasses often passed her door singing in a style quite out of keeping with her sedate upbringing, yet with a fervour and frank enjoyment that took her entirely captive."[4] Her parents strongly objected to her joining the Salvation Army, and her father insisted on filling in her application to become an officer in such a way that she would be rejected.[5] After some persuasion, her parents at last relented, and Cox set off to open the Army's work in France and Switzerland along with several other women. She later took a leading role in the Army's rescue work.[6]

These two life stories were strikingly different. Elijah Cadman was utterly unconcerned about the state of his soul until he heard the Word preached in the open air. He gave up fighting and drinking to engage in the battle against sin in the communities he had always inhabited. His training was acquired as he went, and his dramatic style and energy made him a success. He soon turned to training others. Adalaide Cox, in contrast, had long before found salvation, but she lacked a sphere of labor. Her activities had always been circumscribed by her class position and gender, and these distinctions were reinforced by the Church's teachings and conventions. Given that the home was a woman's sphere, she not surprisingly first glimpsed the Salvationists at work from her own doorstep. She then had to overcome her parents' resistance before she could become an evangelist. By 1881, when Cox joined, the Salvation Army had established formal application proceedings, and her spiritual state, theological understanding, and particular gifts were carefully assessed before she was accepted. Her work took her to France. Later she, along with many other women, pioneered the rescue work that was to become an important sphere of labor for Salvationist women.

Yet Cadman and Cox took paths that were, in many respects, similar. Like all Salvationists, they adopted a special form of dress and relinquished tobacco, drink, and many of the leisure activities their neighbors enjoyed. Their days were filled with God's work. They preached indoors and out, gave out copies of hymns and marched through the streets, sometimes meeting strong opposition. They organized the details of renting halls, meeting expenses, and supervising the work of local officers and soldiers. Their choices set them apart from their respective families and neigh-

borhoods albeit for different reasons. The Christian Mission, and later
the Salvation Army, adopted a structure and practice that combined submission to God's will and discipline with an unusual degree of authority
and responsibility to evangelize the world. The Salvation Army was a part
of wider changes in evangelical culture, but it offered a distinctive response
to the dilemmas facing Victorian Christians. The relationship among what
Salvationists believed, their social, cultural, and religious context, and the
work they did is the subject of this chapter.

THE CHRISTIAN MISSION AT WORK IN LONDON

The East London Christian Mission, like many evangelical Christian organizations, was particularly keen to rescue East London, believed to be
a dangerously neglected mission field. During the early years, the Mission presented its services to other evangelicals as a bulwark against crime,
drunkenness, and depravity. In January 1869 the Mission's newspaper,
the East London Evangelist, described the intense poverty of the East
End, the women "driven into a life of shame and misery" and their children raised "without knowledge of their Maker." "These are those from
whom the ranks of chronic pauperism and habitual crime are systemat-
ically recruited. These as they grow up form the 'roughs' of the streets,
the standing danger of order and society. . . . We must have more stations, more workers, more resources. To procure these, funds are necessary."[7] When the Mission secured the Limehouse Penny Gaff as a new
station, it rejoiced that the walls "which have so often been filled with
coarse songs and ribald jokes may echo in future with hymns of divine
praise."[8]

Anglicans and Nonconformists who established home missions, visiting societies, mothers' meetings, and food dispensaries did so in part
because they believed the working class was degraded, sinful, and dangerously divided from the rest of society. Many of these Christian activists regarded the godlessness of the urban working class as a distinct
threat to the state; the anticlericalism of European revolutionary movements seemed a dangerous portent. Particularly for the state church, the
potential harm seemed serious indeed, and many believed that drawing
the urban working class into the Church's sphere of influence was im-
perative if social upheaval were to be avoided. Many Nonconformists
also regarded regular attendance at worship services and participation
in Christian rites as the essential foundation of individual morality and
social stability.[9]

Many religious publications, including the *Revival* and the *Noncon-formist*, and newspapers like the *Morning Advertiser*, the *Bethnal Green Times and East London Advertiser*, the *East London Observer*, and the *Times* reported on a number of home missions that organized tea meetings, street preaching, and special services for working-class Londoners. The language used to describe the services was very like that used in Christian Mission publications, and seemingly little distinguished the Christian Mission's work from that of any number of other evangelical, home-mission organizations.[10] On April 5, 1869, for example, the *Morning Advertiser* reported on the proceedings at a Christian Mission breakfast attended by eight hundred people. "Good order was preserved throughout and everybody seemed grateful for what he was receiving. One poor fellow was heard to exclaim, 'God almighty knows when I have had such a breakfast' and when he was told he should thank God for it, he said 'I do, sir, with all my heart.'"[11]

These reports emphasized the orderliness and gratitude of the people, the effects of William Booth's strong preaching, and the plentiful hot tea and cakes. The religious press praised the Mission for the good work accomplished. The *Revival* celebrated the "hundreds who have professed to find mercy in connection with our meetings, some have gone to distant lands, some to other churches, and many are now in fellowship with us, hungering and thirsting after the fuller baptism of the Holy Spirit and earnestly striving to bring others to Jesus."[12] In another report the *Revival* described "a navvy, a big burly man, one of the greatest drunkards and blasphemers in Whitechapel. He had deserted his wife and children and given himself up to all manner of debauchery. He was awakened in the open air, and induced to attend theatre services, and was deeply convicted. We have every reason to hope he is soundly converted. He is now living happily with his wife and children and enduring much persecution for Christ's sake. His wife has also found Jesus."[13]

The Christian Mission was, in many respects, part of this body of concerned evangelicals. The Mission's workers regarded the unsanctified state of the inhabitants of the East End as a grave moral crisis. The fundraising appeals of the 1870s stressed the serious threat posed by the unsaved multitudes, and the lists of financial contributors in every issue of the *East London Evangelist* and the *Christian Mission Magazine* suggest such appeals were effective.

Nevertheless, the Mission's most important and ultimately most significant activities set it apart from many of its contemporaries. These differences were evident to other Christians from the earliest years. When the *Nonconformist* praised a Mission gathering, it still noted that "we might dispute the speaker's taste in some matters, we might differ in some of his theological views."[14] Another report distanced writer and reader from the Mission workers and congregations when it noted that a meeting was "not characterized by that calmness, gravity and quiet common among ordinary congregations: the singing is unmistakeably louder; the choruses undeniably longer; the prayers louder and longer and the discourse louder, longer and stronger."[15]

These differences were to become highly visible by the late 1870s, when uniformed Salvationist women and men were preaching and parading through the working-class neighborhoods, but the organization's unique features were present from the beginning. The Christian Mission was not the creation of any larger denominational body. Even its ties with the evangelical organizations and philanthropists that provided the initial financial support were loose and soon broken. It therefore could devise its own structure and practices without appeal to any external body. Its members assumed positions of leadership as there was no other, larger body providing leaders or establishing qualifications for given positions. Similarly, it was not dependent on a parochial structure and could therefore devise circuits or establish and close stations according to shifting demands.

The Christian Mission's theology was different from that of most Anglicans or Nonconformists. The Mission, and later the Salvation Army, were holiness organizations, and that orientation was essential to the creation of its rules and boundaries, to understanding which issues were contested and which were not. Consequently, the Mission and later the Army were harshly criticized by many Nonconformists and Anglicans for both their theological and their practical differences. Not until the early 1890s were Salvationists invited to join interdenominational bodies. Salvationists, in turn, disdained religious rituals that did not lead to sanctification. The ultimate fate, they believed, of a costermonger who never entered a church was to be little different from that of a clergyman who relied only on Church ritual to save him. Not surprisingly, the Army's relations with other churches were often strained.

The Mission and later the Army demanded an ardent, whole-hearted commitment from each member. Faith was to be expressed and affirmed in every aspect of the believer's life. Many churches and chapels attempted to use tea meetings, children's breakfasts, working men's clubs, and mothers' meetings to bring in new members. The Mission and later the Army organized similar services, but they clearly indicated that there was no room for those with a lukewarm commitment who did little more than attend a Sunday service and drop a few coins in the collection plate. They sought a wholehearted commitment from those touched and transformed by the Holy Spirit, and everything they did was based on that premise.

Finally, the Mission and later the Army negotiated cultural and class distinctions in ways that middle-class evangelicals and social reformers rarely agreed with or understood. The rules that governed social reformer Octavia Hill's dwellings, the prerequisites for assistance outlined by the Charity Organisation Society, the behavior expected at the clubs organized for working-class children by churches or settlement workers, the lessons taught at mothers' meetings, all began with the assumption that the values and aspirations of the urban working class led to poverty and disorder. Middle-class philanthropists, social reformers, and clergy regarded their own educational attainments as self-evidently superior; even if their working-class charges could not fully achieve the same standards, they were nevertheless a laudable objective. The Christian Mission, in contrast, was composed of working-class men and women intent on saving souls. Their means and objectives emerged out of their particular theological understanding, class, and community life.

RUNNING A MISSION STATION

The Christian Mission's structure of class meetings, local and circuit preachers, elders' meetings, and annual Conferences was based loosely on the organization of the sectarian Methodists. This structure would have been familiar to its many members who were former Methodists, and it was close to the system the Booths participated in until they left the Methodist New Connexion. By mid-century, however, many Methodists had abandoned the class meeting and attended only Sunday worship services. London, moreover, was exceptional because the Methodists had never been strong there. The Church of England, which claimed nearly half of all church attenders in Inner London, never included any comparable participatory services that members were required to attend. Thus the Mission was at once reviving an older practice and bringing a new type of service to its London membership.[16]

The daily business of the Christian Mission was attended to by the elders' meeting. For example, the April 1870 Croydon Elders' Meeting minutes recorded that seven men and three women met to resolve various problems. Members discussed "the persecution and annoyance to the work and workers from the boys and men outside." It was decided that the gate should be improved and that the hall must be licensed by a magistrate as a place to preach the gospel; such a license would entitle the Mission to request police assistance. In April 1871, Brother Holmes was instructed to reprove Sister Asher because "trifling and laughter was very unbecoming in any meeting of a prayer meeting."[17] Following the 1879 reorganization, all policy and strategy were decided by William Booth with the assistance of his advisors at headquarters. Captains and lieutenants, with the assistance of local officers who volunteered their time, carried out the daily business of the corps. The local officers included a treasurer, secretary, color-sergeant, and bandsman. Together they were responsible for keeping accounts and membership records and implementing the directives from headquarters. The local officers also provided continuity for the field officers, who were moved to a new corps every few months.

The believers' meeting was the spiritual core of the Christian Mission. The first step in membership, required to maintain good standing, it was a training ground for leaders. Members joined "that they may be counselled and watched over and that a record may be kept of their residences so that, in case of absence through sickness or otherwise, they may be visited and cared for."[18] Any individual who attended a believers' meeting for eight weeks was put forward for membership in the Mission. The leader convened the believers' meeting weekly, opening each meeting with prayer and singing. The leader "shall relate his own experience first and then inquire into the experience of the members, one by one, and administer such encouragement, instruction and reproof as their state requires."[19] The Conference encouraged leaders to "avoid a lifeless, formal manner" and to engage in lively singing and brief speaking and prayer.

The believers' meeting was unquestionably intended as a source of spiritual guidance and inspiration for all members. It also had the effect of drawing in and training everyone in public testifying, singing, and speaking. The leaders were chosen from among those who attended the believers' meeting, and thus anyone with the necessary gifts in speaking, singing, and guiding others might assume this position. The leader had to have "clear views of the gospel, have the ability to teach the way of salvation, and be attached to the doctrines and practices of the Mission."[20] The work also prepared members for other offices in the Mission. Soon after it was established, the Mission began to engage its members as exhorters and prayer leaders to carry out open-air and cottage meetings and as local preachers who would retain their paid work and preach for the Mission whenever they could. The Mission also hired others as full-time evangelists. The 1870 Whitechapel circuit plan, which gave the names and addresses of each person in any of these positions, listed eight male and five female preachers and sixteen men and nine women exhorters and prayer leaders.[21] In the first few years, many of these men and women came from other mission organizations. But by the early 1870s the workers were increasingly drawn from among the members. George Scott Railton wrote to one man explaining that the Mission was not seeking evangelists at that time and was "less disposed to do so every year because supply of preachers from amongst the converts of the Mission steadily increases."[22]

The itinerant and local preachers organized open-air services and prayer meetings regularly. Open-air services were to attract a crowd and engage listeners in the message. Preachers were to "let all the exercises be short and lively. It is better to speak several times, with a little singing and prayer between . . . than to speak for a long time, unless specially led to do so by the Spirit." Preachers were instructed to avoid controversial topics and never to speak deprecatingly of any religious body. "Do not rail at papists, infidels, publicans or any class of sinners, or any particular form of error, but with men as sinners in danger every moment of the damnation of Hell and to whom Christ, who died for them, has sent you to offer a present, free and full salvation." At the close of the service, the preachers led the crowd, singing, in procession to a hall. The hymn, it was advised, should be well known. "You had better not sing at all than sing so as to render your effort ridiculous."[23]

The *East London Evangelist* described one Sunday service that began at half-past five in Mile End Road.

> Hundreds appeared to listen with undivided attention. The Word was with much power. . . . We then formed a procession and sang down the Whitechapel Road to the Room. We had an efficient band of singers, and as we passed along the spacious and crowded thoroughfare, singing "We are bound for the land of the pure and the holy", the people ran from every side. From the adjacent gin palaces the drinkers came forth to hear and see; some in mockery joined our ranks, some laughed and sneered, some were angry, the great majority looked on in wonder, while others turned and accompanied us as we went, changing our song to "There is a fountain filled with blood," and then again to "With a turning from sin, let repentance begin; then conversion of course will draw nigh; But til washed in the blood of the crucified Lord; we never shall be ready to die."[24]

Prayer meetings were held at least once a week for those seeking salvation or in need of prayer. Those "deeply convinced of sin and in earnest for salvation" were encouraged to go to the penitent form, a seat set aside for those seeking conversion, while others sang hymns and prayed. Exhorters, leaders, and preachers spoke with penitents, guiding and encouraging them.

Music was essential to all these gatherings. Salvationists sang and played a variety of instruments. Leading a hymn was important, and a strong voice could drown out a hostile crowd. Tambourines were played by women, and concertinas and percussion and brass instruments were played by both men and women. Soldiers and officers composed songs to mark the opening of a corps, to relate a conversion narrative, or to elucidate a theological point. The hymns were regularly published in Salvation Army newspapers and in songbooks. In 1886, the first issue of the monthly *Musical Salvationist*, published by the Army's music department, appeared. Two years later, the Army declared that only music published by the Army was to be played at its services. Besides fostering uniformity and a sacred music tradition different from that of any other body, this requirement created a demand for Salvation Army songwriters.[25] Revivalist standards were found in any Salvation Army hymnbook.[26] All the songs, whether written expressly for the Army or popularized by Moody and Sanky and others, were easy to sing and expressed in words and music a distinct emotional state. Songs were used to sustain a sinner's conviction of sin or to give voice to a convert's hallelujahs.

Mission stations and later corps were required to hold outdoor meetings and processions, prayer meetings for those seeking salvation, and cottage meetings, all on a regular schedule. All Salvationists were to participate in services by leading a hymn, speaking of their experience, or preaching. As Railton wrote, "The system that is generally prevalent in the world, whereby service after service is taken up by one man, and the vast majority of God's people are trained to sit and listen, is a system entirely without sanction in either the Old or New Testament, a system utterly opposed to the very idea of spiritual religion, and which can only minister to idleness and disgrace to the hearers."[27]

Preaching was to be heartfelt and personal. Mission workers received little formal training; the necessary skills were acquired through experience. Railton, the Mission secretary, wrote to Miss A. Woods to encourage her to preach.

> Now all you need is to try and take one line of thought and make enough of it to fill half an hour with anecdotes such as fit the subject. You will find it an easy plan to take for your subjects at first the parables or miracles of Christ. You can find in any one of these a number of different points which will help

you to a good sermon. . . . You may not have the necessary gifts and strength of will needed for one of our evangelists, for we put women to manage stations just as we do men, but no matter where you may be you ought to be a preacher. God can make you one and save souls by you I have no doubt.[28]

Rodney Smith first preached for the Mission in 1877 at age seventeen. He presented himself to William Booth, asking to become an evangelist for the Christian Mission. At the very next meeting Smith attended, Booth announced him as a speaker. Seeing how nervous he was, Booth asked him to just sing a solo. Smith continued to sing at meetings. He recalled that "my schooling, my discipline, was work—visiting people and taking part in meetings."[29] After his conversion in 1876, he experienced "an intense desire to read." He pored over his Bible, struggling to master the language of scripture. He practiced preaching in a field and memorized passages from Isaiah and the Gospels. When he stood up to preach for the first time before over a thousand people at a London meeting of the Christian Mission, he was shaking with fear. He told the crowd, "I do not know what you know about many things but I know Jesus. I know that he has saved me. I cannot read as you can. I do not live in a house as you do; I live in a tent. But I have got a great house up yonder and some day I am going to live in it. My great desire is to live for Christ and the whole of my life to be useful in His service."[30]

Smith continued to preach and soon discovered that "God gave me utterance and I found myself saying things I had never thought about or read about. They were simply borne in upon me and I had to say them."[31] Like Elijah Cadman and many others, Smith struggled to improve his literacy. But he devised his own way to manage the difficult vocabulary of the Bible. "The plan I adopted was this. I went on reading slowly and carefully until I saw a long word coming into sight. Then I stopped and made some comments, after the comments I began to read again, but took care to begin on the other side of the long word. I used to struggle night after night in my lodgings over the hard words and names in the Bible."[32]

Rosina Davies, who joined the Army in 1879, took lessons in grammar and practiced reading the Psalms aloud to improve her speaking. She preached, and "as a rule, I went to pulpits straight from communion with God. I opened my mouth and the Lord filled it with a message. He never failed me and I only wish I could recall what He said."[33] Salvationists believed that extemporaneous preaching broke the stale, worldly conventions that could stifle God's spirit. It also exemplifies their disinterest in the kinds of education and preparation that most clergy relied on when they preached.

Innovation was welcome. John Lawley, who joined in 1878, marched at the head of processions with a stiff leg and snapped his umbrella open at every step. If this maneuver failed to attract attention, he opened his umbrella and raced around in a circle until he gathered a crowd. When he described how the devil attacks sinners, he tore his songbook into shreds and dove off the platform, making swimming motions to illustrate the sea of God's love and pardon.[34] Another officer, struggling to draw a crowd, went every night into the market square and lay motionless in the snow without speaking for forty-five minutes. After a week, a crowd would gather just to watch this odd performance. Finally, he stood and preached.[35] Alfred Tutte, captain at Honiton in 1885, recorded in his diary one successful effort to attract people to the meeting.

> Major in red shirt and helmet carrying the flag; me in sailor's uniform beating a large triangle; one of the comrades in a red jersey and high hat, the other in uniform with two lasses (officers) in single file formed the procession. The place was dead; something was necessary to wake it up. We sang and between each verse I rattled the triangle as loud as ever I could, causing people to flock out in numbers, thinking we had gone off. Their thoughts turned to certainty when about 200 yards from the hall the Major with the flag took to his heels and we followed at top speed to the barracks, the crowd following after. Inside, good meeting. One soul and one the night after.[36]

William Bennett, who joined the Mission in 1872, declared, "I glory in being, in the truest sense, an out-and-out Salvationist, ever ready to jump at any new departure and go to all lengths, however seemingly ridiculous, to attract and convince the lost crowds, which is the true spirit of a Christian Mission Salvationist."[37]

These startling techniques attracted new members, but they were not merely for show. Holiness required a direct, personal experience of the Holy Spirit. Formal ritual and liturgy would never bring the unconverted to God because they were celebrated in the enclosed space of the church, away from the eyes and ears of the people most in need of salvation. Moreover, Salvationists believed such formal ritual rarely brought anyone to a conviction of sin, nor did it point the way to salvation. Conversion was a direct encounter with the Holy Spirit, and Salvationists, like many others in the revivalist and holiness traditions, used music, preaching, and ardent prayer to pull sinners toward God. Salvationist meetings were thus both organized and expressive, spontaneous events. Bramwell Booth described one meeting held on January 16, 1878, in his diary.

> At night Corbridge led a Hallelujah Meeting til 10 o'clock. Then we commenced an all-night of prayer. Two hundred and fifty people were present til 1 A.M.;

two hundred or so after. A tremendous time. From the very first Jehovah was passing by, searching, softening, and subduing every heart. The power of the Holy Ghost fell on Robinson and prostrated him. He nearly fainted twice. The brother of the Blandys entered into full liberty, and then he shouted, wept, clapped his hands, danced amid a scene of the most glorious and heavenly enthusiasm. Others meanwhile were lying prostrate on the floor, some of them groaning aloud for perfect deliverance. I spoke twice in the course of the night; so did Corbridge. He did well. . . . It was a blessed night.[38]

Thus, the Army was both tightly structured and a diverse, even chaotic, organization at times.

MIRIAM AND DEBORAH: THE WORK OF WOMEN

The first Conference of the Christian Mission, held in June 1870 at the People's Mission Hall, 272 Whitechapel Road, brought together twenty-eight men and five women with William Booth in the chair. The Conference established the rules and practices that would govern the Mission until it was reorganized into the Salvation Army in 1879. It determined how the open-air services, the believers' meetings, and the work of local and itinerant preachers would be organized as well as the prayer classes, bible classes, and watch nights. The Conference also assigned individuals to circuits, arranged to open new mission stations, and provided an opportunity to discuss strategies and plans. The 1870 Conference marked the beginning of an established position on women's duties and rights in the Christian Mission. From 1865 to 1870, the Mission had no discernible policy on women members. Catherine Booth was a well-known and active preacher, and she regularly filled large halls to capacity when she preached in London and elsewhere. But it is not clear how her example was initially followed by other women. At the 1870 Conference, the Mission declared it would engage "Godly women possessing the necessary gifts and qualifications" as leaders and preachers or for any other office, and it decided that women could speak and vote at all meetings.[39]

The Mission had already put these principles into action. Eliza Collinridge sat on the Croydon Elders' Committee as early as 1869, and Catherine Booth, Mrs. Collinridge, Miss Short, Mrs. Mathison, and Mrs. Tidman were among the thirty-five voting members present at the 1870 Conference. In the 1870 circuit plan for Whitechapel five of the thirteen preachers were women and nine of the sixteen exhorters and prayer leaders were women.[40] In 1875, Annie Davis, the first woman appointed to run a mission station, was put in charge of Barking, one of twenty-three stations active at that time.[41] The following year, Davis moved to Bethnal Green, and Elizabeth Pollett was put in charge at Kettering, Ellen Hall at Soho, and Mrs. Reynolds at Shoreditch.

These were, in every sense, ordinary working-class women. Ann Blackman, for example, worked as an exhorter for the Mission. She was forty-four years old in 1870, and she lived with her husband, William, a carpenter, and two lodgers.[42] Sarah Pressy, an exhorter listed in the 1872 Whitechapel circuit plan, was the twenty-nine-year-old wife of Thomas, a boot maker. He too was an exhorter for the Mission. They lived with their five children, who ranged in age from five to thirteen.[43] Eliza Collinridge sat on the Croydon Elders' Meeting in 1869, attended the 1870 Conference, and in that year she was a preacher on the Whitechapel circuit. She was twenty-nine years old and lived with her husband, Thomas, a thirty-year-old groom in a livery stable. He too was listed as a preacher in the 1870 Whitechapel circuit plan. They lived in Whitechapel with their two sons, aged four and two.[44] Annie Davis was single and twenty-six years old when she was sent to Barking in 1875. A former Congregationalist, she was drawn to the Mission because of its holiness teaching and the opportunities it offered her.[45]

WOMEN'S ROLE AT MID-CENTURY

The enhanced authority and wide range of religious work for Christian women was an expression of broad mid-century currents. On the one hand, evangelicals were alarmed by the seeming indifference of the urban working class to religion, and they embraced various unconventional methods to attract working-class people to churches and chapels. On the other hand, British women were increasingly willing to press against the constraints and limitations of their sanctioned place; during this period middle-class women established new colleges to prepare women for higher degrees, opened up new professions for women, and began to organize for suffrage and other political rights. Evangelical Christian women, influenced both by a desire to spread the gospel and by the expansion of women's sphere, initiated a range of new organizations, institutions, and practices. Starting in 1850, many churches and chapels organized mothers' meetings, which combined "religious zeal and social conscience." One historian has argued this was the most "pervasive female agency for bringing women together in a regular basis outside the home in British history."[46] The women sewed clothing or household items using goods bought in bulk at advantageous prices, while a leader, usually a middle-class woman, prayed aloud and read from scripture. It was a distinctly female form. It gave middle-class women freedom to evangelize in a sanctioned manner, and it was intended to give poor women both material and spiritual benefit.[47]

The 1830s and 1840s witnessed the growth of new forms of religious community for Anglican women. Churchwomen, both Evangelical and Tractarian, created a number of sisterhoods and deaconesses' houses where single women engaged in philanthropy, mission work, and contemplative prayer. Sisters founded hospitals, orphanages, schools, and benevolent associations, such as the Guild of Brave Poor Things, an organization for the crippled poor. Because the sisters and deaconesses were expected to bring a dowry when they joined and to pay an annual sum toward their expenses, women without means were effectively excluded.[48] The women who participated in such work possessed the leisure to pursue such activities as well as confidence in their own capacity to alleviate the struggles of the urban poor and the conviction that a religious community could best provide the needed structure and support.

In the 1860s and 1870s, a small number of evangelical women, like Catherine Booth, preached by invitation. These were educated, middle-class women who aimed to stir up "cold" Christians and push sinners to a full recognition of their state. All these women remained outside the formal organization of the denominations; they had no voice in denominational decisions, they were never assigned a congregation or circuit, and they enjoyed no regular salary. Their ministry never included communion or baptism. Their work did not lead to an established place in a church or chapel, and it was not necessarily associated with one denomination.[49] This was a female ministry that many Christians could sanction because it was effective and disrupted neither the conventions of femininity nor the established hierarchy of the Church or chapels.

Other women's organizations performed work that was both charitable and missionary. Mrs. Ellen Ranyard's Biblewomen built on the work of older mission organizations, but as a female agency that combined charitable and spiritual work with house-to-house visiting, it was a new departure. The organization's reports emphasized that the work was especially suited to laboring women because "this mission work does not involve any separation from home ties, but can be carried out in the midst of home life and duty."[50] Biblewomen were the first home visitors to receive a salary. Mrs. Collier, appointed as a Biblewoman in 1859, recalled in her autobiography that the salary she received was an important supplement to the money she earned with her mangle.[51] Their work also provided a model for Octavia Hill and other philanthropists of the 1880s.[52]

The independent evangelists, the sisterhoods, the organizers of mothers' meetings, and the Biblewomen all participated in the creation of new forms of Christian womanhood that authorized women to missionize and provide charitable assistance according to the regulations and practices of each organization. Their activities and authority were, nevertheless, constrained by the exclusion of women from positions of prestige or decision making in their denominations as well men's exclusive claim to clerical and sacramental authority. These agencies were more often directed at working-class women than directed by them. Working-class women rarely held positions that would permit them to determine the scope or direction of the evangelical or charitable work they dispensed or received. The Christian Mission built on these initiatives but it granted working-class women and men an unusual degree of authority and a wider range of activities than other Victorian religious organizations did.

The authority and prestige available to women were equally unusual. Working-class voluntary associations, such as friendly societies, trade unions, and political associations, rarely included women in decision-making positions.[53] These bodies were frequently based in workplaces or trades that did not include women on an equal basis in the first place. Women's lower wages often meant they could not afford membership, and many women's occupations were episodic or low-skill and so not included in associations. Many working-class leaders regarded women's marginal status as natural and even as a laudable goal for working-class organizations.[54] For example, in 1877, Henry Broadhurst said to the male delegates of the Trades Union Congress that "it was their duty as men and husbands to use their utmost efforts to bring about a condition of things, where their wives would be in their proper sphere at home, instead of being dragged into competition for livelihood against the great and strong men of the world."[55] Not surprisingly, trade-union organizers frequently complained that women's "apathy, lack of interest and instability" presented grave difficulties and meant few women rose to positions of leadership within unions.[56] Women were also excluded from organizational life because their domestic responsibilities precluded any such activity, although their husbands expected to use their leisure time as well as a portion of their wages for such activities. Working-class suffragists, members of the cooperative movement, and women trade-union organizers all agreed that children and home made any other work, paid or unpaid, difficult.[57] Also many organizations met at times and in places that made women's participation difficult. Women, for example, could not easily attend meetings in the pubs where men gathered. The Salvation Army, in contrast, had a structure and theology that facilitated working-class women's participation and authority.

ENHANCING THE ROLE OF SALVATIONIST WOMEN

In the first five years, Christian Mission women took up work that was very like that of other Christian women's organizations of the period: it was organized in women-only associations for the benefit of other women and usually focused on domestic concerns. The *East London Evangelist* reported in June 1869, "A few sisters, anxious to work for Jesus, have formed themselves into a Christian Pioneer Band, and meet together on Friday evening from seven to eight, to devise and carry out plans of usefulness. They have already established a cottage prayer meeting in one of our darkest streets in Bethnal Green. Other meetings will be added, and they will specially work among children."[58] The *East London Evangelist* reported on other services offered by Mission women. The Christian Women Pioneers established a children's meeting in 1869, and these fourteen women organized eight weekly mothers' meetings that each drew thirty women to the hall to sew, drink tea, and listen as one woman read from Christian writings on various subjects, including housekeeping.[59]

Mary C. Billups, the daughter of a wealthy Cardiff family whom the Booths met when holding revivals in Wales, described the mothers' meetings. One woman, she reported, said her home used to be filthy and scarcely furnished. "Now come into it any time you like. It is clean, I have good bedstead, table and chairs, that haven't their legs broken off and we eat our meals in comfort. But it is all through religion. Praise the Lord!" Other reports credited the meeting with teaching a faith that would give women the ability to withstand great hardship and to fulfill their duties as wives and mothers. One woman said, "There is nothing like religion for making anyone happy. I have sweet time over my washtub with Jesus all the time."[60] Another woman, widowed with several children, said God gave her patience in the face of hardship. "My children know I'm saved and so do my neighbours; my religion has changed my home. Now my children never think of asking me as they used to do for their Sunday penny; but they love to pray and I do believe God will save my children."[61] An attitude that promoted submission to circumstances also marked other reports of mission activity. In a plea for contributions the plight of one family was described. The father was blind, the mother bedridden with dropsy, and the daughter's wages just met the rent. But they were Christians "who appeared happy in their deep poverty."[62]

This quiet submission to poverty expressed in these reports echoes the writing of countless mid-century evangelicals. But as much as these reports expressed a distant, condescending benevolence, men and women active in the Christian Mission were required to transform their own spiritual state, to interpret scripture, and to act on its injunctions. Even a young woman like the daughter in the family who were said to be happy despite deep poverty was expected to guide others and work for the evangelization of her whole community. Her poverty would not be a relief from active service nor exclude her from positions of authority. Submission to God's will and responsibility to save others shaped the work of all Salvationists. Railton described the duty of obedience and active service. "We have got an organisation managed upon the simple business-like principles of a railway, with all the cohesion and co-operative force of a trades union, formed of people whose devotion, determination, and confidence are at least equal to that of the Jesuits, and yet all of whom are left to enjoy and use that perfect spiritual freedom and independence which only the Holy Spirit can bestow on any man."[63]

These expectations would have particular consequences for women through the 1870s. The full denominational authority of women was officially sanctioned at the 1870 Conference, and in that same year the theological foundation of that position was established by a new edition of Catherine Booth's pamphlet on female ministry. This edition, published by Morgan and Chase, was similar in substance to her 1859 pamphlet. All direct references to A. A. Rees and Phoebe Palmer were deleted, but her central arguments remained. The pamphlet was retitled *Female Ministry or Women's Right to Preach the Gospel,* and in it Catherine raised several new points. In particular, she questioned the persistence of error regarding women's preaching. Her approach to scripture was, she wrote, "common sense." Why then had it so long been misinterpreted?

> Surely there must have been some unfaithfulness, "craftiness", and "handling of the word of life deceitfully" somewhere. Surely the love of caste and unscriptural jealousy for a separated priesthood has had something to do with this anomaly. By this course divines and commentators have involved themselves in all sorts of inconsistencies and contradictions; and worse they have nullified some of the most precious promises of God's word. They have set the most explicit predictions of prophecy at variance with apostolic injunctions and the most immediate and wonderful operations of the Holy Ghost in direct opposition to "positive, explicit and universal rules."[64]

Catherine argued that any woman had *the right* to preach "independent of any man-made restrictions." By insisting that preaching was a right unjustly denied to women, she made women's preaching both a theological and a political question. Submitting to God's call to preach put women at the forefront of a battle for religious liberty against a corrupt church that had hoarded spiritual authority for itself. God gave women responsibilities that could not be denied.

Nevertheless, Christian Mission women did face opposition from other denominations, the press, and the communities where they worked. Controversy also erupted within the movement itself. In 1875, just as the first woman was assigned to run a mission station, the Conference was obliged to pass a motion affirming that "the Conference cannot . . . obstruct the admission of females to any work or office in the Mission."[65] For many, this motion presented a challenge. A Salvationist recalled that at one corps she was told that women could speak only when invited to do so. "When we told them . . . that we had been sent to lead, and were going to do so, they naturally kicked; but we just trusted in God, and went right on."[66] When another woman tried to convince her husband to accompany her to a meeting, he replied, "Do you think I am such a fool as to go and listen to a pack of girls?" When he was finally persuaded to attend a meeting, he refused to give into his own longing to go forward to the penitent form. "All I could say in my own defence was, 'I will not be governed by a woman.'"[67] One hymn published in the *War Cry* in 1880 addressed these struggles.

> Take heart, Sister Soldiers, to Jesus be true,
> There's work, and a place in the battle for you;
> Fear not when the lip of derision is curled
> Keep fighting and help us to conquer the world.
> refrain, With blood and fire (repeat three times)
>   We shall conquer the world![68]

The reorganization of the movement as a strict, military-style, command hierarchy effectively silenced much of this debate. When women were placed in charge of corps, their authority was given by headquarters, and no committees or annual Conferences could interfere. Railton argued that the Army's autocratic structure was critical to women's success.

> I am not sure that we ever had an instance of women's successful management in association with a committee of men. A strong-willed man—any man, in fact, with sufficient ability and strength of mind to be successful as an officer, might override and impose his will upon a committee, without offending or driving them away; but no woman could do this without conflicts that would

necessarily destroy her influence, and make her usefulness, on any extended
scale, impossible. I could tell tales as to the struggles of some of those early
heroines with elders and committees. . . . They could never have been sent
out with any prospect of success in a provincial city had they been saddled
with that old machinery.[69]

Again, the intertwining of submission to the Army's discipline and authority and responsibility marked the lives of Salvationists.

Learning to preach indoors and out, to lead a hymn, to guide penitents was a challenge for those whose previous education and work experience seemed to offer little preparation. This was particularly true for
women whose religious experience offered few models of female authority.
Pamela Shepard, for example, was born in Wales in the 1836. When her
husband went to prison, she was left to support her newborn daughter.
He returned home, and two more daughters were born before he abandoned the family. Shepard found lodgings with a friend and worked as a
rag sorter to support herself and her children. She moved to London,
where she joined the Christian Mission. Beginning in 1876, she worked
as the hall keeper and cook at headquarters and was active in the Drunkard's Rescue Society and at Limehouse Penny Gaff station while earning
her living as a laundress. She "opened" Aberdare, Wales, in 1878 with
two of her daughters and Sarah Sayers.[70] Sayers, a forty-year-old widow
and mother of two, had earned her living as a charwoman while she
worked as an exhorter for the Christian Mission.[71] They set off with £5
to cover their initial expenses. Upon arrival, they rented the Temperance
Hall, which held fifteen hundred people. The women preached in the street
to whomever would listen and announced the forthcoming meeting at
the hall. When the crowd in the street pressed toward the two preaching
women, Shepard addressed them in Welsh, insisting that she had a right
to be heard. After the first meeting, they telegraphed headquarters, "Lots
in a pickle and three in the fountain."[72] Pamela Shepard's daughter Kate
went to work in the Rhondda Valley, where she was the first to take the
Salvationist underground and to preach to the miners.[73]

Evangelists were responsible for filling the hall while raising the funds
from the congregation to pay for it as well as related expenses, including the repairs necessitated by large, boisterous crowds. Their own
salaries also came from the funds they raised. If the town was hostile,
they might have difficulty covering their expenses. The women often arrived with little preparation, no local acquaintances, and little knowledge
of the region. This challenge could be exhilarating. In 1879, Hannah
Atkinson and Kate Boyce opened Gateshead. They telegraphed head-

quarters a few days later. "Crowded house six hours. Must get larger place. Hundreds obliged to leave. God is working. Sinners are weeping. Wire back."[74] That same year the journalist W. T. Stead was sufficiently alarmed by the exhausted and fragile appearance of Captain Rose Clapham of Darlington that he wrote to headquarters. William Booth replied with thanks for Stead's "timely warning as we could have formed no idea of Miss Clapham's condition from any of her previous letters." Nevertheless, Booth wrote, "We can only regard this as an inevitable prospect for those who are liable to be suddenly surrounded with a gigantic conflict and victory and we should be compelled to abandon the work altogether if we had not men and women perfectly prepared to face the utmost risk with changeless resolution and a calm confidence in God which is capable of sustaining them to the end."[75] Some limits were recognized. William Booth issued an order against self-starvation and instructed officers to wire headquarters if their funds did not prove sufficient to purchase food.[76]

CREATING A PROFESSION

In 1880, the Salvation Army began to provide formal training. A training home for women, directed by Emma Booth, and another for men, directed by Ballington Booth, opened. At the time of the 1881 Census, there were nineteen women, ranging in age from sixteen to twenty-nine and twenty-five men ranging in age from nineteen to thirty-two at the training homes.[77] The men and women in training were known as cadets. Basic account keeping and other practical skills were taught along with speaking, singing, and Salvation Army theology. Many cadets possessed only the most minimal literacy and arithmetic skills, so this training provided a significant improvement in their education. Cadets developed their preaching skills by conducting "a meeting of a given character, say, a Holiness or a Salvation meeting. Suggestions or criticisms are called for, at the end, from cadets and given, as seems best, by the officer in charge."[78]

In February 1885, the cadets adopted a new means of evangelizing. Two horse-drawn vans were fitted out to carry groups of twelve cadets to rural areas to sell the War Cry, visit homes, and hold meetings. Cadets spent up to two months engaged in this work, a practice that gave the Army a way to reach new areas that could not otherwise support a corps. It also gave cadets training that would help them open new corps.[79] After several months training, cadets were promoted to the rank of lieutenant and sent to assist a corps captain. When a lieutenant had acquired sufficient experience, she or he was promoted to captain and sent to another corps.

Elizabeth Churchill's experience was typical. She joined the Salvation Army in July 1884 at age twenty-one; she was one of 150 cadets at the training home on December 14, 1885. She spent her time "*War Cry* selling, attending meetings indoors and out, in 'on the work', helping with the nursery children, sewing, school work at headquarters, and very many other things too numerous to mention."[80] She spent three weeks with the Cellar, Gutter and Garret Brigade, a branch of the work performed exclusively by women. It was based in several East End communities, including Stepney and Whitechapel, and in Seven Dials. The cadets visited families, nursed the sick, assisted new mothers, and used these opportunities to evangelize.[81] Men did not participate in the Cellar, Gutter and Garret Brigade because this work involved nursing the sick and housecleaning, which were not regarded as suitable tasks for men. Moreover, the Brigade worked with "fallen women," and it was an impropriety for a man to approach a women in a public place or to discuss the particulars of her situation. Churchill recalled in her autobiography,

> When I went into the Gutter brigade, which included two hours patrol in front of the East London Hospital, speaking to and advising straying wilful women, our headquarters was a two-roomed flat in a big tenement building in Bethnal Green. There were five of us. . . . I was instrumental through the Sinner's Saviour of persuading one girl, by name Pollie Dawson, to go to Mrs. [Bramwell] Booth's rescue home at Mare Street, Hackney, where she had a dreadful fight against drink; twice she sent to the Training Home for me to go to her and help her hold on, but eventually she won, and became a Christian, and the last letter I received from her told of the peace she was still enjoying and that she was going to be married to an Army soldier at Clapton.[82]

On February 20, 1886, Churchill was promoted to the rank of captain. Six days later she set off for Little, Lancashire, with Mary Ann Sawyer, another recent graduate, as her lieutenant "to lead and train the soldiers in the devotion of their bodies and souls to the Glory of God and the salvation of the people." When the two women arrived at Little, "the people were more than kind, they were loving, and continually gave us an abundance of food; they packed our hall, every bit of standing room, stairs and window sills; and the sinner's Friend came very near and 180 sought and found Christ." In October 1886, Churchill and Sawyer were sent to Barrow; on arrival they were told "the last officers were lasses and . . . we should go no further as the soldiers were determined not to have lasses again." They were nevertheless so successful this corps petitioned headquarters to permit them to stay longer. The two then went to eleven further postings at Padiham, Carnforth, Nelson, Fleetwood, Fringington, Clitheroe, Blackburn, Haverfordwest, Brading on the Isle of Wight, Fareham, and finally Bishops Waltham, staying from three to six months in each place. Churchill married in 1891, and because "it is the duty of a wife to join her husband's denomination," she left the Army. But she maintained throughout her life "that to be an Salvation Army officer was the best and most satisfying work that one can do."[83]

When they had sufficient experience, women could move to larger, more challenging corps and eventually to other positions. In 1889, Isa Carter was appointed adjutant to direct several London corps. She was brought up a Methodist in Newcastle-upon-Tyne. "But the chapel whose preacher showed Isa Carter the way of salvation did not put her in the way of laying out her life to any advantage. If we showed her the way, and she chose it, is it not a thing to thank God for that the powers of mind and heart she spends on Outcast London were not let go to utter waste?"[84] Polly Ashton, the first female divisional officer, was appointed in 1890. At a large meeting in Luton, she was introduced to the corps captains, who "by their male and female representatives . . . pledged themselves to be loyal and true to their woman leader."[85] Catherine Booth, bedridden with cancer, wrote to Captain Ashton. "In my sick chamber I have heard of your promotion to the command of the division with great interest and with good hope that it may help forward that honourable and useful employment of my own sex in the Master's service, which I have so strongly desired and laboured for, and of which I have been enabled in some measure by the mercy of God, to be an example."[86] Catherine Booth's letter makes clear that Salvationist women were purposefully extending and enhancing women's work.

In the early years of the Christian Mission there were some who believed women's wages should be equal to men's. In an 1876 letter explaining the situation of one sister, Railton wrote, "We do not see why a sister should not receive as much as a brother if she does the work and raises the finances as well."[87] It seems there was no set wage scale in the early days. Elizabeth Pollett was paid more than £1 in 1876, and Miss Woodcock received only 15 shillings.[88] By 1882, however, the situation had changed for reasons that are not clear. The Salvation Army paid its unmarried male captains 21 shillings per week and its lieutenants 18 shillings, while women captains made only 15 shillings and lieutenants 12 shillings. This disparity between men's and women's wages belied the Army's commitment to equality. It also made the position of single women

officers even more precarious than that of their male counterparts, much
like the position of employed single women in any other occupation. Yet
Salvationist women's wages compared favorably with the average wage
of 12 shillings and 11 pence paid to woman workers in nontextile industries in this period. It would not compare with the wages of a London
schoolteacher, who made between £93 and £99 per year. But to women
who had previously worked as laundresses, rag sorters, or vegetable hawkers, the Salvation Army offered significantly improved wages. Many Salvationist women were former general servants, and if they possessed no
special training, their wages were often as low as 5 shillings a week with
food and a bed. The situation for men was different. The average London male artisan earned 35 shillings a week in 1870, and the average laborer could earn 20 shillings, so the Salvation Army offered a reduction
in wages for many men. When Elijah Cadman, for example, applied to
work for the Christian Mission, Railton inquired, "Are you and your wife
fully prepared for reduced income?"[89] It is not surprising that a number
of men who published accounts of their Salvation Army experiences complained of the low wages, but women made no such complaints.

In 1884, the *Pall Mall Gazette* ran a series of articles on "Women Who
Work," and the Army women were included. The *Gazette* argued,

> Nothing has afforded such a demonstration of the inherent capacity of the
> average woman as the fact that in the course of a few years it should have
> been possible to create, chiefly out of servant girls, factory hands, and other
> working women of that class, a regiment of nearly one thousand evangelists,
> each of whom has proved herself quite capable not merely of addressing large
> audiences indoors and out, but the discharge of heavy pastoral work, and the
> management of all affairs, financial and otherwise, of mission stations all over
> the country.[90]

Notably, of the 1,660 women employed as missionaries, scripture readers, and itinerant preachers listed in the 1881 census, just over 15 percent were Salvationists, and by 1884 the Army employed close to one
thousand women.[91] As one woman stationed in Wales said, "As a child
I was very ambitious to grow up and marry a Captain, so that I might
travel and see the world. I've been a Captain, am seeing the country and
the reality far exceeds my imagination."[92]

The professional status of Salvation Army women was also marked
by the uniform, first introduced in 1880. The plain, dark dress and jacket
edged with braid was worn with a black straw bonnet trimmed in black
ribbon. Women also wore red jerseys with mottoes embroidered in yellow and small brooches shaped like a shield or an S.[93] This uniform, with

its obvious military style, conveyed an authoritative professionalism and gave these working-class women a distinctive presence in their communities. One woman recalled that when she put on her first bonnet, she felt "a little singular" and that she "must live up to the appearance of my bonnet and do something extraordinary." But she also feared the ridicule she was sure to meet.[94] The uniform differed from the decorative, colorful clothing favored by many working-class women, and it resembled the styles adopted by advanced women from the 1860s on. Many women professionals, social reformers, and women's rights advocates wore a combination of blouse, jacket, and long, trim skirt, which allowed for greater bodily freedom and dispensed with fussy, ornate styling. Women argued that suits promoted health and allowed for a vigorous, active life.[95] Similarly, Salvationist women enjoyed both the prestige and the practicality of their uniforms. The uniform was also a visual reminder of the self-control and self-denial required of all Salvationists, and it linked Salvationists together, making all their actions a part of their public witness.

Salvationist women were a singular group of working-class women whether regarded as professional, employed workers or as inspired evangelists and preachers who held considerable authority and prestige. Their work was both spiritual and practical, and the Army defended them on both grounds. As an 1877 *Christian Mission Magazine* article proclaimed, "They say it is quite improper for a woman to preach the gospel. What is it proper for a woman to do? Is it proper for them to stand before the public for many hours a day in a shop? The universal practice says that it is. . . . But has woman no better destiny than to stand or sit waiting upon man's bodily needs? Will any one find a reason why women should not stand before the public to offer them the bread of life, the wine and milk of the Gospel and the robes of righteousness?"[96]

THE PROBLEM OF SACRAMENTS

Despite the prominence of women evangelists, preachers, and organizers, the sacraments remained an intractable problem for Salvationists and their critics. Salvationist women possessed none of the qualities usually required for sacerdotal authority: they were not male or formally educated or ordained. The Church of England permitted women to assist only in the pastoral ministry, in work such as visiting the sick and teaching Sunday School, where no liturgical authority was implied or received. Anglicans, of course, believed that only a professional, ordained clergy could legitimate the sacraments. Women were excluded in a special way, for laymen were allowed to speak at services and to assist in Holy Communion by mid-century. The Methodists also distinguished between ordained clergy and lay preachers on the question of sacraments. Since women could not be ordained, they were categorically excluded from the full ministerial role.[97] Salvationists, of course, took little interest in such external qualifications; their perspective was neatly summed up by a conversation a Salvation Army woman had with a man who reprimanded her for preaching.

> "What does an ignorant girl like you know about religion?" he said. "I know more than you do; I can say the Lord's prayer in Latin."
> "Oh, but," she replied, "I can say more than that; I can say the Lord has saved my soul in English."[98]

Still, communion presented particular difficulties. The Salvation Army initially instructed all officers to offer communion monthly. Challenged to explain why women were permitted to perform this sacred ritual, Railton wrote, "In this, as in everything else, the Lord's own principle there being 'neither male nor female' in Christ Jesus is fully acted upon."[99] Yet others saw a woman offering communion as a singular and shocking sight, even blasphemous.[100] One vicar wrote to the *Guardian* to complain. "A few weeks ago . . . the sacrament (if it could be so called) was administered by a woman assisted by two other women. There were a large number present. Everyone in the room was offered bread and wine; but some declined to receive. Comment is superfluous."[101]

Paradoxically, the very theological understanding that made it possible for women to offer communion also led Salvationists to believe that it was redundant. Communion was usually believed to impart or symbolize the presence of the Holy Spirit. If communicants were already saved, as Salvationists believed they must be, communion offered nothing the communicant did not already possess. But the unsaved might mistakenly believe communion could bring the Holy Spirit and thereby ensure salvation. Catherine Booth concluded that communion could pose a danger because people were likely to trust communion as an outward sign of conversion. She wrote, "What an inveterate tendency there is in the human heart to trust in outward forms, instead of inward grace! And when this is the case, what a hindrance rather than help have these forms proved to the growth, nay to the very existence, of that spiritual life which constitutes the real and only force of Christian experience."[102] The Salvation Army ceased to give communion after 1883. That decision both undermined and reinforced a refusal to countenance distinctions between men's and women's relationship to the sacred. This decision removed one aspect of Salvation Army services that was especially offensive to other Christians. At the same time, it emphasized the Army's disregard for the theological principles that were essential to others. By rejecting material forms of receiving grace, the Army underscored the meaninglessness of outward, human physicality and the significance of the transforming grace of the Holy Spirit. The Army claimed to be following the words of John the Baptist, "I indeed baptize you with water . . . but . . . He shall baptize you with the Holy Ghost and with fire." But this decision also denied Salvationist women and men a ritual that many Christians, including some Salvationists, valued.[103]

FIGHTING MEN

The work of Salvationist men was, in many respects similar to that of women, but men faced particular challenges. As much as Christians might regard religious authority as categorically masculine, urban working-class men were not known for their piety or for an interest in religious institutions. By the 1860s several organizations, notably the Boys Brigade and the YMCA, had already tried to bring a Christianity imbued with an ideal of manliness to the working class. These movements drew on the ideals of Thomas Hughes and Charles Kingsley, whose vision of Christian manliness was based on physical vigor, emotional restraint, and an ethic of service.[104] Because these ideals were first articulated in response to the appeal of Anglo-Catholicism among the elite, they did not easily translate into this different context.[105] These all-male organizations offered fighting and games, strength and discipline as means to achieve a Christian state. Since boxing and sports were already popular working-class male pursuits and the religious demands were light, membership did not represent a break with the larger community in the way Salvationist membership did. The sports and camaraderie were the main draw for working-class boys; prayer and hymns were tolerated as the price of admission to the ring or field.[106] Other church and chapel organizations hosted debates and discussions intended to appeal to working-class men. Men's Owns and Pleasant Sunday Afternoons were special meetings exclusively for men. Despite these efforts, women were generally regarded as more pious, and women were the majority at most religious services.[107]

Salvationists responded by attempting to forge a link between working-class manliness and holiness. In 1874 the *Christian Mission Magazine* argued that "gentle, well-meaning faith" would not do for men. A "brawnier manliness" was needed. "Religion will not conquer either the admiration or the affections of men by effeminacy, but by strength. . . . The spirit of religion is the spirit of great power."[108] Salvationists never attempted to nullify or transcend a bodily sense of masculinity or femininity, nor did they seek to alter many of the common prerogatives of masculinity. Instead, they strived to convince men that this faith offered them the possibility of achieving a true manliness. Evangelizing, marching through the streets, preaching on street corners, leading hymns were all to be the elements of an active, energetic, religious life.

By attacking the music halls, pubs, and gin palaces with particular vigor, Salvationists were, in effect, attacking men's use of leisure. When the Army condemned these institutions as sinful, it launched an attack on much of the distinctive, public, and communal aspects of working-class men's culture. Salvationists strived to convince men that drinking, and the wider commercial culture that gloried in drink, made men dependent and foolish. Alcohol was a potent element in men's conversion narratives, and its meaning was rooted in the wider culture of working-class communities. Work mates and neighbors were united in the congeniality of the pub, and having money to spend displayed a man's independence and ability to earn.[109] Alcohol was not just drink; it represented a whole range of activities, especially sports and betting. These activities offered a masculine camaraderie that defined itself through the explicit exclusion of women.

Salvationists asserted that turning from drink to prayer, from flying pigeons to hymn singing, did not necessarily put men in conflict with dominant definitions of manliness. Posters and illustrations in the Army newspapers and pamphlets also played on the masculinity of its converts. The front page of an 1884 issue of the War Cry was dominated by two illustrations. The first depicted nineteen men dressed in rough clothes, kerchiefs tied about their necks and defiant, even surly, expressions on their faces. It was captioned, "Starving on the Husks of Drink and Vice." Below were the same men, neatly attired in uniforms, looking directly at the viewer, many with gentle smiles. These men were "Enjoying and Publishing the Great Salvation."[110] The illustrations testified to the rejuvenating powers of salvation for these ordinary men accustomed to labor and drink, the very men the War Cry strived to reach. Men's testimonies were similar. When they described themselves as former drinkers, gamblers, and fighters, Salvationist men dramatized the depth of the transformation, and they also made another point. When a man testified that he had earned a living boxing and training rats or described how, while he bargained for a bird, he was convicted of sin, he asserted his place within a culture of masculinity that he inhabited.[111] By rejecting that standard, he claimed to be *more* manly. One man asked a meeting, "Do you think now religion unmans me? Do I look any the worse for being a Christian?"[112]

Salvationist men preached in a direct, unadorned manner using working-class idiom and an animated style. When one man came forward to speak at a meeting, a woman said, "Oh, he looks more like a butcher than a preacher."[113] In 1879, a *Daily Telegraph* writer attended his first meeting, expecting gentle remonstrance and persuasion, but he was amazed to see just the opposite.

> He [the preacher] lost not a moment in shilly-shally, but seized Satan by the horns at once, and commenced abusing him in a tone and at a rate which must have convinced the Evil One that he was in the hands of a person who not only had no dread of him, but was hot and eager to rouse him to a fury, and then give him battle to the death. The preacher was a short, thickset man, with short cropped hair, and no shirt collar, and his coat was buttoned over his breast. His gestures were prodigiously energetic, and the consequence was, that before he had preached ten minutes he had worked his wrists well through the coat cuffs—wrists of a size that matched well with his ponderous fists, which except when engaged with the prayer book, were tightly clenched.[114]

The absence of a collar, his large wrists shooting out of his sleeves, and his great energy made his struggle with Satan resemble nothing more than a street fight. This physical, robust, combative preaching expressed Salvationists' conviction that they must convince every listener to flee from Satan and seek God. It drew on the style of urban street vendors and working-class performers as well the preaching of sectarian Methodists and mid-century revivalists. This impassioned style drew considerable attention.

Although Salvationists were certainly not the first or the only street preachers, they adopted such preaching with great enthusiasm.[115] They hawked their faith in front of pubs, in music halls, and alongside the butchers and the costermongers. They borrowed the language of the street vendors when they called out that they had riches without price. They joined the clamor of the street hoping that their words might strike passersby as they worked, shopped, or walked to the pub. They occupied these busy streets despite the sustained opposition of vendors, shopkeepers, and publicans and the competition of others promoting any number of other religious, social, and political causes. In 1876 the Shoreditch mission station reported, "Thank God! That is our song in Brick Lane. The butchers have been trying to stop us again by bringing out their knives and chopping with them upon their blocks, and rattling their irons, while men and boys have shouted and rowed until the noise has been deafening."[116] Preachers had to learn to hold their ground. The resulting behavior could be an advantage. When one preacher was obliged to shout over the voices of the crowd, his voice carried a great distance and reached a young man buying a bird. Ordinarily, "he would not have heard a single sentence, but now he heard it all, not a word was lost."[117] Salvationist men occasionally invaded men's commercial venues directly. One Salvationist went into a barbershop and asked to be shaved. While the barber worked, the Salvationist's three comrades spoke to the barber and the other customers of "their sins and their Saviour."[118]

Salvation Army brass bands were another response to the noise and hustle of the streets. The first brass band was started by William and Fred Fry because "the music seemed to take the devil out of the rowdies at the open-air meetings."[119] Brass bands were already popular. The volunteer forces had brass bands that performed frequently in parks for public occasions as well as in churches, chapels, and temperance societies. The Salvation Army stood out, however, because it "absorbed bands to such an extent that they became one of the features that characterized it," and its bands included women.[120] The bands were valued because they drew a crowd and effectively drowned out the shouts and ridicule with religious music.

These efforts to forge a masculine religiosity met with ridicule in music halls and comic magazines, which depicted Salvationist men as weak, ineffectual, and effeminate. One song, "Obadiah Walked behind the Drum," told of a man who was "rather green" and a "Captain in the Army, the Army of Salvationists I mean."

> One night whilst he was in the South of London,
> He met a girl, and offered her a tract,
> She murmured, "Oh, I'd rather have a drink, sir,"
> And then gave his face a playful smack;
> Like Adam with the apple, he was tempted,
> They went off to a public bar just near,
> And when he'd sampled sev'ral Scotch and sodas,
> By accident he called the lady, "dear!"
>
> At closing time Obadiah was tipsy,
> Of S. and B. he'd had about enough,
> All his tracts were rolled up into pipe lights,
> His watch and chain were in the lady's muff;

And when a bobby found him in a doorway,
Just as the clock was chiming three,
Obadiah Hope was shouting, "Come to glory—!"
The bobby answered, "All right, come with me!"[121]

An 1892 *St. Stephen's Review* illustration depicted General Booth in bonnet and skirt, arm aloft shaking a tambourine, while three imbecilic men cheered and waved (see Figure 6). These depictions ridiculed the very notion of the manly, robust Salvationist.

WOMEN AND MEN

The religious life of Salvationist men was always influenced by the unique prominence of women. Salvationist women, for example, founded the Drunkards Rescue Society in 1874, the first of its agencies charged with spreading temperance.[122] Pairs of women from the Society would lay hold of a man on his way to the public house. They "would arrest his attention, and talk to him, one on one side, and another on the other, thus keeping up a continual fire-fire, and volley of advice. Many a poor fellow was thus extricated from the Devil's clutches, . . . [taken to the hall], surrounded and saturated by such a mighty influence as would drive the Devil out and 'Let the Master in.'"[123] Working-class women regularly fought singly and in groups to stop their husbands from spending wages in the pub, and the Society regularized and, more important, sanctified these efforts.[124]

These efforts formed a sustained attempt to engage women and men, together, in one struggle. Working-class men and women rarely engaged in the same activities or collaborated in organizational or leisure pursuits. Salvationist women, in contrast, assumed positions that would without question bring them into close association with brethren and would give women leadership and authority. The Army was a remarkably heterosocial organization.[125]

Salvationists strived to refashion the relations between men and women, husbands and wives. In the earliest years, it was not clear how membership in the Army would affect marriage and family relations, particularly for women. At the 1878 annual Conference William Booth said, "Elizabeth Agnes Pollett and Ellen Hall have changed their names and their places of abode. I recommended them not to get married but they did not take my advice. They are still with us and willing to do all they can to help. They are not lost and I suppose somebody says in each case they are found. They were good before marriage and they ought to be a good deal better after."[126] The Army soon developed regulations concerning marriage.

In principle, marriage was neither discouraged nor encouraged, but it was a regulated part of Army life and very much part of the mission of an Army officer or soldier. Cadets could not become engaged or marry but were obliged to wait until they were established officers. The *Orders and Regulations for Field Officers* (1886) offered a particular caution to women.

> Female officers ought to be very careful in this matter, seeing that to marry other than an officer removes them from a position of great usefulness and honour, such as they will probably never have the opportunity of obtaining again. And if they are really seeking to spend their lives in that manner which will bring the most glory to their Master, and the largest numbers of souls to His feet, they ought to be very careful not to sacrifice so important a position for any seeming advantages of worldly position, ease, or comfort. Let every female officer who entertains the temptation to take such a step, beware, lest for gratification of earthly feelings, lawful perhaps for others, and lawful for her in different circumstances, she should enter into relations which would drag her down from this honourable and Christ-like career to spend her life looking back on what she has sacrificed with bitter regret if not absolute despair.[127]

Presumably, because wives were expected to join their husband's denomination, male officers would not have faced such difficulties, although no officer could marry outside the Army and maintain that office. This warning makes clear that the authority Salvationist women possessed was precarious and would not be easily reconciled with wifely duty and submission.

All Salvationists were obliged to sign the Articles of Marriage in order to married within the Army. The Articles of Marriage were adopted in 1882.

> 1. We solemnly declare that we do not seek this marriage simply to please ourselves, but that we believe it will enable us to better serve the interest of the Salvation Army.
> 2. We promise never to allow our marriage to lessen in anyway our devotion to God or to The Army.
> 3. We each severally promise that we will never try to prevent each other doing or giving anything that is in our power to do or to give to help the Army.
> 4. We each severally promise to use all our influence with each other to promote constant and entire self-sacrifice for the Salvation of the World.
> 5. We promise always to regard and arrange our home in every way as a Sal-

vation Army Soldiers' (or Officers') quarters, and to train everyone in the faithful service of the Salvation Army.

6. We promise, whether together or apart, always to do our utmost as Soldiers of the Salvation Army, and never to allow it to be injured or hindered by anyone without doing our best to prevent or overcome such injury or hinderance.

7. Should either of us cease to be an efficient Soldier, owing to sickness, death, or any other cause, we engage that the remaining one shall continue to the best of his or her ability to fulfill all these promises.[128]

This public commitment to an active religious life of service was different from the promise required by other denominations. One music-hall routine commented on Salvationists' marriage vows.

The Salvation people are getting on fine.
　　Not really?
　　Yes, really!

They're all getting married—and that's a good sign!
　　Not really?
　　Yes, really!

If a member takes himself a help-mate, no church forms are practiced.
No church forms are practiced when linking their fate,
Except one—and that is that they pass around the plate!
　　Not really?
　　Yes really.[129]

The Salvation Army expected that the marriage vows would be reflected in Salvationists' marital relations. They could dramatically alter domestic life. One of the few hints about Salvation Army marriages is found in a daughter's recollections of her Salvationist parents. The couple met as young officers, married, and had two children. When the husband's work mates were talking about a woman who had just given birth to her tenth child, the men began to tease him about having only two children. He retorted that he would sooner castrate himself than subject his wife to such misery. This man also donned an apron and cooked the midday meal every Sunday so his wife could attend services.[130] Another man, evidently not himself a member of the Army, was summoned in Derby in May 1883 for assaulting his wife. In his defense, he complained that his wife had joined the Salvation Army. As a result, the house was dirty and the children were neglected while she was out at meetings until midnight. His case was dismissed on account of the provocation he received.[131]

The Army, however, would have taken a strong position against this man, not only for his unsanctified state but also because of his violence. The Articles of War, adopted beginning in 1882, which every member was required to sign and abide by, stated, "I do declare that I will never treat any woman, child or other person, whose life, comfort, or happiness may be placed within my power, in an oppressive, cruel or cowardly manner, but that I will protect such from evil and danger so far as I can, and promote, to the utmost of my ability, their present welfare and eternal salvation."[132] This clearly had a wide application, but many men credited the Army with bringing an end to their abuse of their wives. The testimony of one convert given at an 1875 meeting was typical. "If you want to know what God has done for me, go and ask my poor wife, whom I have beaten in my maddened fury until I have endangered her life, and smashed everything I could lay my hands upon."[133] Another women told a crowd, her husband "used to smack me. Thank God, we are both saved and smacking the Devil."[134] Such stories were common in both men and women's testimonies, which also often explained that drink had lead to violence. Historian Ellen Ross has shown that Victorian working-class "husbands were, practically by definition, violent."[135] Working-class communities acknowledged that violence between spouses was commonplace and inevitable. In one 1879 case cited by Ross, a man murdered a young woman before a crowd of onlookers who did not intervene because the man loudly proclaimed she was his wife. And a policeman later explained his inaction, saying, "I thought they were man and wife."[136] Whether or not the Army's strong position against wife assault was successful, the Army nevertheless expected converts to denounce it. No records remain that might indicate whether men were ever disciplined for this offense.

One event suggests that a variety of attitudes toward marriage could be found among Salvationists. In May 1889, a "leading member of the Salvation Army" in Hucknall Tarkand, near Sheffield, sold his wife. A friend "had evinced an affection for the woman and the husband expressed his willingness to part with her. . . . The sum of one shilling was offered and accepted, and the husband subsequently put a halter round his wife's neck and led her to the home of the purchaser."[137] E. P. Thompson suggests that these ritual exchanges persisted "in pockets where the old plebeian culture still endured." These sales, he argues, certainly humiliated women but did not necessarily bring advantage to the husband. Wives earned considerable respect for performing the arduous work essential to the maintenance of the household; this work created an area of "corresponding authority and independence."[138] The Salvation Army echoed other aspects of plebeian culture, and the ambiguous position of women, in turn subordinate and authoritative, was very much part of the culture of this organization. Perhaps it is not surprising that the last known wife sale in England included members of the Army. No comment from the Salvation Army has been found.

The Salvation Army's theology was not intended to diminish distinctions between husbands and wives nor to abolish a wife's submission as given in scripture nor to diminish a husband's prerogatives and responsibilities. Rather, Salvationists strived to make marriage, and all other aspects of a convert's life, part of their effort to evangelize the world. Drunkenness, domestic discord, and violence were at odds with that mission. Submission to God's will required an ordered life that would enable every woman and man to evangelize the world.

QUITTING THE ARMY

The Salvation Army was a disciplined body with a detailed code of conduct. Because no reliable membership figures or lists exist, it is impossible to even estimate how many Salvationists broke with the Army or even what theological or disciplinary issues led to disputes. Salvation Army records do provide service records for a small number of officers. Emma Trigger left domestic service to work as an Army officer in 1878 and resigned from the Army to marry in 1883. Mary Brooks, a widow, resigned in 1882 because of "domestic affairs." Likewise, Joseph Stanway, an unmarried man, left because of his "domestic affairs." Many officers left as a result of illness, and some died in office. Others were expelled or left by request. In a few cases, the records note "misconduct," "idle," or "ran away."[139] Some Salvationists broke away and on occasion took other Salvationists or the Army's property with them. It is impossible to reconstruct these events because the Army's publications state just the bare facts of each case. The *Orders and Regulations for Field Officers* (1886) gave detailed instructions on how to deal with disagreements and disobedience. If, after investigation, it appeared regulations had been broken, the suspected party would be court-martialed, which meant he or she would face a trial by three officers. If the charges were found to be true, the individual was to be disciplined or expelled as necessary. No records of such disciplinary trials have been found.

A small number of former Salvationists wrote memoirs, and some discussed their decision to leave the Army.[140] Rodney Smith, who was a successful officer from 1877, left the Army in 1882. He had spent six months at Hanley, and under his leadership the corps had grown and flourished. At a public meeting, the people had presented Smith and his lieutenant with watches. Bramwell Booth wrote to him shortly after saying it appeared Smith did not wish to remain in the Army as he knew it was forbidden to take gifts, and not only had he taken a gift himself, but he had lead his lieutenant astray. Smith was shocked because he believed he could accept a small gift if the corps were not in debt. He concluded, "I knew in my own heart that I was not a Salvationist after their own. . . . I did not like the uniform, I did not care for the titles nor the military discipline. My style was not Salvationist enough. Still, I succeeded and the Army gave me a splendid sphere for work and an experience which no college or university could have supplied me with."[141]

J.R.R. Redstone joined the Salvation Army in 1880, spent several months at the training home, and was sent out to work in a London corps. His first several corps were challenging but successful. Arriving at one corps, he found fifty names on the roll, but only ten remained and the rest had dropped away. He bought a bell and kettle drum to use in the streets to draw a crowd, and this strategy brought in an additional forty members. In another corps, the building was in such terrible shape all the surplus funds had to be spent on repairs, and nothing was left for other expenses. Redstone struggled to raise needed funds. In all these corps, he found that officers were reluctant to take names off the roll and be held responsible for permitting membership numbers to decline. In 1884, he was sent to Wales, where he had considerable difficulty building the corps. He was asked to resign by Bramwell Booth. He left deeply discontented. "If I had given the people a smooth religion, perhaps there might have been better results for a time, but I dare not do less than my Master commands. I have nothing to be sorry for."[142] He left without being paid and had to borrow money from the major. Another ex-captain, Douglas Beven, also complained about the difficulties of raising funds from those who had so little and claimed the Army took far too large of share of the corps' funds. He complained that the Army required all bandsmen to purchase their instruments from the trade department, although they could be got cheaper elsewhere. He charged that not allowing officers to draw their full salary when the corps was in debt was unjust because even if they left a corps with a surplus, they were not compensated for what they had sacrificed before.[143] These men were all dissatisfied for similar reasons, which arose from the Army's particular discipline and regulations. Undoubtedly others left for reasons that are not recorded, but these three memoirs do capture a sense of the difficulties officers faced and the consequences of the Army's discipline.

The Salvation Army's evangelizing provided working-class women with the opportunity to exercise religious authority and establish a unique professional status within their communities. The Army provided working-class men with an equally significant opportunity to articulate and exemplify a religious life. It was a disciplined, orderly body that required obedience and rectitude from its members. Obedience to the Holy Spirit, however, might bring someone who had never preached before an audience to deliver a sermon or to burst into song before a hostile crowd or to invent a novel way to draw people into a hall. It also might make a listener fall to the ground insensible or leap and shout "glory." This tension between obedience and expression, submission and agency, created a particular kind of evangelical culture that refashioned distinctions between clergy and laity, the church and the world. Salvationist women offered communion. Drunkards and fishmongers became preachers who stood before crowds calling them to salvation. Preaching could begin in the street, a barbershop, or a mission station and was always punctuated with personal testimony and song. Working women and men struggled for souls together as they refashioned the boundaries between married life and religious service. Salvationists submitted to the Army's discipline, which allow them a wide range of spiritual authority as well as a newfound professional status.

Salvationists sharply divided the sinful from the sanctified, distinguishing between holiness and the world. As one Salvationist writer remarked, a "worldly religious man" is "afraid to be thought peculiar, a fool," whereas one who follows Christ "cannot be too 'separate',—his face, dwelling, dress, all he does and says proclaim aloud, 'I am not of this world even as He was not of it!'" The dividing line, "in all it[s] yawning reality, dividing the saved from the unsaved, the alive from the dead," shaped all that Salvationists sought to be and to do.[144] As one hymn writer expressed it,

My old companions said, "He's undone!"
My old companions said, "He's gone mad!"
But Jesus made me glad, Bless His Name![145]

FIVE

Authority and Transgression

The Lives of Maud Charlesworth,
Effie Anthon, and Rebecca Jarrett

The Hallelujah Lasses seized what was categorically denied to women: authority both sacred and secular. They claimed a right to preach equal to that of men. They preached on street corners and from platforms, creating new spheres of public work for women. The activities of these women were strikingly innovative in the urban communities of late Victorian Britain. Salvation Army theology taught that holiness, the first and most important criterion for religious office in this life and salvation in the next, was available equally to men and women. This doctrine opened significant new ground to women, and it challenged educated, ordained men's monopoly on spiritual authority. But it did not necessarily mean women could easily assume new positions within this organization or the wider community. There were no simple or obvious models available to working-class women to represent themselves as spiritual authorities or to distinguish themselves from dominant working-class notions of femininity. During the 1870s and 1880s, British women of all classes "repeatedly spilled over and out of their ascribed, bounded roles, costumes, and locales into the public streets and wrong parts of town, engaged on missions of their own."[1] Salvationist women drew their inspiration from culturally available conventions of femininity and authority, in ways that were challenging and at times contradictory. Their transgressions prompted observers to associate the Hallelujah Lasses with disorder and sensationalism but also to recognize their likeness to praying mothers and chaste providers of spiritual and material needs. The dramatic effects of juxtaposing the images of Madonna and Magdalene allowed the Army to capitalize on women's performances to expand its constituency in the 1870s and 1880s.

GENDER, DISORDER, AND SACRED AUTHORITY

The dominant model of female authority was domestic and maternal. As Deborah Valenze's work on sectarian Methodists shows, working-class women had used their domestic and productive labor to justify an increased public role during the early nineteenth century. Sectarian Methodist women claimed their religious activities to be an extension of their critical social and economic position in laboring households. Their religious convictions also served to challenge the divisions between productive labor and domestic labor, divisions that were associated with the spread of industrialization.[2] Plebeian women had likewise claimed that their family duties required them to take political action in the Owenite movement or in bread riots.[3] These actions occurred in the first decades of the nineteenth century; by the last third of the century, the social and economic context that had fostered such activity was largely eroded by the spread of urbanization and industrialization. However, clear cultural continuities remained. Catherine Booth drew on the female Methodist preachers for inspiration. The memory of their activities no doubt lingered well into the 1860s in the communities of the north and Midlands, where many Salvationist women were raised.

Motherhood remained an essential source of authority for working-class women. Because it included both spiritual and practical authority, Salvationist women could build on and expand motherhood as a justification for their own authority. Mothers were the most significant family figures in conversion stories. Many converts, both men and women, evoked the image of their mothers praying for their souls during their reckless youths or at the moment of their conversion. Having the care of their own souls and the souls of their children gave women a spiritual authority that was at once empowering and a terrible responsibility. A mother's prayers and righteousness could ensure a child's place in heaven. Yet if they failed, they bore responsibility for their children's eternal torment. A mother was also responsible for providing food and other necessities. A woman's ability to earn and to stretch small sums of money assured her family's survival. This practical aspect of motherhood was reflected in the naming of women leaders as "mother." Catherine Booth never held a rank but was known as the Army Mother. Women in charge of the training home and rescue homes were frequently referred to as mother. This was similar to the Methodist practice of calling women of "exemplary courage and devotion to the cause" Mothers in Israel.[4] There was no masculine equivalent in either movement. To speak of working-class women's spiritual authority in domestic terms was a powerful metaphor that was evocative of women's real authority in everyday life.

The vision of devout and chaste Salvationist women laboring for souls runs through countless Salvation Army publications as well as in sympathetic press reports. The autobiography of a young Londoner, Elizabeth Flint, offers such a perspective on Salvationist women. She contrasts the choices of her two sisters, Mabel, a Salvationist, and Doll. Mabel wore her uniform with black, thick stockings that concealed her legs, and her bonnet made her face "pale and peaky."[5] Her boyfriend Erbie was also active in the Salvation Army, and Mrs. Flint commented, "Working for the Lord! The Lord must be hard up taking on people like Erbie."[6] The family was uneasy with Mabel's serious convictions, and, in an effort to convince her to give up the Army, her sister Doll bought her a soft, green dress and a red hair ribbon. Mabel refused both. Doll focused her ambitions on an escape from poverty and toil to a clean, sunlit home with modern conveniences. She intended to acquire all these amenities through the men whose attention she so easily attracted with her sheer stockings and bright, stylish clothes. Both choices were potentially dangerous. The family warned Mabel that her morose appearance and serious concerns would hardly attract a promising mate, and Doll's sexual availability could leave her disgraced before her family and community.[7] Each sister negotiated between the narrow possibilities open to working-class women.

Flint's comparison stressed the chastity and self-denial of Salvationist women and their repudiation of bodily, commercial pleasure. Flint's story also suggested that both sisters made unconventional choices that separated them from their wider community. In a more comic vein, one musical comedy, The Shop Girl (1894), portrayed a group of shop girls who are taken to a Salvation Army meeting to learn how to resist temptation. They laugh at the Hallelujah Lasses and proclaim "their own determination to 'Frolic, flirt and spoon.'"[8]

Mothers were not the only icons of feminine authority invoked by Salvation Army women. As the Hallelujah Lasses proceeded through the streets—singing, stopping to pray and to preach—they used their bodies, costumes, musical instruments, song lyrics, and the spoken word to convey their messages. Still, women occupied the streets only with difficulty.[9]

Working-class women had to use the streets to travel to work, to the marketplace, and to the homes of neighbors or kin. Women used courtyards and alleyways to dry clothes or visit neighbors. But the legitimate use of the streets was limited to such maternal and domestic duties. Girls did not play street games that were permissible for boys, and respectable girls would not loiter in the street or dance or sing to the music of street performers.[10] Preaching and singing drew on images of righteous mothers saving souls, thus clearly remaining within the bounds of conventional domestic responsibilities. But Salvationists also took their religious convictions outside the usual confines, seizing and occupying the streets to save souls.

Hallelujah Lasses drew attention to their cause by their own spectacular displays. They also drew on representations of prostitutes and disorderly women to express their position in the public realm, to speak of life and death, of vulnerability and purity. Eliza Haynes unbraided her hair, put flowing ribbons in it, and hung a sign around her neck saying "I am Happy Eliza." Thus attired, she paraded through the streets of Marylebone.[11] Two women in Hackney put on their nightgowns and paraded in the streets to announce a meeting, to "the immense sensation of the whole population."[12]

Streaming hair, flowing ribbons, and nightgowns attracted attention and encouraged spectators to question women's presence in the streets. Wearing a nightgown in the street suggested sexual invitation. Neat hair covered by a hat was a sign of order and decency; those too poor to buy a hat covered their heads with folded newspapers. Insane women were often depicted without hats, their hair long and unkempt. Haynes's appearance thus would link her with disorder and even insanity. She defied, moreover, Paul's injunction that a woman "that prayeth or prophesieth with her head uncovered dishonoureth her head" (1 Cor. 11:5). For centuries, these verses were among the most frequently used to assert that women's preaching was unscriptural. Haynes's action could therefore be both a social and theological challenge. Yet the Hallelujah Lasses' religious purpose was obvious. When Salvationist women walked and prayed in Piccadilly, where no respectable woman would go, their Quaker-like bonnets and the "S" on their collars identified them with the Salvation Army. One young woman, walking alone in Piccadilly, discovered her "quiet dress seemed sign enough to denote we belonged to the Salvation Army."[13]

The Hallelujah Lasses' manipulation of the image of disorderly women may be interpreted in several ways. First, the association of female religious enthusiasm with sexual license had a long, rich tradition.[14] Thus the association was virtually inescapable and demanded a response. Second, the prostitute was among the few available models of a "public woman." Third, and most important, images of disorder allowed the Hallelujah Lasses to express their own purity and the power of their mission. Prostitutes were associated with disease, putrefaction, and death. They were the "seminal drains" through which all society's excretions were washed away, ensuring the purity of other women and society as a whole.[15] Prostitution was linked to cities for, as one social critic wrote in 1857, "prostitutes are as inevitable in vast collections of human beings as are sewers, sinks and cesspools."[16]

The Hallelujah Lasses at once employed and reversed these images. These urban missionaries said they would "net the gutters" and "sweep the social sewers" seeking those rushing to death and destruction.[17] But when all those found in the sewers and gutters came to the Hallelujah Lasses, they were purified. Like prostitutes, the Lasses went where other women would not go and acted as vessels through which society's filth and disease would pass. Unlike prostitutes, however, they were agents of cleanliness and sanctification. If prostitutes saved society by siphoning off its waste, the Hallelujah Lasses could do even better by purifying the pestilence and banishing death.

THE BISHOPS' ACCUSATIONS

Hallelujah Lasses played off these associations with prostitutes and public women, while pamphlet writers and newspaper editors criticized and ridiculed them. The implications of the Salvationists' impropriety suddenly became of paramount importance in 1882. On May 9, the Convocation of Canterbury accepted a request from several bishops to consider the possibility of cooperation with the Salvation Army. A few bishops, most notably E. M. Benson, then bishop of Truro and later archbishop of Canterbury, believed the Salvation Army had succeeded in reaching the very groups the Church had failed to touch. The bishops proposed a cooperative union with the Army that would be beneficial to all concerned. A committee consisting of Benson, Lightfoot of Durham, Westcott of Cambridge, Canon Wilkinson, and the Rev. Randall Davidson, the archbishop's chaplain, was appointed to study the question. The committee attended Army meetings, visited the training homes, and solicited opinion from around the country.[18] With a few exceptions, the clergy admired little about the Army's methods. They regarded any sort of cooperation between the two bodies with horror. The committee's report was never filed. Benson was reluctant to complete it, saying it was "a hopeless task" because the opposition to the Army was so widespread.[19] When he was offered the archbishopric, he was able gracefully to abandon the project.

The investigation was important for the Army because it provoked clergy to discuss the Salvation Army, the proceedings receiving extensive publicity. Women celebrating the sacraments, children singing a hymn to the tune of "Champagne Charlie," or men rolling about on the floor in a flood of emotion shocked and offended these gentlemen.[20] The most serious allegations concerned sexual impropriety. These charges, hinted at before,[21] could not be ignored when made by men such as Canon Farrar in his sermon at Westminster Abbey and reprinted in the *Guardian*. He criticized the Army's "sham titles," "ludicrous stage properties," and drums, tambourines, and processions. "Dangerous fanaticism" throughout history, including the fourteenth-century flagellants, the *convulsionaires* of France, the Ranters, and the Salvationists always shared certain religious characteristics. These included, "the same prominence of women and children—the same wild hymns and tunes—the same indifference to regular clergy and the sacraments—the same morbid exaltation of religious feeling—the same physical excitement."[22] A few weeks later, the *Saturday Review* reported one clergyman's claim that "immorality has resulted from the meetings in which the young mingle and excitement runs high."[23]

These accusations exploded at the Upper House of the Convocation in April 1883. According to the record of the meeting, Dr. Markness, bishop of Oxford, stated that the Army "called for holiness of life on the part of its members; but its action had led to deplorable consequences and to unholiness of life. It was impossible to suppose that there could be holiness of life when young persons of both sexes were called together in exciting meetings, held up to a late hour at night, and permitted to go away without control." [24] Dr. Atley, the bishop of Hereford, confirmed this assertion.

The accusation sparked an immediate response. Catherine Booth addressed a meeting at Kensington Town Hall to answer the charge. She claimed there was no evidence whatsoever to support the bishops' vilification and complained that they ought first to have verified the truth of the accusations. She added that the attacks on Salvationists had risen. "The roughs had kicked one of their lieutenants and left him for dead, abusing him with the very words of the Bishops in their mouths."[25] According to the Salvation Army's official historian, the bishops of Oxford and Hereford, when challenged, conducted a survey in the two counties and admitted they found not a single case of immorality arising from the Army's meetings. The charges eventually "dissolved themselves as did calumnies against the early Christians."[26] Historian Stuart Mews has confirmed that a "detailed survey was conducted, which vindicated the Army."[27]

There was, however, another conclusion to this story. The Salvation Army conducted its own survey of the corps to determine the truth of these allegations.[28] It requested the corps captains to report how many meetings they held each week, how many attended, and how many illegitimate births occurred "owing to the association together of young persons at our services." Twenty-one corps replied that twenty-eight births had occurred in connection with the Army's services, and several admitted rumors of more. Only Portsmouth reported none, while Winsford recorded the highest number, three.[29] Several captains wrote explaining the women's circumstances. Captain Savage of Boston wrote that a young woman was left alone with her mother's "paramour" while her mother was in jail for theft. He made "an attack on her virtue and the result was a child but this man was never in any of our meetings." The captain declared another case to be "very damaging" because both parents were active Salvationists.[30] Captain Taylor of Alverstone believed that while two unmarried mothers in his corps did attend Army meetings, "these both would have happened with or without the Army being in town."[31]

It is not clear whether any other of the more than three hundred corps received the survey or why these twenty-one responses were saved among Archbishop Benson's papers. Attached was a letter from Salvation Army headquarters asserting that "we find only twenty-eight cases in which illegitimate births *are said* to have occurred in connection with our services."[32] Given that it was not rumors but the corps captains who said the births occurred, this information would only have damaged the Army's already battered reputation. Perhaps because of Archbishop Benson's high regard for the Army, he decided not to publicize this information. At the 1883 Convocation, the bishop of Oxford presented "the carefully prepared statement of three sad cases of . . . young women having lost their characters through attending the nightly meetings of the Salvationists."[33]

These surveys suggest that the Army did not attract just the chaste and respectable. Historians have argued that in the early nineteenth century, an illegitimate child was accepted by the community, especially if the father acknowledged his responsibilities. But after 1840 an illegitimate birth meant economic and social ruin for a woman. Chastity and respectability became firmly linked.[34] For the bishops of Oxford and Hereford, a pregnancy out of wedlock cast the Salvation Army in a poor light. Although it is impossible to know the precise circumstances in each case, Salvation Army meetings apparently attracted those who did not entirely adhere to its tenets or even wider community standards of respectability. For some who attended its meetings, a pregnancy out of wedlock was not necessarily incompatible with active membership. The surveys would suggest some Salvationists reinterpreted the Army's tenets to suit their own beliefs but nevertheless found the meetings attractive. Certainly Salvationists were not the only unmarried mothers attending a place of worship. But the Army was condemned by contemporaries not because it inculcated workers with a middle-class mentality, as some historians have argued, but because it failed to civilize them at all. The surveys suggest some corps captains also suspected that the meetings provoked the very opposite of the spiritual transformation they intended.

The allegations of sexual impropriety lingered even after the bishop of Oxford publicly retracted his statement. The press, in particular *Lloyds,* regularly printed stories of men and women arrested for drunkenness or disorderly conduct who claimed a connection to the Army. *Lloyds* printed detailed reports of Salvationists summoned to support their children, the birth of children to unmarried women, or any other similar improprieties they could unearth. The papers ignored the *War Cry*'s insistence that most of those individuals had never had any connection to the Army.[35] But those small disturbances were overshadowed by a second scandal that again called into question the propriety of Salvationist women, and this time the indiscretion was linked to the Booth family.

THE "MAIDEN TRIBUTE OF MODERN BABYLON"

In July 1885, prominent journalist and editor of the *Pall Mall Gazette* W. T. Stead wrote a series of articles entitled "The Maiden Tribute of Modern Babylon," which described the dark underworld of London's vice emporiums. Stead was determined to demonstrate how easily an innocent child could be taken into prostitution. He had acted in cooperation with the Booth family, who took a great interest in the social issues surrounding prostitution as a result of their involvement with the Army's rescue work. They hoped to force the government to increase protection for children and to create harsher penalties for those involved in the vice trade. Stead's most sensational revelation focused on a child allegedly procured for £5 from her drunken mother and defiled in a brothel. The story was not strictly true. In fact, Bramwell Booth, his wife, Florence, and William and Catherine Booth had convinced Rebecca Jarrett, a former prostitute and brothel keeper who had been rescued by the Salvation Army, to act as a procuress. Jarrett went to Lisson Grove and negotiated with the mother of thirteen-year-old Eliza Armstrong to engage Eliza in employment, the exact nature of which was unclear. Eliza was examined by a midwife to confirm that she was a virgin, and thus innocent and of good character, and she was then sent to work as a servant for a Salvationist family in France. It is not clear where her mother believed Eliza was going or how much money changed hands. But Stead and the Booths believed their point was proven. An innocent child had been removed from her home and could have been forced into prostitution.

When Stead published his version of these events, partly true and partly fictional, in the *Pall Mall Gazette,* Eliza's mother recognized her daughter's story in the details. She applied to the police court to have her daughter returned. This application led to a police investigation, and Jarrett, Stead, Bramwell Booth, and several others were charged with abduction of a child under sixteen. Jarrett, Stead, and the midwife were also charged with indecent assault because of the midwife's examination of the child. The case turned, in part, on whether Mrs. Armstrong willingly sold her daughter into prostitution, as Jarrett maintained, or had arranged for Eliza to go into service, as Mrs. Armstrong alleged. The court found them guilty and sentenced Jarrett to six months, Stead to three months. Bramwell Booth was acquitted. After her release from prison, Jarrett returned to her life as a Salvationist.

The case did lead to important legal changes. Parliament passed the Criminal Law Amendment Act, raising the age of consent and increasing police powers to prosecute prostitutes and brothel keepers.[36] Salvationists had argued that this was a critical step in the campaign against prostitution, and they had taken a prominent role in pressing Parliament to pass this legislation. The officers and soldiers played only a small role in the drama. Still, it had a significant impact on the whole Salvation Army. First, the Armstrong case made the Hallelujah Lasses a familiar sight to readers of almost any newspaper. The uniforms, bonnets, and red guernseys were already common in the landscape of urban working-class neighborhoods. Now they enjoyed broad recognition. Second, the campaign brought rescue work to the forefront of the Salvation Army's mission. Whereas it once occupied only a small section of the *War Cry*, the progress of the rescue work was reported regularly and in detail after 1885. The Salvation Army represented the rescue work as urgent, a compelling extension of its spiritual mission. In January 1886, the *War Cry* declared, "The work of purifying and rescuing must go on at all costs—if it means a Bramwell Booth in the dock, a Stead in Holloway jail, or a Jarrett in a cold prison cell."[37] In 1885 the rescue work had a staff of four; by 1888 a staff of seventy ran ten rescue homes housing 212 women.[38] The Salvation Army gained the reputation as "the largest, the most successful and to some extent the most innovative rescue organization in Britain."[39] It also gained the Salvation Army a place in national bodies, such as the National Vigilance Association, in which it had previously not been included.[40]

But as much as the Maiden Tribute case raised public awareness of the Army's rescue work, it also sparked public outrage. Jarrett and Bramwell Booth were attacked by angry spectators outside the court. In the streets crowds drowned out Salvationists' preaching with cries of "Where is Eliza?" and even assaulted uniformed Salvationists. The story of a laboring man's daughter abducted and seduced was a familiar Victorian narrative, and in this case the Salvation Army was cast in the role of procurer. The music halls offered their own take on these events. Marie Lloyd sang "Buy Me Some Almond Rock" about a woman who had been "asked out, and without doubt I'm dying to make a start."

> Only fancy if Gladstone's there,
> And falls in love with me,
> If I run across Labouchere,[41]
> I'll ask him home to tea. . . .
> I heard in truth that General Booth
> is going to be M.C.
> And if he is, 'twill be good "biz",
> No end of fun there'll be. . . .
> Randy pandy, sugary candy
> Buy me some almond rock.[42]

THREE LIVES

These events created a particular challenge for Salvationist women. They exercised their spiritual and sacred authority within a context complicated by accusations of sexual impropriety, excessive public prominence, and expectations of maternal affection and spiritual responsibility. They were at once fulfilling their role as righteous mothers and violating the limitations on sanctioned speech and action. The biographies of three women associated with the Army suggest how these issues shaped their careers as Salvationists. Maud Charlesworth, daughter of an Anglican clergyman, joined the Salvation Army in 1882 despite her father's vigorous objections. She took up work the Church would never have allowed, opening the Army's work in France and Switzerland and preaching all over England. She married Ballington Booth in 1886, and together they directed the Army's work in the United States. The second woman, Effie Anthon, was the daughter of a woman redeemed in the Army's rescue home and adopted by a middle-class educator and supporter of the Army. But Effie was soon in need of the Army's rescue work herself, and, contrary to the outcome in most publicized cases, she failed to achieve any lasting change in her spiritual life. Her story illustrates the immense consequences sexual sins entailed and the limitations of the Army's rescue work. Last, Rebecca Jarrett, prostitute and brothel keeper, came to the Army when her health collapsed, and there she found redemption and a new life evangelizing other fallen women. Her participation in the Maiden Tribute case made her notorious and earned her six months in jail. After her release, she continued to work in the Salvation Army's rescue work until her death. In some respects, each woman differed from the typical Hallelujah Lass, but these particularly well-documented lives reveal how Salvationists negotiated the tensions their work and lives engendered.

MAUD CHARLESWORTH

In 1885 the Rev. Samuel Charlesworth published a book in which he lamented that his "loving, truthful and dutiful" daughter Maud was "entirely alienated from me and her relatives and former friends; she has deserted her home, forsaken the Church of her youth." [43] (See Figure 7.) She had joined the Salvation Army. After repeated attempts to "rescue my child from what I felt to be a most demoralising influence," he resorted to the publication of *Sensational Religion as Resorted to in the System Called the "Salvation Army" in Its Influence upon the Young and in Its Effects upon the Duties and Claims of Home Life.* Four years later his daughter, Maud Charlesworth Booth, published her autobiography, *Beneath Two Flags,* which detailed her own experiences in the Salvation Army. The father's and daughter's competing accounts of the Salvation Army were concerned particularly with the public prominence of Salvationist women and their enhanced authority. At stake were two interpretations of Christian womanhood.

Samuel Charlesworth's family included one prominent member, his sister, Maria Louisa Charlesworth, author of many widely read religious books, including *Ministering Children* and *The Female Visitor to the Poor*. Writing was among the few forms of socially sanctioned public speech for middle-class Christian women, and Charlesworth's writing gained a national audience. Her books described "the moral and religious force emanating from the truly religious woman" who used her gifts in modest, feminine ways to guide the poor and wayward.[44]

Maria Charlesworth's notion of feminine Christianity was shared by her brother and his wife, Maria. Mrs. Charlesworth's devotion and faith were recorded in her husband's biography of her, *Memorials of a Blessed Life* (1882), published after her death. He dedicated it to his three daughters, "as sharers in the work, and the faith and the hope of their beloved Mother." Maria Beddome had married Samuel Charlesworth in 1857, and they moved to Limehouse, East London, soon after. Mrs. Charlesworth became involved with the local factory women. Charlesworth wrote,

> The young women working in these were wont at their meal-time to sally forth into the street, walking arm in arm [in] wide-spread rows, singing and talking boisterously, and often profanely, so as to create much annoyance. Mrs. Charlesworth yearned over these poor stray ones; she saw the employers and obtained permission to come to the factories during the hours of dinner and tea to talk to the workers. At first she met with the rudest reception and most noisy interruption. . . . In one factory for making sacks, the women were often violent; . . . sacks and tin cans would be thrown downstairs after them. . . . Gradually the better disposed of the men and women became listeners, then earnest hearers . . . until at length some fifty or sixty would sit quietly round the now loved and esteemed teacher . . . and eagerly drink in the words of truth and life.[45]

The work eventually grew to include bible classes, prayer meetings, and a believers' meeting. Mrs. Charlesworth also worked with the Mildmay Mission and with Mrs. Ranyard's Biblewomen. Twelve years in Limehouse, "with its mineral factories, stagnant canals, and thick fogs," took their toll on her weak constitution, and she "fell asleep in Jesus" on November 7, 1881.[46]

Samuel Charlesworth's rendition of his wife's life expressed a view of feminine religiosity very like that found in his sister's books. Mrs. Charlesworth assumed no authority within her husband's parish. She taught exclusively in sanctioned settings outside the church, and she did not preach. She worked primarily with women. She shared a dangerous environment with the workers, but her health could not withstand it;

her death thus exemplified both her delicate nature and sacrifice and the presumed class differences between her and the other inhabitants of Limehouse.

The Rev. Samuel Charlesworth sincerely hoped his three daughters would follow in his wife's footsteps. But the Salvation Army offered another path. The Christian Mission began work in Limehouse in 1868, and when they were not permitted to use the street for open air services, the Rev. Charlesworth allowed them to use the church garden. Ironically, in 1882, when William Booth wished to convince Bishop Benson that the Mission's work was a benefit to the Church, he informed the bishop that Mrs. Charlesworth of Limehouse found the membership in her bible class much increased by its work.[47] But the Christian Mission grew into the Salvation Army, and the Rev. Charlesworth's opinion changed. He deplored the flags, the "prominent allusion to those with formerly abandoned lives," and the name of Jesus Christ being "so irreverently alluded to."[48] But Maud took a great interest in this organization. Her mother wrote to her at school in 1881,

> Do not come home too full of the Booths and the Army. I do so hope you will try to keep your mind from being taken up with this one subject, and try to throw your heart into our work, where I trust you will help me. I shall be so glad of your help this week, but if you are thinking only of the Army, other sober work will seem dull to you. I have not called on Mrs. Booth and I do not think we are very likely to know any of the Booths.[49]

In her autobiography, Maud recalled that she first saw the Salvation Army "marching the streets through snow or rain, kneeling upon the hard ground, or sitting crowded together in a poor, broken-down theatre, with the poorest and the lowest of that large East London parish." From others she soon learned when the Army passed to "smile with derision and . . . to repeat tales which had lost the little spark of truth with which they started." Still, she was drawn to the Salvation Army. "Kneeling in the solemn stillness of my father's church, perched upon a high hassock in our pew, through what to me was rather a weary service, I used sometimes to hear the stillness broken by singing in the streets with this refrain: 'Oh you must be a lover of the Lord, Or you can't go to heaven when you die!'" This refrain remained with her and she began to attend the services until, "in an Army hall, I saw Jesus my Saviour as I had never seen him before and gave up my life entirely to God—my God, the Army's God, and the drunkard's God. There I received into my heart the love and fire that have sent me forth to do God's will, and to follow the steps of Christ of Calvary."[50]

Her father claimed religious thoughts were not the sole attraction of the Army. At an Army meeting Ballington Booth, William and Catherine Booth's second son, then twenty-four years old and a prominent officer in the Army, held her hand when inquiring about her soul. "The twofold cord of religious feeling and love attachment so closely woven into her young life, so tightly drawn around her, was sufficient to draw her from her once loved home, and her father and sisters, and her former church associations."[51]

After Maud left school in 1882, she convinced her father to permit her to go to Paris with Catherine Booth, the Booth's eldest daughter, then twenty-three years old and in command of the Army's work in France.[52] Florence Soper, who was later to marry Bramwell Booth and direct the Army's social service work, Adalaide Cox, also active in rescue work, and Arthur Clibborn, who married Kate Booth in 1887, were among the group chosen to open the work in Paris. Samuel Charlesworth agreed to pay £100 for board and instruction in French and German if Maud would refrain from wearing the uniform, and only visit the poor. Maud immediately began selling the *War Cry* in front of the Opera House, and she sent the first £25 of her tuition to Salvation Army headquarters as a donation. Her father was horrified. His daughter was among those women street sellers who were "seen as the most abandoned class of women in Paris."[53] When he remonstrated with Maud, she said he had never forbidden it. But, he replied, "I could never dream of your engaging in such an unfeminine, indecorous work."[54] Salvationist women were aware of the association with the street vendors whom Charlesworth deplored. When it was proposed that officers sell the Army's newspaper in the streets of Paris, one woman recalled the shame she felt. "Brace the insults and ignominy of a Paris boulevard?" But, with the thought of Christ's sacrifice before them, the women began to work the streets, "as blessing always succeeds a sacrifice."[55]

In December 1882, headquarters decided to proceed to Switzerland, a Protestant country that would presumably welcome the Salvation Army. Kate Booth and Maud were among those sent to open the work. Kate Booth received a special title, La Marechale, that she would continue to use for many years. Immediately, rowdy crowds disrupted the meetings and attacked Salvationists in the streets. The Swiss authorities banned Salvation Army meetings in January despite laws guaranteeing the free exercise of faith and individual liberty. When the Salvationists moved to hold meetings in private residences, these too were banned. Kate Booth and Maud Charlesworth were both taken into custody, questioned for four hours, and expelled from Geneva. They appealed this decision to higher authorities and were told the court was scandalized by their activities when scripture so clearly forbade women's preaching. La Marechale replied:

> It is contrary, you tell me, to your sense of what is right and becoming that young women should preach the Gospel. Now, if Miss Charlesworth and I had come to Geneva to act in one of your theatres, I have no doubt we should have met with sympathy and approval from your public. We could have sung and danced on your stage; we could have dressed in a manner very different from, and much less modest than, that in which you see us dressed; we could have appeared before a miscellaneous audience; . . . we should have got money; . . . and you would all have sat and approved. . . . But when women come to try and save some of the forty or fifty thousand of your miserable, scoffing irreligious population . . . then you cry out that it is unseemly and immodest. You would not bring your wives and daughters to hear us speak of Jesus, though you would bring them to hear us if we danced and sang upon the stage of your theatre.[56]

The courts ruled against the Salvationists.

Comparing Salvationist women to actresses was apt. Both professions brought an unusual degree of publicity to women who stood on a platform or stage addressing an audience, and it was that very connection that so horrified many critics of the Army. The comparison also made use of what was distinctive about Salvation Army services, the theatricality and sensation used to draw crowds. After the authorities expelled the Salvationists, one theatrical paper reportedly wrote, "Our theatre has lost a formidable rival, and the crowd is beginning to find its way back to us."[57] In fact, Kate Booth's defense made use of the aspect of the Salvation Army that Samuel Charlesworth deplored most. At Army services, he asserted, "sensation was the motive power, excitement the sustaining force"; these emotions left the believer's spiritual life "morbidly excited and superficially expanded."[58] The Hallelujah Lasses engaged in none of the private, modest Christian service exemplified by Charlesworth's wife and sister.

La Marechale returned to Switzerland, where she was jailed for continuing to hold Salvation Army meetings. Disputes with the Swiss government continued until 1884.[59] The Army succeeded in gaining widespread publicity, if not support, for its work in Switzerland. The newspapers followed the case, the *War Cry* devoted considerable attention to the events, and numerous tracts were written by Army supporters.[60] Maud Charlesworth spent the next year addressing Salvation Army meetings across England about her Swiss experiences. She lived in the home of William and

Catherine Booth, much to her father's dismay. He wished for her to come home, but William Booth reportedly told him, "Your daughter is ours, and she will be ours for life; you may force her to go home and break her heart and send her to an early grave, but she will be ours to death."[61] Samuel Charlesworth regarded this reply as a grave affront to his fatherly prerogatives, but the Salvation Army expected all its members to put their duty to God and the Army first. William Booth was consistent in this requirement; he refused all contact with his daughter Kate and his sons Ballington and Herbert when they left the Salvation Army.

Samuel Charlesworth strenuously objected to the militarism and authority assumed by those without justification of education, ordination, or status. He argued,

> [If the Army] chooses to make young girls vain and ridiculous by dubbing them Marechales, Majors, Captains, Lieutenants, Aides-de-Camp etc. the weakness and folly of such an absurd practice deprives it of harm. But when . . . bearded and moustached young men [are] dressed in uniform with naval and military titles, allowing them to be so addressed and spoken to among strangers ignorant of the deception, I say that such conduct is not only religiously a fraud but socially and nationally a grievous wrong.[62]

Maud found the authority and sacrifice allowed her in the Army compelling. When Salvationist women went out to rescue the fallen, "this was to be our battlefield through the dark hours of the night. Straight into the midst of the crowd we stepped, the light showing up our uniform, the 'S' upon our collars and Army badge upon our bonnets making us conspicuous in contrast with the gay crowd."[63] To those who said no respectable woman would act this way in public, she wrote, "I can only thank God I belong to the Salvation Army—a people who are not 'respectable' but who, as midnight soul-seekers, are winning the gratitude and love of the lost, and leading their sisters back to the paths of virtue, righteousness, and peace."[64]

Maud recognized the Salvation Army as a unique opportunity for women. When Maud was still at school, her mother's letters acknowledged that the ordinary parish work expected of a clergyman's daughter would seem "dull" after the Salvation Army. Certainly Maud would never have addressed a congregation, worked the streets, or been arrested had she remained in the Church.

Maud wrote of one fourteen-year-old girl who was working as a nursemaid; saved at an Army meeting, she was immediately drawn into the work and given opportunities for meaningful, public work. She soon began to read fluently and to address public meetings.

Apart from the Army, she probably would have married in her native village, and have lived a narrow life, with no opportunity and possibly no desire for anything higher. In her Army life in England, as soldier, cadet, and field officer, she constantly came under the influence of higher and stronger characters and intellects and absorbed more than she realized, until she was thrown upon her own responsibilities as commanding officer of a corps.[65]

One of Maud Charlesworth's companions in France and Switzerland, Nettie Wallis, wrote an account of her decision to join the Army. She felt a call to foreign missionary service, but without training in languages and few resources she did not know how she would fulfill her call. She went to hear Catherine Booth preach in London and knew that the Salvation Army was the answer. She joined the Army and soon after learned that "I need not go very far to find the heathen. There they are—only two hours passage across the Channel."[66]

In October 1883, William Booth wrote to Samuel Charlesworth seeking his permission for Maud to marry Ballington Booth. Charlesworth strongly objected to this union, and he even threatened to appeal to the Court of Chancery for an injunction. Maud refused her father's entreaties to break the engagement and return home. Samuel Charlesworth's objections to this union were twofold. He could not "sanction the Army's notion of marriage" because it insisted that commitment to the Army must come first. A husband, therefore, could be sent to India, a wife to the United States and the children left with strangers. He also objected to the Booths.

Mr. and Mrs. Booth raised themselves from a position of poverty and obscurity to one of wealth and eminence by industry, thrift and ability. . . . I should have been the last person, I hope, to have recalled or commented on their antecedents of indigence and meanness; but when they have made the profession of religion the stepping stone from a very low and poor condition to one of great responsibility, publicity and influence, they have laid themselves and their schemes and doings open to investigation and criticism by all who are injuriously and prejudicially affected by their conduct.[67]

Maud ignored her father's objections, and in September 1886 she married Colonel Ballington Booth. Tickets to the service were sold at 2 shillings, 6 pence, and a "Great War Demonstration" and wedding breakfast followed.[68]

Samuel Charlesworth believed he had been robbed of his daughter. The Salvation Army offered her excitement, sensation, authority, and romance, none of which the Church could condone. Bereft of his daughter, he recalled that Maud was once "a most loving, dutiful and truthful

Figure 1.   Catherine Booth. Courtesy of The Salvation Army National Archives.

Figure 2.   William Booth. Courtesy of The Salvation Army National Archives.

Figure 3.   George Scott Railton. Courtesy of The Salvation Army National Archives.

Figure 4.   Elijah Cadman. Courtesy of The Salvation Army
National Archives.

Figure 5.   Adalaide Cox. Courtesy of The Salvation Army
National Archives.

Figure 6. *St. Stephen's Review* cartoon of William Booth. Courtesy of the British Library.

Figure 7. Maud
Charlesworth Booth.
Courtesy of The Salvation
Army National Archives.

Figure 8. Effie Anthon.
Courtesy of Queen Mary
and Westfield College,
University of London.

Figure 9. Florence Soper Booth. Courtesy of The Salvation Army National Archives.

Figure 10. Salvation Army brass band. Courtesy of The Salvation Army National Archives.

Figure 11.   Emma and Frederick Booth-Tucker.
Courtesy of The Salvation Army National Archives.

girl; the joy and cheer of my home life, an affectionate companion and a sympathising helper in my parochial work in schools and among the poor."[69] Maud Booth moved far beyond the confines of the private, decorous work her father offered. She traveled in Great Britain and in Europe renting halls, creating publicity, preaching, and dealing with souls in concert with other Salvationist women. With her husband, Ballington, she commanded the Army's work in the United States from 1887 to 1896. Maud Booth wrote for the U.S. *War Cry* and began a program designed to assist released prison convicts. She became known as a "powerful public speaker who could electrify large crowds," and she became so famous that one manufacturer obtained her endorsement of a product, the "Vapo-Cresolen Lamp."[70]

Maud's authority, like that of other Salvationist women, was derived from a sensational public presence so unlike the respectable femininity exemplified by her mother and aunt. Preaching, selling newspapers in the street, accepting a salary were all unthinkable for a middle-class woman. Maud Charlesworth even married a man with none of the marks of gentility. She was, in effect, relinquishing all claims to respectable middle-class womanhood. Maud Charlesworth Booth's vocation was a part of wider social and cultural changes that shaped women's lives. Her mother and aunt had worked with Ranyard's Biblewomen, organized bible classes and mothers' meetings, all innovative work in the 1860s. But Salvationist women were, in some respects, "new women"—activist, urban women who created new professional opportunities for other women and sought to broaden their cultural and political landscape. Middle-class journalists, teachers, artists, and office workers rode bicycles; attended lectures, theater, and political meetings; subscribed to publications aimed at this expanding readership; and took part in the commercial possibilities of city life. Some chose celibacy and career, while others attempted to broaden the confines of permissible sexuality and family life.[71]

Maud Booth and other Salvationist women shared some of these aspirations. They found a professional career in the Army that offered an opportunity to exercise responsibility and to advance to positions of authority. They moved freely through the urban streets, meeting with prostitutes, drunks, and others they would not otherwise encounter. They also rented premises for meetings, budgeted for and paid expenses, advertised meetings, and supervised the activities of soldiers and junior officers. Women like Maud Charlesworth, who came from middle-class families, would have rarely ventured out without a chaperon before they joined the Army and certainly would not have talked to prostitutes in the streets. Many of these women did not marry, instead spending years living with another officer or living communally in an Army home. This physical and social independence demonstrated their steadfast commitment to enhancing and expanding Christian women's activities. Salvationist women also shared with other professional women an ethic of service. Historian Dina Copelman argues that professions were defined both by the expertise required and by the mission to serve, but, of the two, "service . . . dominated women's claims to professions."[72] Salvationist women acquired education, special training, and a considerable range of employment opportunities, but service remained the preeminent goal.

Historians have argued that the "new woman" was middle class and that working-class women shared neither her aspirations nor her achievements. Salvation Army women, who were predominantly working class, may modify this perspective.[73] Although middle-class women, like Florence Soper Booth and Maud Charlesworth Booth, received high-ranking supervisory positions in which their superior education and class status were evidently used to fullest advantage, many working-class women also assumed positions of authority, and tensions erupted with their families and communities too. In 1879, for example, two Hallelujah Lasses "opened fire" on the small Welsh mining town where eighteen-year-old Rosina Davies lived. She was the daughter of a miner, raised Primitive Methodist. Although the Primitives had once eschewed distinctions between "respectable and rough," as her chapel became "more organized," it was filled with only the respectable, and they were "too respectable for open air work."[74]

Davies was immediately drawn to the Salvation Army's outdoor services, and she determined that she had to get saved. But her horrified mother locked her in the house and forbade her to attend any more meetings. It was not that she opposed Christianity; the freedom and publicity associated with Salvation Army women appalled her. "Mother feared all the excitement and freedom was a stepping stone to a worldly stage of life, and as I was different from the rest of the family, difficult to manage, she thought there must be stricter discipline." But Davies escaped and went to a meeting. "I came home radiant with the joy of surrendering myself to Christ." As she knelt to pray, her mother began to beat her with a birch rod. "She gave me another stroke, thinking I was hardened, and I told her I was not hurt because Jesus bore the strokes for me. . . . My beloved mother! She suffered more than I did. She feared her little girl was going astray, and she wanted to save my soul."[75]

Davies left to join the Army, and, with fellow officer Sarah Webb, she opened the Army's work in several communities. She took lessons in grammar and practiced reading the Psalms aloud to improve her speaking. Throughout she found "persecution, zealous prejudice, and selfish unwillingness that a Girl evangelist should come into the arena and fight the Good Fight in public."[76] Another working-class Salvationist, Martha Chippendale, was beaten by her father when she came home and announced that she had been saved. The next day she asked whether she might attend another Salvation Army meeting. He told her, "I'll hammer you every time you go," and so he did. The other mill girls mocked her swollen face and jeered at her when she said grace before meals. When Chippendale finally announced to her mother that she intended to become a Salvation Army officer, her mother replied that a good daughter would never leave home until she was married.[77] These working-class women faced familial restrictions not unlike those endured by Maud Charlesworth. Submission to God's will was a call to active service; those who heeded the call relinquished the restrictions that had once confined them for a different, and often arduous, set of demands.

EFFIE ANTHON

In 1888 Constance Maynard (1849–1935) received a letter from Captain Ellen Pash. The two women had studied at Cambridge together as part of the first generation of women to receive a university education. Pash was now a Salvation Army officer, and Maynard was headmistress of Westfield College, which she had founded in 1882. Captain Pash told her of a six-year-old girl, Effie, in an Army orphanage in Paris; the Army hoped to place her with a good family (see Figure 8).[78] The child was born to an Italian woman who had become pregnant when her family's clergyman had been asked to sit up with her when she was ill. The family sent her away in disgrace, and the Salvation Army found her two years later, "homeless, friendless, and totally unfit to support herself and her child, . . . nearly out of her mind with anxiety, shame and despair." She was sent to live with Mrs. Josephine Butler at Winchester, where she was converted and reclaimed. She proceeded to Paris as a cadet to work in the orphanage where her daughter was then living. The daughter came to know her mother by name, although she had been told her mother was dead. In 1888, it was determined, probably by leading officers in the rescue work, that Effie should be adopted, and the Army contacted four Salvationist families who had given their names as ready to adopt the next foundling. Effie would go to a miner, "though all agreed she seemed utterly unsuited to the humblest ranks."[79] Captain Pash hoped Maynard would know a more suitable family.

Constance Maynard was a respected pioneer in women's education and an evangelical. She founded Westfield College not only to guide young women in their intellectual life but to offer higher education in a Christian context. Like many women of her class, Maynard kept several concurrent journals that detailed various aspects of her life. As soon as she received Captain Pash's letter, she began to write a diary that would eventually chronicle her relationship with this child in six volumes. These diaries are among the few remaining sources on Effie's life. They contain letters from her and others and lengthy descriptions and reflections by Maynard. The diaries leave many questions unanswered, and the perspective of the mother is completely absent. Although only a fragmentary picture emerges from these diaries, they nevertheless allow a glimpse of one life that did not follow the prescribed path set out in Salvation Army conversion narratives. Effie's relationship to the Salvation Army began with her mother's reclamation, and eight years later she returned to the Army's rescue workers in need of reclamation herself. This child's life contained many of the struggles and tensions common to Salvationist women's conversion narratives, but her story was not resolved. She was never able to sustain the change that holiness ought to have made, and the Army eventually gave her up.

At the time, there was no legal way for a biological parent to sever all ties to a child, nor was there a way for another person to receive a permanent legal claim to a child.[80] The Salvation Army's adoption services were an outgrowth of the rescue work. Wherever possible, a mother was expected to provide for her child, but in exceptional cases the Army arranged adoptions.[81] It is not clear why this child was counted as such an exception.

At thirty-nine years of age, Constance Maynard knew her professional choices required that she sacrifice motherhood unless some unusual circumstance made it possible. Particularly after her father's death in September 1888, the tremendous sacrifices of family and emotional ties her professional and intellectual life demanded seemed ever more onerous. Shortly after her father's death she told her sisters she was considering adopting a child, preferably a child of six, leaving "the trouble of babyhood" to someone else. She told them, "I do *want* a child, but I shall not tell anyone whatever, or look in an orphanage, or take the least step towards it, only (I give you warning!) if one is thrown at my head I will catch it."[82] Captain Pash's letter seemed providential.

Maynard replied to the letter, expressing an interest in the child and asking Captain Pash to bring her to visit. When Effie was brought to Maynard's home, Maynard immediately thought "of course she won't do." Her spectacles (intended to correct a squint), her shabby frock and darned stockings, her "rough untutored manner" hardly appealed to Maynard.[83] But as the day wore on, the small child charmed Maynard, and she decided to begin to consider adopting her. Initially, Maynard hoped that she would be allowed a trial period of six months when the child "should be returnable to the S.A. without accusation or explanation,"[84] but she was not able to convince the Salvation Army to agree to this trial. She arranged for a legal contract, signed before a lawyer, in which the mother would relinquish all her rights and Maynard would agree to support the child until she was eighteen. Maynard promised "so to train the child that she should serve in that holy war against sin and Satan, in which I, the adopting parent, am already labouring to the best of my powers."[85] The lawyer reminded Maynard that the mother could not legally relinquish her rights but advised that it was best not to inform her of this legality.

The lawyer, Captain Pash, Maynard, the child, and her mother met in a lawyer's office in November 1888. When Maynard told Effie that the woman who she was supposed to know only as a cadet at the Paris orphanage would be there, she was pleased. She told Maynard, "She will be there? She is my friend and I love her. She gave me many things, a doll, a small horse and many other things."[86] When Maynard and the child entered the room, Maynard thought she saw the mother start. After some minutes observing her, Maynard thought "her beauty [was] of an unintellectual and animal type, to my mind," a view that would eventually influence Maynard's perception of this child.[87] The papers were signed, and the mother wept. When they left, Effie asked why the woman had wept so much. Maynard replied by asking what she thought. "I do not know but I believe she must have lost something very precious. She cries a lot."[88] Maynard seemingly did not reflect on what the child might make of this odd meeting, nor did any of the Salvationists involved in the adoption wonder what effect witnessing this proceeding might have on Effie. Soon after she was baptized in the Church with the name Stephanie Anthon. Her initials, S.A., honored the Salvation Army, and Anthon was invented because it translated as "crown of flowers."

Effie began life with Maynard in the home of Mrs. Moore at Wimbledon. Problems erupted immediately. Effie was too rough, she told lies, and she would not attend to her lessons. Soon, Effie had to be moved to another place and then another. On a holiday in France with Maynard and one of Maynard's favored students, Miss Campbell, Maynard was deeply dismayed by Effie's need for a constant audience, her rudeness, and her dishonesty.[89] One morning over breakfast at the hotel, another visitor asked Effie how she liked France. She replied that she liked it, "but Auntie likes England better and I think I do too." The man replied that she was a fortunate girl to be visiting France with her aunt. Effie then said, "leaning forward as if she was saying something she thought everybody ought not to hear, 'At least I call her Auntie, you know, but she's my Mother really.'"[90] Her comment certainly highlighted her ambiguous status as did Maynard's choice of France because she wished to see how much Effie remembered of the language and the country from the four years she had lived with the Salvation Army there.

Maynard tried everything she knew to reform Effie's character. She chastised her for rudeness, lies, and disobedience; told her that her behavior was sinful; and sought ways to make her obedient and humble. When she was ten, Effie spent a holiday as a servant in an attempt both to punish her and to teach her humility. The first week she resisted, telling her mistress "she was a lady, not your servant as you seem to think."[91] The second week she was more tractable but did not seem to take this lesson in humility as seriously as Maynard had hoped. Maynard was disappointed that she enjoyed domestic work, adopted a cockney accent, and took a great interest in the local goings-on.

All these efforts were consistent with Maynard's evangelical Christianity. She hoped her lessons would make Effie more tractable and humble, less self-interested and more concerned with morality. She believed such changes were a matter of choice. Effie had only to seek right. Salvationists would have agreed that any individual, no matter how sinful, could with true repentance be utterly transformed by holiness. Maynard also considered Effie's behavior to have an ethnic taint. She believed it was the "false, vain, untrustworthy Italian that shows in Effie." She wondered whether Effie did not suffer from a "moral idiocy" that came to her from her antecedents. Her unfortunate moral character might well be overcome but only with the help of a strong Christianity.

Maynard gave up any hope that Effie would attend Westfield much less join Maynard in any professional capacity. Instead, she set her expectations much lower. Effie briefly attended a school that trained orphan girls to be servants, hospital matrons, and teachers. From the start,

Effie consistently broke rules, mistreated younger children, and fell behind in her lessons. Finally, in January 1894, a teacher discovered her in
bed with other girls teaching them "filthy and disgusting tricks."[92] The
school immediately isolated Effie and summoned Maynard. They told
Maynard the only way to deal with such a problem was to take the child
away immediately to impress on the other children the horror of this sin.
Two other girls were expelled with Effie. From that point forward, Effie
was never free of that taint. When Maynard approached Dr. Barnardo,
a philanthropist renowned for his child-rescue work, in September 1896
about Effie, he told her that a child who could not "be classed with other
children [was] not a child for him, . . . and he would no more take her
than if she were in the midst of small pox."[93]

The orphanage sent Effie to Brighton to work as a domestic servant
and companion to an elderly woman; expectations for her were thus reduced again. Rather than attending a school that would prepare her to
be a Board schoolteacher or nurse, she was given a position as a general
servant. She also took on a new name, Annie, that was to stay with her
as long as she served as a domestic servant. She was only twelve years
old, so she had to attend the local Board school. Maynard despaired over
the changes this new situation wrought in Effie. Her speech became like
that of the people around her. "When I hear the slow, slovenly accent, I
feel as if she had cut the last strings that bound the course of her life to
mine."[94] Maynard told Effie that she must now stop calling her Auntie,
"that she was no real relation. . . . I told her to speak *of* me as Miss Maynard and to *address* me as Godmother."[95] Maynard stopped bringing
Effie to Westfield College to visit, and she wondered when she saw Effie
cleaning a grate that she had once cuddled this child in her bed.

Effie went to work for an elderly woman who kept one lodger. She
was responsible for daily marketing and general cleaning. Later Maynard would discover that the freedom this position allowed her provided
an introduction to a number of new experiences including a sexual relationship with the lodger. This situation came to an end in September
1896. Effie wrote to Maynard informing her she had stolen money from
her employer and needed to find a new situation.

After some searching, Maynard approached the Salvation Army. She
reflected in her diary, "The outcasts are their prize, and they will keep
my E., through any thing and everything. Here she is, liar, thief and of
intolerable insolence, and so unclean in mind that she must touch no other
child, here she is and no one will take her."[96] Maynard met with Major
Mary Bennett, the officer in charge of Clock House in Walthamstow, to

discuss Effie's case. She felt she was "among *heavenly* sort of women, where the very highest ideal of conduct and the very sincerest love to those who had the basest ideal went hand in hand."[97] She visited the rooms, "clean and neat and airy," and watched the girls sewing outfits for service or doing fine work for sale, projects that made the home nearly self-supporting. The young women at Clock House were, like Effie, most often living apart from their parents, unmarried, and working class, and their most common prior occupation was domestic service.[98] Maynard believed the Army would succeed with Effie because of its simple theology and clear, unequivocal demands. On October 23, 1896, Effie entered Clock House.[99]

The Salvation Army Women's Social Services began informally in 1881, when Mrs. Cottrill of Whitechapel Corps began to open her home to young women seeking to escape life on the street and to settle them in respectable situations. When her husband objected to sharing his breakfast table with streetwalkers, the Army rented a house for the work. In January 1884 the *War Cry* announced that the "special aim of this Home is to save young girls who are just entering upon the paths of sin and shame. . . . We rely entirely on spiritual influences for leading them on in their desires and efforts to lead a new life." The home targeted prostitutes, young girls "in danger," and "girls who have been ruined and forsaken but who are opposed to leading an immoral life."[100] Pregnant women gave birth in the home until 1886, when the Army established its first separate maternity facility.[101] Like other rescue missions, the Salvation Army tried to redeem women who had taken a wrong step. If no one aided these women, Salvationists believed, they would have no alternative but to resort to the streets, thus endangering their souls, the souls of their children, and the moral environment of the whole community.[102] The Salvation Army preferred to take "previously respectable" women over those who were diseased or addicted to drink. "First fall" women were most likely to succeed in finding work or marrying and potentially joining the Salvation Army.[103] As the work expanded, the Army rented other houses including Clock House, where Effie lived.[104] The residents took in laundry and sewing, thus helping to support the home and acting on one of the rescue work's founding principles—that each woman should contribute as much as possible to her own redemption.[105]

The first director of the work was Florence Soper Booth, wife of Bramwell Booth. Historian Ann Higginbotham has noted that the most prominent women in the rescue work were from middle-class families. These women included Florence Booth, daughter of a physician; Adalaide

Cox, daughter of an Anglican clergyman; and Mary Bennett, daughter of a solicitor who had trained in painting and sculpture.[106] The work may well have appealed to these women in particular because it had for some time been an aspect of middle-class women's philanthropy and the Army allowed them considerable authority. For Maynard, it brought her into to contact with women whose education, professional careers, and religious convictions resembled her own. These women shared an independence and zeal for reform that set them apart from most of their contemporaries. They had much in common with other women in the last quarter of the century who established institutions like settlement houses, sisterhoods, and nursing programs, which provided single women with professional service work and shared living arrangements. Yet Maynard was aware of the social distance between her work at Westfield College and the work of a Salvation Army officer. Maynard regarded the rescue work as "the most spotlessly beautiful of all the work of the S.A.," but she wondered at the life the officers led among fallen women; the "bare floors, the rough meals, the unvarying routine, are all as *nothing* compared with the unending companionship of these poor low girls."[107] She admired their faith and love. "If anyone *should* desire the life of Obedience, Poverty and Chastity, here it is in such perfection, that the sisterhoods seem in comparison to be only playing at it."[108]

Salvationists believed that a woman's reclamation could not begin until she was converted. Effie was converted almost immediately. On October 28, Effie wrote,

My dear Godmother,

I reached here quite safely, after waiting about half an hour I found Cadet. I am very glad you have sent me here for something lovely has happened, I have done what you have prayed for eight years at least, I have given myself to God, and O I am so happy and so glad to be able to give you joy, by telling you your prayers are answered. I often think of two lines that I have read many times. . . . "Moment by moment, let down from heaven, Time opportunity, guidance are given." Here is a fresh opportunity and by God's help I will make the best of it. . . . They are all so kind here. . . . Major [Bennett] is kindly going to let me be office girl and I am going to do my best to please God and you and all here.[109]

The Army's holiness theology taught that true conversion enabled an individual to know and act on God's will. Effie's conversion therefore would be judged against her subsequent behavior.

Maynard was deeply impressed by the religious work accomplished by the Army, but her description of it also expresses her clear sense of its limits.

> Surely it has all the real ingredients of a convent. . . . There is the strict rule and enclosure and the *endless* services, where the thoughts of religion are at their barest and simplest, Sin Confession Pardon Holiness—here is their whole gospel. The reiteration of these primary thoughts was the holding up [of] the Crucifix, Jesus in His death being the one thing they *know* and *feel* and impress on these wretched girls. The endless singing of hymns and shrill Choruses (for altogether there must have been *hours* of singing in the day) with its putting into their mouths over and over words far too high and holy for them. . . . Over and over they sing "Bless His Holy Name", "Praise the Lord!" . . . and when they pray the simple prayers are almost drowned in the response of the others. . . . The highest of all ideals is put straight before them and they are expected to actually attain it, hour by hour and that is nothing less than a walk with God, an absolute relinquishing of the old self and all its desire and a being yielded wholly to God to be dwelt in by Him.[110]

Maynard continued to be concerned about Effie's education and arranged for her to spend half a day at a small school costing 15 shillings a week. Effie, however, rebelled against the school, refusing to attend, neglecting her work, and speaking rudely to the teachers. As a result, she was expelled. At the same time, Bennett wrote, it was discovered that "she has given way to that wicked habit . . . and she has actually said that she wished we would bind her hands when she goes to bed at night. Of course this very plainly shows there is no real conversion about the girl and until this, she will be the same."[111] Effie also stole 2 shillings and 6 pence from the major's drawer.

A few weeks later another letter arrived from Bennett. "I do not think you knew she was a fallen girl? but this is so. It happened when she was living at Brighton through a young man lodging in the same house."[112] Maynard lamented that she "would she had died rather than this. . . . Even as quite a child, she had no natural modesty, no shame, but that it should come to this when she was only just 13 seems incredible."[113] Maynard found herself unable to write to or visit Effie. "I do not want to act as a disciple of Christ should not, but there is surely a human as well as a divine side to such a thing as this."[114]

Maynard visited with Bennett, who informed her that Effie's story had emerged when, after seven or eight weeks of rebellion against the home's discipline, "she was driven into a corner as it were, and trying to say all she could think of to shock us, and one day in a fit of desperation she said to Ensign Martin that often when she was sent out on messages she went into the Public House and sinned with a man who lived there and gave her money. We knew this couldn't be true (and indeed it was not) but that she knew more than she should was very evident. . . . Ensign pressed her a little and truth came out."[115]

Maynard confessed how repelled she felt, and Bennett replied that when she had entered this work, she too felt shock at what she learned. Still, Maynard visited that day with Effie and told her that this sin could not be undone. For some time, she said, she had hoped Effie would come and live with her again, but this was now impossible. "She had raised a barrier between us that was insurmountable." After they prayed together, Maynard embraced her and thought, "My Effie, still mine, though defiled, worse than murdered."[116]

Some months later, Maynard received further communication from Bennett that revealed that Effie was again subject to her old habits. Another girl at the home also under the "tyranny" of this sin "had to be sent to an asylum as hopeless and is still there, half idiot, half lunatic, languishing out her life, inaccessible to higher influences. In the opinion of the officers, E. has been with in measurable distance of this terrible fate." Maynard was warned that it would be unwise to take Effie out at Christmas as she had hoped because she was not yet able to resist sin fully. The consequences of her inability to resist, the officers warned Maynard, were severe indeed. "It is evident that in their opinion everything, spiritual and moral progress, courtesy, intellect, physical health, even her very eyesight, depend on this one secret habit."[117] These connections between masturbation and other bodily ailments were well established among medical professionals as well as the wider public. An 1863 study found a high rate of masturbation among tubercular patients, and connections were drawn between other physical and mental disabilities and the exhaustion that followed masturbation.[118] As historian Barbara Robinson has argued, "Nineteenth century health teaching was dense with images of pollution and contamination. . . . Masturbation was a contributor [to] the national 'degeneration.'"[119] Salvation Army officers were instructed to watch young soldiers for signs of this vice. A 1903 memorandum, circulated to all commanding and local officers, warned that "thousands of young women die today from no other cause. Thousands are today in the lunatic asylum; young yet hopeless idiots, just because of this one vice."[120]

In 1898, Effie began to learn typing and shorthand in preparation for work in an Army office. She did not enjoy it and found the sedentary life difficult. Effie complained to Maynard of near constant headaches and a pain in her side that she could not account for, but these complaints did not seem to raise any serious concern among the officers at the Clock House. She also confessed to Maynard that "I do worry now about my own father and mother, and lay awake sometimes wondering and worrying about them. I long to know what they were like in feature and character and I want to know all about myself and them before I was six."[121]

Maynard wrote to Major Bennett in June, asking whether Effie might not be given other work and noting that Effie preferred scrubbing to shorthand. Major Bennett replied that it was impossible "and the height of folly and presumption to question it." Effie soon took matters into her own hands. She ran away to Maynard. When Maynard asked why she had come, she replied, "I've come to my only friend" and "I didn't mean ever to go back."[122] She had broken open a collection box and took 2 shillings from it to pay for her journey. That afternoon, Maynard brought Effie back to Clock House, where Major Bennett insisted that it was God's will for Effie to learn shorthand and refused to discuss it. When Major Bennett asked Effie what she had to say for herself, she replied "nothing," and Major Bennett decided that Effie could not return for at least a fortnight, perhaps never. Maynard arranged for an acquaintance to take Effie as a general servant. Effie longed to return to the Army. The officers at Clock House decided after a few weeks to readmit Effie, and she returned there exactly two years after she was first admitted.

In the spring of 1899, Effie asked Maynard whether she could wear the Army uniform, noting that Major Bennett supported her request. Maynard felt it was too early for her to make a clear decision for the Army and wished that Effie would wait until she was at least twenty-one. Maynard went to see Mrs. Bramwell Booth and insisted that she wished Effie to continue her training in domestic service, nursing, and other skills. She argued that "every one of their best officers have been partly trained outside, Mildred Duff, Maggie Hare and all I can think of." She wished Effie to make a real choice at twenty-one. Mrs. Bramwell Booth replied "the very same touch that made her a Christian . . . will make her a Salvationist . . . and to risk one risks the other. Why should she choose? . . . There is nothing to choose. You are half-hearted in making her a Salvationist, that's what it is." When Maynard inquired about Booth's daughters and asked whether she might want them to attend Westfield, Booth replied, "I wouldn't risk it, very *very* dangerous." Maynard recorded in her diary that she would now "buy her [Effie] a concertina and pay for her lessons and set her up as a proper Salvationist."[123] In the summer of 1901, however, Effie's health began to deteriorate dramatically. Her feet collapsed, and she could barely walk. She was anemic and fainted easily. She continued her training in the Army, but her weak health remained a barrier to success in any area.

On January 20, 1903, when Effie turned twenty-one, Maynard told "her who she was." Effie took great interest in the news that her mother had recently given birth to a son, as was reported in a Salvation Army publication. Maynard did not reveal in her diary whether Effie remembered her mother from the orphanage or from the scene in the lawyer's office, but she did report that Effie said little. The next day Effie set off for the training home to enter as a cadet.

She described the training home as "very regular and spic and span." She received daily marks in conduct, lessons, practical religion, and peddling. "I am top for Lessons my darling and I feel it is all your love and goodness in giving me such a lovely education." In August 1903, she "claimed from God the blessing of a clean heart, . . . a life wholly given to God without reserves and living a good holy life up to the light one has." Six months later she was ready to be commissioned, but her poor health, especially a growth on her neck that was very painful, required that she take a temporary position. More seriously, she had confessed that some months back she "fell again . . . under the enemy that at one time trampled down her life." She had resisted since, but this confession nevertheless meant she had to wait for her commission. When Maynard wrote to offer her two weeks at the seaside to recover her health with the hope that she would be commissioned in six months, Effie responded with a letter Maynard considered "rough and self-assertive." She claimed her health was the only barrier; she had been "privately commissioned," which she said was just as good, and she did not wish to go to the seaside. Maynard sent the letter on to the head of the training home, Colonel Lambert. She replied, "She is indeed a very strange girl and unless her conduct is more satisfactory will never have the privilege of a commission."[124]

During these months, Effie had a position at 259 Mare Street, Hackney, at the Army rescue home. Work among the "fallen," the Salvation Army believed, was most effective when it included women who had themselves been redeemed. Effie must have appeared to be living a life of holiness that would serve as an example to others. The officers told Maynard that Effie was concerned about her mother, and when she learned that her mother might be coming to England, she expressed a strong desire to meet her. Maynard wrote to Effie explaining that if her mother's husband and friends found out she had a grown daughter, "the poor thing would be covered with shame and disgrace and no one knows what she might do." Effie did not reply to this letter, disappointing Maynard. "I had written with my heart and it gives me a sense of shallowness. She cannot distinguish great things from small."[125]

In February 1904, the growth on Effie's neck was diagnosed as tuberculosis, and it was decided she must undergo an operation. She was sent to Dover to recuperate. When she was able, she went to Dorking to assist with Salvation Army Sunday services, where she "played the Autoharp and sung 11 solos and spoke on Peter's Denial and conducted the after meeting." Soon after she returned to her duties at Clock House; however, Bennett (now a brigadier) informed Maynard that "she had given way to her old sins and this had led to telling lies and taking money from the boxes."[126] She was brought before all the officers at the home to confess, and they were asked to decide whether she could remain among them or instead should become a ward maid at the infirmary. She was forgiven. She also wrote to Maynard to confess and seek forgiveness.

> I know you will be grieved, but still I do not wish to hide it any longer, I have tried to cover it up long enough. First of all I have given way for a long time to my old besetting sin (you know what I mean) then I have been untruthful and deceitful and also dishonest. Dear Mistress, perhaps you will think I have never been really good, but I have only given way to the first [which] has led to all these terrible sins and downfall. . . . The money I have taken I am going to replace as soon as possible. I never should have believed that I could have fallen so low and got so far away from God and now dear Mistress seeing I have told you and seeing Brigadier has forgiven me and given me another chance and seeing that Christ has wiped it out with His blood, may I ask you my dearest friend and Mistress to forgive me too.[127]

She kept her rank as lieutenant with the understanding that she would be "a different woman, never again to be held a slave to the devil."[128] She was unable to meet this standard however, and in May she lost her stripes and was sent out as a ward maid. The Women's Social Services chose this work for her because it was hard but interesting and had been the redemption of another girl in an even worse state. It also happened to be the same work her mother was doing at the time of Effie's adoption.

Maynard responded by feeling "drawn to her as never before since she was a little child."[129] Effie did not, however, get on well at the hospital. Disliked by the other servants and mistrusted by her superiors, she seemed destined for trouble from the outset. In August she was dismissed, and she wrote Maynard, "I always have been a failure and I suppose always will be. I don't care now what happens to me. I shall never again try to be good, it is all rubbish. I shall just please myself and go my own

road. I don't care what becomes of me now. Your wretched, Annie."[130]
She found herself a position as a cook-general. Her health remained poor,
and she wrote that "I am thoroughly wearied out by the close of the day,
and feel in the morning as if I had no rest whatsoever." The tubercular
growth on her neck reappeared. Still, she returned to the Army's meetings and soon sought again the blessing of a clean heart.

Effie's illness was a constant difficulty. The tumor on her neck continued to grow and to cause her pain. Maynard wrote in her diary that
she chided Effie, telling her that the Salvation Army authorities told her
that Effie "always could have been well had she tried, that all her weakness and illness was due to her own wickedness. . . . If she persevered in
right for some 2 or 3 years more I believed that after all I should see her
fresh and strong and bright as she ought to be."[131] Effie replied, "Do you
always think of the wickedness when you think of the ill health? If my
poor suffering body always reminds you of a depraved heart, I feel as I
should never again want to tell you of my health, for oh I want you to
forget all that."[132]

Over the next several years, she moved from situation to situation,
unable to satisfy either her employers or herself. Her health grew worse;
subsequent surgeries on her neck did nothing to relieve the pain. Maynard's relationship with Effie increasingly suggested that she thought of
Effie as a dependent social inferior. For example, on Effie's birthday one
year Maynard sent her nightdresses, "which have shrunk very much but
are still sound."[133] She was disappointed with the indifferent thanks she
received. Maynard continued to send Effie a small monthly allowance,
but their correspondence tapered off because Maynard was consistently
dissatisfied with Effie's deceptions, instability, and seeming ingratitude.

Finally, in 1915, Effie became so ill with tuberculosis she had to move
to a workhouse infirmary. In November, Maynard wrote to suggest a
visit in the coming weeks, and the staff replied that Effie was near death,
conscious only at intervals. Maynard went to her immediately. Although
Effie was beyond speaking, Maynard recited poems Effie had loved as a
child.[134] On November 15, Maynard received a telegram, "Stephanie Anthon, 4–30 this morning."

The story of Stephanie Anthon's unfortunate life highlights aspects of
the Salvation Army's work not often revealed by the Army's own publications. Published conversion narratives never hint at the kinds of troubles that beset Effie. The Salvation Army first took Effie in because her
mother was a fallen woman, and her own fall brought her back to the
very rescue work that had saved her mother. Her mother was, by the

standards used to judge Effie, a redeemed woman, but she had to relinquish her daughter and keep her past a secret. Indeed, few conversion
narratives describe a woman's sexual past, although many women recounted incidents of drunkenness, criminality, and domestic violence in
detail. The Salvation Army separated Effie from her mother when she
was four and told her that her mother was dead. Although her mother
cared for her at the orphanage only a few months later, this deceit seemingly troubled no one except perhaps Effie. She often asked Maynard
about her mother, but she had to wait until she was twenty-one to hear
about her parents. She longed to meet her mother and brother, but neither Maynard nor the rescue-work officers permitted it lest her mother's
secret be revealed. The confusion and loss Effie so clearly felt could not
be contained by a conversion narrative of fall and reclamation. Neither
did the Army's narratives tell of other repeated conversions that were
seemingly genuine but failed to effect any sustained change in habit or
behavior. Effie's letters to Maynard express a passionate desire for a new
heart, but whatever change she effected was fleeting and her conversion
failed to achieve what the theology promised.

Effie was regarded by Maynard, several employers, teachers, and Salvation Army officers as naturally unfit to be a lady and a potential danger to her peers. Maynard's confidence in the Salvation Army as an appropriate setting for Effie's redemption was based on her belief that the
Army spoke to the lowest strata of English society with its simple theology, repetitive emotional services, and strenuous physical work. Its
relationship to working-class culture was a strength, but it was also a
severe limitation. Maynard recognized that Salvationist women shared
the reforming zeal of women educators, social-purity activists, and
women's rights advocates like herself. But the Salvationists were active
in working-class settings, which were at a great distance from Maynard
and her associates at Westfield College. Salvationist women combined
aspects of Victorian feminism with evangelical holiness theology, and this
combination had consequences for their perspective on social class. Unlike Maynard, the officers were utterly unconcerned with Effie's career
prospects or accent. They wished only to assure her salvation. Maynard
thought this view to be shortsighted, but they regarded her concerns as
far more shortsighted because she placed at risk Effie's steady progress
toward holiness. Her opportunities might be limited, but what did it matter if she were reclaimed?[135]

Effie's life was beset by her ambiguous status. She was, in turn, Maynard's daughter, niece, goddaughter, and dependent charge. As Effie grew,

the expectations of Maynard and others lessened, and she became solidly working class in her position and aspirations. Her "besetting sin" excluded her from the life Maynard hoped to share with her and sent her back to the Salvation Army, but the same problem resulted in her dismissal from the Army. Effie's life also illustrates the ambiguous nature of a "fallen" woman. Maynard sent Effie to Clock House because her "secret vice" had been revealed, but it was only some months later that the full extent of her sexual experience became known. At thirteen Effie could not have legally consented to sexual relations because the Criminal Law Amendment Act, which the Salvation Army had supported through the Maiden Tribute events and the subsequent campaign, raised the age of consent to sixteen.[136] Still, the guilt was firmly Effie's, and forgiveness was hers to seek. Her sexual sins were linked to all her other bodily infirmities and character faults by Maynard and the Salvation Army officers. Dishonesty, theft, and other failings were regarded as secondary effects of her real sin. Even the tuberculosis that killed her was merely a physical sign of her secret sin, which only she could relinquish. It is difficult to determine what might be counted as the cause of Effie's "fall" because it could be one of many and the details remained mysterious. Yet it was evidently the defining fact of her life.

REBECCA JARRETT

The autobiographical writings of Rebecca Jarrett (c. 1850–1928), the prostitute and brothel keeper saved by the Salvation Army, are among the very few Salvationist conversion narratives that in any way describe an illicit sexual past. Her life story was unusually well documented because she played a key role in the Maiden Tribute scandal of 1885. Just after the trial, Josephine Butler published a biography of Jarrett in which she attempted to defend Jarrett's actions throughout the case. Butler was a leader in the campaign to repeal the Contagious Diseases Acts and an important feminist and social-purity activist. She was a friend to Catherine Booth and wrote several informative, admiring articles about the Salvation Army, including an 1883 pamphlet in support of Maud Charlesworth and Kate Booth's work in Switzerland. Her biography offers a particular version of Jarrett's entry into prostitution and her years as a brothel keeper. Jarrett's life became a starting point for Butler's wider discussion of the sexual politics of the 1880s. Its polemical purpose was sharper and narrower than that of the usual Salvationist biography.[137] It would, the publishers asserted, "modify those bitter and hard feelings towards this good woman which some good and sincere people think themselves justified in cherishing. On the other hand, the many who have not lost faith in her general veracity, or the genuineness of her new life, will be amply strengthened in their belief by this plain and unvarnished statement of facts."[138]

This version presented a story of seduction familiar to Victorian readers. The tale of a maiden, daughter of a respectable laboring man, seduced by an upper-class libertine was common to street ballads, penny novels, theatricals, and Victorian fiction. The story stressed the profligacy and exploitation of the rich and the weakness and virtue of the poor.[139] Butler's version of Jarrett's life drew on these themes.

Butler recounted how Jarrett's father was a respectable, prosperous tradesman who failed in business because of drink and died soon after. Her mother was left with seven children, and she cared for them as well as she could. Jarrett went into a good position as a servant when she turned fifteen. There, a gentleman visitor "with flattery and presents led her to meet him in the evening unknown to her mistress." After visiting her mother and brothers one evening for tea, she "was met by this deceiver and led away from the path of virtue."[140]

When she could no longer hide her pregnancy, she was forced to leave her place. She gave birth to a daughter and later a second child and lived with her lover as his mistress. He finally took her to Manchester and placed her in a "house of ill fame to get a living for herself and her two children, which she did for twelve months, carrying on a sinful career and giving way to drink and all kinds of vice."[141] Injured in a fall, she had to enter a hospital. When she was released, she discovered one child had died and her lover had sent the other away to school but refused Jarrett the address because of the bad life she was leading. Her "heart turned to bitterness; . . . the one thing she had been longing for and living for, she had been deprived of—to hear the voice of her children. One fond word from them would have woke up her mother's heart within her, and made her try to do better."[142]

She moved to London and opened a brothel. The girls she brought there were "led to believe they are being taken to some of their friends, and when they enter they find the house filled with poor unfortunates; and then with drink they are overpowered, and the seducer gains his purpose." At last Jarrett became too ill from the effects of drink to continue, and she went to live in a boardinghouse run by a Salvationist woman. The landlady prevailed on Jarrett to allow the local captain to visit, and Jarrett eventually agreed to go to London and enter the rescue home where

she was saved. After her conversion, she began mission work among prostitutes in association with the Army and Butler. Butler revealed that Jarrett received no salary for her work with the "fallen." Her home, "of
very humble description," and her "very plain" food were provided, and
she wore Butler's discarded dresses and boots.[143] All these revelations were
intended to demonstrate Jarrett's sincerity and Christian purpose. But they
also highlight the social distance between Jarrett and the other principal,
middle-class actors in the Maiden Tribute case. While Jarrett was in jail,
Butler went on holiday in Italy, and Stead was allowed to keep a servant
with him in jail and to receive regular visitors.[144]

Butler described Jarrett as a mother, something no other source mentioned, and she argues that losing her children made Jarrett lose all hope
and her aspirations for a better life. In this version, Jarrett's own mother
bore no responsibility for her fall. She is last glimpsed in Butler's story
in her domestic setting, serving tea to her son and daughter. Jarrett was
seduced by a middle-class man, and her story became one of class exploitation. This polemical purpose of Butler's obviously shaped the story.

But two other versions of Jarrett's life challenge Butler's story. After
her release from prison, Jarrett returned to her life as a Salvationist, and
she later wrote an account of her fall, conversion, and the Maiden Tribute case. Two versions are extant, one handwritten and one typescript,
and they contain significant differences. Further details of Jarrett's life
are found in Florence Soper Booth's diary of 1885–86, in which she
recorded details of Jarrett's conversion, her actions in the Maiden Tribute scandal, and her career in the Salvation Army. The differences among
these many versions of Jarrett's life suggest what could be discussed, what
was obscured, and how the very public spectacle of the Hallelujah Lasses
had sharp limits.

Jarrett's handwritten autobiography is undated but was written when
she was seventy-nine years old. The spelling is unconventional, and few
sentences are marked by capitalization or periods, but the handwriting
is clear. Like many conversion narratives, Jarrett's opens with the words,
"Her experience written by herself for God glory not for my Glory for
herself but for God alone."[145] But, unlike most women's narratives, which
are silent on sexual matters, Jarrett's moves immediately to describe and
account for her sexual past. Her mother was left a widow with seven
children. One brother worked at Woolwich dockyard, one daughter went
to Australia, never to be heard of again, two sons went to sea and were
lost, and two others died of cholera. Jarrett was left alone with her mother,
who had to "keep her home on for me and her self she had to work hard

for her living." Jarrett recalled that her mother was "very proud of my hair Poor old mother I had very fair hair then it took her some time to wash it and keep it clean."

Her mother used to take her to out to Cremorne Gardens, a Chelsea pleasure garden known for gambling, drinking, and "the immoral character of its female frequenters," according to complaints made to the Chelsea Vestry.[146]

> I had to bring my poor mother home the worse for drink on Sunday night. I was only 8 or 10 years of age you wonder why so young I got in the way of an impure life That was why I left my home so early to begin my life of sin and degradation. At Cremone I got my money was well-known. At age 13 I was standing looking at buses being filled with people at the Public House in Chelsea an old man stood at my side doing the same I was I thought til he said to me would you like a ride in a bus I said will you bring me home again he said I will I went in the bus with him he took me too Hyde Park got out there went into the Park it was quite dark I could not see him but I found as he was moving what his meaning was I got away from him and run home.

The narrative offers no other explanation for Jarrett's life. Her "fall" thus appears to have been occasioned by her drunken mother, who left her in a dangerous place, and by her naive acceptance of the man's offer.

She next relates that she took to drinking so much that she did not even care for food; doctors told her she would die if she did not stop. One day she saw a large sign announcing a Salvation Army meeting, and she went out of curiosity. Her dress and hat with a large blue feather drew the attention of the Salvationists; they spoke with her and inquired where she was staying. When they later visited her, they convinced her to go to London with them and enter the Army's rescue home. "They never had such a bad drink case, fancy. from a girl of 13 or 14 right up to 35, too old to be taken to a home I was taken to the London Hospital kept their for 10 weeks came out cured and well been watched with the greatest care by the S.A. and Mrs. Josephine Butler. . . . My aim directly was to try to help others which I did try at the time of the Armstrong case." She described how she was asked to prove "I could get a poor girl of 13," and she did. "The mother was in the Public House drinking with the money I had just given her; . . . she did not even come over to bid her good bye." She took the child to the home of a "real titled lady so I was sent to prison for six months."

Despite her good intentions, angry mobs treated Jarrett roughly when she appeared at court; the court gave her a heavy sentence, and she suffered very harsh conditions in jail. She recalled that "I was treated by all the [Salvation Army] officers with the greatest kindness and care and respect the dear old *Army Mother* walked with 90 ladies with many more names to get me out." Salvationists sent her a warm vest and four shawls. After she left prison, she attempted to continue in rescue work, but "it was too trying just comming my self off prison. . . . I should have lost my reason but my precious friend Mrs. Bramwell Booth held on to me." She ended her narrative with this expression of gratitude: "Here I am 40 years since I first entered the Salvation Army in Hanbury St., a poor drunken broken up woman Mrs. General and Mrs. Bramwell Booth did not look at that side I was degraded sunken down low by drink their work was to try and raise me up. . . . I am near 79 years in age but I am closing my earthly life with sincere gratitude to the Salvation Army and the precious officers for their care and devotion to me." This narrative is only thirteen pages long and offers few details about Jarrett's conversion or her subsequent life. It does, however, suggest that Jarrett believed drunken mothers had left her and Eliza Armstrong in peril. In neither case does she even mention a father. Both girls were thirteen at the time their "fall," real or staged, began. The Salvation Army rescued them both with the maternal concern and guidance a good mother ought to have given.

Jarrett wrote a second, extended version of her life. There is nothing to explain why she wrote this second version. It might have been produced for publication, although there is no evidence it appeared in print. It is also possible she produced it for her Salvation Army associates. The writing style is similar to that in the handwritten version. A different perspective, however, of Jarrett's childhood and of her mother's role in her fall emerges. In this second version, her widowed mother was struggling to make ends meet, and "she got me in the way to look for my share." She took Jarrett to Cremorne Gardens. "I was only 12 years of age. My mother was a bit proud of me. I was inclined to be tall very fair hair blue eyes. I remember had round my neck a string of great blue beads she kept me clean that was my attraction. I never walk the streets she was very particular and kept me very clean."[147] This passage evokes the standard vision of prostitutes as women in dressy, showy clothes, but Jarrett insists on her youth and cleanliness, neither of which characterizes the prostitute. This juxtaposition suggests maternal care gone wrong, a mother who kept her daughter clean but for the wrong reasons.

Her two brothers were at sea. When they arrived home to find their mother drunk and their sister employed in this way, they turned Jarrett into the street, although she was only sixteen. "Turned out a lot of the fellow were waiting to see what was really going to happen so when I got turned out I was lodged for the night in a coffee shop near Victoria Station." One man took her to Buxton to live with him; she stayed two years before they returned to London. "But of course coming back to London I was so well known in Cremore Gardens that other came and found out where I was living they came the one who had kept me over 2 years got upset about it and left and only 19 years old then but I seemed to get one if one left me I soon got another to take his place. I never see my Brothers or Mother again." Although her mother introduced Jarrett to prostitution and even supervised the conditions of her work and although her brothers only made matters worse by sending her away, she cautions the reader. "Some of you will say as you read this what a *bad mother* she must have had but Please *dont* she was a good mother it was my wretched father doing He left her several times and lived with other women my poor Mother was left with 8 children; . . . she took to drink, it was the trouble that drove her to it.[148] Her mother cannot be praised, however, for her prayers, her faith, or her example of godliness. In so many Salvation Army conversion narratives, women and men credited their mothers with laying the foundation for their eventual conversion. Jarrett, in contrast, was converted in spite of her mother.

Jarrett knew drinking had put her health in grave danger, but she did not know how to stop. "It made me have a bit of life and the men who were keeping me would not have kept me if I was always in bed so I had to get more and be as bright as I could."[149] No rescue homes would take a woman past twenty-five, and as she was now thirty-eight, she was well beyond their range of concern. When she saw a board advertising a Salvation Army meeting with Major Oliphant and Captain Cadman however, she went in and slipped into a seat at the back. Her feathered bonnet revealed her life to all. She fainted in her seat, and the Salvationists came to assist her.

This description makes use of conventions familiar to any reader of Victorian fiction or social commentary. Jarrett wore showy clothes as she had as a girl, but she was now sick and weak, and her life was fast coming to an end. Social commentators, doctors, and social reformers regularly predicted the prostitute's decline to be as quick as it was inevitable. The doctor and widely read author William Acton wrote of "those miserable creatures, ill-fed, ill-clothed, uncared for, from whose misery the eye recoils, cowering under dark arches and among bye-lanes," a picture that was widely recognized and accepted.[150]

The Salvationists did not shun Jarrett. They asked where she was staying, but she was reluctant to tell them. "Those strange bonnet on some
with tambourines in the hands, the folks in the hotel would think I had
gone off my head." Finally her need of help overcame her fears. She gave
them her address. When they all arrived at her hotel, the man she was
living with thanked them, gave them some money, and told them he had
done all he could for Jarrett. The Salvationists then took her to London
and directly to a doctor. When she arrived at the Army rescue home, "a
lovely young mother with red jersey on she rose up and *kissed* me said
I have been waiting for you dear. . . . Its memory is very sacred to me it
was the welcome the frozen up heart got a bit of." She spent some time
in London with Mrs. Bramwell Booth, and then she was sent to Winchester, to Mrs. Josephine Butler's rescue home, where Effie Anthon's
mother also resided in the mid-1880s. She concluded that "it was not
the preaching that done the work in my poor *soul* it was the care and
trouble they all took of me *My God* reward them it worked in me and
gave me a real *Salvation.*"[151] Jarrett's rescue was the work of women,
notably the "young mother" who welcomed her.

Jarrett prayed to "be made a good woman and truly brake away from
the drink." This was accomplished "not by preaching but by works."
She began visiting public houses to speak to young girls in Portsmouth.
One place she visited she found "there in bed was an old man with two
young children neither was 12 years of age as I knew the mother was
out working at the wash tub I made them both go home I sent up the
vigilant man."[152]

Bramwell Booth called her to London and took her to see W. T. Stead,
who asked her to prove that it was possible to procure a child in London. She put on "some very showey thing and went into the street," where
she noticed a pretty girl. She spoke with the child's mother and asked
whether she could take the child away for £2. The mother agreed. "That
Mother never asked me what I wanted her for or where I was going to
take her even asked when she would see her again she had got the money
there I could take her where I liked or do what I liked with her but *thank
God* I was a converted woman showing up the wrong and trying to do
His Blessed work. . . . When I found it was for a public show I felt it but
the dear General and his dear wife was true and loyal to me." After
charges were laid, the police began to search for her. A lawyer accompanied her to Bow Street, where she was taken to jail. "It was poor Mr
Stead with his papers that did it all the S.A. had nothing to do with it
they let Mr. Stead have me to be the poor tool to show it up; . . . it was

a most trying time for me and only just been *converted* the men I had been living with who had kept me as their woman now they jeered at me for making myself such a fool."[153]

She was charged with abduction, and for "ten or thirteen days" rode from jail to court in a Black Maria and endured the proceedings. She faced a court where her past was brought up; "in fact things have been so raked up they know more than I can remember." She noted the irony that had she not been converted she could have "taken her way and done just what I liked with" Eliza Armstrong.[154] In fact, Eliza was living with a Salvation Army family in Paris and selling the *War Cry* in the streets.[155] Meanwhile, "the men who had lived with me stood near me and called me all the horrid names they wanted me to slip out and go back with them."[156] The Army officers stood by her.

Jarrett was forced by the court to testify. Her testimony was unclear, perhaps untrue. She said that Stead had not written what she had told him, but the court also revealed that during her testimony she did not give accurate addresses for the brothels she claimed to have run. She refused to say more than that she was unwilling to have her past brought out. She was discredited as a witness, and the judge told the jury she was "one of those women who are led to exaggerate their own guilt for the purpose of glorifying or exaggerating their present merit."[157]

She was convicted and spent six hard months at Millbank Prison. After her release, she continued with rescue work in the Salvation Army. She related a number of cases she had been involved in during the forty years since the Maiden Tribute case and expressed her ardent hope that the work at 259 Mare Street would continue. She closed, "*God Bless the reader* of this history it is not a make up but a real case. Your humbly a sinner saved by *grace*, Rebecca Jarrett."[158]

Further details of Rebecca Jarrett's conversion and work in the Salvation Army emerge from the diary of Florence Soper Booth, known to Jarrett as Mrs. Bramwell Booth and often mentioned in Jarrett's autobiographies as a source of support and affection. Florence Booth was the director of the rescue work (see Figure 9). The most significant detail Florence Booth's diary reveals is that Jarrett remained in contact with her brothers and her mother at least until 1885, when she entered the Army's London rescue home. Her mother was an important, if shadowy, figure in her conversion.

In January 1885, Florence Booth recorded that Rebecca Jarrett, then living at the rescue home, had left her a note telling her she was unable to continue "trying this new life." "On Sunday when she saw her mother . . . she did not tell her mother where she was, but she said she was living by herself, her mother said she was living right and keeping herself honestly that she would be willing to go into Fulham Infirmary and let the Brothel be given up." Florence Booth, Catherine Booth, and several officers all went to Rebecca Jarrett, prayed with her, and implored her to take this as "a clear and open door from the Lord." She continued to insist she could not stay at the rescue home and began to pack her bags to leave. Florence Booth recorded her words of admonishment.

> She must go facing the truth—that she was turning her back on God and heaven and deliberately chose sin and hell and that she would go to hell with her mother's soul and the souls of the poor girls she would get into the brothel and the young men etc. That she must go now telling herself and us the same truth that she would acknowledge when we all stood around the throne. Suddenly, to my surprise for I thought she was lost she broke down bitterly. Said I will give it all up and fell down on her knees sobbing. She prayed to God to save her. . . . She said she would write to her mother that very night and tell her to come away and leave the brothel.[159]

After some weeks of silence, in May 1885 Florence Booth noted that Jarrett was working in Portsmouth and at Josephine Butler's home in Winchester and that this work was difficult.

On June 2, 1885, only five months after Jarrett's conversion, she took Eliza Armstrong from her mother. Five days later, Florence Booth recorded, Jarrett's brothers came to visit her at Winchester. Over the next few weeks, as the *Pall Mall Gazette* story took hold of the public imagination and legal proceedings began, Jarrett grew more depressed. Florence Booth gave her a pillow embroidered with the words "Counted worthy to suffer for Jesus sake."[160] Her next visit with Jarrett was in jail, "a most disagreeable stinking hole" where they could speak only through a small square grating under observation of a "low looking man."[161]

Florence Booth described her distress at the court proceedings and Jarrett's difficult testimony. No one except for Jarrett's close associates realized that she refused to reveal the actual addresses of the brothels she ran because her mother and brothers continued to run one brothel. When confronted in court, she only said, "I am not going to tell you where I did live, I am willing to go through any punishment; anything concerning the case I am willing to answer truthfully and honestly, but as to my past life I am not going to do it; . . . you forced that lie out of me."[162] Her brothers' visit to her when the case began may have been a request to protect their interests.[163] Even in her autobiographies, written years later, she did not reveal the role her mother and brothers played in her life, and the typescript version claimed she never saw them after she left home at sixteen.

But the role of the mother was, as historian Judith Walkowitz argues, central to the many versions of this story.[164] In court, Mrs. Armstrong faced aggressive cross-examination, but she maintained she never sold her child into prostitution. She presented her neighborhood not as one where mothers willingly sold their daughters into prostitution but as a community that did not tolerate bad mothering. She testified that a "good many people stopped me in the street" and "spoke to me rather angrily" about her daughter. Her struggle to get her daughter back was essential if she were to maintain her own place in that community and save the street from a "bad name."[165] Her mothering was very much on trial in her neighborhood and in court. But it is clear that Jarrett associated Mrs. Armstrong's seeming drunken indifference to her daughter's fate with her own mother's role in her "fall." Jarrett's mother's active participation in her life as a prostitute was seemingly so distressing that even forty years later she did not mention it. She did describe the Salvation Army rescue workers as another source of maternal care that led both herself and Eliza to safety.

Florence Booth continued to mention Jarrett in her diary after she was released from prison, and it is clear Jarrett struggled for some years. In 1886, she was "overcome with temptation and done wrong." She was sent by the Army to the United States for some time but did not manage well. In March 1887, she returned to England and went to stay with Captain Elijah Cadman and his family.[166] Florence Booth's diary breaks off soon after, but Jarrett did remain in the Salvation Army until her death in 1928.[167]

Josephine Butler's life of Jarrett differs fundamentally from the versions presented by Jarrett or from what can be found in Florence Booth's diaries. Historian Seth Koven argues that for nineteenth-century evangelicals "truth consisted of that which could lead a person to God's saving grace. . . . 'Truth' could be quite different from 'fact' because facts, not animated by God's love, in themselves lacked the power to save."[168] The "truth" of Jarrett's life became a demonstration of how women were brought into a life of prostitution and that the maternal love so often denied them was the wellspring of their salvation. Butler's biography, however, could not contain the facts of Jarrett's life within that moral. Neither of Jarrett's own conversion narratives were any more forthcoming about her mother's role in her life. It is also possible she too was a mother and excluded that detail from her narratives. Public sexuality and maternal responsibility were contradictory, too vexing and complicated to be revealed in any of the versions of her life. If Salvationist conversion narratives combined biography, theology, and a call, Jarrett's was no exception. Her theology stressed the redemptive power of action, of engagement with sin, and her call was to other women to join this movement of missionary mothers who rescued the fallen. Her silence concealed the difficulties and tensions such work engendered.

The Hallelujah Lasses' work was fraught with tensions. Their spiritual authority and sensational public prominence sparked accusations of sexual impropriety and apostasy. For a woman to preach was unscriptural. For her to do so clad in a nightdress or with her hair loose and uncovered while banging a tambourine and hawking the *War Cry* was an outrage against social and theological convention. These women willingly entered the fray, relishing the opportunity to mingle self-expression and self-sacrifice.

For some women these sexual, public images too literally described their position. Effie Anthon struggled to remove the taint of sin, but she could not. Salvationists could attribute Effie's failure to relinquish her "secret sin" only to her unwillingness to accept God's love. Rebecca Jarrett became a respected Salvationist, but her story could not be explored fully within the conventions of Salvation Army conversion narrative.

Ironically, the Criminal Law Amendment Act of 1885, passed in the aftermath of the Maiden Tribute scandal, increased penalties against brothel keepers and effectively destroyed the "brothel as a family industry."[169] This law made the relationship that Jarrett never explained between the members of her family obsolete. Her participation in the Maiden Tribute scandal did open up other kinds of work for women. This case caused the Salvation Army to dramatically expand the rescue work, and women, both rescuers and rescued, filled the new homes. This work occupied a uniquely female branch of the Salvation Army, and it soon required special funds and a periodical to chronicle its activities; in addition, it created a link between Salvationist women and other social-purity activists and rescue workers. Stronger ties between Salvationist women and feminists, for example, led the Army to come out in support of women's suffrage. This support also brought the Salvation Army to the attention of a wider public. The Women's Social and Political Union, a leading suffrage organization founded in 1906 by the Pankhursts, took the Salvation Army as the "main inspiration" for its "revivalist methods, advertising and management."[170] Salvationist women were not directly concerned with the struggles of the Victorian women's movement. They were, nevertheless, a part of a wider nexus of women activists and reformers, and these working-class evangelists engendered many of the same tensions and opportunities as the "new women" and feminists. Ray Strachey, in *The Cause: A Short History of the Women's Movement in Britain* (1928), wrote, "The Hallelujah Lasses were not consciously preaching feminism; they were looking for souls to be snatched from sin and damnation; they were wrestling with drunkenness, vice and degradation; but as they went about their business they taught that other lesson too, in that quiet and practical fashion which best carries conviction."[171]

SIX

Robbing the Devil of His Choice Tunes

Converting the Culture of Working-Class Neighborhoods

In the early 1880s, the music-hall performer Herbert Campbell sang one of the many popular songs about the Salvation Army.

> From the Salvation Army I've had such a treat
> I wish they'd make other arrangements.
> Ev'ry Sunday they make such a row in the street,
> I shall have to make other arrangements.
> I'm told in a shriek and a yell and a roar,
> We shall meet again when this life is o'er.
> If I've got to meet them on the Golden Shore,
> I'd rather make other arrangements.[1]

Punch in 1890 expressed similar sentiments in a poem that lamented, "Quakarian calm is obsolete; but oh! who can resist, the tow-row tow-row tow-row of the loud Salvationist?"[2] Uniformed preachers and ecstatic services provided endless fodder for songs and jokes in the music halls and comic magazines. While the halls parodied Salvationists, the Army borrowed the music-hall tunes, the language and gestures of theatrical performers, and the advertising style of the circus.

Unlike many Victorian Christians, Salvationists had religious convictions that did not encourage a withdrawal from the world. Instead, it promoted an engagement with it and the working-class neighborhoods of late Victorian cities. They were lively, diverse, commercial, and residential communities with a variety of social, commercial, political, and religious influences. This varied and changing neighborhood culture challenged

Salvationists to articulate their religious vision in an urban working-class idiom to capture the attention, and the hearts, of the working class. Salvationists strived both to revitalize well-established Nonconformist traditions of sobriety, virtue, and independence and to infuse commercial entertainment with a Christian morality. The Salvation Army's innovative negotiation of varieties of popular politics, culture, and religion demonstrates the vitality of the movement, and it helps account for the Army's notoriety and popularity. It also complicates easy assumptions about a secularized working class or the incompatibility of working-class popular culture and religion.

SAVED IN THE CITY

The Christian Mission, and later the Salvation Army, shaped a battle plan to suit the culture and geography of Victorian working-class neighborhoods. The East End was the first battleground. Because it was the location of the permanent headquarters and the training ground for officers, it continued to be among the Army's most important sites. Throughout the later nineteenth century, the East End was among the most persistently difficult areas to evangelize for any mission. William Booth wrote of the East End, "Turn what way you will, you may walk for miles, and everywhere you will find a dense population given up to all kinds of wickedness."[3] Home missions, special services, settlement houses run by clergy and volunteer workers developed special programs for the East End and similar working-class urban areas. Still clergy and laity despaired over the thousands of women and men seemingly indifferent to the claims of religion.[4] Salvationists determined that it was necessary to adopt whatever means "appear most likely to accomplish the object we have in view," and these means included many old evangelizing techniques as well as many innovative methods that excited attention and brought in crowds.[5]

The Army's programs were distinctive because of its particular understanding of sin, which shaped all the work. Sin resided in the hearts of transgressors, and only the Holy Spirit could dislodge it. It could be seen in a person's body, actions, and words. After conversion, the Holy Spirit filled the body, mind, and spirit of the penitent, banishing evil. Holiness removed "original sin, or inward corruption of the heart."[6] The penitent was then "filled with the spirit and kept daily, hourly, obedient."[7] A hymn writer expressed it this way:

> Once I heard a sound at my heart's dark door,
>   And was roused from the slumber of sin:
> It was Jesus knocked, He had knocked before;
>   Now I said, "Blessed Master, come in!"[8]

The change wrought by the Holy Spirit altered not only the spirit but also the body. As one convert wrote, "He saved me. . . . He received *all, all! my body, soul,* and *spirit.*"[9] Conversion could even transform a person's visage. The Hallelujah Phrenologist proclaimed that "the love of God in a man or a woman's face sheds a ray of heavenly glory upon its possessor's features."[10]

Sin was most often understood as bodily sin, such as fighting, gambling, and most of all drinking; it not only was in individual hearts but also flourished in the public houses, streets, and courtyards. The Salvation Army marched through neighborhoods, preached in marketplaces, and sang hymns in front of pubs because these places generated sin. At the 1876 annual Conference, William Booth told the Christian Mission that a mission station "is not a building or a chapel or a hall; it is not even a society but a band of people united together to mission, to attack, to christianize an entire town or neighborhood."[11]

This strategy also drew on beliefs about the significance of the urban environment that were common in this period. From the second half of the nineteenth century, Victorian social commentators often claimed that the crowding, filth, and disorder of urban life made city dwellers "more vulnerable to organic disease and to the temptations of immoral behavior."[12] In the minds of Salvationists, the "conversion" of penny gaffs, music halls, and circuses replaced their pernicious influence with the balm of salvation. This transformation was illustrated by the Mission's report of the opening of a mission hall in the premises of the Limehouse Penny Gaff.

> During the whole of the opening services, a great crowd was assembled outside the place. Some who had come to show their dislike of the new order of things indulged in the language of the most horrible description; numbers of children whose morals had completely disappeared under the old pernicious influence of the gaff, and were fast ripening into juvenile drunkards and thieves, every now and then shouted out expression [with] which—with painful precocity—their lips had become familiar; but among the crowd there were many who seemed to ponder thoughtfully over the change, listening with quivering lips and moistened eyes to the hymns of praise and salvation which arose from the band of believers congregated within the building. . . . Nearly all seemed to belong to the humbler classes . . . their clean and orderly appearance testifying to the social improvement which had rapidly followed their

conversion. . . . The work of religious teaching is invariably followed by a vast amount of social regeneration.[13]

The belief that Christians must reform this culture they deplored had a long history, but attitudes to leisure were changing in the later nineteenth century. Plebeian Methodists of the early nineteenth century had already struggled to suppress village festivals, drinking, and blood sports because of the brutality, drunkenness, and waste of time they associated with such pursuits.[14] For instance, in 1850 the *Bible Christian Magazine* listed as sins "ballroom, card table, village wake, the race course, the bowling green, the cricket ground, the gin palace or the alehouse."[15] But the second half of the nineteenth century was a period of transition and innovation in popular leisure in two ways. By mid-century, urban leisure was a combination of casual, local entertainment and well-organized, capitalist business ventures. At the same time, Nonconformists and Anglicans relaxed the prohibitions against leisure, in part in response to these changes in leisure itself.

Urban neighborhoods were increasingly subjected to vigorous renewal and reform after 1850. Philanthropists, social reformers, clergy, local governments, and Parliament devised diverse strategies to rebuild older neighborhoods, which were regarded as unsanitary, dens of crime and vice, and potential hosts to revolutionary activity. At the same time, thousands were displaced to make way for new railways and other building schemes. A shift to open streets and new kinds of housing destroyed the old rookeries and created new kinds of public street culture that were more visible and accessible to outsiders. These changes were accompanied by a movement to provide rational recreation for the urban working class. Philanthropists and social reformers created amenities like public parks and libraries.

Entrepreneurs sensed potential profit in shaping how city dwellers might spend the leisure created by shorter hours of work and a small increase in wages. These innovators created a number of new commercial forms of entertainment. The London pleasure gardens were revitalized with new attractions like American bowling at Cremorne Garden. Railway companies began to offer cheap excursion fares to horse races and the seaside, and seaside towns built new attractions. Mechanics institutes, temperance societies, and Sunday Schools began to take advantage of these new opportunities by organizing their own day excursions to glimpse the beauty of the natural world or engage in healthy exercise.[16]

This period also marked the beginning of music hall. For many years, saloon theaters and penny gaffs had offered programs of drama, farce, singing, and dancing. In 1838, nearly one hundred penny gaffs in London offered a mixed program to predominantly young audiences. That these premises were usually licensed to sell drink and tobacco distinguished them from other kinds of theaters. Music halls grew out of these venues. In 1860, the London Music Hall Proprietors' Protection Association was formed to protect the halls, a recognition of the substantial investment involved. In 1866, London had thirty-three halls with an average seating capacity of fifteen hundred and a capital investment of £10,000. The brewing firms were often involved in financing the halls. By the end of the century, there were 328 London halls licensed for music and one or more in each provincial city. The increasingly commercialized market was also evident in the arrival of artists' agents and the large salaries paid to the most popular performers.[17] Performances were on a vast scale. In an 1884 play about a horse race, horses tore across the stage and out the side door. Cabs and omnibuses on stage were not uncommon. In 1876 two hundred children were on stage for a London production of "Bo Peep."[18]

Even while this new, commercial entertainment was becoming popular, older, less commercial and capitalized forms of entertainment persisted. The local public houses offered drink, conviviality, and gossip. Keeping and racing birds was popular even with those who did not actively participate but who could still enjoy the spectacle and the betting. Blood sports had declined in popularity, but some rat baiting and cock fighting continued. Boxing, long a sport of working men, was growing in popularity. In the 1880s, working men's boxing clubs formed in many towns and cities, and the establishment of the Amateur Boxing Association in 1880 offered men increased opportunities for competition. Many public houses held fights nightly and spectators could enjoy the fight, place bets, and drink.[19] Despite all these opportunities, historian Andrew Davies cautions that many of these leisure pursuits were available only to those with money to spare. Robert Roberts, in his account of Salford, described how poverty shaped leisure. "Summer evening leisure for men without the few coppers to go to the tavern meant long, empty hours lounging between kitchen chair and threshold. How familiar one grew in childhood with those silent figures leaning against door jambs, staring into vacancy waiting for bedtime."[20]

During the first half of the century, most denominations saw their work as direct competition to amusements and leisure pursuits. As Hugh Cunningham argues regarding Methodists of the early nineteenth century,

they "met to worship God, to save people from sin, not to offer them a
relatively harmless way of amusing themselves. And if they mounted
counter-attractions, this was a missionary gambit, a proclamation of a
different way of life, not an alternative way of amusing oneself." By the
late nineteenth century, however, denominations were "operating in a
competitive leisure market."[21] Many chapels came to believe that "everything is religious which is not clearly irreligious" and consequently organized evening concerts, cricket clubs, and evenings that included a meal
followed by a speaker and lantern slides or hymns. Many East End clergymen took "a keen interest in anything of a sporting and/or violent nature, especially boxing which had the advantage of being both."[22] Still,
some clergy continued to disapprove of all such amusements. The Rev.
Archibald Brown, pastor of Chatsworth Road Baptist Chapel, urged his
congregation to find amusement in Christ and told them the Book of
Deuteronomy is not really dry once one gets into it, but most clergy dismissed him as an ill-tempered religious melancholic.[23]

A SPIRITUAL WORLD

The Salvation Army was neither fully part of the communities it evangelized nor fully outside them. Its language and theology were embed-
ded in a world-view Salvationists shared with other laboring people. In
particular, the Army's theology resonated with common notions of the
spiritual world that many other denominations rejected. Salvationists believed that those who heeded Christ's warnings would enjoy a personal
relationship with God in this life and salvation in the next. Those who
lived in sin would suffer the torments of hell evermore. They envisioned
God as ever-present in this world, intervening in the daily workings of
human affairs. To elite Christians, this was an archaic view of divine providence. They believed providence operated generally and predictably
through "general and immutable laws of cause and effect."[24] Salvationists believed the Holy Spirit would speak to and act on individuals during the course of their lives in order to guide them or punish them. Many
conversion narratives described a moment when God spoke to a penitent, directing and guiding that person. The Holy Spirit was not always
gentle. Captain Condy was converted as a young man while working as
a farm laborer in Devonshire. His master's daughter, who "laughed aloud
at me for praying aloud in the stable, was in a little time a corpse." A
publican "who took a prominent part in an attack upon the Army not
long ago" was reportedly run over and killed on the spot. In 1893, it

was reported that a woman in Salisbury "was scoffing and reviling the Army . . . when immediately she began to spit up blood and was carried to the infirmary, cursing and swearing. On her arrival there, she had lock-jaw and died within two hours."[25]

This concept of providence harmonized with the beliefs of many laboring people. Spirits were generally believed to inhabit the world, interfering with human affairs and making themselves known through appearances and signs. It was commonly believed that manifestations of nature, like the aftermath of a storm or the patterns in a burning fire, could affect the course of events or portend the future.[26] A Shropshire man testifying at an 1879 inquest into the death of his wife told the court that he knew she was in distress by the crack in the loaf of bread when he removed it from the oven.[27] William Lovett, the labor leader, recalled his early confidence in the existence of ghosts. When he expressed his doubts later in life to the baker in his native village, the man retorted that he must be an infidel because the Bible spoke of ghosts.[28] Such beliefs were not limited to laboring people.

John Wesley believed "the giving up of witchcraft is in effect giving up the Bible." He lamented any "giving up to infidels one great proof the invisible world; I mean that of witchcraft."[29] The Methodist Joseph Barker, writing in the 1840s, claimed "thousands and thousands of people in the Methodist society still believe" in ghosts, witches and pixies.[30] Reginald Nettel has observed, "There were two cultures at work among the Primitive Methodists: a folk culture that had not yet been turned by intellectual influences and the cult of the Bible as the Word of God, absolutely true and therefore invincible. Put them together and the force of creation gets to work with new fervour."[31] Historians John Rule, Barrie Trinder, and James Obelkevich have all argued that the success of early Methodism was due, in part, to its ability to translate folk beliefs into a religious idiom. The Cornish miners were receptive to Wesley "not because he demanded a new rational view of the world, but because he did not."[32]

This world-view was also represented in the millenarian prophets of the early nineteenth century, including Joanna Southcott, Luckie Buchanan, and Richard Brothers. These "sincere earnest, Christians, dependent for guidance on a literal interpretation of the Bible" strived to understand the upheavals of the French Revolution and the economic transformations of the early nineteenth century with the aid of biblical prophets and the book of Revelation.[33] Their fervent, emotional prophecy foretold destruction and salvation. Several female prophets assumed the mantle of the "Woman Clothed with the Sun," who "being with child cried, travailing in birth, and pained to be delivered" (Rev. 12:1–2). This passage was read as the signal of the Second Coming, which would overthrow this world and herald a new life. These biblical passages were employed by the prophets and their followers to interpret the turbulent political and social world they inhabited.[34]

Salvationists inherited aspects of this spiritual world-view. Certainly Salvationist theology did not regard the world as the result of a rational order of general laws but as a potential chaos in which an individual's only protection was God's love. Holiness saved the soul from Satan's schemes and God's vengeance. Theirs was not the enlightened faith cherished by the middle class. Salvationist preaching assumed a belief in a spiritual world, in heaven and hell and providence. These convictions would have corresponded to the beliefs of those born in rural areas or small towns to Methodist parents of the same generation as Lovett and Barker. For these people, divisions between sanctioned, religious practice and other means employed to control events were not necessarily meaningful. For example, Sarah Williams's study of Southwark in the later nineteenth century reveals that "individuals could insist on the regular attendance of their child at Sunday School and still cut a lock of the hair of that same child, place it between two slices of bread and give it to a passing dog as a cure for the child's whooping cough."[35] While an Anglican clergyman might dismiss Salvation Army theology as absurd superstition, his criticism was irrelevant in an urban working-class context. The inhabitants of the working-class communities the Army evangelized did not make a division between a rational, respectable religion and an equally rational, secular world-view but struggled to interpret the profoundly spiritual world they inhabited. Unlike the evangelists and clergymen who visited working-class neighborhoods to dispense whatever spiritual guidance and material aid they had, Salvationists had a theology that was, at least in part, an aspect of the neighborhood culture they strived to convert.

THE MILITARY METAPHOR

Battle pervaded the descriptions of the work of the Salvation Army from the earliest years, and military language soon dominated all aspects of the organization. While this language described the Army's relentless battle with sin, it also evoked images of bodily health and imperial strength that were an important part of the wider culture. Right from 1865, evangelizing was described as a battle. The Whitechapel mission station reported in April 1871, "The opposition in the open-air has been dreadful; but leaning on the mighty arm of Jehovah, we have been enabled to stand our ground and have not once beaten a retreat."[36] An 1874 article addressed to "our leaders and our brethren in the battle-fields" reminded everyone that "this is no pleasant promenade . . . but a stern hand-to-hand conflict with the most horrid forms of evil and indifference and the most diabolical opposition of hell."[37] Captain Rudduck reported in 1880 that as soldiers and officers at Bethnal Green "stoned the entrenchments of the enemy during the day, numbers of them barricaded themselves behind the windows. Our soldiers fired at every point and with such precision that the shots managed to get between the chinks of the window frames and the folds of the curtains right in the hearts of many of a case-hardened sinner."[38]

Although such language certainly functioned as a metaphorical device that dramatized and glorified the struggle, it also arose out of a belief that music halls and pubs bred and propagated sin. The Army was engaged in a battle for territory. Its success would signal a victory in this life and the next. This language pervaded all aspects of the organization by 1879. Its prayer meetings were called knee drills, its tracts *Hallelujah Torpedoes,* and its preachers captains and lieutenants engaged in "hand-to-hand conflict" in battlefields everywhere. A song written by Captain William Baugh to the tune of "Camptown Races" expressed the enthusiasm for combat.

> Salvation Soldiers live to fight!
> Oh yes! Oh yes!
> Against the Devil with all their might,
> Fight in Jesus' name![39]

The military language had several meanings. The Bible is replete with military images, and Christians have drawn on these for centuries in many contexts. But militarism had particular attractions in later Victorian England. This language was expressive of the rough, physical world the working class inhabited. In this world violent deaths at work and at home were not uncommon. Daily life, even at its best, often involved intense physical exertion whether one was at work at the docks or carrying babies and food up many flights of stairs. Work mates and neighbors fought frequently, and the fights outside pubs at closing time were a part of what historian Jerry White has termed the "street theatre of working-class neighborhoods."[40] Quarrels between husbands and wives were a daily

occurrence in every working-class neighborhood.[41] A music-hall performer sang,

> If our street's not quite Belgravia, it is lively you'll allow,
> You're always right to see a fight, or hear a jolly row;
> Black eyes are just as plentiful as berries on a tree.[42]

Physical combat and struggle, then, were very much a part of Salvationists' lives, and it is not surprising that this military language was
embraced.

Militarism was also a central aspect of a wider English political culture. In 1859, the Volunteer Force was founded, and by 1863 over two
hundred thousand men had enlisted. The Volunteers were overwhelmingly working-class men. While conservatives embraced the patriotism
of military service, laboring men could see the Volunteers as a bulwark
against the tyranny of Louis Napoleon and his repression of the working class. Volunteers enjoyed the "show, the dress and the camp," according to one observer, and others noted the appeal of seaside excursions, football, and drinks after a meeting. The Volunteers were widely
recognized; they often appeared at state funerals and visits, and their brass
bands were important to making that musical style popular.[43]

The significance of the military was not only social and political. The
urban community and the dying physical body were linked in countless
literary metaphors as well as through the real presence of deadly disease
in Victorian cities. Social critics and politicians regarded the military as
an antidote to the wasting body of urban man. Historian Michael Budd
argues, "The most easily referred models of robust physicality were military in character."[44] England was a great imperial power in the late
1870s, and the possibility that war might break out at any time made
the military prominent and topical.[45] The British military was essential
to imperial dominance. National and racial strength and the healthy soldier's body underscored racialized "Englishness." Thus, military service
was associated with manliness, robust health, citizenship, independence,
and a vigorous body that could withstand the enervating effects of urban life.[46]

The name *Salvation Army* evoked all these associations. In 1878,
George Scott Railton in an article for the *Christian Mission Magazine*
wrote, "We are a volunteer Army." Bramwell Booth objected that he was
not a volunteer but a regular. William Booth substituted the word *Salvation,* and this striking name was soon adopted.[47] When the name was
introduced in the *Salvationist,* General Booth proclaimed, "Everyday it

[the Army] is becoming fierce and determined and courageous and confident and every day more and more a Salvation Army."[48] Military names were soon created for every aspect of the work, codifying language that had existed informally for at least a decade. As one hymn proclaimed,

> To serve the King of Kings I have enlisted,
> His solider brave and true I intend to be;
> Although for years His power I had resisted,
> I sought and found his glorious liberty.[49]

The Army thus associated itself with all that the Volunteer Force represented. It too would take men and women made feeble by unhealthy living and invigorate them, body and soul. For the many Salvationists who had little opportunity to hope that they would ever enjoy political power or even the franchise, the Salvation Army offered a place in God's army.

The Army's program included a route to healthy, invigorated bodies through discipline, order, and regulation. Total abstinence from alcohol was required, and Salvationists were encouraged to improve their diet. The Booths were strong supporters of hydropathy, a water cure offered at several English spas, and in the 1880s some officers suffering from fatigue or illness were sent to hydropathy clinics to recover. The *Local Officer* carried frequent advice on diet and health. Corps members were urged to wash often because anyone who "is *not* careful to keep his or her whole body and clothing clean can have no influence for good."[50] In 1902, *Vim*, a monthly magazine "devoted to promoting health and vigor of the mind and body," included testimonials about the Salvation Army's use of body-cleansing bath equipment.[51] The link between health and holiness was especially clear in the choice of food. Bramwell Booth argued that a vegetarian diet should be followed because it is "favourable to purity, chastity, and a perfect control of the appetites and passions," all qualities of holiness.[52]

Salvationists were by no means unique in these beliefs. U.S. evangelicals and religious reformers, including Sylvester Graham, Ellen White, and Mary Baker Eddy, were particularly involved in health reform. Hydropathy, vegetarianism, and total abstinence were especially popular causes. But few such reformers were to be found among England's working class. Working-class people were notoriously attached to a diet that many social reformers regarded as wasteful and not sufficiently nutritious.[53] The Salvation Army promised a path to renewed spiritual and bodily vigor that would strengthen a convert for the struggles to come.[54]

RECRUITS

Regardless of the circumstances, it was never easy to induce sinners to seek salvation, and it was particularly difficult in communities where the circumstances of life did little to foster religious adherence. Richard Free, a Church of England missionary in the Isle of Dogs, observed, "In the East End to be ever so remotely suspected of 'religion' is so unfashionable that only persons of exceptional character dare run the social risk."[55] John Eldred remembered of his Bermondsey childhood that his mother went through a "period of aspiration" during which she purchased a piano and an accordion and began to attend services at a hall, "where members of one of the smaller sects held their meetings." Eldred himself was marked off by his expensive boots, which convinced the other children that he was "an oddity, a foreigner, at whom, necessarily and properly, one should heave bricks."[56]

Conformity to neighborhood standards not only saved a family from ridicule but also secured their place in the neighborhood network of sharing and communal solidarity. Families lent and borrowed household items, helped each other care for the sick, aided those out of work, and shared useful or interesting gossip. Neighbors also shared hallways, toilets, and communal boilers for doing laundry.[57] To be marginalized or excluded from the community was risky for families who relied on the support of neighbors to survive unemployment, illness, or an ordinary shortfall. The threat of exclusion was a powerful inducement to remain aloof from religious institutions. Most children were baptized and attended Sunday School, and the majority of marriages were solemnized in the church; but few residents of Stepney or Bethnal Green attended church or chapel services. The clergy dispensed various kinds of relief, which were often tied to a visit from a Church official.[58] Although the clergy despaired over low attendance rates, that did little to effect the variety of ways the working class utilized the churches.[59]

Neither the Christian Mission nor the Salvation Army fostered such instrumental, distant relations between itself and the larger community. The Army demanded ardent, engaged commitment from its followers, and it constantly strived to extend its reach. This was not, however, an easy undertaking. Many evangelists from a wide range of missionary and church societies stood on street corners, preaching and singing. When a crowd gathered, they exhorted the people to consider the state of their souls and attend services at the local hall.[60] The Salvation Army sought ways to draw listeners in as a way of distinguishing themselves from the clergymen whom no one took much notice of and of capturing those souls they believed were rushing toward hell.

One of the most significant features of the Salvation Army was the relationship of its members to the wider community. As soon as people were saved, they were asked to stand before a crowd and relate their experience of conversion. The 1874 Conference declared that because "people are peculiarly amenable to the influence of their own neighbours and acquaintances, it is desirable more than ever to form bands for missioning the streets, for house to house visitation, and for tract distribution."[61] Salvationists valued entire sanctification above all else. If the spirit of God pervaded an individual, he or she was ready to preach and testify regardless of previous sinfulness, lack of education, or inexperience. This strategy meant converts had to dedicate themselves not only to personal righteousness but also to evangelizing their communities. It also meant that all converts were responsible for evangelizing their own families, fellow workers, associates, and friends. The emphasis on personal relationships in the work of evangelization set it apart from the work of such men as the Rev. Richard Free, who chose an East End church because he sought "real experience." He was puzzled by the local culture. He recalled that he failed to "make myself as far as possible one of them."[62] The Salvation Army agreed that such social distance was virtually insurmountable. An 1874 *Christian Mission Magazine* article entitled "Rough Labourers for Rough Work" declared, "If working people's hearts and minds are to be reached, it must be by the agency of their own fellows in labour and suffering. A clergyman may labour in his parish for a lifetime to accomplish what some working men could do in a few months, supposing there were an equality in spiritual power."[63]

THE STRUGGLE AGAINST POPULAR LEISURE

The military language and structure aptly expressed Salvationists' very real struggle against a wider, working-class culture. The pubs, music halls, and penny gaffs were well-entrenched institutions that would be dislodged only with difficulty. Like their evangelical predecessors, Salvationists regarded most working-class leisure with horror. An 1870 report on Shoreditch stated, "It is soul-sickening to meet youths, men in the prime of life, and even old men (whose grey hairs look ripe for the grave) with birds under their arms on their way to eternal death."[64] In 1869 the Christian Mission published a story about a young boy who followed a preacher who attended the theater. On his deathbed the boy told the preacher, "I followed you like a slave, until I was happy nowhere but in the atmosphere of the accursed theatre. Curses on it! Curses on it! It has drained me of every good; sapped my virtue; destroyed my soul."[65] The view that such pastimes as bird keeping and theater led to eternal damnation appeared to most Victorian Christians as rather old-fashioned and rigid. But even if the Army seemed to share a horror of sinful amusements with serious Christians of an earlier era, its strategy for pulling sinners away from the snares and temptations of popular leisure was strikingly innovative.

The Salvation Army literally appropriated theaters, music halls, and public houses for religious purposes. The theaters the Salvation Army "converted" were lively and encouraged audiences to participate. People would talk, drink, and eat throughout the performance, and people would often come and go, meet friends, and move to a new seat. In 1873, a thirteen-year-old boy fell into the pit of a theater and died. The inquest revealed that young men often passed each other over, from section to section, or rolled from the top seats down toward the front.[66] Only in the 1870s did music halls begin to provide fixed seats, lower the lights, and cease allowing the audience to promenade during the show.

The Christian Mission created its own style with elements borrowed from these performances. It borrowed the name "free and easy" as well as elements of the program. The meetings began with a hymn, followed by a prayer and a narration of the mission's work. The "free and easy" then commenced. An 1871 *East London Observer* writer who attended a "free and easy" departed while it was in "full blast," noting, "Like the secular free and easies, the religious ones maintained the character for being late!"[67]

The "capture" of the Grecian Theater and Eagle Tavern, City Road, was an important campaign in the battle with popular entertainment. The Eagle was a popular hall. Marie Lloyd, the renowned music-hall performer, appeared there in her early years.[68] On June 29, 1882, the *War Cry* announced its purchase. Soon after, a fund was established to raise the £16,750 necessary to secure the lease.

A leaflet was published urging the public to support the campaign.

Converts who have drunk, and danced and sinned there repeatedly in the dark days of their former life assure us that the souls of more young people have gone down to destruction through the scenes of revelry which have been witnessed on these premises than from any other popular resort in London.

Standing amidst a dense working-class population . . . and known far and wide, the building will give us the opportunity far superior to anything we have hitherto had of gathering tens of thousands of the worst people together and we trust that a great many of those who have formerly been seen there dancing their way to destruction will be found on the same spot rejoicing in the Lord and leading others to Him.[69]

The pamphlet went on to document the Salvation Army's gains over the previous year, which included 114 new corps and 328 more officers. The Archbishop of Canterbury had contributed £5, the General Secretary of the Wesleyan Missionary Society sent £20, and the Queen expressed her "satisfaction that you have been . . . successful in your efforts to win many thousands to the ways of temperance, virtue and religion." Her Majesty declined to contribute to the fund. Further funds were raised by charging the over six thousand people who attended the wedding of Bramwell Booth and Florence Soper one shilling admittance.

On September 27, 1882, the *War Cry* announced that three thousand people had gathered to open this new hall.[70] In November a "Salvation Spectacle at the Grecian Theater" was reported. A prostitute, a young boy, a "respectably dressed lady," and four deaf men were converted in one evening.[71] A Salvationist who went under the name the "Hallelujah Midget" composed a song for the occasion. He took the tune from "Pop Goes the Weasel."

> Up and down the City Road,
> In and out the Eagle
> That's the way the money goes,
> Pop goes the Weasel.[72]

Salvationists instead sang,

> Jesus fills me with His love,
> He shall shout in Heaven above,
> Glory, glory, glory.
> We've turned the Eagle upside down,
> Glory, Glory, Glory
> And sent the dancers out of town,
> Glory, Glory, Glory.[73]

Four years later, an Army poster announced a meeting offering "Thrilling Scenes Nightly at the Old Grecian!" It promised "Salvation For Costers, Cabmen, Cats-meat-men, Loungers, Lords and Stealers, Policeman, Pirates and Political Agitators." At 8 o'clock, Major McKie, "more on the Spot than Ever," would have a "Pitched Battle in the Pit." "200 Warriors in Red & Blue will be there with their swords! Come & See This! Don't Fail! Marvellous. Climax of Climaxes. Pelion on Ossa.

(Do you know what *that* means? For information, apply 'Grecian') and two brass bands on top of that. Songsters of the Feminine Persuasion. Thousands of Angels in Attendance. Shouts of Joy and Great Peal on the Chimes of Heaven!"[74]

The conversion of the Eagle and Grecian did not pass without notice. On the day it opened, the *East London Observer* reported that an "immense force . . . fully 6000 persons" thronged the street.

> Headed by brass bands and banners, the Army proceeded, three and four abreast, along City-Road, their progress retarded by the unruly mob, who derided and jostled them as they passed along. On reaching the Eagle gates some difficulty was experienced in entering but with the aid of the police, and after some sharp skirmishing and much crushing, the Army entered and, with cheers, secured possession of their new premises.[75]

The Army was obliged to keep the license that maintained it as an inn, tavern, or public house; when it failed to serve alcohol, the landlord brought the Army to court in an attempt to compel it to use the premises as licensed. After years of legal proceedings, the Army ceased operations in the late 1890s.[76] The Army's loss of the hall was regretted more than it was regarded as a failure. Thousands crowded the hall, and the attention it generated was unrivaled.[77]

The Salvation Army "captured" the Eagle and Grecian because it was believed to be utterly sinful; not only was it full of sinners, it also produced sin. And if the Holy Spirit could cleanse the hearts of sinners, so too could the music halls be hallowed. Though the words of the music-hall songs were sinful, the tunes were easy to sing and popular. As William Booth said in 1877, "I rather enjoy robbing the Devil of his choice tunes."[78] The buildings were even better. With seating for thousands, lighting, and a stage, they had few rivals. The theaters and music halls were among the best-known buildings in any neighborhood. The working class visited them far more regularly than they did the churches and chapels, and they seemed to find the atmosphere quite congenial.

Many of the Army's preachers adapted theatrical techniques to attract those who might otherwise never attend religious services. Their exploits were often spontaneous and rarely emanated from headquarters or a divisional officer despite the Army's strict hierarchy. Most were organized locally and expressed the energy and creativity of a corps or an individual. Corps used posters, street displays, broad theatrical gestures, and visual effects to dramatize their mission. Posters advertised the spectacular possibilities. A poster announcing a talk by Billy McLeod, a former prizefighter, proclaimed he had been "conquered by Jesus"; yet it included a large illustration of McLeod in the ring and promised he would speak on his "youthful days, crooked pals, early scrapes, booze and swagger, . . . scenes in the dock, execution of a companion for murder," and other chilling topics.[79] A poster produced in the early 1880s proclaimed the arrival of a "Yankee Lass" at Scarborough. She was "a Wonder! Dressed in American Costume! With a Turban on her Head! Splendid Singer, Good Talker, and Proper Tambourine Player!"[80] Salvationist preachers often took names that promised startling sights and sounds to those who came to a meeting. The *War Cry* announced a meeting with the "Salvation Midget, 40 Pounds in Weight, 40 inches in Height, 40 Years in Age!" Another article described a service with the "Army Midget," where the "Converted Wife Beater" told how he went to hear "the Salvation Fiddler and he got the Devil fiddled out of him, and for three years he never struck his wife."[81]

One 1882 outdoor meeting in Hull included "two 'Blood and Fire' flags flying, thirty-seven musicians, brass instruments, banjos, fiddles, tambourines and cymbals, all making a mighty stir."[82] John Lawley, who began working with the Mission while he was still in his teens, liked to tear his song book into shreds to show how the Devil attacked sinners or to dive off the platform and make swimming motions to illustrate the sea of God's love and pardon.[83] In 1890, the Willesden Green corps organized a procession.

> The two plucky lass officers looked quite majestic when fixed up in a marble mason's trolley, which served as a war chariot. The driver too, in his red guernsey and white helmet, was quite a 'draw.' In each side of the chariot were lasses waving flaming torches. These were followed by the band and corps and the effect was further enhanced by about a hundred and fifty of the native small fry, howling and yelling as if they were trying to compete with Barnum's amiable speciums of natural history.[84]

Announcements of the appearance of the "Salvation Midget," the "Converted Sweep," and the "Saved Drunkard" suggested the possibility of hearing a conversion story replete with daring sins or seeing a man so remarkable that he might otherwise be glimpsed only in a penny gaff. As one observer commented, "People go to see the Hallelujah Giant who weighs thirty-three stone with the same feeling that they go to see Tom Thumb and the Siamese Twins."[85] The music and spectacle attracted even those who took no interest in the theology that inspired them; the Army hoped only that they might stay long enough to be converted.

The music halls also had another, immensely important appeal. Peter Bailey has argued that in music hall "pleasure is represented as an abundance. In the grand style of its architecture and amenities, the hyperbole of its address, and the scale and variety of the programme, music hall was the site and occasion for liberality, profusion, and plenitude, however bogus."[86] Music hall was thus especially appropriate. The Army not only wanted to widen the appeal of Christianity but also strived to convey that God's love was so immense, so utterly transformative that anyone could be saved in an instant. The style and language of music hall were widely recognized and comprehended, and it thus offered a powerful means to communicate, with sounds, gestures, and words, essential elements of Army theology.

Salvationists adapted various musical styles and tunes to their own purposes. Brass bands were immensely popular in this period (see Figure 10). The Army's first brass band was formed in 1878 by the Fry brothers, and soon the Army began to sell instruments and offer musical instruction.[87] Many of the songs played or sung at Salvationist meetings were standards from U.S. camp meetings, and some were known as "negro spirituals." Many were popularized by Moody and Sanky. Gypsy Smith, for example, met Sanky in London in 1873 and was impressed by his work; Smith soon began singing in a similar style at Christian Mission meetings.[88] Versions of these songs were found in many eighteenth- and nineteenth-century Baptist, Methodist, and Congregationalist hymnals on both sides of the Atlantic. Some were written by eighteenth-century evangelicals including Charles Wesley and Isaac Watts, but even these writers used well-known choruses, or congregations simply added them later. The songs favored by Salvationists were usually simple and repetitive. These characteristics allowed any listener to join in. They were also easy to adapt to a particular situation. For example, they sang,

Is there anyone here like weeping Mary?
Call to my Jesus and He'll draw nigh.
Oh, Glory, glory glory Hallelujah,
Glory be to God who rules on high.
Is there any body here like sinking Peter?
Is there any body here like faithless Thomas?[89]

This revival standard could be easily adapted by a song leader who wished to address a particular person or situation.

The Army also took dozens of music-hall tunes and wrote new lyrics for them. These tunes were well known and easy to sing. At the same time adapting these tunes allowed Salvationists to criticize the ideals presented in the halls. One of the most popular music-hall figures, George

Leybourne, made famous the song "Champagne Charlie" during the late
1870s and 1880s.

> I've seen a deal of gaiety,
> Throughout my noisy life,
> With all my grand accomplishments
> I could never get a wife.
> The thing I most excel in is
> The P.R.F.G. game,
> A noise all night, in bed all day,
> And swimming in champagne.
>
> Chorus
>
> For Champagne Charlie is my name,
> Champagne Charlie is my game,
> Good for any game at night, my boys,
> Good for any game at night, my boys,
> For Champagne Charlie is my name,
> Champagne Charlie is my game,
> Good for any game at night, boys,
> Who'll come join me in a spree?[90]

This song was about a swell. Typically, as Peter Bailey has shown, "the
swell was a lordly figure of resplendent dress and confident air, whose
exploits centered on drink and women; time, work and money scarcely
intrude as the swell struts his way across town in the company of other
'jolly dogs.'"[91] The song was one of "action and release." Freed from
his daily labor, the swell spent his evenings on the town, "combining the
fashionable with the fashionably disreputable."[92] He defined masculinity through gesture, dress, the consumption of champagne, and the company of other men.

Captain William Baugh took this well-known tune and gave it new
words in 1882; he called his song "Bless His Name He Sets Me Free!"[93]

> I was a slave for many years, and conquer'd by my sin,
> I tried and pray'd, in doubts and fears,
> but still was wrong within.
> I heard that Jesus died to save,
> From every sin set free,
> I gave up trying there and then, and oh, He set me free!
>
> Chorus
>
> Oh, Bless His Name He sets me Free [repeat]
> Oh the blood, the precious blood,
> I'm trusting in the precious blood.

And now I live to God alone, I live to do His will;
I give myself to God away,
That He my soul may fill.
He takes the offering as it is,
And makes it as He will,
And through the Lamb I've constant peace,
For Jesus says "Be still!"

And though the world and hell unite
My peace to overthrow,
My trust is in the living God,
Who makes me white as snow.
The precious Blood now cleanses me,
And Jesus keeps me right;
My will is swallowed up in God,
I'm walking in the light.

This song clearly illustrated the Army's theology, and it tore down every aspect of the swell. The song suggested that instead of providing escape from toil, drink and the pleasures of the swell enslaved men. Freedom was not action or release but rather a tranquillity found when the individual will was overtaken by God. If the swell was defined as much by the company he kept as by his behavior, then men ought to closely examine their own companions. Similarly, when the lyrics urged men to walk in God's light, they suggested that men might find a better self in the community of the Salvation Army. The song became popular and was strongly associated with the Army. One Anglican clergyman complained that ever since the Salvation Army came to his village, "one hears the most sacred words shouted out" to the tune of Champagne Charlie.[94]

New words were written for countless other songs; "Daisy Give Me Your Answer Do" became "Jesus I Love Thee with All My Heart." Songs were rewritten to commemorate a local event or special occasion. These adaptations made the Army's music memorable and associated it with what was popular and current in a community. The Salvation Army perspective in these songs also countered what was popular and admired by music-hall patrons.

IMPERIAL SPECTACLE

By the 1880s, the Army included a wide range of cultural expression in its services. Its spectacle came to include a glimpse of the imperial exotic. At the 1885 annual meeting at Exeter Hall, "the congregation was entertained, amongst other things, by the novelty of a sacred duet on the

bagpipes and by a Chinese convert performing his devotions in full heathen costume on the platform."[95] The *War Cry* description of the attractions at the Alexandra Palace anniversary celebrations in 1887 resembled descriptions of a circus freak show. "There were tents to be seen,
natives to be stared at and Hindoos to be shaken hands with." The "ex-
jail birds" led by Major John Lawley recalled "snatches of their cell experiences" and the bonds they had "endured for Christ's sake" when arrested for their work in the Army. The "Foreign Demonstration" included
converts from the Army's work in India, "a robed, head-shaven, smil-
ing converted buddhist priest, the tamed devil dancer and the Cinghalese
publican." The commissioner's "Hindustani Secretary" sang "that touch-
ing, 'I'm clinging to the Cross' again. It was as fresh as ever." There were
also "four Swedes, one Norwegian, and three Finns, and like everyone
else, they spent one of the happiest days in their lives."[96]

The Booth weddings were of particularly grand proportions, occasions
that highlighted the Army's imperial reach. The *War Cry* announced
Emma Booth's engagement to Frederick Tucker in March 1888 (see Figure 11). Once married, the couple were to proceed to India, and an Indian theme ran through the ceremony. Tickets were sold to soldiers,
officers, and friends at prices ranging from sixpence to five shillings, with
the proceeds to go toward a fund to assist "the tremendous claims of the
Heathen world upon the Army."[97] The wedding, on April 9, 1888, was
described as an "imposing spectacle." Salvationists and others crowded
into the Congress Hall, full of "eager interest in a strange sight and desire to see every bit of it."[98] Mottoes and Bible verses covered the walls,
and the pillars were decorated to resemble palm trees. Band members
wore turbans of red, yellow, or blue. Officers from the Indian corps in
Indian dress along with "Tamils and Cingalese" sat on the platform, wel-
coming the bride. The groom appeared barefoot, in a calico robe and
turban with a begging bowl.[99] "Effect was aimed at in each detail and
in all the setting of this sacred service."[100] That effect, the *War Cry* continued, was intended to remind the couple and all the spectators of their
duty to God. That duty included bringing the unregenerate to God, and
this dramatic service was meant to further that aim.

The twenty thousand spectators who attended the day's festivities at
Alexandra Palace or the many guests at this wedding were able to see
people who they might otherwise only hear about, and this encounter
took place in a setting that emphasized every Salvationist's important
position in Britain's imperial program. The Salvation Army's international reach could be extended by every new convert, every prayer of-

fered for the Army's success, every penny given to its programs. Thus the Army reminded all converts, no matter how humble, that they might take part in the glory of the imperial quest and affirm their position as British Christians by offering salvation to heathens at home and abroad. These events brought the empire before these observers and emphasized the superior, metropolitan location of British Salvationists.[101]

WOMEN AND THEATER

The Hallelujah Lasses were, by definition, a theatrical spectacle. Women preachers were controversial; women preachers in uniform, playing the tambourine, and singing were shocking. In the nineteenth century, in fact, the term *public woman* was used interchangeably for both performers and prostitutes; this usage suggested a series of associations among publicity, impropriety, and inauthenticity.[102] The way in which public speech and sexual impropriety were linked in public culture was not unique to the nineteenth century. The accusation of sexual indecency leveled against women preachers is as old as Christianity itself.[103] Salvationist women who stood before the public to preach, particularly in a style that so obviously borrowed from popular theater, could not help but invoke all these associations.

The Army did not invent the name Hallelujah Lasses, but as soon as crowds started to use it, it was found on countless posters and advertisements, including one poster that advertised "The Exhibition of the Hallelujah Lasses."[104] An even more explicit association with theater was made in 1886, when twenty lasses in London designed what they called "a theatrical set" to illustrate the differences between a drunkard's and a Salvationist's home. The drunkard's home was depicted at a "gloomy haunt, dark and dreary and comfortless" in contrast to the "pretty little Salvation parlor," which had a tambourine, a teapot, and a saucer on a table with a chair and curtains on the window. The lasses used the set to act out the changes that would be wrought by conversion.[105]

The Army's use of this association is best exemplified by Eliza Haynes. When she was unable to draw a crowd to the Marylebone hall, she unbraided her hair, put flowing ribbons in it, and hung a sign around her neck saying "I am Happy Eliza." She also drove around the streets on the luggage rack of a four-wheeler, playing the fiddle and handing out flyers for upcoming meetings that announced "Happy Eliza and the Salvation Brass Band."[106] The *War Cry* described her first meeting as "Happy Eliza on the Stage."[107] She became a sensation, with the newspapers reporting on her activities and the police following her. A music-hall song was written about her and performed at the Crystal Palace. The song tells of a man who joined the "Hallelujah Band" because of these "buxom lasses young and fair."

> They call one Happy Eliza, and one Converted Jane
> They've been most wicked in their time, but will n'er do so again;
> They said pray come and join us and I was just in the mood,
> They're Hallelujah Sisters and they're bound to do me good.
>
> I know that good those young girls are, but strangely to relate,
> Altho' they're often deep in thought, they don't forget the plate,
> For money they can't do without, nice things we all crave
> Besides they ought to make some bunce [money], as through the streets
> they rave.[108]

The spoken last line asks listeners to join the Army, but "mind you must not interfere with my pet lambs, they're my own especial property." If the singer's appreciation of the charm of the Lasses was perhaps not quite what the Army intended, it was predictable given how Happy Eliza had captured public attention. And the Army had no hesitation about capitalizing on this perception.

Haynes was drawing on an increasingly sexualized popular commercial culture. Peter Bailey has argued that barmaids of the 1860s and 1870s exemplified a kind of contained, commercialized sexuality. Hired for their appearance and charm, these young women worked behind the counter, which gave them an aura of glamorized distance. This "parasexuality" played a part in the expanding service sector and commercialized leisure of the later nineteenth century.[109] Eliza Haynes, a publican's daughter, could not have failed to recognize the tensions evoked when a woman preacher made herself a public spectacle. Another music-hall song archly combined ridicule of Salvationist women's morality and theatricality. "Sister 'Ria" told of a "pious girl" who used to "go converting all along the giddy Stand; She bought herself a tambourine, to bang both night and day; and she would sing and dance in such a fascinating way."

> But 'Ria was missing one fine day,
> And very sad to tell,
> Not only her, but other things
> Had walked away as well.
> Some wicked individual
> Had tempted her you know,
> To leave the mighty Army,
> And become a real live "pro."[110]

This flamboyant style borrowed from popular theater and music hall to appeal to audiences with dramatic gesture, music, and spectacle. This repertoire was simply not available to either the sectarian Methodists of the early nineteenth century or the independent women evangelists of mid-century. Moreover, these urban working-class women were not bound by conventions of middle-class gentility, nor did they need to fear offending a denominational body that permitted women to preach only under carefully delineated conditions.[111] Indeed, the Salvation Army's leaders recognized the extraordinary attraction of women preachers. Catherine Booth commented in 1886 that women could more easily gain attention because "generations of suppression of women, and the consequent prejudice and curiosity with respect to her public performances, conspire immensely towards attracting the people."[112] This attraction was recognized by Bramwell Booth. When the Coventry corps had trouble filling the hall, the chief of staff gave various suggestions and then concluded, "If there is no other plan of working the place we had better send lasses."[113]

SENSATIONALISM

Unlike virtually any of their contemporaries, Salvationists appealed to working-class audiences by borrowing some of the elements of working-class culture with a real appreciation of their attractions. The brass bands, music-hall songs, street performances, and daring women all appealed to the senses. The use of such cultural elements was widely called sensationalism, and it was, George Scott Railton asserted, the best way to reach the people. "Millions of sinners have been appealed to for many a long year, and have become so callous and indifferent, that a very earthquake of sensation alone can suffice to arouse them . . . The Bible, the one great record of truth, is beyond doubt the most sensational record in existence."[114] An 1883 *War Cry* article insisted that sensationalism was not only the Army's way but God's way to reach his people. "Why did the Lord, when He wished to attach a people over to Himself, come down amid thunder and lightening, on Sinai and make even the best of them all 'exceedingly fear and quake'? . . . What if not that the only religion God cared about was one that continually moved the worshippers in the most sensational manner conceivable?"[115]

These efforts placed the Army at an enormous distance from other Christians. Certainly sectarian Methodists and other evangelicals had used sensational means to stir cold hearts and ignite a desire for salvation, but by mid-century most sectarians had eschewed such methods.[116]

One contributor to the January 1883 *Primitive Methodist Quarterly Review*, which was hardly the most conservative publication, asserted, "There is no defense that can be offered for [the Salvation Army's] irrelevant exercises or their outrageous advertisements; these things are wretched accretions and corrupt fungi, which will certainly drop off with the winds of criticism and the frosts of adversity." Another contributor opined that "the effect of such advertisements is to render the people who demand them incapable of any religious life, as they destroy the very foundation of religion in the human soul—reverence."[117]

These criticisms reveal the wide gulf in theology between Salvationists and their contemporaries. Salvationists embraced a bodily faith, in which salvation was known through a physical encounter with God; in this encounter penitents could weep, shake, fall into unconsciousness, or levitate. To reach sinners, Salvationists had no hesitation about using the same bodily senses that penitents would use to express the presence of the Holy Spirit. It clearly stated, however, that these encounters must be directed toward salvation. Corps were not permitted to hold "entertainments or recitations" organized with the intention of pleasing the hearers. While churches and chapels were busy organizing entertainments, the *War Cry* insisted, "we cannot too carefully guard against the coming in amongst us of anything which would prevent our saying truly that we meet together always and only for Salvation purposes."[118] The methods used to attract sinners and glorify God could include a brass band, a rousing song with shouted responses, and a woman preacher with a sign around her neck racing through a neighborhood. The intention, purpose, and effect made all the difference. One hymn printed in 1880 in the *War Cry* clearly explained that "noise is not sin."

> Some say I am too noisy,
> I know the reason why,
> And if they felt the glory,
> They'd shout as well as I.[119]

The Army drew audiences. The Salvation Army boasted of it; observers noted it. When the soldiers and band of the Marylebone corps proceeded through the streets on Boxing Day 1887, the *War Cry* commented on the effect. "The route, as usual, was thronged with hundreds of eager spectators who pressed closely to the sides of the column, making it every now and then, rather difficult to get along. . . . We doubt whether the Marylebone Theater near by . . . could boast of such a packed gathering as filled our place on Boxing Night."[120]

Conversion was the goal, but the methods often resulted in confusion. Matthew Callaghan, a laborer from Maida Vale, was charged in February 1882 with being drunk and disturbing a Salvation Army meeting. "The prisoner said 'They had a fiddle playing on the stage. It did not look like a chapel.'"[121] *Lloyds* reported in April 1882 that the Oxford Street Corps applied for a summons against a man who disturbed the meeting by shouting and screaming. When the captain stated that the hall was licensed for religious services, the magistrate, Mr. Newton, asked, "But don't you sing and dance there?" The captain replied, "We sing but we don't dance." The summons was granted. The following day the residents of Oxford Street appeared before Mr. Newton to inquire what action they might take against the Salvation Army's disturbances. One resident complained that "the shouting, raving and playing of brass bands is simply intolerable and not only that, but it has a tendency to bring the Word of God into ridicule." Mr. Newton suggested they apply to the Court of Chancery for an injunction to restrain the Army.[122] The magistrate's response in both cases and *Lloyds*' juxtaposition of the two court cases suggested that the Salvation Army had more in common with those who disturbed its meetings than with the respectable residents of Oxford Street.

The Salvation Army's "capture" of the Eagle and Grecian along with other such buildings extended the connection between the Army and the purveyors of mass entertainment. In 1886, the premises were assessed for the poor rate. The Salvation Army appealed the decision, claiming that it was exempt as a religious institution. Bramwell Booth spoke before the Middlesex magistrates.

> We acquired the premises in 1882 and converted them to religious purposes. We used to sell Salvation papers but that has now been discontinued, and the music license has been allowed to lapse. No uniforms were kept or sold. . . . The theater is used only for religious public service and we charge 1d for admission to "reserved" seats. . . . Cross-examined by Mr. Poland:
>   During the present year we have had tambourines, whistles, drums and bones. I do not know about drums. I do not think we have had castanets and bones. I think it impossible that we have "bones" like the "Christy Minstrals." Probably banjos and concertinas. I do not know whether in May last an entertainment was given by "Blind Jemmy" who performs. "Blind Mark" does perform sometimes upon the harmonium, and "Blind Johnnie" sings and accompanies himself on the banjo. It is quite possible that as an inducement for people to come an announcement is made that these persons are going to perform on these instruments.[123]

The court upheld the levy of the poor rate in this case and in similar cases in Worcester in 1884 and Plymouth in 1883.[124]

The close association between the Army and the music hall was also acknowledged by the celebrated singer Marie Lloyd. She commented to critics in 1897, "Why if I was to try and sing highly moral songs they would fire ginger beer bottles and beer mugs at me. They don't pay their sixpences and shillings at a Music Hall to hear the Salvation Army."[125] Salvationists *were* pelted with ginger-beer bottles when they performed, but they would surely have been pleased to be recognized as the alternative to music hall.

THE PRINTED WORD

The Salvation Army borrowed other aspects of popular culture in order to reach those unmoved by sermons and church ritual. The design and content of the Christian Mission's periodicals, the *East London Evangelist* (1868–1869) and the *Christian Mission Magazine* (1870–1878), resembled those of other religious periodicals of the day such as the *Revival* and the *Primitive Methodist Quarterly Review*. Small enough to be held easily, the magazines were designed in a plain, regular style. Article titles were displayed in large type, but the typeface was otherwise uniform and there were no illustrations. The *War Cry*, however, borrowed the freshest and most innovative aspects of new journalism, including its large newspaper format, startling headlines, and plentiful illustrations.

The content of all these publications borrowed plebeian literary forms, particularly the broadside. Broadsides were a source of information and entertainment for laboring people from the eighteenth century to the mid-nineteenth century. They contained woodcut illustrations and text printed in bold, distinctive typeface. These designs were used over and over. The broadsides were diverse and included songs, ballads, stories of executions and shocking murders, and strange tales.[126] William Corbridge, an evangelist from the earliest years of the Christian Mission, borrowed from two broadsides: "Railway to Heaven" and "Railroad to Hell."[127] In simple rhyme, these broadsides compared life to a journey on a train. Passengers might choose to ride on a line that "from heaven to earth does extend, where real pleasures never end." On that train, "Jesus is the first engineer; He does the Gospel engine steer; The preachers of the sacred Word, Co-workers with their dying Lord." Others might choose to "ride into Hell in our pride, on railroads of sin with blue Devils inside." Corbridge wrote a sermon that borrowed this theme and built on it. It was later reprinted as a tract entitled *The Up Line to Heaven and the Down Line to Hell*.[128] It proclaimed,

TICKETS ARE FREE! . . . But in order to get a first class ticket you must have a first class start; give up sin, live holy, and you will have a first class ride, and this will ensure a first class heaven. . . . The Steam Power is the Holy Ghost living in us; and with good stokers . . . the spirit accompanies our praying, preaching, singing and processions, then drunkards, swearers, thieves, liars, and harlots are convinced and converted.[129]

The broadsides reminded readers,

When we behold the flag that's white,
It cheers the heart, for all is right;
But when green we do behold,
Caution it says and be not bold.[130]

Likewise, Corbridge warned of "green lights" shone by praying mothers and Sabbath-school teachers, which are ignored by the passengers to hell. He represented the Christian Mission as the red light of danger. William Booth shouted out danger and called on everyone else to do the same. "Shout it out in your meetings, shout it out in the open air; in all your processions, in every road, in every street, in every court, yard and alley. . . . They have stamped their feet on the blood of Jesus; shout danger. They have stamped on their mother's prayers; shout danger. . . . Never mind the respectable; try to save them. Never mind the professionals; shout salvation; salvation for everyone. Salvation now."[131]

The striking, repetitive language and vivid imagery aimed to capture the listeners. Undoubtedly, many who heard the sermon or who later read the tract knew the broadside Corbridge echoed. Readers could situate this tract in a tradition well known to working-class readers and distinguish it from other traditions such as the tracts of Hannah More. No one could confuse More's tracts with a broadside or a penny novel. Her tracts did not have the same startling stories, use the same dramatic language, or have the same graphic design as the broadsides or penny novels, and her theology was also different from that of the Salvation Army.[132] The Army's strategy encouraged readers to employ their own cultural knowledge to interpret Corbridge's sermon.

George Scott Railton was the author of numerous tracts. In *The Salvation Paper Mill*, he used a style similar to that of Corbridge. "In God's great mill I saw some rough and dirty refuse had been collected and turned into clean paper. That refuse of drink and poverty, and crime, the refuse of degraded men and women, who lived and died in sin, had been gathered up and successfully sent through the great 'Salvation Mill.'"[133] The "history of the rags" extended his theme. "At one time I was a fearful drunkard, and hardly knew for several years what it was to be sober at night. I am so glad the rag-collectors picked me up in the streets of G——, for since I have been to their 'Salvation Mill' I have been so wonderfully changed, and turned into such a nice sheet of paper, I can hardly ever believe that I was ever a rag at all."[134] This tract drew on the daily lives of laboring people and linked salvation and sin to their experience of work and to the common articles of daily life.[135]

The Salvation Army also borrowed from the graphic design of broadsides and posters. *The Up Line to Heaven and the Down Line to Hell* was cleverly designed. Each page was divided in two. The text began on the left side on page one, and the reader read down the left half of each page to the end and then turned back to page one to read down the right side of each page. The design dramatized the choice, made at the outset, between heaven and hell, salvation and sin. The striking mix of typefaces and the use of bold type to emphasize key phrases were reminiscent of the design of broadsides.

Other designs were borrowed, particularly those for posters advertising popular entertainment— music halls, amateur fights, and circuses. The design and text of the Army's posters were intended to capture the eye of even those hostile to religion. Some of the posters were such careful reproductions that people reputedly mistook them for music-hall and circus announcements and were quite surprised when they attended the event.[136]

The Army also borrowed widely from the advertisements directed at the working class. Attempts to market goods on a national level to working-class consumers were new, and the Salvationists were pioneers in their willingness to appropriate this style and language.[137] Consumerism and advertising were used in two related ways. First, beginning in the 1860s, the Christian Mission used advertising language and style to describe salvation. For example, one page of the *Christian Mission Magazine* in September 1874, an advertisement for the "Christian Passengers' Assurance Company," offered a "Paid Up Capital and Reserve Fund: The Love of Jesus Christ Our Lord." It asked readers to "apply for further information to any insured person. . . . Do not believe representatives of any one not insured in this Company." Along the bottom a warning directed at all those without insurance cautioned that they "may die at any moment, in which case they will lose both body and soul in hell! INSURE AT ONCE!" A February 1877 article called on readers to "Claim Your Legacy" that has been "left to the Church by its Saviour, consisting of New Jerusalem stock; but the greater part of it remains unclaimed."[138] These ads thus linked salvation to an eventuality that any working-class person understood and felt deeply: if preparations for death were not made, calamity would result. Many working-class families purchased death insurance even when it meant less money for food because falling short of money for a proper funeral was a terrible dilemma for any family.[139] Similarly, an 1882 ad offered "Valuable Employment" to "thousands of men and women willing to forsake their Old Master, the Devil, and accept Jesus instead."[140] Again, the most commonplace experience offered a way to speak of conversion.

Salvation was described in concrete, material terms, as a state everyone should visibly demonstrate. One young woman who wore her uniform everywhere was called an "Advertising Christian."[141] Consumption could represent what salvation could offer. The *War Cry* reported on a domestic servant who, despite the persistent opposition of her mistress, was determined to join the Army. She "ordered a 'Hallelujah bonnet,' a tambourine, and a ribbon as tokens of her determination." These objects offered her a way to visibly insist on her desire to join the Army. Objects that were part of someone's past life, like feathers, flowers, pipes, tobacco pouches, and brooches, given up "for Christ sake" were often displayed at meetings to demonstrate what had been relinquished.[142] Conversion was also represented through the change in consumption that it occasioned. One man, for example, testified that since his conversion, "my poor wife gets a joint of meat now on a Saturday night instead of a black eye. Glory be to God! it is the Lord that has done it! and that landlord knows that I am converted, for he gets his rent instead of cursing and the little lambs are going to school next week."[143] Another man testified that he knew his wife was serious when she purchased a Salvation Army bonnet, and so "I threw my pipes, tobacco and pouch into the fire, gave up my glass and got salvation for myself."[144]

In urban working-class families, Ellen Ross has argued, "work, money and food were interchangeable, or nearly interchangeable signs." A "good husband" or a "good wife" was one who provided for the family's material needs. Given how difficult that could be, when it was achieved everyone recognized the devotion and love it represented.[145] When working-class men and women described their conversion in terms of consumption and material goods, they evoked powerful associations of love, devotion, and commitment.

The Salvation Army took advantage of the profitable possibilities of a consumer culture aimed at working-class people. The *War Cry* advertised Salvation Army tea priced at 2 shillings a pound and a variety of pocket watches from £1 15s to £2 12s.[146] Salvationists could purchase red and white quilts with the Army emblem, Salvation Army towels, or toilet soap.[147] The Army also offered "cartes de visite" (small photo cards) of the Booth family and books on a variety of topics. Proceeds from the sale of all these items benefited the Army, materially and symbolically. Like similar products, the soap, bonnet, or quilt proclaimed the owner's adherence to the Army and personal salvation. It suggested that salvation was, in a sense, a consumer product that could be chosen from among the array of products available. Religion could be "a force competing for a market share according to new rules governed less by mercantile controls and elite institutions . . . than by market forces and the sheer power of public opinion."[148] All this commercialism on the part of the Army was based on a vision of urban working-class people as frustrated consumers, caught up in squandering their money on drink and other indulgences. If they could be induced to use their money to express the deeper pleasures of God's love and family ties, they might live wholly different lives.

The push toward consumption was not always successful. In 1884, the *Pall Mall Gazette* reported on the Central Criminal Court case of William Astely, aged twenty-two, who had stolen several letters containing valuable securities. "The prisoner, in defence, said he had been led astray by the Salvation Army, who were always telling him he could not go to Heaven unless he had a uniform. He took the property in the letters in order to pay for the uniform."[149]

The Salvation Army was a neighborhood religion. Its music, militarism, preaching, and pamphlets were all borrowed from the culture of working-class neighborhoods. Salvationists took a distinct stand on popular culture and leisure. Unlike other denominations, they abhorred the notion that congregants might come to church to be entertained. But they embraced aspects of working-class entertainment that other Christians eschewed for their low, vulgar sensationalism. Salvationists' criteria were strictly practical. What effected conversions was adopted; what did not was ignored. Holiness, revivalist theology was the ground for their convictions. God used sensationalism, and so too should Christians if all the souls rushing to hell were to be saved. Because conversion came through the body, Salvationists' music, preaching, testimonies, and street processions were intended to move penitents to sing, clap, stamp their feet, and shout until the Holy Spirit swept through them. The Salvation Army's methods were striking and innovative, earning them a significant following and impassioned opposition from clergy, magistrates, local governments, and many residents of the neighborhoods Salvationists strived to transform.

Disorderly Champions of Order

Opposition to the Salvation Army

By the early 1880s, Salvation Army processions of uniformed officers playing musical instruments, women preachers opening new towns to the Army's work and even spreading its reach into France and Switzerland, the wide circulation of the *War Cry,* and the street frays between Salvationists and youth gangs brought the Salvation Army national prominence. Its work was widely reported in the *Times, Lloyds,* the *Pall Mall Gazette,* and the local papers wherever it was active. Further attention resulted from the Church of England committee formed under the direction of the bishop of Truro in 1882 to investigate the possibility of a union between the Church and the Salvation Army. Although the impossibility of such a union was soon clear, the investigation focused national attention on the Army's work.[1]

The Salvation Army stood in uneasy alliance with middle-class evangelists, philanthropists, and social reformers. It was one part of later-nineteenth-century evangelicalism and a sharp challenge to the long-established practices and beliefs of the evangelical movement. Not a middle-class mission attempting to civilize the urban poor nor a movement suited to those aspiring to the petite bourgeoisie, still the Army's mission paralleled Church and chapel efforts. Both strived to bring Christianity to the urban working class. Thrift and temperance enabled its followers to live by standards that middle-class philanthropists would have deemed appropriate. Some converts might save money for the material objects associated with a respectable life. Still, donning a uniform to attend sensational services would do little to affirm such a respectable demeanor. By the early 1880s, many observers became convinced that the similarities between Salvationists and other missionary movements were superficial. Some believed the Salvation Army was dangerous. A flood of pamphlet literature criticizing the Salvation Army appeared. These social critics, journalists, and clergy denounced the Army's theology and practices, pointing to the threat they posed to Britain's religious and political culture. These pamphlets criticized the Salvation Army for much the same reasons as those given by local governments and magistrates who used the law to contain the Army. This pamphlet literature reveals the significant divisions among nineteenth-century Christians and the Salvation Army's place in those divisions. It also makes clear the gravity attached to evangelizing the urban working class.

The Salvation Army was a neighborhood religion, but Salvationists were neither fully of the communities they evangelized nor outsiders. The Army borrowed its music, preaching style, buildings, language, and organizational structure from institutions and practices that were a familiar part of urban working-class landscapes. Yet, its relationship to the wider communities remained unstable. Some trade unionists and labor leaders admired the Salvation Army's ability to organize its adherents into well-disciplined corps, while others deplored its theological approach to poverty. Some deemed it irrelevant, while others found its services blasphemous. Working-class women and men thronged into Salvation Army halls; some found the services moving, while others gawked and laughed. Salvationists did not necessarily fear opposition because it could serve to build the movement, and Salvationists often embraced "persecution." In some communities, opposition was casual and limited to tossing rotting vegetables and fish. In other instances, young men organized themselves into "Skeleton Armies," which initiated serious, well-organized street frays.

The opposition mounted by pamphlet writers and the legal opposition of magistrates and local governments coincided with attacks by street gangs. The Army stimulated a kind of informal alliance of these unlikely allies, who were united in their desire to clear Salvationists from their neighborhoods. Their opposition allowed the Salvationists to present themselves as the champions of the working class, resisting an unjust church and state—a position that echoed a long tradition of Nonconformist, egalitarian radicalism.

A SENSE OF IMPENDING CRISIS

In the 1880s, Christians of all denominations agreed that the working class teetered on the edge of an abyss. Andrew Mearns's *The Bitter Cry of Outcast London* (1883) was one call to action that galvanized immediate attention and concern. Mearns, a Congregationalist minister, claimed that miserable living conditions were the cause of urban working-class irreligion. How could the poor, whose dwellings were crowded, filthy, and crawling with vermin, be expected to concern themselves with religion? Although some efforts had been made, the "flood of sin and misery were gaining."[2] This concern was not new. But in the 1880s it occurred against a backdrop of fear that missionary efforts, legislation, and urban reform were not addressing the problems of chronic unemployment, miserable housing, and growing working-class discontent. The Paris Commune seemed perilously close to many clergy, journalists, politicians, and employers as they observed with growing alarm the mass demonstrations of workers or the formation of groups like the Social Democratic Federation in 1883.[3] The language used to describe poor, urban neighborhoods changed. The word *slum* came into common usage in the late 1870s and became the standard term used by journalists in the 1880s. The slum evoked a "teeming wilderness, perpetually spilling over and extending its boundaries." It was a "showcase of imagination" that philanthropists, clergymen, missionaries, and politicians used to define issues and pursue goals.[4]

The London City Mission, the Open Air Mission, Ranyard's Biblewomen, the Metropolitan Tabernacle of C. M. Spurgeon, and the Mildmay Mission had long strived to bring Christianity to the urban poor, each perceiving the need for relentless work in urban working-class communities.[5] In the 1890s, Charles Booth noted that in London, "the poorer parts especially, in almost every street there is a mission; they are more numerous than schools or churches, and only less numerous than public houses."[6] By 1914, two hundred thousand district visitors were at work in England.[7] Newer efforts were a direct response to the sense of impending crisis in the 1880s. The Charity Organisation Society (COS), the work of Samuel Barnett and his colleagues at Toynbee Hall, and the Forward Movement were prominent and influential examples. Each of these organizations attended to souls and bodies, dispensing food and boots with spiritual guidance. Each one also articulated a call for social reform in its work.

The COS was founded to bring order to the vast array of charitable provision and to exemplify a new approach. Charity, according to its leaders, ought not to consist of simply giving money to support the poor but rather must promote citizenship. The poor should be helped to become self-supporting, ethical citizens, and the wealthy should voluntarily give to enable the poor to achieve this goal. The COS distinguished between the "deserving" and "undeserving" poor through personal interviews and home visits. Drinkers, those considered fit to earn sufficient wages, or anyone whose need would continue, such as the elderly or widows with young children, were excluded. These distinctions earned the COS the nickname "Cringe or starve," but it was a strong influence on British social policy in this period.

Toynbee Hall offered a different approach to poverty and irreligion. The Rev. Samuel Barnett opened this settlement house in 1884 with the intention of finding means to bring the wealthy and poor into contact in order to overcome class division and promote mutual responsibility and respect. The settlers were primarily recruited from Oxford University. No women were included because Barnett feared they would appear to take over and drive away the men. The residents of Whitechapel would learn "self-restraint and fellowship" from "following the example set by one's betters." Barnett eschewed the COS's distinction between deserving and undeserving, arguing that everyone would benefit from an improved environment and education.[8] Other organizations devoted their efforts to a particular problem. The 1880s, for example, was the key period for organizing women's efforts to stop prostitution through rescue homes or midnight street visits, during which women, often evangelicals, approached the fallen. Others established schemes to help the unemployed to emigrate.[9] The Salvation Army participated in this evolving and competitive arena of Christian evangelizing and social reform, and its growth served as a threat and an example to others.

OPPOSITION FROM THE ESTABLISHMENT

During the Christian Mission's first decade, the London papers described it in congenial, if rather condescending, terms. Its work was clearly comprehensible and deemed appropriate. The *Nonconformist* reported in 1867 that the hall was dingy and gloomy, but "the nearly two thousand people, belonging to the poorest and least educated class, behav[ed] in a manner that would reflect the highest credit upon the most respectable congregation that ever attended a regular place of worship."[10] The *Bethnal Green Times* expressed satisfaction with the Christian Mission, where "men are continually being saved from a life of confirmed vice, and 'converted' into loving fathers and respectable citizens."[11] This attitude was no doubt facilitated by the language of the early Christian Mission publications. William Booth described the East End and its inhabitants in terms common to Victorian social investigators and reformers, who characterized members of the urban working class by their desire to drink, their lack of domesticity, and their rejection of constituted authority, particularly the police and the Church.

William Booth's first published description of the Christian Mission's work, *How to Reach the Masses with Gospel* (1872), depicted filth sliding among the social, moral, and psychic domains in a style common to that of Friedrich Engels, Charles Dickens, and Mearns.[12]

> Of the teeming multitudes who crowd the squalid homes, if *homes* they can be called, which fill our Whitechapel courts and lanes, comparatively few, probably not one person out of ten, ever enters a place of worship. . . . In the very centre of this ocean of depravity and wretchedness, the Christian Mission has its headquarters, and to win these multitudes from the gin palace, the theatre, the concert hall, and the infidel lecture-room, to Christ and usefulness and heaven, is its special work.[13]

This pamphlet portrayed the poor as unwilling heathens; they lacked the appropriate housing for decency and privacy. When presented with the gospel, many would listen eagerly and could be quickly convinced to seek salvation. The East End desperately needed evangelists who could rescue souls from Satan's grip. Booth ended his pamphlet with a request for prayers and donations.

As the Mission style grew more spectacular, it became a more visible and dramatic organization, and the press commentary changed. The *East London Observer* of March 17, 1877, commented that it did not usually discuss religious questions.

> But this "Salvation Fair" episode is of such an unusual character that we may be pardoned for mentioning it in this department. It has not been confined to the mission hall alone, but has been thrust before the public in a way eminently calculated to rob the cause it intended to benefit of much that is beautiful and to be admired. The promoters of the fair have not scrupled to enter the camp of the enemy and appropriate all that might be regarded as attractive. . . . We shall not attempt a description of what takes place at this hall. . . . It is lamentable that such scenes should be perpetrated in the name of religion; grievous that there is no civil power to stop such an exhibition, a sin that money intended to rescue the masses should be perverted to such a purpose, and any man, pretending to point to paradise should convert this mission hall into a prefatory pandemonium.[14]

These criticisms of the Christian Mission soon were repeated elsewhere and expanded again and again until the early 1890s. The Army was denounced as a blasphemous body of notoriety seekers promulgating unsound theology. These charges were made in the press, from pulpits, and in a mass of pamphlet literature published between 1880 and the early 1890s. The writers may have agreed that evangelizing the urban poor was a pressing need, but they deplored the direction taken by this once-promising movement. The 1880s witnessed the most widespread and relentless criticism. With a heightened sense of danger among the propertied classes should efforts to Christianize the urban working class fail, the Salvation Army's beliefs and practices appeared to them ever more threatening. As one pamphlet writer said, "The religion of the churches had exercised . . . almost no influence whatever," yet the Salvation Army had a "remarkable effect."[15] What that effect might prove to be was the subject of intense debate.

Language marked an immense gulf between Salvationists and their critics. The familiar, common language adopted by Salvationists offended many Christians who upheld a distinct form of address and vocabulary for things sacred. One critic complained, "We find them speaking of spiritual matters with the greatest nonchalance, making the Holy Name of God, his attributes, and holy things in general appear ridiculous."[16] A Gateshead clergyman described a Salvation Army service in a letter to the *Guardian*. "Shouting ejaculations, closely bordering on irreverence, prayer expressed in shockingly familiar language, over excitement, inexpressibly distasteful, I confess, it was to my own feelings."[17] One London clergyman objected to the language "deliberately selected and approved by the leaders of the movement as a means of catching the eye or the ear"; such language led people to attend services or purchase the *War Cry* solely for amusement.[18] Frances Power Cobbe, a prominent feminist activist,[19] also believed that "bringing the holiest things into the general carnival of equality and jocosity" was not "trifling or innocuous." Where once the subject of religion was avoided, public house crowds now laughed at the Salvation Army and "the most sacred names and deepest human feelings and hopes come in for their share of ridicule."[20] Albert Muspratt in *The Salvation Army: Is It a Benefit to the Cause of Religion?* (1884) contrasted the "ignorant and illiterate" officers of the Salvation Army with the learned clergy of other denominations. John Price, in his 1882 pamphlet *The Salvation Army Tested by Their Works* acknowledged that "ungrammatical English or even some vulgarisms, which lowlived characters cannot be expected to drop on short notice" might be excused, but he advised the Army to "postpone *public ministry* until a decent language has been acquired."[21]

These criticisms, repeated again and again, were the result of two different understandings of the place of sacred texts and language. Salvationists used daily, familiar language to evangelize. They saw nothing wrong with preaching in a barbershop, diving off the platform to dramatize a point, or drawing a parallel between the road to salvation and a ride on a train. If listeners recognized themselves in the stories and if laughter or shared experience made the message compelling, the preaching was a success. The *War Cry,* William Booth's *Doctrines and Disciplines,* and personal advice to new officers made it eminently clear to all Salvationists that words, spoken or sung, were to be plain, clear, and engaging. Words were the route to conversion. The Army did not advocate sustained Bible study or partaking of the sacraments but rather pleaded with penitents to seek salvation immediately. The more striking and arresting Salvationists' words, the more powerful their work. What critics reviled as a blasphemous carnival the Salvationists believed was the reason for their success.

Salvationists, moreover, had a particular sense of the usefulness of working-class language, popular music, and other aspects of daily life in working-class communities. Holiness theology did not regard the individual soul as irredeemably sinful from birth to death. Even the worst sinner could be infused with God's presence, able to act as God's agent on earth.[22] Likewise, no musical form, dress, or style of address was categorically profane. Whatever elements of the larger culture could be converted to the saving of souls ought to be employed. William Booth claimed, "Some perhaps will call my taste vulgar, but mind I am a utilitarian; I go in, not for the ornamental, but the useful."[23] In contrast, clergymen were immersed in a tradition of church music and liturgy that sharply demarcated the spiritual from the mundane. To those accustomed to the language of the Book of Common Prayer and the King James Bible, the language of Salvation Army preaching was shocking. One critic, John Price, argued, "Nothing less than a thorough consciousness of spiritual deficiency could induce them to have recourse to such carnal and eccentric expedients for attracting large audiences. A brass band playing tunes never before associated with religion . . . will naturally draw people together out of curiosity."[24]

The *Saturday Review,* in an article entitled "Booth's Dancing Dervishes," described the *War Cry* as a mixture of "blasphemy and buffoonery."[25]

The clergy and most Nonconformist ministers were educated men unfamiliar with the culture of the urban working class. Salvationists scorned attempts to remove people from their daily lives or to rely on those who knew nothing of the lives of working people to lead them to salvation.[26] High Churchmen attempted to attract the poor of London's East End with richly decorated churches and ritual that would distract people from the monotony of their daily lives.[27] Salvationist preachers instead emphasized their connections to local communities by such means as adopting names for themselves like the "Hallelujah Fishmonger." Their speech was "vulgar" in that it both was the language of the working class and was emotional and broad. Such language was not usually associated with the clergy; using it made plain the Army's disregard for education and ordination and its overriding concern for a sanctified soul.

This difference is also evident in the criticism of the Army's decision not to offer communion. As we have seen, the Army leadership believed people often mistook communion or baptism as a means to salvation. They insisted penitents should seek only inward grace.[28] Anglicans and most Nonconformists viewed the sacraments as the divinely ordained means for Christians to obtain grace. As one Christian critic of the Army insisted, "Attendance at the Lord's supper is . . . enjoined in the New Testament, and is as necessary for feeding and strengthening our spiritual life as eating natural food is necessary for strengthening our natural life. . . . The movement among the 'Army' then which denies these things . . . is but one of zealous men; for if God does a work it is sure to be in full accordance with his revealed will."[29]

An Anglican clergyman, Wyndham Heathcote, who worked with the Salvation Army for a few years between receiving a degree from Oxford and returning to the Church, witnessed Salvationists returning to the penitent form seeking "more of God." This, he asserted, was "plainly a demand for communion."[30]

Salvationists believed each individual was responsible for his or her own soul. No outward forms or ministerial functions intervened between the individual soul and sanctification. Only the converts could know the state of their souls and declare themselves fully sanctified. Critics decried the loss of humility that resulted from this theology. One clergyman asserted, "Everyone is made the judge of his own state; and . . . the instant and public professions *must* be destructive of that humility that accompanies true repentance."[31] Critics especially condemned the *War Cry* corps reports that detailed conversions achieved with the aid of the Holy Spirit. "Judging from the *War Cry* . . . any one number of that vain-glorious periodical would convict the writers and actors of an amount of boasting . . . hardly consistent with having the Spirit at all."[32] To rely only on an individual's own word regarding the state of his or her soul meant the "convert of yesterday is often the teacher of today." "Has the holy reverence that breathes in every word anything in common with the unseemly familiarity, with the rushing into that presence with the assurance of equals, . . . with the light and easy use of sacred names suggestive to most (to say the least) of levity and unseemliness . . . and say even of profanity?[33]

The Army's sensational services came in for especially harsh criticism. One writer described the "nonsensical rhymes they call hymns" sung with "clapping of hands and stamping of feet, and intemperate bawlings out of Hallelujahs." These "noisy meetings" were often "prolonged until bedtime, not counting their half-night and all-night services for both sexes, which we think no prudent parents would allow their sons or daughters to attend."[34] Charles Waller in his 1882 pamphlet, *The Salvation Army: How Should the Thoughtful Christian Judge This Movement,* asserted that in the Army "sensationalism is too prominent. . . . It is objected that there is something coarse and irreverent in the appeals to the senses made by the Salvation Army. What devotion, it is asked, can be stirred by the confused noise of brass instruments, drums and tambourines?"[35] Benjamin Newton argued that all Christians have a duty to seek things "that are TRUE, full, completely, perfectly true, we are also to seek things that are of 'good report.' . . . Surely no one will affirm that there is anything 'venerable' or of 'good report' in the screams, dancing and gesticulations that characterize the meetings of this body. . . . To please and excite the flesh by stimulating its propensities and gratifying the cravings of the eye and ear, may and does, prepare the way for Satan."[36] An 1883 article in the *Saturday Review* suggested that all "fanatical movements" appeal to the "sensuous emotions, pandering to the love of excitement." But "nothing could be carried out more precisely on the music-hall plan, nothing could be devised less likely to encourage a spiritual habit of mind."[37] In a more ironic tone, a letter to the *Daily Telegraph* asked whether the "dramatic artists earning their living by the exercise of an honourable profession" at the Grecian Theatre could indeed be as "injurious to the public morals than some of the exhibitions of the Salvation Army."[38]

The participation of women in the Army's sensational, dramatic services was particularly denounced. Churchmen had long argued that women's weaker nature rendered them especially susceptible to sexual indulgence when in the grip of religious hysteria. In particular, sects with unconventional gender arrangements and unusual worship practices, such as seventeenth-century Quakers and the Shakers, endured persecution.[39] It is hardly surprising that clergymen accused the Salvation Army of fostering sexual immorality. Salvationist women received little notice from the press or critics during the first fifteen years of the Army's work. By the 1880s the Army was far larger and more prominent, its music-hall tunes and sensational services well known. Equally important, a wider movement of women who were opening professions for women, broadening women's educational opportunities, and demanding a voice in local and national politics was increasingly visible. Thus, the Hallelujah Lasses were associated with both an old threat of female sexual and religious excess and a contemporary, and growing, movement of women activists.

Neither of these associations seemed to make the Hallelujah Lasses a likely vehicle of religion and order for the "heathen masses." Writers presented the scriptural passages conventionally used to uphold a prohibition on women's preaching to demonstrate that women should remain in private and in subjection to men. "That most exalted type of womanhood, the Blessed Virgin Mary, kept all the sayings of Jesus, and pondered them in her heart, doubtless while she busied herself about her household duties."[40] But the ecstatic, emotional Salvationist meetings raised particular worries that went beyond the scriptural prohibitions against women's preaching. Instead of leading women to a life of righteousness, it was feared that the Army lured them into a whirl of activity, excitement, and eventual ruin. It drew women in with false promises and exploited a desire for sensation that, once stimulated, was difficult to relinquish. "Can it be safe or right to call women (and young women too) by the hundreds into positions which must of necessity break down all 'shamefacedness'? Is there nothing wrong in placing young women in positions that must minister cruelly to their vanity, that love [of] admiration and display so inherent in our poor humble nature, as women?"[41] Price reproved women for abandoning their "native sense of decorum and feminine retiredness" in order to preach "with studied attitudes and gesticulations only fit for the stage."[42] To prove how un-Christian it all was, another critic asked readers to imagine "the Blessed Virgin Mary heading the procession with a tambourine."[43]

The Booth family came in for particular criticism. It was leveled at the structure of the Salvation Army, which concentrated authority in the hands of one family, and at the publicity members of the family received. Several former Army officers wrote pamphlets with titles such as *The New Papacy* and *General Booth: The "Family" and the Salvation Army, Show-*

ing Its Rise, Progress, and Moral and Spiritual Decline; these pamphlets condemned the Booths' excessive control over the movement. The Booth children were particularly resented. S. H. Hodges, a former Army officer, remarked that the attention paid in the *War Cry* to the Booths' illnesses was a means to draw attention and sympathy to themselves.[44] William Booth, undoubtedly the most well-known Salvationist, was often targeted for ridicule by *Punch* and other comic magazines. An 1883 *Punch* cartoon depicted him dressed in a costume half-way between that of Robin Hood and a cowboy, playing a horn. It was captioned, "'General' Booth: His Own Trumpeter."[45] Critics condemned the Booths for using the children's marriages to advertise the movement and to lavish attention on themselves. One critic mocked the *War Cry* for comparing Emma Booth to Joan of Arc and printing her verbatim conversations with God.[46] Several writers took exception to the Booths' sons-in-law "stultifying their manhood and slighting their ancestors" by adding the Booth name to their own.[47] Another former Salvationist asserted that their doing so "is looked upon as being an irrefutable proof of the pride on 'The Family's' part, and the humiliation of men who have been chosen as husbands."[48]

William Booth's power and authority were ceaselessly criticized. Some contrasted his humble beginnings with his present power, while others compared the General's authority with the Pope's hold over the Roman Catholic Church. One pamphlet, *Pope Booth: The Salvation Army A.D. 1950* (n.d.), imagined the world in that year if the Salvation Army continued to expand. "Pope Booth" now ruled even the British king. Pubs, concerts, and theaters were long ago outlawed, and all the publicans sent to the North Pole. All other denominations were suppressed, the ministers in hiding.[49] Balliol College, Oxford, was now a home for invalids, and St. Paul's Cathedral, a clothing depot. A man not dressed in Army garb "was immediately surrounded by a half-score of women rattling tambourines over his head, and screaming dreadful allusions to his sinful life, and declaring he was lost!"[50] The narrator went on to meet a group of men, mostly ministers, who told him William Booth had amassed such a fortune and such power that he and his successors were able to enforce this system. The men were plotting a second Reformation. The author ended with the warning that "dreams come true" and Christians should not mistake the Army for a benign organization.

The author of *The New Papacy* also regarded the Army as a real threat, declaring, "Almost in a decade we have seen a leader emerging from the darkest obscurity, moved by the best objects, no doubt, in the first instance, but elevated to a position as paramount and despotic and to a power over the lives and actions of his followers more absolute than those of the Pontiffs of Rome herself."[51] This writer warned that while Protestants feared Rome, "in our midst and right on our hearthstones there is a growing up power as absolute and dogmatic as that of the Papacy, whose object expressed by its actions, and not hidden . . . in the secret councils of its leaders, is like that of Rome, the destruction by absorption of every Christian denomination amongst us and the bringing [of] all into subjection [to] the heirs and successors of the Booths."[52]

The Salvation Army was not just compared with Rome but was more generally accused of having a foreign, un-English spirit. Cobbe complained that along with the Salvation Army came "the I-am-as-good-as-you-and-better sentiment which comes to us with every steamer from the Atlantic and which may unhappily shortly rise up amongst us like a bad gas out of the Channel Tunnel from Paris—[it] may be driven back by healthier breezes."[53] The Reverend Cunningham Geike worried that the Salvation Army might undermine England's "splendid national character," which he believed to be the best on earth. Formed over the ages by the Church of England, the national character could only be harmed by "the fantastic doings of Mr. Booth."[54]

Anti-Catholicism was widespread in nineteenth-century England. Long-held prejudices against Catholics were exaggerated in the second half of the century by the presence of Irish immigrants, the creation of a Roman Catholic hierarchy in England, and disputes within the Church of England over ritualism. Many believed with Cardinal Newman that "as English is the natural tongue, so Protestantism is the intellectual and moral language of the body politic."[55] The Protestant nature of the constitution that emerged in 1688 was said to give the British people their religious and civil freedoms. These rights were threatened by the politics of Roman Catholicism, which was thought to stand for absolutist monarchy and a primary allegiance to the Pope rather than to the state or monarch. Many believed that God's providence had allowed the British their imperial power so that they could spread their political institutions the world over.

The Salvation Army was associated with Roman Catholicism despite the obvious theological differences. William Booth was thought to enjoy absolute allegiance from all Salvationists, who were obliged to promise that they would "be a true solider of the Army 'til I die."[56] He held his position as General for life and would appoint his successor. This structure was thought to closely resemble that of the Roman Catholic church and the supreme authority of the Pope. Both were expansive movements that, it was thought, attracted converts at the expense of all other denominations and even individual liberty. Both were thought to address the senses and imagination, dealing in feeling and symbols not in a rational or intellectual faith. Roman Catholicism was often accused of childishness and of being fit only for the lower grades of civilization. The Salvation Army's critics made much the same accusation.[57]

Accusations of hoarding money linked the Salvation Army to anti-Catholic prejudice and also to anti-Semitism. The author of *The New Papacy* noted that the Salvation Army profited from the sale of the mandatory uniforms as well as of the quilts, teacups, and pocket handkerchiefs marked with the Salvation Army symbol. William Booth was accused, like the Pope, of using his position to obtain money. The Reverend Geike remarked that his leadership position carried with it "many advantages not exclusively spiritual."[58] Anti-Semitism was evident in this criticism and was often intertwined with the anti-Catholic message. Cartoons in comic magazines during the 1880s depicted Booth's features in a conventionally anti-Semitic manner. An 1882 cartoon in *Entr'acte* depicted William Booth with an exaggerated hooked nose, long beard, and wild eyes scooping up money and hoarding it in boxes. An 1892 *Punch* cartoon depicted William Booth with similar, exaggerated facial features and a demonic grin, with his arms outstretched, pulling on puppet strings attached to crowds of Salvationists.[59] Victorian images of Jews focused on facial features, a prominent nose, dark hair, penetrating eyes, or an apparent ability to haggle over prices and to acquire and lend money. William Booth's facial features evidently evoked "Jewishness" to many observers who then linked the wealth he supposedly controlled with the ethnic characteristics his face suggested.[60]

If religious life were associated with order, discipline, and allegiance to the state and constituted authority, then the Salvation Army had no place in the evangelization of the urban working class. Whether papal conspiracies or Jewish acquisitiveness was the charge, William Booth was accused of a foreign deceit that would threaten England's national character. Salvationist women usurped a place denied to them by the Bible and tradition. The sensational meetings did little to teach self-restraint to those whose excesses were regarded as the source of poverty and social disorder. The language of Salvationist preaching and hymns threatened the respect and dignity with which all things sacred were to be held. These critics cautioned all Christians to stand aloof from this growing movement. The dean of Carlisle asserted the Army's teachings led to "the subversion of the social system and [tended] directly to the uprooting of every Christian church."[61]

These critics made known their strenuous objections to the Salvation Army in print and from pulpits, making use of well-established and dignified means to make their fears known. Meanwhile, in the streets, young men, alone and in gangs, indulged in time-honored ways to rid a neighborhood of a nuisance. They threw bricks at Salvationists, mewed like cats when they sang, poured beer over their heads, and attacked the preachers. Although the street gangs that attacked Salvationists were not likely to read the oppositional pamphlets or newspapers, they nevertheless expressed some of the same criticisms. At times, street gangs, magistrates, local governments, and middle-class inhabitants of the towns invaded by the Salvation Army worked in an informal and unintentional alliance.

NEIGHBORHOOD OPPOSITION

From the earliest years, the Christian Mission met with opposition. Converts were taunted at home, at work, and in the streets. When John Allen was converted, his whole family was incredulous. His sister thought it would not last, but when it did, she ceased to see him. His wife "professed to be converted about a fortnight after him; but she soon fell back into sin, and remained for years a foe within his own household, testing to no small degree his courage and patience."[62] One Whitechapel worker prayed, "Lord thou knowest everyone is against me—my family, my shopmates, my wife and the devil; but thou art more than all that can be against me."[63] A Shoreditch man was pelted with boots by the other residents of his house when he kneeled to pray.[64] Work mates and employers were also likely to ridicule the converted. One convert testified, "I do feel so happy now . . . though my mates get round me and make a game of me, and sometimes they pelt me when I'm at work, and call me a "ranter," yet I don't mean to give it up."[65] Domestic servants were particularly vulnerable to their employers, who expected their own standards of social behavior and dress to be upheld. An 1882 *War Cry* article reported that a young woman was dismissed from her position for wearing a "Hallelujah bonnet" and an "S" on her collar.[66]

The opposition that Christian Mission and Salvation Army evangelists most frequently described and struggled with came from groups in the streets, large and small, organized and spontaneous. Young men poured beer on the Salvationists as they preached, pelted them with rotting vegetables, and fought with their fists and their words to keep the Salvationists away. This kind of opposition was primarily, though not

exclusively, working class. An 1880 letter to the *Christian* from Charlotte Mason, a resident of the West End, described one evening at the
Marylebone corps under Captain Eliza Haynes, "Happy Eliza." The
"well-dressed rabble that crowded into the hall . . . commenced talking
in loud tones, shrieking, laughing, whistling, and in fact, doing everything to disturb the meeting." These were not, she noted, "roughs" but
"young men and women, such as will probably be demurely sitting in
churches and chapels on Sunday, or in halls, 'piously' singing, 'We are
the holy flock of God.'" This kind of ridicule was usually short-lived and
likely to bring considerable sympathy to the Salvation Army.[67]

Most of the street frays carried out by working-class women and men
centered on drink. The public house was the critical site of evangelizing
and of the defense of the culture of drinking and conviviality. The Salvation Army believed drink made men brutal, prone to fly into rages, to
beat their wives, and to give all their wages to the publican. In order to
save drunkards, open-air services were held in front of breweries, theaters, and above all pubs. Elijah Cadman described the effect his preaching had at a public house in Hackney. "They threw two paper bags of
flour at us, which made us black and white, and then brought beer, the
potboy putting this to a brother's mouth, but he pushed them away."[68]
At Bethnal Green an open-air service was disturbed by "women from
upstairs windows hurling publicans cans on the heads of the Lord's
people; children screaming, men and women yelling, altogether creating
such a scene as will not soon be forgotten."[69] In Whitechapel in 1884,
a captain who called herself Deborah gathered a group in front of a public house called the Blind Beggar. They sang a hymn, but when the publican realized she would also preach, he told them to move on. "We were
delighted to find his efforts brought us a larger crowd than we should
otherwise have had and we did our best to make them see how drink
and the devil were deluding them."[70]

The police frequently moved the mission workers on, often at the request of businesses that objected to the loud, boisterous crowds that gathered. When two Christian Mission preachers refused to leave Three Colt
Lane, police took them to the station and charged them with obstruction. They distributed tracts to all the policemen and prayed aloud until their release. In court, a publican himself strengthened their resolve
to carry on. The *Christian Mission Magazine* reported that he had told
them "he hated drunkenness as much as we did, but it was unpleasant
to have such hard things said against his trade *when he had so much
money invested in it.*"[71] The Mission workers were released with a prom-

ise that they would not obstruct the street again for six months. In 1880, two London Salvationists preaching in the street were arrested and charged with causing a disturbance and insanity.[72] These struggles persisted into the 1890s in many locales.[73]

Such opposition was neither intense nor threatening to the movement; in fact it was often seen as a wonderful means to bring in new converts. When the Female Pioneer Band preached at Bethnal Green, two young women "rushed up with something in their hands to throw at the speaker; but the Spirit of God met them, and looking in the face of one of the Sisters, they burst into tears, and running into our hall, threw themselves at the feet of Jesus."[74] Similarly, in 1877 a policeman roughly forced Elijah Cadman to move. That policeman was soon found speaking at the Mission hall.[75] These conversions were especially prized. Such people would not come because they believed, but when they came to disrupt, they heard the message anyway. One young man told the Whitechapel corps, "For weeks I persecuted the people of God. About fourteen of us used to come on purpose to upset the services, but God upset me."[76] Opposition could be part of God's plan if it provided opportunities for salvation. As one mission worker declared when a bag full of gunpowder was tossed at him, "Our number will increase for we have the devil on the spot and people will run to see the Devil when they won't stop to hear the truth."[77]

MARTYRDOM

Jesus said, "Blessed are ye when men shall revile you, and persecute you, and shall say all manner of evil against you falsely for my sake; Rejoice and be exceedingly glad: for great shall be your reward in heaven; for so persecuted they the prophets who were before you" (Matt. 5:11–12). Salvationists interpreted this passage as a guide to action. Many embraced persecution as a means to strengthen and bear witness to their faith. Captain Emily Carpenter wrote to headquarters to reassure everyone that despite the alarming press reports about a recent riot she had received only a black eye and some kicks.[78] When Captain Barrett was jailed for obstruction at Wigston, he kept a diary of his prison experience. He began with "Blessed are they which are persecuted for righteousness sake for theirs is the kingdom of heaven." He quoted passages from the Acts of the Apostles about Paul's persecution of the Christians, his conversion, and his subsequent imprisonment. Barrett reflected on the Jewish captivity in Egypt and on David, who had prevailed against a seemingly stronger enemy. Scattered among these reflections were Barrett's comments on the poor food, the difficult work of picking oakum, and the hard boards that made his bed.[79] When Alfred Tutte was imprisoned in 1887, he recorded in his diary that he felt "despondent and downcast" until he prayed. "I told . . . the Lord that he was able to make brown bread and skilly as sweet and pleasant as roast duck and green peas, and He satisfied my soul and body. I revelled in God's love and felt willing to suffer for any extent for Him."[80]

In June 1885, Lieutenant Annie Bell was imprisoned in York Castle, and her experiences exemplify the many meanings and uses of persecution for Salvationists. She was fined 20 shillings and costs for singing in the public marketplace of York. "This libel on English justice she rightly refused to endorse," the *War Cry* reported, and she chose to go to prison rather than pay the fine.[81] The constable pointed out to her that a Christian magistrate had sentenced her, and she asked, "Was it not the same sort of Christians that got Jesus Christ crucified?" She was brought to prison and all her clothing and possessions were taken from her. She was told to bathe but not given any means to dry her hair. She was dressed in thin prison garb so ragged she did not know how to get into it until some other prisoners helped her. The doctor accused her of being drunk the night before. The chaplain told her the Salvation Army was a mockery of religion and assured her that he knew she had pinned her summons on her breast and had ridden around the market on horseback. Her hair would not dry in her damp and chilly cell, and she was given nothing but bread and skilly to eat. She remained her in her cell and was put to work at sewing. She was released when the bishop of Durham paid her fine. He was reported to have said that while he deplored the Salvation Army's excesses, he admired its "magnificent enthusiasm."[82] A letter to the *War Cry* commented,

> Just think of the treatment of this harmless girl by the magistrate, the parson, and the policeman. Satan tried to have Daniel devoured by the lions, and his companions burnt because they stood firm for God, and this is the offence of Annie Bell. If magistrates are right in these cases then Jesus must have been wrong, when He told His disciples to go into the streets and lanes of the city, and to the highways and hedges to compel the people to come in. If The Salvation Army had the spiritual control of our prisons, there would be little need of magistrates, parsons, and policemen such as these.[83]

Bell's time in jail allowed her to exemplify the virtues of patience in suffering and devotion to evangelizing the lost whatever the cost to herself. Salvationists relished the opportunity to demonstrate their righteousness in comparison with the magistrate's injustice and the clergyman's insults. They considered evangelizing to be a pressing duty that was long ago abandoned by other Christians concerned only with their own comforts. The Army's willingness to compare its officers with biblical prophets and martyrs offended the magistrates and clergy. But for Salvationists persecution demonstrated their effectiveness and offered them the opportunity to strengthen their faith. As Salvationists described sin primarily in bodily terms, bodily self-sacrifice was regarded as an especially valued way to demonstrate faith. In 1888, the *War Cry* described getting pelted and hit as a "rare privilege."[84] It is not surprising that urban working-class women and men, who would inevitably know hard labor, violence, and want of food or shelter, would embrace such experiences as redemptive means to transform their communities.

ORGANIZING THE OPPOSITION

Opposition to the Salvation Army after 1880 was more organized and politically charged than the informal, episodic opposition of the first fifteen years of the Army's work. The Army had entered a period of extensive growth. New corps opened, the number of officers and soldiers grew substantially, the Army became more prominent and visible in the streets, and its military character made it distinctive. Public notoriety accompanied this success. The extensive press coverage and pamphlet literature targeted the Army's theology and methods. By the early 1880s, caricatures of the Booths and Salvation Army officers appeared in comic magazines with a large working-class readership, like *Fun, Moonshine,* and *Alley Sloper's Half-Holiday.*[85] Salvationists became stock figures in music halls. As the Army became more recognized and singular, opposition to its work became more focused, organized, and widespread both in the streets and in the courts.

Local opposition to the Salvation Army was a part of a wider neighborhood life. Salvationists worked in communities where disruption and fights were commonplace. Domestic violence permeated working-class family life, and disputes between work mates and neighbors often ended with fist fights. Street fights between rival gangs "provided a systematic means for young men to prove themselves against their peers, and affrays were invested with great significance by the participants."[86] The Salvation Army worked within this culture of public fighting. An evangelist reported in a Christian Mission newspaper in 1869 on the work in Ratcliffe Highway, London.

Much opposition has been encountered; at first, the persecutors contented themselves with ridiculing and mutilating the tracts that they were given, tearing them into shreds and throwing them over the speaker. . . . On Sunday the twenty-first, a meeting was again held. . . . When Brother Rose was speaking, about one hundred Irish fell upon them; one young man, very well dressed, seized him up, another struck him with a heavy blow on the cheek, and the whole party were being much knocked about when four policemen came and compelled the preachers to desist.[87]

A music-hall song described a similar scene.

To see a perfect Pantomime, I'll tell you where to go,
Just ramble round our quarter when the lights are getting low;
The p'lice dare not go down there, so we fairly have our fling,
You bet your boots we're up to snuff, and up to anything!

The Army of salvation came to save our souls one day,
They were not many minutes there before there was a row;
And when the row was over at the length the only things we found,
Was a cap, some whiskers and three legs were laid upon the ground.[88]

All this opposition might suggest that Salvationists were despised outsiders whose presence was resisted by drunken crowds and police alike. Gareth Stedman Jones argues in an influential article that while "Salvationists paraded up and down the main streets" of every poor borough in London by the turn of the century, it was nevertheless "inescapably clear that middle-class evangelism had failed to recreate a working class in its own image."[89] Victor Bailey has likewise argued that "opposition to the Salvation Army included . . . the so-called 'rough' working-class who were determined to defend their entertainments and who were hostile to the self-righteous cult of respectability."[90]

But these disputes were not a simple question of unctuous outsiders imposing their values on lively working-class neighborhoods. The disputes between Salvationists and the larger community were very much part of urban street life. In the dispute in Ratcliffe Highway, for example, the Irish were no doubt defending their faith as well as their street. Others defended the pubs and music halls that many Salvationists themselves had once frequented. Even if the Army typically described its opponents as sinful, degraded, and heathen, Salvationists and "heathens" alike were drawn from the same occupations, streets, and even families. To many observers, there was little to distinguish Salvationists from the gangs that attacked them.

The Army's moral rectitude and religious ecstasy created complicated relationships to neighborhoods, police, and local government. William Booth insisted that Salvationists obey the law, but when police and local authorities attempted to stop their street preaching and processions, they resisted and indeed courted opposition. William Booth declaimed in 1872, "Ours is an extraordinary work and therefore we try to accomplish it with extraordinary means. . . . The greatest curse on the church here is respectability. It sits like a nightmare on every branch of it, crippling all its energies, compressing its vitality, and shutting the Holy Ghost out of it."[91] It was not clear to clergy, local authorities, or the press that the Salvation Army would bring Christianity to the "heathen masses," but everyone agreed it bred rowdyism and disorder.

The neighborhood opposition to the Salvation Army had two consequences. On the one hand, an unintentional alliance of middle-class property owners, local authorities, and the street gangs emerged. While no party sought this alliance, it appeared to be perfectly obvious and effective from the perspective of the Salvationists. On the other hand, these odd alliances enabled the Army to use the diversity of the opposition to vigorously assert its place in working-class neighborhoods. The Army argued for its rights against a repressive church and state. When Salvationists stood as champions of laboring people, they assumed a place in the long tradition of plebeian, Nonconformist egalitarianism.[92]

In a number of locales, young men formed "Skeleton Armies" to pursue Salvation Army processions; they mocked and often attacked the Salvationists. By 1882, Skeletons in some towns had adopted uniforms and flags. Commissioner George Scott Railton remembered that the term *Skeleton Army* was first used in Weston super Mare in 1881.[93] It soon became the general term for the opposition. The precise origin of the term is obscure. Bailey argues that the name was "derived from groups like the 'Skull and Crossbone Boys,' organisations which celebrated Guy Fawkes' night."[94] Obviously, it was a play on the name Salvation Army, which had been adopted in 1879. The name *Skeleton* can be read as a multiple parody. It ridiculed the Salvationists' concern with life after death and the other-worldly austerity the Salvationists practiced. It may also have alluded to the frequent accusation that the Booths bilked money from their followers to enrich themselves and left their impoverished followers to starve. The Army was the Skeletons' particular target. Other missionary societies, like the Christian Community, the Open-Air Mission Society, and the London City Mission, instructed their brethren to go quietly among the people and to avoid arousing a commotion in order to win the trust and confidence of the unredeemed. Occasionally, these evangelists did meet with ridicule or opposition, but they did not count it in their favor.[95] Salvationists expected to rouse the devil and infuriate sinners.

The Skeleton Armies were not random; they staged theaters of opposition that echoed the Salvation Army's language and style. Skeletons attacked the elements that most strongly identified the Salvationists and distinguished them from other Christians: their hats and uniforms. They destroyed the objects that marked out Salvationists: the flags and musical instruments. In Rugby, opponents entered the barracks, stole the flag, cut it up, and distributed the pieces.[96] The attacks, moreover, took place especially when Salvationists were preaching and marching. In Hastings, Captain Beaty was kicked so violently she was bedridden for weeks. Her death a few years later was said to be caused by the internal injuries she sustained.[97]

The violence was not directed so much at windows or pews because Salvationists did not confine themselves to their buildings. To smash the drum was to challenge the Army's vaunted success in transforming the culture of the working class. To steal the caps and tear the uniforms denigrated the status of the Salvationists and ridiculed their claims to righteousness. Furthermore, such violence defied the Salvationists' claim to special protection. When men crowded into the Chelsea hall in 1887, they spat, sang, drank, smoked, and swore. When they emerged intact and unchanged, they thereby legitimated their own behavior and flaunted the weakness of the Army's position.[98]

At the same time, these riotous disputes were a defense of public space and institutions against the reclamation efforts of the Salvationists. Yet it was the Salvationists' utter lack of respectability and unseemly religious practices that their working-class opponents most frequently ridiculed.[99] In Honiton opponents of the Army published a newspaper, the *Skeleton,* and the few surviving issues offer a glimpse of the opposition.[100] The December 16, 1882, edition commented on a *War Cry* article about a captain who suffered a wounded head and disabled arm after a skirmish in the street.

> If this is a specimen of the "religion" and of the "Captains" who furnish reports for the *War Cry* save us from their intercession. What can respectable people think of a man of this type, who talks about "out flanking the devil," "you're all going to 'ell" and in the same breath mutters "Praise the Lord" or "Hallelujah" with an expression on his face that would lead one to suppose that butter would not melt in his mouth? What can we designate such proceedings but a rotten stinking hypocrisy.

The newspaper described a music-hall clog dancer who "enlightened the wicked 'unsaved' ones before him by saying he used to clog dance to such as them, but in future, he'd clog dance to Jesus!" The writer proclaimed, "If our Redeemer were to descend now there would be a greater clearance than the occasion on which He cast out the Buyers and Sellers from the Temple."[101] *The Skeleton* also insisted that the Salvationists often assaulted their opponents. Though "they said they would save us from Old Nick and sin," it soon became clear "all they liked most was females and money."[102] The paper also contained vulgar jokes about the Army, acrostics in the style favored by the *War Cry,* and damaging stories about Salvationists drawn from other papers. The charges of hypocrisy, immorality, and corruption were standard features of anticlericalism, but clearly these writers were neither anti-Christian nor secular. They did not regard the Salvationists as a body of respectable Christians bent on saving souls but as loud, boisterous, self-serving hypocrites.

The Army invariably countered that this opposition was instigated and supported by publicans and brewers.[103] In 1874, it stated, "Drunken men are instigated, and bribed with liquor, to annoy and if possible break up our meetings."[104] Bramwell Booth, chief of staff, complained to the Home Secretary in 1881,

> In nearly every town where there has been any opposition we have been able to trace it more or less, to the direct instigation, and often the leadership of either individual Brewers and Publicans, or their employees.
> The plan adopted is by treating and otherwise inciting gangs of roughs . . . to hustle and pelt, and mob the people.[105]

Although accounts in the *War Cry* and the local press suggest that publicans may have offered beer to men who would attack Salvationists, it is also clear that the opposition was diffuse and had no central organization. No doubt many who attacked Salvationists were drunk, but that was hardly an unusual state for many working-class men.[106]

The Army's claim, however, had rhetorical power whether or not the drink trade actually organized opposition to it. It suggested that the opposition was orchestrated by corrupt business interests and that the violence was carried out by men blinded and duped by drink. The opposition was therefore not an expression of local interests or of reasoned objection but was merely self-interest of the basest kind. This claim made the opposition seemingly extraneous to local communities, acting in its own interests against the material and spiritual needs of working-class neighborhoods. That rhetoric also resonated with radical and liberal opposition to the drink trade and made its assertions both intelligible and credible. It continued a long history of opposition by working-class Non-conformists whose temperance and frugality were part of a "logic of collective self-help."[107]

Opposition also arose from perceptions of the Salvation Army's work. In 1888 the Reverend W. Adamson, vicar of Old Ford, testified before the House of Lords Select Committee on the sweating system. He claimed that sweating was an old problem in many East London industries, but it was made worse by the Salvation Army when it offered to make matches at a half pence per gross lower than the usual price. It was said to have also taken in laundry at a lower than usual cost. In a letter to the *Times,* Adamson claimed he had heard about this practice at a meeting of the COS, "from the curate, the scripture reader, and mission women, and from the poor women who worked on the boxes." He further asserted that when the Army offered to take in laundry for 4 pence per dozen, "the 'Skeleton Army' caused great excitement, and even groups of young women, angry at the supposed complicity of the Salvation Army with the reduction, were to be seen and heard in the streets."[108] The Salvation Army immediately appeared before the Committee and published a denial in the *Times,* pointing out that it had never taken in laundry or made matches at any price.[109] It is difficult to determine whether such perceptions of the Salvation Army were as widespread as Adamson claimed, but his claim did receive extensive coverage in the *Times,* and it may well have contributed to the mistrust of the Army.

The particularities of the opposition to the Salvation Army created some rather unusual, though short-lived and unintentional, alliances, which Salvationists used to great advantage. As the attacks on Salvationists increased and intensified in towns and cities across Britain, middle-class Christians became increasingly alarmed by this dynamic organization. While clergymen and magistrates despised the unruly crowds that attacked Salvationists, the Army was often regarded as the more serious threat to public order. The pamphlet writers became aware of the Salvation Army in part because of the neighborhood opposition to it. A letter from "Common Sense" to the editor of the *Torquay Directory and South Devon Journal* argued that the Army's religious practice was hardly Christian. "I have never understood why, if they are right, we should not have some Sunday an Indian Fakir with a tom-tom or some dancing dervishes performing on the Strand, they would doubtless do good by alluring idlers from the public houses and as to religion, the Fakir would most probably consider himself far in advance of the Salvationist."[110]

Working-class youth gangs were unlikely to derive their ideas from these pamphlets. Still, the combination of working-class opposition and published criticism of the Army increased both the attention given to the Salvation Army's work and the perceived threat it presented to good order. The police and magistrates frequently acted on their conviction that the Salvationists were the cause of the disturbances. During the 1888 Torquay disturbances, a magistrate accused the Salvation Army of being little more than a money-making concern.[111]

At times, the police simply ignored the disturbances, as this report from Stoke Newington, published in *The Daily Telegraph* in 1881, attested.

> Yesterday morning . . . the bands issued forth in the afternoon. . . . The largest marched to the Shakespeare. . . . Here the division of about 20 persons, male and female, began to sing but before the end of the first verse a crowd of roughs had gathered round and began a counter chant. At the third verse someone issued forth from the tavern with a can of beer in his hand, and making use of a foul expression, offered it to the Salvationists. This was a signal for a general riot and in a few moments the members of the Army were attacked, knocked down, and shamefully used. Acting under the orders of their captain, the band gave no blow in return but avoiding their brutal assailants as best they could, covered the retreat of the women. There were over five hundred persons present, but not a single hand was raised in defence of the band. . . . One young girl yesterday was seriously injured, two of the men were much hurt, and nearly every member of the band had been robbed of some article of property. All of this took place within a stone's throw of two large police stations.[112]

Salvationists were frequently charged with obstruction, fined, or jailed. In Torquay and Eastbourne, the local governments enacted bylaws specifically aimed at forbidding the Salvation Army's musical processions on Sundays, and they persisted in enforcing them. Crowds justified the attacks on Salvationists because the Army was in fact breaking the law. The presence of the police at Army processions only highlighted the tensions Salvationists created when they boldly defied the laws and were attacked by boisterous and drunken crowds.[113]

THE EASTBOURNE DISTURBANCES

The implications of the informal and unintentional alliances that emerged among street crowds, clergy, police, and local governments were especially clear in Eastbourne, where a corps opened in 1890. Eastbourne was a well-established, respectable seaside town in Sussex. Its climate was said to be the healthiest in England. Its first pier was built in 1866, and its population grew from 5,795 in 1861 to over 10,000 in 1871. The railway opened the town to many others who came on cheap excursion fares. It had the reputation for being more respectable than many resorts, even genteel. Like other seaside towns, including Brighton, Blackpool, and Southend, Eastbourne was host to a "massive growth in leisure facilities, much of it the work of energetic financiers and entrepreneurs. . . . Theatres, music halls, pleasure gardens, penny-in-the-slot machines, zoos and musical facilities of all kinds sprang up in the resorts."[114] The combination of commercial leisure, substantial crowds, and a lively street culture made Eastbourne an ideal spot for Salvationist evangelizing.

But as soon as the Army arrived, town residents started to complain. The Eastbourne ratepayers complained to the Watch Committee that the Army's "assemblies diminish the trading value of our properties and those of us who let lodgings find it detrimental to the letting of apartments and the comfort of visitors."[115] They urged the Watch Committee and Borough Council to enforce the by-law prohibiting Sunday processions. The local government and ratepayers objected strenuously to the expense of hiring additional police to protect all involved when the law clearly forbade the processions. The Army persisted. In June 1891, the Watch Committee reported "there was considerable hustling, pushing and shouting and the Police had difficulty getting the Army into their barracks. The disturbances were made very much worse by the Salvationists themselves and a number of others who [were] attending for the purpose of defending them." Fourteen Salvationists, ten men and four women, were charged with disturbing the peace and fined £5 each. Two were jailed.[116]

In August 1891 at Eastbourne, one man kicked a Salvationist drum and tried to put his head through it, while another man took a tambourine from a Lass and struck her with it.[117] Women were singled out for particular treatment.

> [Men] would deliberately walk up to a woman in the streets and pour a torrent of foul obscenities into her ear. . . . Miss Edith Maynard says, "The language used by the men to myself and the other women has been of the vilest character. . . . You have only to be known as a Salvationist in Eastbourne to have the filthiest language used to you. Whether in uniform or not, or whether in the marches or going about town on business, it makes no difference."[118]

Soon, street processions culminated in near riots. In September 1891 a group "endeavoured to take the instruments and capture the banner. Three or four caps were taken from the Salvationists and thrown down the beach. The flagstaff was broken and the larger half went in the same direction." Later that same day and again in the evening, the Salvation-

ists marched, and more struggles ensued.[119] On another occasion, the
police asked the Salvationists to disperse, but they instead fell to their
knees and began to pray. "The crowd then made a rush at them, and . . .
not having sufficient strength of Police present, and seeing the danger of
them being swept into the sea, four mounted men went into the crowd
and separated the people from the Salvationists."[120] During the worst
period, upward of a thousand people crowded the streets to participate
in and encourage the frays.

The crowds who attacked the Army were like many Salvationist men
with respect to age and occupation. They were typically working men,
bricklayers or grocers' assistants or those in more marginal positions such
as flower hawkers or costermongers. Their ages ranged from the mid-
teens to the early thirties. Thus each side could easily recognize the other,
and they might well have known each other from work or the neighborhood.[121] These street fighters resembled the "scuttlers" of Manchester and Salford, who formed neighborhood-based street gangs to resist
"incursions upon their own territory in order to defend their honour."
These "theatres of hostility" displayed a "conception of manliness . . .
centred on toughness." This status was derived from both displays of
fighting prowess and the "capacity to drink heavily."[122] The attacks on
Salvationists were, in part, one of many contests between rival models
of gender. Skeleton gangs were intent on humiliating teetotal Salvationist men and assertive Salvationist women.[123]

In contrast, the Eastbourne ratepayers were propertied, lower-middle-class and middle-class people, including a coal merchant, a dental
surgeon, and a greengrocer. The residents who complained of the uproar
the Army caused in the streets included a tea dealer, a glass and china
dealer, a paperhanger and an undertaker.[124] These inhabitants of Eastbourne desired no alliance with the crowds of young laboring men who
attacked the Salvationists. They confined their complaints to letters and
petitions to the local government and the press. But their actions still
worked in concert with those of working-class youths to intensify opposition to the Army and strengthen the resolve of the local government
to continue fining and jailing Salvationists who broke the by-law.[125]

Just as important, the combined opposition of ratepayers and youth
gangs provided the Salvation Army with a way to interpret the opposition to their evangelism and to resist it. In a September 1891 letter to the
Times, the mayor of Eastbourne declared that "the magistrates, and the
Town Council have done, and are doing, and will continue to do, their
duty in endeavouring to maintain law and order and to prevent distur-

bances of the peace, and it is surely not too much to ask the Salvation Army to refrain from breaking the law." Bramwell Booth responded four days later. He complained,

> [The mayor had nothing to say about] the thieves and rowdies, the prize fighters and boozers who have been allowed to gather together Sunday after Sunday, primed with liquor for the attack on inoffensive women and men, who are known never to return a blow, and who may, therefore, be struck by any coward. . . . It is admitted our people have suffered the spoiling of their goods, that their clothes have been torn off their backs in the open streets, and they have been mobbed, and hooted, and stoned, and carried fainting from scenes that would have disgraced Magdala or Coomassie.

The *Times* commented that the Salvationists, "these disorderly champions of order," had only themselves to blame if their "liberty . . . has been restrained," for the fines and imprisonments are the "very proper penalties they have incurred as lawbreakers."[126]

The Army's rhetoric fused some of the language and symbols employed by working-class radicals and plebeian Nonconformists of an earlier generation with the particular concerns of Salvationists. Salvationists responded to ratepayers' petitions and attacks in the streets by proclaiming that they were the champions of the people, engaged in hand-to-hand combat with a repressive state, a corrupt church, and the vicious drink trade, which enslaved working people. The crowds were, Salvationists argued, not a genuine part of the neighborhood but rather deluded men lured by publicans into acting on behalf of a corrupt world.

Like the supporters of the Tichbourne Claimant, who protested against an unjust legal system, Salvationists called for "fair play."[127] "The magistrate on the bench . . . becomes a convenient agent between the priest in his cassock, the worldling with his big gold chain, and the jailer with his keys[,] and persecution, skulking under the aegis of prosecution, points with pious pride to its veneration for the maintenance of the Law, the preservation of the Church, the stability of the throne and the honor of God."[128] Salvationists linked the persecution they suffered to the persecution of Protestants under Mary Stuart, the slanders and harassment experienced by early Quakers, and the struggles of Evangelicals who protested against slavery, thereby placing themselves in a long tradition of struggle for religious and political liberty. They complained bitterly that Salvationists could not get a fair hearing in court. As Bramwell Booth, the chief of staff, proclaimed in an 1890 *War Cry* article on Eastbourne,

> The attitude of the persecutors in this trial is well-known; they have not hesitated at any cruelty they could inflict, or any indignity they could impose

upon the weak and inoffensive men and women of a country village who have
come before them for conscience's sake. . . . The power of our opponents is
also a matter for serious contemplation. They have all the favour of wealth
at their back. . . . They have the advantage of being able to fight with the
people's money—an increase in the local rates being always a most handy
way of paying costs! . . . We are poor! Our opponents know it. . . . They
thought they could crush us by bringing wealth and influence to bear against
poverty and simplicity.[129]

They complained Salvationists were jailed for obstruction and disorderly
conduct on little evidence, while the drunken, riotous crowds were ignored or encouraged.

When the Army finally succeeded in overturning the laws that restricted their rights to march and evangelize on Sundays, they celebrated
with grand processions, banners, and music that displayed their rightful
place in the public thoroughfares. When Salvationists gathered in 1888
to celebrate John Roberts's release from a Torquay jail, they held aloft
a banner that depicted a Salvationist in prison garb slaying a vulture.
Next to him stood Liberty, holding a Bible and wearing a cap of liberty.
Five brass bands marched through the streets to a hall where the local
paper reported over a thousand people gathered to greet Roberts.[130] Their
caps of liberty and colorful banners celebrating justice and liberty would
have been instantly recognizable to a whole range of nineteenth-century
radicals. Salvationists thus insisted on their place in a long history of religious radicalism that very much made them a part of these communities, however marginal and despised they might have been.

Hugh McLeod has argued that the most distinctive feature of nineteenth-
century, urban religious life was conflict between rival sects and between
believers and nonbelievers.[131] From that perspective, the Salvation Army
can be seen as a significant example of a movement formed expressly to
oppose the staid complacency of other Christians and of nonbelievers.
The Army regarded leisure pursuits as its principal rivals, while its ability to use leisure institutions as its inspiration was a major facet in its
success. Equally important was Salvationists' ability to mine an older
Nonconformist radicalism; by doing so they were able to express their
spiritual vision, respond to their opponents, and link themselves to that
older tradition.

The resistance to the Salvation Army cut across class and denominational lines. Middle-class Christians despaired over the possible impact of Salvationist women and men in the communities where they

opened fire. The Salvationists and the Skeletons each tried to dominate working-class neighborhood life and to assert the authority to interpret it. Skeletons did not object to Salvationists simply because they were religious but because they were disreputable and blasphemous. Salvationists were also to be despised because they challenged widely accepted notions of masculinity. To cover Salvationists in beer and chase them away from the pub was a way to assert disdain for Salvationist masculinity as well as the right to dominate the neighborhood. The combined force of all its opponents worked to contain the Salvation Army and to offer Salvationists a way to resist and interpret their critics. Thus, working-class religiosity was woven into larger struggles over gender, popular leisure, and neighborhood life. The relationships among religiosity, respectability, and class cultures were fluid and contested.

Far too often, religion is relegated to what happens in church and politics to what happens in trade unions or parties, and thus the diverse and contested nature of working-class religion, politics, and culture is diminished. Church attendance has too often been the measure of religiosity, and the Victorian middle class has been seen as the possessors of whatever religious life can be discerned.[132] But, as Thomas Wright wrote in 1873, workers' "common sense tells them that to make church-going the be-all and end-all, as a text of religion, is to confound religion with one of its most mechanical sides."[133] If instead we consider alternatives such as belief, the formation of political analysis, attitudes toward power, ideas about rights and liberty, and, as the Salvationists would insist, a personal experience, then religion's influence can be discerned in a new light. While it is clear that the Salvation Army did not succeed in converting the working class as a whole, it is also clear their efforts sparked conflict within working-class neighborhoods and with other Christians, a conflict that reveals how much evangelizing the "heathen masses" mattered to all concerned.

Postscript

The Legacy of the Salvation Army

The year 1890 was a turning point for the Salvation Army. Its leadership changed, and it launched a social services wing that would divide the organization in two and soon dominate the public perception of the Salvation Army. On October 4, 1890, Catherine Booth died. Fifty thousand people filed past her coffin, and thirty thousand people lined the streets of London to watch her funeral procession wind toward Abney Park cemetery. She was eulogized in the national press, and the *Bible Christian Magazine* hailed her as "the most famous and influential Christian woman of the generation."[1] The Salvation Army had lost one of its most important theologians and preachers; as an example of female leadership and authority, she had inspired thousands of Salvationist women. William Booth lost his evangelical partner. He began to withdraw from much of the daily work of overseeing the Army. He traveled to Canada, Australia, South Africa, and the United States to see the Salvation Army in action. In his later years, he was limited by ill health and fatigue to more ceremonial than organizational responsibilities.

William Booth remained general of the Salvation Army until his death on October 20, 1912. But by the 1890s the responsibility of overseeing the work at International Headquarters fell to Bramwell Booth, chief of staff, and a small circle of senior staff. The Booth children chafed against the autocratic leadership of their brother, complaining about decisions they might have accepted from their father but not from Bramwell. Ballington and Maud Booth resigned their commissions in

1896 over disputes about their leadership in the United States and the degree of control exercised by Bramwell over a country he had never visited. They went on to found the Volunteers of America, a philanthropic organization.[2] Herbert had similar complaints about Bramwell's leadership; he and his wife resigned in 1902 after several successful years in Australia. He began work as an independent preacher in the United States, Canada, and England.[3] Katie and her husband, Arthur Booth-Clibborn, resigned in 1902. They had disputed Bramwell's decision to send them to Holland in 1896 and had differences with Salvation Army doctrines concerning pacifism and faith healing. The Booth-Clibborns spent a few months residing at a community called Zion, near Chicago, led by an evangelist who claimed to be the second coming of the prophet Elijah. They later returned to England with their ten children, and Katie began a career as an independent evangelist that was to last until her death in 1955.[4] Emma and her husband, Frederick Booth-Tucker, led the Salvation Army in the United States from 1896 to 1903. She was hailed as a great orator, and under their leadership the U.S. Army grew considerably. Emma died in an accident on the Topeka and Santa Fe Railway on October 28, 1903. Her husband remained with the Army until his death in 1929, and several of her children went on to hold prominent leadership positions in the Army.[5] Lucy Booth married a Swedish Army officer, Emanuel Daniel Hellberg, in 1894; the couple remained Salvation Army officers, although they received scant attention in the *War Cry* or in official Salvation Army histories.[6] Marian, who never enjoyed good health, took no active part in the Salvation Army. By 1903, only Evangeline and Bramwell continued to hold leading positions, and they too were to be divided by a dispute over his leadership in 1929.[7] Evangeline became general in 1934. A new generation of leaders had been created.[8]

The second important event of 1890 was the publication of William Booth's *In Darkest England and the Way Out*. England's "submerged tenth," its poorest citizens, was ignored by nearly everyone. Booth likened the cannibals and pygmies of Darkest Africa to these denizens of Darkest England.[9] England, he claimed, had sufficient wealth to end their misery, and he proposed to show the way. His solution would be "as wide as the scheme of Eternal Salvation as set forth in the gospel. . . . If the scheme . . . is not applicable to the Thief, the Harlot, the Drunkard, and the Sluggard, it may as well be dismissed without ceremony."[10] Existing programs, including those established by the Poor Law, charity, and trade unions, either were ineffective or helped too few. Booth proposed to es-

tablish City, Farm, and Overseas colonies. The City colonies would gather
together the destitute, provide for their immediate needs, and commence
with moral and spiritual rejuvenation. They would then proceed to the
Farm colonies, where their health would be recovered and their character reformed. From there they would be favorably placed to find employment at home or in the Overseas colony. In addition, Booth proposed
to extend the Army's cheap food depots and shelters. He also wanted to
expand the Army's industrial factory, where men trained as carpenters,
cobblers, and so forth. Here they would receive food and shelter until
they had sufficient skills to find regular work.

Little in *Darkest England* was wholly original in any sense. The book
emerged from "the fusion of ideas of the social-imperialist movement,
anxious to use the Empire to combat urban degeneration, and the 'social gospel' wing of Nonconformity, notably its emphasis on rural
panaceas."[11] Booth's notion that the countryside and farm work provided a healthful, invigorating change for the enervated urban worker
was common to many of his contemporaries. In 1888, for example,
Samuel Barnett proposed establishing a farm colony that would remove
the poor from overcrowded cities. Social imperialists proposed a variety
of schemes to reduce poverty through emigration, and Keir Hardie and
Annie Besant were both promoting the idea of country farm colonies as
a solution to urban unemployment. The work of Andrew Mearns and
George Sims provided much of the material on which Booth rested his
case.[12] Indeed, many who championed Booth's scheme believed it combined the best of Christianity, socialism, and political economy.[13]

The idea that Britain's "heathen masses" were a group apart, un-
touched by civilizing influences, echoed sentiments found in earlier Salvation Army publications. There were always two perspectives. On the
one hand, the *Christian Mission Magazine* and *War Cry* optimistically
addressed East End inhabitants as potential converts and described meetings led and attended by eager, serious working-class women and men.
On the other hand, these same publications often described East End inhabitants as scarcely human and thoroughly indifferent to the Army's
evangelizing. The *War Cry* of May 30, 1885, described a "midnight ramble around London." The writer saw "low-browed, fierce looking men
and women, with such faces as scarcely seem to belong to their sex, dirty
public houses, as full as they could be, old, grey-haired men tottering
both with age and drink. . . . Youths with dogged looks that told of the
prison barber, drunken labourers, vagrants, thieves, and vagabonds
passed and repassed me."[14] Another article borrowed its title—"Horri-

ble London"—from George Sims. "Creeping along under midnight lamps go a motley crowd of human beings, in an ill-starred crew who, as if born of the night, in the night find their support and pleasure; creatures whom the daylight shames and drives into their holes like rats of the baser sort."[15]

These descriptions capitalized on the unknown, savage nature of the slum dwellers. Their bodies were not gendered in the usual way. Their habits were foreign to both writer and reader. Although the Salvation Army had been active in the East End for twenty years, the *War Cry* acknowledged that many slum dwellers were unknown to them and often hostile, more like the inhabitants of the Salvation Army's foreign outposts than like other civilized Britons. Optimism persisted. In February 1887, the *War Cry* reported on the work of new "slum corps" at Borough, Walworth, and Rotherhithe. "Prejudice is being swept away and souls gloriously converted. . . . By faith we can see a great army rise out of the London slums."[16]

These reports, and indeed the existence of special slum corps, were designed to respond to the particular conditions in London. In the poorest districts of London, where workers were classed predominantly as unskilled or semiskilled, the economic depression of 1884–87 was devastating. The chronic housing shortage, the decline of older industries, and cyclical depression undermined the economic position of many laboring people. Especially after the Trafalgar Square riots of the unemployed in February 1886, it was clear that the dissatisfied, angry poor might pose a threat to middle-class society. Throughout 1886–87, the economic distress and the presence of small, vocal socialist and labor organizations, seemingly ready to mobilize the working class, struck fear in many a property owner's heart. The Salvation Army's work strived to meet both material and spiritual needs in order to diminish the distress that led to political disturbances.

In February 1886, just after the Trafalgar Square riots, William Booth, who rarely commented on politics, published an article on socialism. The article demonstrated both the Army's sense that socialism posed a real threat and the Army's desire to present itself as an alternative. London, Booth wrote, had an extraordinary concentration of wealthy and poor. Socialism was one solution to that inequality, but, he asserted, it remedied one wrong with another. No one ever willingly relinquished wealth; any attempt to redistribute resources would "disturb the very foundations on which society is built up." Moreover, it contradicted scripture, which promised rewards to the righteous and punishment for the wicked. Also, socialism "clashes with what is revealed to us in the condition of the eternal world. There are different grades and conditions there." He proposed instead "Salvation Socialism." Because sin caused vice, misery, and poverty, the solution was to make people good.[17]

Booth's notion that sin was the cause of misery and poverty was far from original. The Salvation Army's solution, however, was shaped by its evangelicalism and differed from the approach of the COS, which had dominated the discussion of charity and social welfare since the 1870s. The COS sought to divide the undeserving from the deserving poor. The undeserving would be given no assistance but the workhouse, where regularity and thrift would be forced on them. The deserving poor would be given charitable assistance that would foster self-reliance and virtue. In contrast, William Booth believed even the most thoroughly unregenerate individual could be transformed by the Holy Spirit and no one should be denied the spiritual and material care needed to effect conversion. The form that assistance might take was open to question, and throughout the 1880s and 1890s the Salvation Army's answer was refined continuously.

The Darkest England scheme extended and formalized elements already present in the Army's work.[18] During the preceding six years, the Army had already established rescue work, shelters, food depots, and other programs to relieve distress and to exert a religious influence on those believed to be too burdened to seek it on their own. From 1884, the Salvation Army slowly shaped a dual mission of evangelizing and social services. In 1884 a rescue home was opened in East London.[19] By 1888, a staff of seventy ran ten rescue homes housing 212 women.[20] In November 1884, the *War Cry* announced the establishment of slum outposts staffed by the women training-home cadets. The Lasses slept in a room in Seven Dials that was very like the other rooms in the neighborhood. They spent their days, "visiting from house to house, storey to storey, room to room, washing the little ones, scrubbing the rooms, nursing the sick, listening to the heart-rending tales of woe, taking God, salvation and hope to dark hearts."[21] They served the immediate, material needs of the poor while urging the people to consider their souls and come to a Salvation Army meeting. This Cellar, Garret and Gutter Brigade sought special donations of clothing, tracts, and money to continue its work. Also in 1884 the Salvation Army began to visit recently released prisoners and to help locate missing family members.

The Army fashioned its own response to both the match girls' strike of 1888 and the 1889 dock strike. After the match girls' strike, the Army set up a hygienic match factory that would not use the dangerous chemicals that caused "phossy jaw" and would pay 4 pence per gross instead of the usual 2 1/2 pence. The boxes were covered in slogans such as "Love Thy Neighbour" and "Our Work Is for God and Humanity." The matches were more expensive than any others, and soon only Salvationists, "members of other denominations, Co-Operatives, and Trade Unions" purchased them. The factory closed in 1894.[22] During the 1889 dock strike, the Salvation Army offered farthing meals to strikers and their families, serving up to seven thousand meals daily for the duration of the strike from its cheap food depot in West India Dock Road, Limehouse, established in 1886.[23] Ben Tillett, leader of the dock strike, later recalled that the Salvation Army was "destined to serve a very useful purpose of a commissariat character" during the strike.[24] The *War Cry* noted with satisfaction that the Army's efforts had greatly reduced distress and earned the gratitude of the trade unions.[25]

Although neither its goals nor its programs were derived from the socialists or the labor movement, the Salvation Army was "the beneficiary of an emerging working-class consciousness" that was also important to labor and socialist organizing.[26] E. P. Thompson described the 1880s as a "profoundly ambiguous moment when Salvationism ran in double harness with London Radicalism and the early labour movement."[27] These efforts prompted some within the labor movement to support the Darkest England scheme. Tillett was present when William Booth sought financial support for the scheme at an Exeter Hall meeting in November 1890. *Reynolds Newspaper*, a widely read working-class newspaper, the radical London daily the *Star*, and the *Labour World*, all came out in support of the scheme.[28] *Justice*, the Social Democratic Federation newspaper, and *Commonweal*, the Socialist League newspaper, did not support the scheme. Historian Victor Bailey argues that those in the socialist and labor movements to "whom socialism meant economic justice, greeted *Darkest England* as an important addition to the library of social reform."[29]

Although its ideas and programs were not unprecedented, *In Darkest England* proved to be a striking book.[30] It capitalized on the enormous public interest in Henry Morton Stanley's *In Darkest Africa* and, like much contemporary social criticism, racialized the very poor by linking them to the inhabitants of Britain's imperial conquests. The lurid frontispiece depicted Salvationists pulling drowning men and women from the raging sea of starvation and unemployment and leading them upward to the City, Farm, and Overseas colonies. Booth used clear and vivid examples. He stated, for example, that his goal was to bring the clothing, food, and shelter of everyone up to the standard of those provided to the London cab horse, a graphic comparison mentioned repeatedly by reviewers.[31] An outstanding fundraiser, William Booth was already well-placed to enact his plan. He was able to raise over £100,000 by January 30, 1891. The book went into its fifth printing by November 1891, and the considerable profits were invested in the scheme.[32] Salvation Army officers were ready to commence work. The Army already enjoyed a certain public prominence, which it capitalized on. Much of the proposal was never enacted, and other programs were soon abandoned. But in whatever respect the Darkest England scheme was successful, it drew on the Army's present strengths and on a range of contemporary ideas and schemes. Ultimately, it enhanced the Salvation Army's reputation.

But this new direction effected a great change and altered the Salvation Army's relationship to clergy, middle-class donors, journalists and social critics as well as the working-class women and men it hoped to convert. It brought Salvationists to the attention of those who previously had no particular reason to take notice of their activities. Trade unions charged the Salvation Army with sweating and undercutting union wage rates at its workshops. The Army responded that these workers were unskilled and untrained and were given the equivalent of union wages in the form of a bed and food in addition to their wages, but it did nothing to satisfy the unions.[33] However, the social wing, with its own commander and staff, slowly gained the respect and confidence of many government officials, social critics, and clergy. In 1910, Rider Haggard published an admiring book about the Army's social work, *Regeneration*. This book included statistics, interviews, and Haggard's own observations of the work. After two hundred pages describing the social services, he noted that the Army was a religious organization but "little has been said to me" about the Salvation Army's theology. In 1911, Beatrice and Sidney Webb, Fabian socialists and influential shapers of British public policy, published *The Prevention of Destitution* and included a lengthy, admiring discussion of the Army's Hadleigh Colony, where three hundred able-bodied men resided. The Webbs suggested that even if one disagreed with the Army's religious sentiments, its work was effective and carried out at a lower cost than the state's projects.[34]

Observers of the Salvation Army in the 1880s would not have been able to have taken so little note of its theology and religious practices because they permeated all aspects of its work. The observers in the 1890s looked at the Salvation Army's accomplishments in strictly practical terms, a perspective no observer a decade earlier had ever taken. Admiration for the Army's social services was widespread. During the 1909 debates regarding the Royal Commission on the Poor Law, some members of the government, social-imperialists, and the Fabian section of the labor movement considered offering state subsidies to the Salvation Army for its work with the unemployed. Although this proposal was never acted on, that it was even discussed demonstrates that the Salvation Army was regarded as a serious, efficient, and deserving agent of social reform ten years after it began its Darkest England scheme.[35]

In 1904, William Booth was received by King Edward VII, and he was granted an honorary doctorate from Oxford University in 1907.[36] During World War I, the Salvation Army equipped and staffed ambulances at the front and ran services for soldiers and officers. As biographer St. John Ervine has argued, until the establishment of the social services, William Booth was just "the leader of a noisy sect whose members were continually in trouble with the police at home and abroad."[37] Afterward, he became a celebrated man, well respected as the leader of a successful social service program.

The Salvation Army was no longer only a religious movement made up of the people it sought to save. Salvationists could regard some people as the recipients of social services even if they hesitated to accept its evangelical message. Middle-class Christians who might find the Army's services vulgar nevertheless willingly contributed to its social programs. Its officers now included trained social workers. New converts could not immediately be set to work in quite the way they were in the 1860s through the 1880s because more extensive education and training for this work came first. Corps captains continued to serve in the ways they always had, but the Salvation Army's public prominence was derived from its social services.

The culture and character of the Salvation Army as explored in the preceding chapters changed. The Salvation Army moved from being a sensational, revivalist sect at odds with the Church, police, and local governments to being a religious organization with a social service wing that was often the more prominent part and with strong ties to other Christian and state-run agencies. Some might see this change as the inevitable secularization of a religious movement as it is absorbed by a modern, urban society and abandons its former evangelical fervor to join a growing state-sponsored bureaucracy.[38] But any attempt to distinguish a short-lived "religious" period from the "social" or "political" aspects of the Salvation Army's mission misses its most dynamic and distinctive features.

The Salvation Army was among the first denominations to proclaim "women's right" to preach the gospel, and under its aegis thousands of working-class women assumed a spiritual authority that defied injunctions requiring female silence and submission. The Hallelujah Lasses stood in the streets, claiming spiritual authority for themselves while calling on others to repent. They drew on the urban working-class culture that surrounded them to create an evangelizing style that expressed their religious convictions. These convictions were not limited by institutional boundaries nor were they focused on the interpretation or creation of texts. Rather, they were expressed in words and through the body in dramatic conversions, sensational and physical preaching, and a willingness to withstand the opposition of street gangs and the indignity of jail. Salvationist women contributed to the Victorian social-purity movement and the expansion of women's employment, and they offered one model of reformed gender relations that addressed many of the conflicts that plagued working-class urban households. The Salvation Army's integration of aspects of Victorian feminism and evangelical Christianity introduced these ideas into new circles, bringing working-class women in particular into a wider women's movement. After the vote was won in 1918, many leading suffragists "went on to champion women's leadership in religious contexts," supporting women's ordination and preaching themselves.[39] The Hallelujah Lasses were pioneers in establishing an authoritative, public, religious voice for women.

Salvationist men, in turn, offered a masculine religiosity that stressed temperance, frugality, and discipline, all of which were at odds with pervasive notions of manliness. Salvationist men acquired military-style uniforms and titles but within a remarkably heterosocial organization that encouraged women and men to struggle against sin side by side. Salvationists revitalized older traditions of Nonconformist sobriety, plebeian righteousness and radicalism in a new, urban context. Enthusiastically borrowing from the repertoire of popular culture, they created a uniquely urban working-class religious movement. Salvationists' embrace of popular culture inspired other twentieth-century preachers, including Aimee Semple McPherson, and prefigured the work of evangelists like Billy Sunday.[40]

Salvationists' holiness theology offered one response to spiritual and material struggles in an idiom borrowed from working-class neighborhoods. This theology stressed an individual, bodily encounter with the

Holy Spirit that would transform the convert's very nature. A religion that did not make a convert shake, weep, and shout did not have the power to transform that person into a Christian, ready to do battle with sin. Its evangelical, holiness theology, dramatic bodily conversions, and the steadfast commitment to a strict behavioral code all link the Salvation Army to the Pentecostal movement of the early twentieth century. By the late twentieth century, Pentecostalism was the fastest growing branch of Christianity and included one in four Christians worldwide.[41] As an early example of this movement, the Salvation Army was part of one of the most significant developments in twentieth-century Christianity.

Notes

ABBREVIATIONS

BL   British Library, London
CMM   *Christian Mission Magazine*
ELE   *East London Evangelist*
WC   *The War Cry*
SAHC   Salvation Army Heritage Centre, London

INTRODUCTION

1. "Salvation Soldiers Live to Fight," sung to the tune of "Camptown Races"; words by Captain William Baugh, WC, 7 October 1882, 1.

2. The Salvation Army offers an interesting opportunity to investigate questions of class, religion, and imperialism. The imperial aspects of the Salvation Army's work, however, fall outside the bounds of this particular study, which is focused on working-class community and culture in Britain. I briefly consider the meaning of the Army's imperial mission to its working-class converts (see Chapter 6), but this aspect of its work certainly deserves further attention. On the Salvation Army and empire, see Rachel J. Tolen, "Colonizing and Transforming the Criminal Tribesmen: The Salvation Army in British India," *American Ethnologist* 18, no. 1 (February 1991): 106–25. Jeffrey Cox is completing a book on British Christian evangelizing in India, including the work of the Salvation Army.

3. The statistics for 1878 are given in the *Northern Daily Express*, 12 April 1879, 4. Statistics for 1884 are from Robert Sandall, *The History of the Salvation Army*, vol. 2 (1950; reprint, London: Salvation Army, 1979), app. M. I have avoided the terms *sect* and *denomination* to describe the Salvation Army for two reasons. First, extensive debate about the precise meaning of both terms has not

resulted in any clear agreement, and use of either term may imply a position that I do not intend to endorse. See Bryan R. Wilson, ed., *Patterns of Sectarianism: Organisation and Ideology in Social and Religious Movements* (London: Heinemann, 1967). Second, the Salvation Army's concerns extended far beyond its own membership, and its members strived to create a transformative movement. The terms *organization* and *movement* suggest that goal.

4. Hugh McLeod, "Introduction," in *European Religion in the Age of Great Cities, 1830–1930,* ed. Hugh McLeod (London: Routledge, 1995), 24, argues that conflict is a key feature of nineteenth-century urban religious life.

5. *Church* refers to the Church of England, and chapels are the Nonconformist houses of worship.

6. Charles Booth, *Life and Labour of the People in London,* 7 vols., Religious Influences, 3rd ser. (1903; reprint, London: AMS Press, 1970).

7. For an overview of the secularization debate, see Steve Bruce, ed., *Religion and Modernization: Sociologists and Historians Debate the Secularization Thesis* (Oxford: Clarendon Press, 1992). On the decline of religion in England, see, for example, A. D. Gilbert, *Religion and Society in Industrial England: Church, Chapel and Social Change* (New York: Longman, 1976). An important new perspective on religion is Sarah C. Williams, *Religious Belief and Popular Culture in Southwark, c. 1880–1939* (Oxford: Oxford University Press, 1999).

8. E. P. Thompson, *The Making of the English Working Class* (London: Penguin Books, 1968), 13, 411–12. Thompson's argument echoed the work of Elie Halevy, *History of the English People in the Nineteenth Century,* vol. 1 (1913; reprint, London: Ernest Benn, 1960), which argued that religion was a bulwark against social unrest and revolution in England. A provocative reading of Thompson's interpretation of Methodism is Barbara Taylor, "Religion, Radicalism and Fantasy," *History Workshop Journal* 39 (1995): 102–12. Thompson's later work, notably *Witness against the Beast: William Blake and the Moral Law* (Cambridge: Cambridge University Press, 1993), takes a rather different perspective on religion.

9. E. J. Hobsbawm, *Primitive Rebels* (New York: Norton, 1959); E. J. Hobsbawm and George Rude, *Captain Swing* (Harmondsworth, Middlesex: Penguin Books, 1973); E. J. Hobsbawm, "Religion and Socialism," in *Workers* (New York: Pantheon Books, 1984), 37–38, 46.

10. See, for example, Robert Colls, *The Pitman of the Northern Coalfield: Work, Culture and Protest, 1790–1850* (Manchester: Manchester University Press, 1987); Thomas W. Laqueur, *Religion and Respectability: Sunday Schools and Working Class Culture* (New Haven, Conn.: Yale University Press, 1976); John Rule, "Methodism, Popular Beliefs and Village Culture in Cornwall, 1800–1850," in *Popular Culture and Custom in Nineteenth Century England,* ed. Robert Storch (London: Croom Helm, 1982), 48–70.

11. Deborah Valenze, *Prophetic Sons and Daughters: Female Preaching and Popular Religion in Industrial England* (Princeton, N.J.: Princeton University Press, 1985), 17. Robert Colls, "Primitive Methodists in the Northern Coalfields," in *Disciplines of Faith,* ed. Jim Obelkevich et al. (London: Routledge & Kegan Paul, 1986), 322–33, also persuasively argues that the emphasis on politics does not allow historians to appreciate what Methodists accomplished.

12. Gareth Stedman Jones, "Working-Class Culture and Working-Class Politics in London, 1870–1914: Notes on the Remaking of a Working Class," *Journal of Social History* 7, no. 4 (summer 1974): 471. Roland Robertson, "The Salvation Army: The Persistence of Sectarianism," in *Patterns of Sectarianism: Organisation and Ideology in Social and Religious Movements,* ed. Bryan R. Wilson (London: Heinemann, 1967), 49–105, argues that the Salvation Army offered social mobility to its members. I argue that Stedman Jones and Robertson's argument is based, in part, on a flawed analysis of the class basis of the Salvation Army (see Chapter 3).

13. Robert Sandall, *The History of the Salvation Army,* vols. 1–3 (1947, 1950, 1955; reprint, London: Salvation Army, 1979); Arch Wiggins, *The History of the Salvation Army,* vols. 4–5 (1964, 1968; reprint, London: Salvation Army, 1979); Frederick Coutts, *The History of the Salvation Army,* vol. 6 (1973; reprint, London: Salvation Army, 1979).

14. These biographies include Harold Begbie, *The Life of General William Booth, the Founder of the Salvation Army,* 2 vols. (New York: Macmillan, 1920); Catherine Bramwell Booth, *Catherine Booth: The Story of Her Loves* (London: Hodder & Stoughton, 1970); Frederick St. George de Latour Booth-Tucker, *The Life of Catherine Booth: The Mother of the Salvation Army,* 2 vols. (New York: Fleming H. Revell, 1892); Richard Collier, *The General Next to God* (London: Collins, 1965). The most recent biography of Catherine Booth is Roger J. Green, *Catherine Booth: A Biography of the Cofounder of the Salvation Army* (Grand Rapids, Mich.: Baker, 1996). Green's biography is the most scholarly, critical, and thorough. The best biography of William Booth remains St. John Ervine, *God's Soldier: General William Booth,* 2 vols. (London: Heinemann, 1934).

15. Both books neglect the Booth personal papers, held at the British Library, London, which are essential, and neither cites the extensive personal papers of Salvationists held at the SAHC. Horridge includes several local studies of the Salvation Army's work that are very valuable. However, he cites documents that are identified only as "previously unpublished letters and papers, copies in the author's possession" (237, n. 88). Such unusual citations for significant material do not inspire confidence. Neither author fully made use of the national or provincial press to examine the wider context in which the Salvation Army worked. Glenn K. Horridge, *The Salvation Army, Origins and Early Days: 1865–1900* (Godalming: Ammonite Books, 1993), and Norman H. Murdoch, *Origins of the Salvation Army* (Knoxville: University of Tennessee Press, 1994). Laura Lauer, "Women in British Nonconformity, ca. 1880–1920: With Special Reference to the Society of Friends, Baptist Union and Salvation Army" (Ph.D. thesis, Oxford University, 1998) is an important study that compares Salvationist women with other Nonconformists. Edward H. McKinley, *Marching to Glory: The History of the Salvation Army in the United States, 1880–1992* (Grand Rapids, Mich.: Eerdmans, 1995), is an important scholarly study that includes some background on the Salvation Army in Britain. More recent work on the American Salvation Army includes Lillian Taiz, "Hallelujah Lasses in the Battle for Souls: Working- and Middle-Class Women in the Salvation Army in the United States, 1872–1896," *Journal of Women's History* 9, no. 2 (1997): 84–105; Lillian Taiz, "Applying the Devil's Works in a Holy Cause: Working-Class Popular

Culture and the Salvation Army in the United States, 1879–1900," *Religion and American Culture* 7, no. 2 (1997): 195–223; Diane Winston, *Red Hot and Righteous: The Urban Religion of the Salvation Army* (Cambridge, Mass.: Harvard University Press, 1999).

16. In his influential study, *Class and Religion in the Late Victorian City* (London: Croom Helm, 1974), Hugh McLeod examines class differences in church attendance; the absence of the working class from religious institutions is an important element in this study. McLeod examines the Salvation Army as one example of a movement that failed to reach the working class. K. S. Inglis, *Churches and the Working Classes in Victorian England* (London: Routledge & Kegan Paul, 1963), ch. 5, is among the most concise and insightful treatments of the Salvation Army's history.

17. John Kent, *Holding the Fort: Studies in Victorian Revivalism* (London: Epworth Press, 1978).

18. Victor Bailey, "Salvation Army Riots, the 'Skeleton Army' and Legal Authority in the Provincial Town," in *Social Control in Nineteenth-Century Britain,* ed. A. P. Donajgrodzki (London: Croom Helm, 1977), 131–253, and Victor Bailey, "In Darkest England and the Way Out: The Salvation Army, Social Reform and the Labour Movement, 1885–1910," *International Review of Social History* 29 (1984): 134–71.

19. Dean Rapp, "The British Salvation Army, the Early Film Industry and Urban Working-Class Adolescents, 1897–1918," *Twentieth Century British History* 7, no. 2 (1996): 157–88.

20. For example, Jeffrey Cox, *The English Churches in a Secular Society: Lambeth, 1870–1930* (Oxford: Oxford University Press, 1982); Donald Lewis, *Lighten Their Darkness: The Evangelical Mission to Working Class London, 1828–1860* (London: Greenwood Press, 1986); McLeod, *European Religion in the Age of Great Cities.*

21. Hugh McLeod, *Piety and Poverty: Working-Class Religion in Berlin, London and New York, 1870–1914* (New York: Holmes & Meier, 1996), xxiii. See also Hugh McLeod, "New Perspectives on Victorian Working-Class Religion: The Oral Evidence," *Oral History* 14, no. 1 (1986): 31–49, which suggests that the oral-history evidence presents a different picture of working-class religion than the one often presented by historians.

22. Callum Brown, "The Mechanism of Religious Growth in Urban Societies: British Cities since the Eighteenth Century," in *European Religion in the Age of Great Cities, 1830–1930,* ed. Hugh McLeod (London: Routledge, 1995), 241, 242.

23. Sarah C. Williams, "The Language of Belief: An Alternative Agenda for the Study of Victorian Working-Class Religion," *Journal of Victorian Culture* 1, no. 2 (1996): 314.

24. Work that has influenced my own understanding of the history of faith and belief includes Caroline Walker Bynum, *Fragmentation and Redemption: Essays on Gender and the Human Body in Medieval Religion* (New York: Zone Books, 1991); Cheryl Townsend Gilkes, "Together and in Harness: Women's Traditions in the Sanctified Church," *Signs* 10, no. 41 (1985): 678–99; Lawrence Levine, *Black Culture, Black Consciousness: Afro-American Folk Thought from*

Slavery to Freedom (New York: Oxford University Press, 1977); Phyllis Mack, *Visionary Women: Ecstatic Prophecy in Seventeenth-Century England* (Berkeley: University of California Press, 1992); Lyndal Roper, *Holy Household: Women and Morals in Reformation Augsburg* (Oxford: Clarendon Press, 1989); Mechal Sobel, *Trabelin' On: The Slave Journey to an Afro-Baptist Faith* (Princeton, N.J.: Princeton University Press, 1988). See also essays in Susan Juster and Lisa MacFarlane, *A Mighty Baptism: Race, Gender and the Creation of American Protestantism* (Ithaca, N.Y.: Cornell University Press, 1996), and in Paul E. Johnson, ed., *African-American Christianity: Essays in History* (Berkeley: University of California Press, 1994). For an influential discussion of the problem of belief, see Thomas Kselman, "Introduction," in *Belief in History*, ed. Thomas Kselman (Notre Dame, Ind.: University of Notre Dame Press, 1991).

25. Valenze's study of plebeian Methodism, *Prophetic Sons and Daughters*, uncovers the "sacred worldview of laborers and relate[s] [it] to contemporary economic and social change" (6). In her conclusion, Valenze comments that, "to the discerning eye, promoters of plebeian righteousness and humble virtue were still at work in the Salvation Army missions of late nineteenth-century cities" (281).

26. My understanding of these dynamics has been influenced by Robin D. G. Kelley, *Race Rebels: Culture, Politics and the Black Working Class* (New York: Free Press, 1994), and by James Scott, *Domination and the Art of Resistance* (New Haven, Conn.: Yale University Press, 1990).

1. THE ROOTS OF THE SALVATION ARMY

1. Catherine Bramwell Booth, *Catherine Booth*, 23; Booth-Tucker, *The Life of Catherine Booth*, 1:33–42.

2. Catherine Mumford Booth Papers, BL, manuscript diary, May 30, 1847, BL Add. Mss. 64806, f. 158.

3. Mumford, diary, May 24, 1847, f. 156.

4. Mumford, diary, May 21, 1847, f. 155.

5. Mumford, diary, May 13, 1847, f. 153.

6. Mumford, diary, February 6, 1848, f. 183.

7. Ervine, *God's Soldier*, 1:307.

8. The pledge was a written promise to abstain from alcohol; it was widely promoted by evangelicals and temperance advocates.

9. Quoted in Mary Ryan, *The Cradle of the Middle Class: The Family in Oneida County New York, 1790–1865* (New York: Cambridge University Press, 1981), 99.

10. Lyn Miller, "Chastening: Susan Warner's Theology of Pleasure in *Wide, Wide World*" (unpublished paper, Divinity School, Harvard University, 1993).

11. Valenze, *Prophetic Sons and Daughters*, 36.

12. Membership in a class was compulsory for Methodists. The class ticket was evidence that an individual was a member in good standing and could partake of communion and the other benefits of membership in the chapel. Rupert Davis, *Methodism* (Harmondsworth, Middlesex: Penguin Books, 1963), and Booth-Tucker, *The Life of Catherine Booth*, 53–63, 72–88.

13. Mumford, diary, May 30, 1847, f. 167; Booth-Tucker, *The Life of Catherine Booth*, 49–50.

14. William Butler, *A Short Account of the Life and Death of Ann Cutler* (1796), cited in Valenze, *Prophetic Sons and Daughters*, 53.

15. Valenze, *Prophetic Sons and Daughters*, 54.

16. Ibid., chs. 3 and 4.

17. Ibid., 178.

18. Quoted in W. H. Jones, *History of the Wesleyan Reform Union* (London: Epworth Press, 1952), 20.

19. Kent, *Holding the Fort*, 78.

20. Richard Carwardine, *Transatlantic Revivalism: Popular Evangelicalism in Britain and America, 1790–1865* (London: Greenwood Press, 1978), 120–28.

21. *Facts Are Stubborn Things: An Illustration of Conference Methodism in the Bacup Circuit* (n.p.: Printed for the General Wesleyan Reform Committee, n.d.); *A Faithful Verbatim Report of the "Fly Sheets," by a Wesleyan Minister Who Is Not Yet Expelled* (Birmingham: William Cornish, 1849); *A Few Facts about the Wesleyan Conference Expulsions* (Hastings: W. Ransom, n.d.). See also Carwardine, *Transatlantic Revivalism*, and Kent, *Holding the Fort*.

22. Booth-Tucker, *The Life of Catherine Booth*, 48.

23. Kent, *Holding the Fort*, and Rev. James Caughey, *Showers of Blessing from Clouds of Mercy; Selected from the Journal Writings of the Rev. James Caughey* (Boston: J. P. Magee, 1857).

24. Ervine, *God's Soldier*, 1:32.

25. William Booth Papers, SAHC, unpublished letter to unknown friend, London, 1849.

26. Catherine Mumford Booth Papers, BL, letter to William Booth, May 13, 1852, BL Add. Mss. 64799, f. 3.

27. Catherine Mumford Booth Papers, BL, letter to William Booth, May 25, 1855, BL Add. Mss. 64802, f. 101.

28. William Booth Papers, BL, letter to Catherine Mumford, December 1, 1852, Add. Mss. 64799, f. 26.

29. Ervine, *God's Soldier*, 1:61–63.

30. Catherine Mumford Booth Papers, BL, letter to William Booth, February 7, 1853, BL Add. Mss. 64799, ff. 119–22.

31. Ervine, *God's Soldier*, 1:64–69.

32. Ibid., 1:54–59; see also Catherine Mumford Booth Papers, BL, letter to William Booth, March 17, [1853], BL Add. Mss. 64799, ff. 150–53.

33. Ervine, *God's Soldier*, 1:65–94. Catherine Mumford Booth Papers, BL, letters to William Booth, from March 20, 1853, to September 22, 1853, BL Add. Mss. 64800, and from September 24, 1853, to January 19, 1855, BL Add. Mss. 64801.

34. William Booth Papers, BL, letter to Catherine Mumford, December 1, 1852, BL Add. Mss. 64799, ff. 25–26.

35. Ervine, *God's Soldier*, 1:93–122.

36. Catherine Mumford Booth Papers, BL, letter to William Booth, May 2 [1855], BL Add. Mss. 64802, f. 84.

37. Catherine Mumford Booth Papers, BL, letters to William Booth, May 1853, BL Add. Mss. 64800, ff. 55–67.

38. Catherine Mumford Booth Papers, BL, letter to William Booth, December 16, 1852, BL Add. Mss. 64799, ff. 60–61.

39. Catherine Mumford Booth Papers, BL, letter to William Booth, April 12, 1853, BL Add. Mss. 64800, ff. 41–43.

40. Catherine Mumford Booth Papers, BL, letter to William Booth, March 17, [1853], BL Add. Mss. 64799, ff. 150–53.

41. Catherine Mumford Booth Papers, BL, letter to William Booth, [January 8?9? 1854], BL Add. Mss. 64801, ff. 88–92.

42. Catherine Mumford Booth Papers, BL, letter to William Booth, [June 13, 1853], BL Add. Mss. 64799, f. 9.

43. Catherine Mumford Booth Papers, BL, letter to William Booth, December 12, 1852, BL Add. Mss. 64799, f. 52.

44. See, for example, Catherine Mumford Booth Papers, BL, letters to William Booth, December 5, 1852, December 27, 1852, and February 20, 1853, BL Add. Mss. 64799.

45. Ervine, *God's Soldier,* 1:110.

46. Catherine Mumford and William Booth Papers, BL, letter to her parents, January 5, 1856, BL Add. Mss. 64803, f. 107.

47. Dale Johnson, "The Methodist Quest for an Educated Ministry," *Church History* 51, no. 3 (September 1982): 304–20.

48. Valenze, *Prophetic Sons and Daughters,* Afterword.

49. Catherine Mumford Booth Papers, BL, letter to William Booth, [after June 13, 1852], BL Add. Mss. 64799, f. 10.

50. Catherine Mumford Booth Papers, BL, letter to Rev. David Thomas, 1855, BL Add. Mss. 64806, ff. 199–201. There is no record of his response to this letter. It is even possible that it was never sent. The date of this letter has generated some controversy. Booth-Tucker, *The Life of Catherine Booth,* gives the date as 1853. He quotes her as writing, "In your discourse on Sunday morning" (118), whereas the manuscript letter reads, "I had the privilege of hearing you preach on Sunday morning April 22nd –55." Catherine Bramwell Booth, in her biography of her grandmother, *Catherine Booth,* gives the date as 1850. Norman Murdoch, "Female Ministry in the Thought and Work of Catherine Booth," *Church History* 53 (September 1984): 348–62, agrees with Catherine Bramwell Booth. Christine Parkin, "A Woman's Place: Catherine Booth and Female Ministry," in *Catherine Booth: Her Continuing Relevance,* ed. Clifford W. Kew (London: Salvation Army, 1990), states that "this letter has been assumed to come from 1853, but Catherine Bramwell-Booth dates it as 1850" (8). Roger Green, *Catherine Booth,* points to a presumed error in my 1992 dissertation, where I gave the date of this letter as 1855; Pamela J. Walker, "Pulling the Devil's Kingdom Down: Gender and Popular Culture in the Salvation Army, 1865–1890" (Ph.D. diss., Rutgers University, 1992). Green suggests that "Catherine was mistaken in other dates and may have been mistaken here" (307, n. 2). Does Dr. Green mean to suggest that Catherine did not know the year when she sat down to write her letter? Neither Parkin nor Murdoch consulted the original letter, but Green's citation indicates that he did. I do not know why the date of this letter

should be disputed. Other evidence, particularly a letter to William written April 9, 1855, on the subject of women's place, which mentions Thomas, suggests that she was thinking deeply about this subject at that time. There is absolutely nothing to support any other date than the one clearly given in the text of the letter.

51. I have retained all the original spelling.

52. Ervine, *God's Soldier,* l:125.

53. *Methodist New Connexion Conference Journal* (Methodist Archives and Research Centre at the John Rylands University Library, Manchester), May 21, 1855, entry 78.

54. Catherine Mumford Booth Papers, BL, letter to William Booth, April 9, 1855, BL Add. Mss. 64802, f. 66.

55. See Adam Clarke, *Adam Clarke's Commentary on the Old Testament* (London: Joseph Butterworth and Son, 1825), and Samuel Dunn, *Christian Theology by Adam Clarke with a Life of the Author* (London: Thomas Tegg and Son, 1835).

56. Catherine Mumford Booth Papers, BL, letter to William Booth, April 9, 1855, BL Add. Mss. 64802, f. 67.

57. Ibid.

58. Ibid.

59. Ibid., f. 68.

60. Ibid., f. 65.

61. Ibid., f. 71.

62. In addition, the usual salary in 1862 for a superintendent was £76, so William was comparatively well paid. See Rev. William Baggaly, *A Digest of the Minutes of the Institutions, Polity, Doctrines, Ordinances, and Literature of the Methodist New Connexion* (London: Methodist New Connexion Bookroom, 1862).

63. See letters of support for William's work in the *Methodist New Connexion Magazine,* April 1854, 209; June 1854, 353; January 1855, 33; February 1855, 94; March 1855, 148 and 152.

64. The holiness movement began in New York, and one of its principal figures was Charles Finney. The doctrine of holiness, or entire sanctification, was derived from Wesley, but Finney gave conversion a definite structure and formula. Charles G. Finney, *Lectures on Revivals of Religion* (New York; Leavitt, Lord, 1835); Caughey, *Showers of Blessing,* and John Wesley, *A Plain Account of Christian Perfection* (Bristol: William Pine, 1770). See also Carwardine, *Transatlantic Revivalism*; Nancy Hardesty, *Women Called to Witness: Evangelical Feminism in the Nineteenth Century* (Nashville, Tenn.: Abingdon Press, 1984), 49–50; Keith J. Hardman, *Charles Grandison Finney* (Syracuse, N.Y.: Syracuse University Press, 1987); Kent, *Holding the Fort,* ch. 1; Mary P. Ryan, "A Women's Awakening: Evangelical Religion and the Families of Utica, New York, 1800–1840," in *Women in American Religion,* ed. Janet Wilson James (Philadelphia: University of Pennsylvania Press, 1980), 89–110.

65. *Methodist New Connexion Magazine,* October 1855, 540.

66. Catherine Mumford Booth Papers, BL, letter to her parents, October [1855], BL Add. Mss. 64803, f. 33. For a brief period, she wrote to her parents; perhaps they had reconciled during that time.

67. Catherine Mumford Booth Papers, BL, letter to her parents, October [1856], BL Add. Mss. 64803, f. 162.

68. Ervine, *God's Soldier*, 1:197–212; Catherine Mumford Booth Papers, BL, letter to her parents, November 12, [1855], BL Add. Mss. 64803, ff. 59–60.

69. Booth-Tucker, *The Life of Catherine Booth*, 1:299.

70. Ibid., 1:308.

71. Catherine Mumford Booth Papers, BL, letter to her mother, [June 1858], BL Add. Mss. 64804, f. 121.

72. Methodist New Connexion, *Minutes of the Annual Conference of the Methodist New Connexion* (London: Methodist New Connexion Book Room, 1858, 1859, and 1860). See also Ervine, *God's Soldier*.

73. Gateshead Society Members' Class Register, Tyne and Wear Archives Service, Newcastle-upon-Tyne.

74. See Catherine Mumford Booth Papers, BL, letter to her mother, February 8, 1858, BL Add. Mss. 64804, ff. 82–85.

75. Catherine Mumford Booth Papers, BL, letter to her mother, [September 18, 1858], BL Add. Mss. 64804, f. 142. As a child, her eldest son was called by his first name, William. He began to use his second name, Bramwell, in his teens. I have referred to him throughout as Bramwell for the sake of clarity.

76. Catherine Mumford Booth Papers, BL, letter to her mother, August 22, 1859, BL Add. Mss. 64805, ff. 21–23.

77. Ervine, *God's Soldier*, 1:271.

78. Hardesty, *Women Called to Witness*, 16; Anne C. Loveland, "Domesticity and Religion in the Antebellum Period: The Career of Phoebe Palmer," *Historian* 39 (1977): 455–71; and Charles Edward White, *The Beauty of Holiness: Phoebe Palmer as Theologian, Revivalist, Feminist and Humanitarian* (Grand Rapids, Mich.: Francis Asbury Press, 1986).

79. *Wesleyan Times*, 3 October 1859, 644.

80. Catherine Mumford Booth Papers, BL, letter to her mother, January 21, 1861, BL Add. Mss. 64805, f. 97.

81. Phoebe Palmer, *Four Years in the Old World* (New York: Foster, Palmer Jr., 1867).

82. Catherine Mumford Booth Papers, BL, letter to William Booth, April 9, 1855, BL Add. Mss. 64802, f. 66.

83. Carwardine, *Transatlantic Revivalism*; Kent, *Holding the Fort*; Paul Gilroy, *The Black Atlantic: Modernity and Double Consciousness* (Cambridge, Mass.: Harvard University Press, 1993).

84. Frances Willard, Lucy Stone, and Antoinette Brown were all active in the holiness movement. See Hardesty, *Women Called to Witness*, 14, 47, and 97. See also Barbara Brown Zikmund, "The Struggle for the Right to Preach," in *Women and Religion in America*, ed. Rosemary Radford Reuther and Rosemary Skinner Keller (San Francisco: Harper & Row, 1981), 193–241. For other aspects of women and holiness, see Jean Humez, "'My Spirit Eye': Some Functions of Visionary Experience in the Lives of Five Black Women Preachers, 1810–1880," in *Women and the Structure of Society*, ed. Barbara Harris and JoAnn McNamara (Durham, N.C.: Duke University Press, 1984), 129–43, and Gilkes, "Together and in Harness."

85. Hardesty, *Women Called to Witness*, 63–76.

86. James Everett, *The Midshipman and the Minister; the Quarter Deck and the Pulpit* (London: Hamilton, Adams, 1867).

87. Arthur Augustus Rees, *Reasons for Not Co-operating in the Alleged "Sunderland Revivals"* (Sunderland: Wm. Henry Hills, 1859), 5.

88. In response to an assertion that he could not "bear that any good should be done by others than myself, or in another way than my own," Rees gave the well-known passage from Virgil, "can there be such anger in heavenly spirits," a reference to the anger of the goddess Juno against a "pious man," and followed with a phrase of his own invention, "can there be such anger in revivalists"; ibid., 15. My thanks to Professor John Lenghan for translating these two passages for me.

89. Ibid., 9.

90. Ibid.

91. Ibid., 14.

92. This criticism was echoed in Rev. Dr. Jarbo, *A Letter to Mrs. Palmer in Reference to Women Speaking in Public* (Northshields: Philipson and Hare, 1859), and it was to become a standard criticism of the Salvation Army in later years.

93. Catherine Mumford Booth Papers, BL, letter to her mother, December 25, 1859, BL Add. Mss. 64805, f. 48.

94. The first edition of the pamphlet was published locally, but I do not know the precise publication details. She wrote to her mother, "I am in the hands of a *man*, a printer and if this is a specimen of printers, I hope to keep out of their hands in future." Ibid., f. 45. No known copy of that pamphlet has survived. The second edition was published in London by George J. Stevenson in 1861. See also Booth-Tucker, *The Life of Catherine Booth*, 1:337.

95. This pamphlet is most probably changed only slightly from the first edition, judging from her correspondence with her mother. It is, however, significantly different from the edition published in 1870: Catherine Booth, *Female Ministry: Women's Right to Preach the Gospel* (London: Morgan and Chase, 1870; reprint, London: Salvation Army Publishing, 1975). Scholars have based their analysis of this pamphlet exclusively on the third edition. Murdoch, *Origins of the Salvation Army*, makes use of that third edition and does not use the Rees pamphlet. Horridge, *The Salvation Army*, does not include any of these pamphlets in his discussion of women's preaching but claims that "women's equality" was one of the "twenty different facets" of militarism in the Salvation Army. Horridge offers no further explanation of how women's equality might be understood as an aspect of militarism. Green, *Catherine Booth*, is the most recent of the biographies, and it makes use of both the second and the third editions as well as relying heavily on my 1992 Ph.D. dissertation: Walker, "Pulling the Devil's Kingdom Down." The third, 1870, edition was made more widely available when it was reprinted in Donald W. Dayton, ed., *Holiness Tracts Defending the Ministry of Women* (New York: Garland, 1985), and excerpted in Dale Johnson, ed., *Women in English Religion* (Lewiston, N.Y.: Mellen Press, 1983). Booth-Tucker, *The Life of Catherine Booth*, 1, ch. 17, also cites the third

edition. His is a partisan biography, and he may have chosen to use that edition because it was written after the establishment of the Christian Mission. The following discussion is based on the second edition of the pamphlet and thus differs substantially from other writing on Catherine Booth's work. I am grateful to Dr. Dorothy Thompson, Dr. Hugh McLeod, Dr. Richard Carwardine, and the librarians of the Methodist Archives and Research Centre at the John Rylands University Library, Manchester, for helping me find the Rees and earlier Booth pamphlets.

96. Catherine Booth, *Female Teaching: or, the Rev. A. A. Rees versus Mrs. Palmer, Being a Reply to a Pamphlet by the Above Gentleman on the Sunderland Revival*, 2d ed. (London: George J. Stevenson, 1861), 6.

97. Ibid., 3.

98. Ibid., 4.

99. Ibid., 22.

100. Ibid., 14–15.

101. Ibid., 22.

102. Many nineteenth-century leaders of charismatic and revivalist movements put a greater emphasis on Jesus's life than on the authority of Paul, and Catherine was no exception.

103. Catherine Booth, *Female Teaching*, 32.

104. On Adam Clarke, see Clarke, *Adam Clarke's Commentary*, and *The Dictionary of National Biography*, vol. 4, ed. Sir Leslie Stephen and Sir Sidney Lee (1921; reprint, Oxford: Oxford University Press, 1973), 413–14. Catherine also cited the Anglican Daniel Whitby, the Methodist Philip Dodderidge, Alfred Barnes, and Mrs. Phoebe Palmer. She also used, but did not cite, a letter from J. H. Robinson to the *Methodist New Connexion Magazine* of March 1848, especially in her analysis of 1 Cor. 14:34–35 and 1 Tim. 2:11–12. See Catherine Mumford Booth Papers, BL, letter to her mother, April 23, 1861, BL Add. Mss. 64805, ff. 112–13. Her scriptural argument resembled that of U.S. holiness advocates associated with Oberlin College. See, for example, Antoinette Brown, "Exegesis of 1 Corinthians XIV: 34–35 and I Timothy II: 11–12," *Oberlin Quarterly Review*, January 1849, 358–73, and Luther Lee, *Women's Right to Preach the Gospel: A Sermon Preached at the Ordination of Rev. Miss Antoinette L. Brown* (Syracuse, N.Y.: Published by the Author, 1853). Catherine made no mention of these texts, and it is probable she did not read them. They had a similar theology and used many of the same theologians to buttress their case, which would account for the similarities.

105. In his *Remarks on the Ministry of Women* (1808), Hugh Bourne, the founder of Primitive Methodism, made an argument from scripture similar to Catherine's; in John Walford, *Memoirs of the Life and Labours of the Late Venerable Hugh Bourne* (London: T. King, 1855), 1:173–77. I am grateful to Professor Deborah Valenze for pointing out this similarity to me.

106. Rev. Robert Young, *North of England Revivals: The Prophesying of Women* (Newcastle-upon-Tyne, 1859).

107. Catherine Mumford Booth Papers, BL, letter to her parents, December 25, 1859, BL Add. Mss. 64805, ff. 45–48.

108. An excerpt from this book was published in *The Bible Christian Magazine* in December 1859, and it is possible that Catherine read it as she was completing her own pamphlet.

109. Phoebe Palmer, *The Promise of the Father; or a Neglected Spirituality of the Last Days* (Boston: Henry V. Degen, 1859), 1.

110. Ibid., 9.

111. On Mrs. Palmer, see Harold E. Raser, *Phoebe Palmer: Her Life and Thought* (Lewiston, N.Y.: Mellen Press, 1987), and Loveland, "Domesticity and Religion in the Antebellum Period." On earlier women who also used this logic, see Merry E. Weisner, "Women's Defense of Their Public Role," in *Women in the Middle Ages and Renaissance,* ed. Mary Beth Rose (Syracuse, N.Y.: Syracuse University Press, 1985), 18–21. The tensions between passivity and self-assertion were also present for women in the spiritualist movement. See Alex Owen, *The Darkened Room: Women, Power and Spiritualism in Late Victorian England* (London: Virago Press, 1989).

112. Catherine Booth, *Female Teaching*, 30.

113. Mack, *Visionary Women*, 136.

114. WC, January 4, 1890, for example, states that Catherine Booth comforted her daughter, whose infant was ill, with a promise to raise the child in heaven; her remarks suggest that the child would grow older in heaven and that Catherine would retain her maternal sensibilities.

115. Valenze, *Prophetic Sons and Daughters,* documents that sectarian Methodist women, for example, utilized the passage "But God has chosen the foolish things of the world to confound the wise; and God hath chosen the weak things of the world to confound the things which are mighty" (1 Cor. 1:27).

116. Catherine Mumford Booth Papers, BL, letter to William Booth, September 3, 1860, BL Add. Mss. 64802, f. 143.

117. Ibid., f. 142.

118. On this shift, see, for example, "Letters on Revivals," *Methodist New Connection Magazine* 23 (June 1855): 318, and "Why Revivals Are Redundant," *Bible Christian Magazine* 25 (January 1860): 31–35.

119. Catherine Mumford Booth Papers, BL, letter to William Booth, April 9, 1855, BL Add. Mss. 64802, f. 68.

120. Catherine Mumford Booth Papers, BL, letter to her parents, December 7, 1857, BL Add. Mss. 64804, f. 57.

121. Catherine Mumford Booth Papers, BL, letter to her mother, December 23, 1857, BL Add. Mss. 64804, f. 63.

122. Historian Dina Copelman, *London's Women Teachers: Gender, Class and Feminism, 1870–1930* (London: Routledge, 1996), xv, argues that women teachers active in London in the 1870s and 1880s were mainly the daughters of artisan and lower-middle-class parents. Parents "prepared daughters for occupations and in general did not consider paid employment inappropriate for women. This meant that women from these strata did not view employment as a product of feminist struggle." Catherine Booth likewise did not view employment per se as a divisive issue nor did she believe that it would cause loss of status for a woman. She did, however, regard preaching as a particular employment that had wide-reaching implications for women.

123. Catherine Mumford Booth Papers, BL, letter to her parents, December 23, 1857, BL Add. Mss. 64804, f. 63.

124. Catherine Mumford Booth Papers, BL, letter to her parents, August 23, [1860], BL Add. Mss. 64805, f. 62.

125. Catherine Mumford Booth Papers, BL, letter to her parents, September 24, 1860, BL Add. Mss. 64805, f. 75.

126. Booth-Tucker, *The Life of Catherine Booth*, 1:376.

127. Catherine Mumford Booth Papers, BL, letter to William Booth, September 13, 1860, BL Add. Mss. 64802, f. 149.

128. Catherine Mumford Booth Papers, BL, letter to her mother, December 31, 1860, BL Add. Mss. 64805, f. 93.

129. Catherine Mumford Booth Papers, BL, letter to William Booth, [mid-1860], BL Add. Mss. 64802, f. 145.

130. Bethesda Methodist New Connexion, Leaders Meeting Minutes, May 30, 1860, Tyne and Wear Archives Service, Newcastle-upon-Tyne.

131. *Wesleyan Times*, 20 August 1860, 541.

132. Catherine Mumford Booth Papers, BL, letter to her parents, September 24, [1860], BL Add. Mss. 64805, f. 76.

133. Ervine, *God's Soldier*, 1:45.

134. Catherine Mumford Booth Papers, BL, letter to her parents, February 11, 1861, BL Add. Mss. 64805, f. 102.

135. Ibid., f. 99.

136. Ibid., ff. 101–2.

137. Catherine Mumford Booth Papers, BL, letter to her parents, October 7, 1856, BL Add. Mss. 64803, f. 153.

138. Catherine Mumford Booth Papers, BL, letter to her parents, October 22, 1857, BL Add. Mss. 64804, f. 47.

139. There is no extant record of the Conference decisions except for a brief record left in the minutes.

140. William Booth letter to H. O. Crofts, June 14, 1861, Annual Committee Report Book of the Methodist New Connexion, June 9, 1862, Methodist Archives and Research Centre at the John Rylands University Library, Manchester.

141. Annual Committee Report Book of the Methodist New Connexion, June 9, 1862, Methodist Archives and Research Centre at the John Rylands University Library, Manchester.

142. Ibid.

143. William Booth, letter to H. O. Crofts, n.d., Annual Committee Report Book of the Methodist New Connexion, June 9, 1862, Methodist Archives and Research Centre at the John Rylands University Library, Manchester.

144. Catherine Mumford Booth Papers, BL, letter to her parents, [June 1861], BL Add. Mss. 64805, f. 120.

145. Booth-Tucker, *The Life of Catherine Booth*, 1:390–537; Ervine, *God's Soldier*, 1:230–71.

146. Catherine Mumford Booth Papers, BL, letter to her mother, October 18, 1861, BL Add. Mss. 64805, f.156.

147. Catherine Mumford Booth Papers, BL, letter to her parents, January [1862], BL Add. Mss. 64806, f. 5.

148. Ibid.

149. Ervine, *God's Soldier*, 1:270.

150. Catherine Mumford Booth Papers, BL, letter to her mother, January [1862], BL Add. Mss. 64806, f. 1.

151. Booth-Tucker, *The Life of Catherine Booth*, 1: 535; Ervine, *God's Soldier*, 1:262.

152. Catherine Mumford Booth Papers, BL, letter to her mother, [December 1864], BL Add. Mss. 64806, f. 135–36.

153. ELE, March 1869, 81.

154. Booth-Tucker, *The Life of Catherine Booth*, 1:359–61.

2. CREATING THE SALVATION ARMY

1. Ervine, *God's Soldier*, 1:281.

2. Revival, 13 July 1865, 27.

3. Revival, 27 July 1865, 59–60.

4. ELE, October 1868, 3.

5. WC, Christmas Issue, 1886, 9.

6. D. W. Bebbington, *Evangelicalism in Modern Britain: A History from the 1730s to the 1980s* (London: Allen Unwin, 1989), 107–14; Carwardine, *Transatlantic Revivalism*; Cox, *The English Churches in a Secular Society*; Gilbert, *Religion and Society in Industrial England*; Kathleen Heasman, *Evangelicals in Action: An Appraisal of Their Social Work in the Victorian Era* (London: Geoffrey Bles, 1962); Inglis, *Churches and the Working Classes*; Kent, *Holding the Fort*; Laqueur, *Religion and Respectability*; Lewis, *Lighten Their Darkness*; McLeod, *Class and Religion*; John Shelton Reed, "Ritualism Rampant in East London: Anglo-Catholicism and the Urban Poor," *Victorian Studies* 31, no. 3 (spring 1983): 375–404.

7. For example, *The Book and Its Mission* 28 (June 1857): 12–15, in an article entitled "The London Heathen and Their Missionaries," mentions Seven Dials and Wardour Street as the worst centers of heathenism in London. On Dickens, see P. J. Keating, "Fact and Fiction in the East End," in *The Victorian City: Images and Realities*, vol. 2, ed. H. J. Dyos and Michael Wolff (London: Routledge & Kegan Paul, 1973), 585–602.

8. Lynn Lees, *Exiles of Erin: Irish Migrants in Victorian London* (Ithaca, N.Y.: Cornell University Press, 1979), 46.

9. Gavin Weightman and Steve Humphries, *The Making of Modern London, 1815–1914* (London: Sidgwick and Jackson, 1983), 77–89.

10. *Revival*, 26 April 1862, 132.

11. Alan Mayne, *The Imagined Slum: Newspaper Representation in Three Cities, 1870–1914* (Leicester: Leicester University Press, 1993), 130. For other views of evangelism to London's working class, see Flora L. Freeman, *Religious and Social Work amongst Girls* (London: Skeffington and Sons, 1901); In *Perils in the City* (London: Headly Bros., 1909); Adalaide Ross, *Manual for Workers of the East London Association for the Care of Friendless Girls* (London: Hatchards, n.d.).

12. William Booth, *Report of the Christian Mission*, October 1867 (London, 1867).

13. William G. McLoughlin, *Modern Revivalism: Charles Grandison Finney to Billy Graham* (New York: Ronald Press, 1959), 25. Historians have debated how innovative Finney and Caughey's methods were and the degree to which they were indebted to earlier Methodist practice. See McLoughlin as well as Kent, *Holding the Fort,* and Carwardine, *Transatlantic Revivalism.* William and Catherine Booth clearly regarded Finney and Caughey as exceedingly important innovators however much they might have borrowed from prior practice.

14. Finney, *Lectures on Revivals of Religion* (1835), 149–51, in McLoughlin, *Modern Revivalism,* 86.

15. Ibid., 167, in McLoughlin, 87.

16. Kent, *Holding the Fort,* 78, and Carwardine, *Transatlantic Revivalism,* 117–18. Caughey's work was an important issue during the "Fly Sheets" controversy. See Chapter 1.

17. Carwardine, *Transatlantic Revivalism,* 120.

18. Quoted in George Scott Railton, *Twenty-One Years' Salvation Army* (London: Salvation Army, 1889), 4.

19. Booth-Tucker, *The Life of Catherine Booth,* 1:539–40.

20. Ervine, *God's Soldier,* 1:277.

21. Ibid., 1:283.

22. William Booth's biographer, St. John Ervine, states that the Booths' combined income in these years was £400–500 per annum. He notes that this sum is far greater than the £200 Dr. Cooke, the eminent leader of the Methodist New Connexion, earned during the same period. Ervine gives no source for this figure, and it is difficult to determine how he arrived at it. The Booths were, according to Ervine, £85 in debt in the summer of 1865; it is not clear how they would have incurred such debt when their income was by any measure substantial. It is also noteworthy that the Booths employed only one servant at this time, as did most of the better-paid artisanal and clerical households. Ibid., 1:270–71.

23. *Revival,* 20 November 1862, 233–34.

24. *Revival,* 30 June 1864, 412.

25. Quoted in Booth-Tucker, *The Life of Catherine Booth,* 541.

26. *Revival,* 31 August 1865, 129.

27. Ibid.

28. *Revival,* 7 September 1865, 149; 3 May 1866, 241; 17 May 1866, 278; 7 June 1866, 317; 12 July 1866, 20; 2 August 1866, 66.

29. William Booth, *How to Reach the Masses with Gospel* (London: Morgan, Chase and Scott, [1872]), 77.

30. Ibid., 78. Mary Billups and Jane Short, two middle-class women who worked with the Booths and at times lived with them, were probably two of the women he was referring to.

31. See, for example, *Revival,* 17 August 1865, 106; 28 September 1865, 180; 7 June 1866, 328–29.

32. Sandall, *The History of The Salvation Army,* 1:52 and vol. 1, app. I.

33. The members of the Council were Samuel Morley, MP; Captain Fishbourne; George Pease of the Stock Exchange; the Rev. J. H. Wilson, secretary of the Home Mission Society; the Rev. W. Tyler, minister of the New Town Chapel; the Rev. Robert Ashton, secretary of the Congregational Union; Samuel Mor-

gan; Richard Chase; Captain W. E. Smith, secretary of the Evangelisation Society; and Gawin Kirkham, secretary of the Open Air Mission. In addition, he appointed a Committee to assist him. They were Nathaniel James Powell, Charles Owen, John Alfred Merrington, John Eason, George Hamilton, John Lee Dale, Edmund Ives, W. H. Crispin, and C. S. Mitchell. Ervine, *God's Soldier,* 295.

34. Ibid., 1:304–5.

35. *Tower Hamlets Independent and General East End Advertiser,* 6 February 1869, 5; ELE, November 1868, 18; ELE, February 1869, 71; CMM, April 1870, 57.

36. Ervine, *God's Soldier,* 1:310–11.

37. Quoted in ibid., 1:312.

38. Quoted in ibid., 1:312–13.

39. Ibid., 1:322.

40. Sandall, *The History of the Salvation Army,* 1:76 and 80.

41. Booth, *How to Reach,* 83.

42. Francis Crossley Papers, SAHC, William Booth, letter to Mrs. Crossley, October 16, 1899. See also Edward Mynot, "Frank Crossley—Saint or Sinner?" *Manchester Region History Review* 11 (1997): 52–59.

43. Ervine, *God's Soldier,* 1:508, 2:820.

44. *Nonconformist,* 10 April 1867, 290.

45. *Tower Hamlets Independent and General East End Advertiser,* 23 November 1867, 6.

46. *Nonconformist,* 10 April 1867, 290. A similar perspective is given by a visiting nurse in East London. She recalled that one of her clients was a strict Baptist who enjoyed chatting about religion with the Roman Catholic and Jewish peddlers. But the Salvation Army officers, who would have gladly visited her, were "too rough and elementary and she shrank from them with a silent aversion." Margaret Loane, *An Englishman's Castle* (London: Edward Arnold, 1909), 28.

47. *Tower Hamlets Independent and General East End Advertiser,* 23 November 1867, 6.

48. *Nonconformist,* 4 November 1868, 1077, and *Bethnal Green Times and East London Advertiser,* 29 February 1869, 2.

49. Christian Mission Conference Minutes, SAHC, June 30–July 1, 1873. The report also listed 329 members at Shoreditch, 272 at Poplar, 100 at Croydon, 50 at Tunbridge Wells, 30 at Portsmouth, and no figures for Hastings, for a total of 1,081 members and another 167 on trial.

50. William Booth, *How to Reach,* i.

51. Eileen Douglas and Mildred Duff, *Commissioner Railton* (London: Salvation Army, n.d.), 27.

52. Railton, *Twenty-One Years' Salvation Army,* 39.

53. See the Christian Mission Conference Minutes, SAHC, 1870 and 1871, and the reports in CMM. See also William Booth and G. S. Railton, *Behind the Pigeon Shop* (London: S. W. Partridge, [1868]).

54. The information here and in the next few paragraphs on the Mission's structure and doctrine is drawn from the Christian Mission Conference Minutes, SAHC, June 15–18, 1870. See also Booth, *Report of the Christian Mission,* and William Booth, *Rules of the Christian Mission* (London, n.d.).

55. Even the wording was identical in much of the document. See Baggaly, *A Digest of the Minutes,* 220–23. Norman Murdoch, "Evangelical Sources of Salvation Army Doctrine," *Evangelical Quarterly* 59, no. 3 (July 1987): 237–38, has traced the similarities between 1865 Christian Mission statements of doctrine and the doctrines of the Evangelical Alliance, set out in 1846. I agree that the two statements contain important similarities, but the differences are equally significant.

56. "In like manner also, that women adorn themselves in modest apparel, with shamefacedness and sobriety; not with braided hair, or gold, or pearls, or costly array. But (which becometh women professing godliness) with good works." 1 Tim. 2:9–10.

57. Sandall, *The History of The Salvation Army,* 1955 reprint, vol. 1, app. F.

58. Bebbington, *Evangelicalism in Modern Britain,* 151–80; Carwardine, *Transatlantic Revivalism,* 189–91; Kent, *Holding the Fort,* 313–28; McLoughlin, *Modern Revivalism,* 82–83, 103–5, 110–11. Murdoch, "Evangelical Sources," notes that the U.S. influence on the Salvation Army has been largely ignored. He suggests that "Bramwell Booth may have given the best explanation of the reason why the Army has failed to note this link when he wrote, 'some of the opposition which developed in the long run against the Booths was originally due to a prejudice against "foreigners," particularly these evangelists from the United States.' Identification with American revivalists was not popular in England" (243).

59. William Booth, *The Doctrines of the Salvation Army* (London: Salvation Army, 1891), 62.

60. Ibid., 74–83. See also "Holiness," CMM, April 1871, 49–53, and May 1871, 64–68; and Catherine Booth, *Holiness: Being an Address Delivered in St. James Hall, Piccadilly, London* (London: Salvation Army, n.d.).

61. William L. Andrews, ed., *Sisters of the Spirit: Three Black Women's Autobiographies of the Nineteenth Century* (Bloomington: Indiana University Press, 1986); Hardesty, *Women Called to Witness;* Cheryl Towsend Gilkes, "The Politics of 'Silence': Dual-Sex Political Systems and Women's Traditions of Conflict in African-American Religion," in *African-American Christianity: Essays in History,* ed. Paul E. Johnson (Berkeley: University of California Press, 1994), 80–110, and Humez, "'My Spirit Eye,'" 129–43. African-American and English women had different religious cultures and therefore took up this theology in different ways. Its influence, however, was felt in both contexts by midcentury, and women on both sides of the Atlantic were aware of and influenced by each other's preaching and written work.

62. These women were not strangers. Geraldine Hooper preached at the Christian Mission in April 1872 (*East London Observer,* 13 April 1872, 6). Hooper was an Anglican, a popular preacher, and the author of equally popular penny tracts. She died in 1872 at the age of thirty-one. See Olive Anderson, "Women Preachers in Mid-Victorian Britain: Some Reflections on Feminism, Popular Religion and Social Change," *Historical Journal,* 12, no. 3 (1969): 471.

63. See Anderson, "Women Preachers in Mid-Victorian Britain."

64. *The Book and Its Mission,* October 1857.

65. *Missing Link,* 1 November 1866.

66. F. K. Prochaska, "Body and Soul: Bible Nurses and the Poor in Victorian London," *Historical Research* 60, no. 143 (October 1987): 336–48, and F. K. Prochaska, "A Mother's Country: Mothers' Meetings and Family Welfare in Britain, 1850–1950," *History* 74, no. 242 (October 1989): 379–99.

67. "Female Preachers," Christian Mission Conference Minutes, SAHC, June 15–18, 1870, n.p.

68. See Chapter 4.

69. The Circuit Plans for 1870 and for 1872, the Christian Mission at Whitechapel, SAHC, are the only two extant, but it is probable Whitechapel was roughly similar to the other circuits. It is difficult to be certain of the number of women because some of the names are no longer legible. See also Croydon Elders' Meeting Minutes, the (East London) Christian Mission, SAHC, October 23, 1869, and the minutes of the Shoreditch Elders Meeting, the (East London) Christian Mission, SAHC, January 26, 1872. For Annie Davis's appointment, see CMM, July 1875, 192.

70. George J. Stevenson, *Historical Sketch of the Christian Community, A.D. 1818–1826 by One of Their Members* (London: George J. Stevenson, 1868); Rob Roy, *"Go Out Quickly" into the Streets and Lanes of the City* (London: Open Air Mission Society, 1855); Bebbington, *Evangelicalism in Modern Britain*, 119–20; Lewis, *Lighten Their Darkness*.

71. Robert Nye, "The Bio-medical Origins of Urban Sociology," *Journal of Contemporary History* 20, no. 4 (October 1985): 659–75; Gareth Stedman Jones, *Outcast London: A Study in the Relationship between the Classes in Victorian Society* (Oxford: Clarendon Press, 1971), ch. 16; Peter Stallybrass and Allon White, *The Politics and Poetics of Transgression* (London: Methuen, 1986), ch. 3.

72. Booth, *How to Reach*, 5–6.

73. Reported in CMM, July 1876, 145.

74. Cox, *The English Churches in a Secular Society*; Reed, "Ritualism Rampant in East London"; Brian Harrison, "For Church, Queen and Family: The Girls Friendly Society, 1874–1920," *Past and Present*, no. 61 (November 1973): 107–38; Gerald Parsons, "A Question of Meaning: Religion and Working-Class Life," in *Religion in Victorian Britain*, vol. 2, ed. Gerald Parsons (Manchester: Manchester University Press, 1988), 63–87.

75. John Burnett, *A Social History of Housing, 1815–1985*, 2d ed. (London: Methuen, 1986), 150.

76. M. J. Daunton, *House and Home in the Victorian City: Working-Class Housing, 1850–1914* (Baltimore: Arnold, 1983), and M. J. Daunton, "Public Place and Private Space: The Victorian City and the Working-Class Household," in *The Pursuit of Urban History*, ed. Derek Fraser and Anthony Sutcliffe (London: Arnold, 1983); this author persuasively argues that these two types of housing fostered different relationships between public and private space and that the shift was part of a conscious middle-class effort to reshape working-class habits. For the Salvation Army, however, both kinds of streets provided a route to a large potential audience. See also James Winter, *London's Teeming Streets, 1830–1914* (London: Routledge, 1993), for a description of how Londoners used their streets.

77. Ellen Chase, *Tenant Friends in Old Deptford* (London: Williams and Norgate, 1929), 58.

78. *Morning Advertiser,* 15 April 1869, 3; *Christian,* 4 August 1870, 11; CMM, August 1870, 121.

79. A penny gaff was an inexpensive theater that offered a variety of music and often the display of people with especially unusual physical traits.

80. Brian Harrison, *Drink and the Victorians* (Pittsburgh: University of Pittsburgh Press, 1971); Peter Bailey, *Leisure and Class in Victorian England, 1830–1885* (London: Routledge & Kegan Paul, 1978); Peter Bailey, ed., "Making Sense of Music Hall," *Music Hall: The Business of Pleasure* (Milton Keynes: Open University Press, 1986); Andrew Davies, *Leisure, Gender and Poverty: Working-Class Culture in Salford and Manchester, 1900–1939* (Buckingham: Open University Press, 1992); Penelope Summerfield, "The Effingham Arms and the Empire: Deliberate Selection in the Evolution of Music Hall in London," in *Popular Culture and Class Conflict, 1590–1914,* eds. Eileen Yeo and Stephen Yeo (Sussex: Harvester Press, 1981), 209–40.

81. Rule, "Methodism, Popular Beliefs and Village Culture," 48–70, and Barrie Trinder, *The Industrial Revolution in Shropshire* (London: Phillimore, 1973), 292–93.

82. Summerfield, "The Effingham Arms and the Empire," 221. See also Davies, *Leisure, Gender and Poverty.*

83. *East London Observer,* 6 April 1867, 2.

84. *East London Observer,* 15 April 1871, 4.

85. John K. Walton, *The English Seaside Resort: A Social History, 1750–1914* (New York: St. Martin's Press, 1983), and James Walvin, *Beside the Seaside* (London: Allen Lane, 1978).

86. Statistics for 1878 and 1879 are given in the *Northern Daily Express,* 12 April 1879, 4.

87. Railton, *Twenty-One Years' Salvation Army,* 63.

88. Ibid., 65.

89. CMM, September 1878, 236.

90. Ervine, *God's Soldier,* vol. 2, app. III.

91. It was, in fact, altered several times. See ibid., vol. 2, Epilogue, and 2:1046–49, 1078–90.

92. See, for example, J. J. R. Redstone, *An Ex-Captain's Experience of the Salvation Army* (London: Christian Commonwealth Publishers, [1888]), and S. A. Hodges, *General Booth: "The Family" and the Salvation Army, Showing Its Rise, Progress, and Moral and Spiritual Decline* (Manchester: Printed and Published by the Author, 1890).

93. CMM, September 1878, 323.

94. CMM, November 1878, 281; see also Sandall, *The History of the Salvation Army,* 2:38.

95. Charles Fry Papers, SAHC, Fred Fry, letter to Mr. Hawkes, February 20, 1928, and "The Autobiography of Charles William Fry," manuscript, n.d. See also Sandall, *The History of the Salvation Army,* 2:113–14.

96. The General, *Orders and Regulations for Field Officers* (London: Salvation Army, 1886), ch. 7, sec. 5.

97. "Explanation of Terms," ibid., i.
98. Ibid., ch. 7, sec. 5. In some instances, a divisional officer might be a staff captain, and other adjustments were not unusual.
99. SAHC, Articles of War.

3. CONVERSION

1. Geo. R., *The Salvation Navvy: Being an Account of the Life, Death and Victories of Captain John Allen of the Salvation Army* (London: Salvation Army, 1880), 9.
2. Ibid., 15.
3. Ibid., 17.
4. Ibid., 33.
5. Ibid., 10.
6. This phrase is taken from Mack, *Visionary Women.*
7. On working-class autobiography, see Gretchen Galbraith, *Reading Lives: Reconstructing Childhood, Books, and Schools in Britain, 1870–1920* (London: Macmillan, 1997), and David Vincent, *Bread, Knowledge and Freedom: A Study of Nineteenth-Century Working-Class Autobiography* (London: Europa, 1981).
8. Jones, "Working-Class Culture and Working-Class Politics," 471.
9. Stephen Humphries, *Hooligans or Rebels?: An Oral History of Working-Class Childhood and Youth, 1889–1939* (Oxford: Basil Blackwell, 1981). McLeod, "New Perspectives on Victorian Working-Class Religion," notes that Humphries "is mainly concerned with religion as a tool of authority," but he "tends to underestimate the complexity and ambivalence of many people's attitudes" (32). Elizabeth Roberts, *A Woman's Place: An Oral History of Working-Class Women, 1890–1940* (Oxford: Basil Blackwell 1984), like Humphries, uses oral evidence but presents a picture of working-class religiosity very like the one suggested by the Salvationist conversion narratives of two decades earlier.
10. Regina Gagnier, *Subjectivities: A History of Self-Representation in Britain, 1832–1920* (Oxford: Oxford University Press, 1991), 152.
11. Chana Ullman, *The Transformed Self: The Psychology of Religious Conversion* (New York: Plenum, 1989), 152.
12. Philip Greven, *The Protestant Temperament: Patterns of Child-Rearing, Religious Experience, and Self in Early America* (New York: Knopf, 1977).
13. There is a rich literature on Puritans, some of which is distinctly critical of Greven's approach. See, for example, Charles Lloyd Cohen, *God's Caress: The Psychology of the Puritan Religious Experience* (New York: Oxford University Press, 1986).
14. Paula Fredricksen, "Paul and Augustine: Conversion Narratives, Orthodox Traditions and the Retrospective Self," *Journal of Theological Studies* 37, no. 1 (1986): 33. Fredrickson also makes the important point that Paul does not convert to Christianity, as there was, at that time, no Christianity. Paul himself referred to his experience as a prophetic call. See also Joe E. Barnhart and Mary Ann Barnhart, *The New Birth: A Naturalistic View of Religious Conversion* (Macon, Ga.: Mercer University Press, 1981); V. Bailey Gillespie, *The Dynamics of Religious Conversion* (Birmingham, Ala.: Religious Education Press,

1991); Richard H. Hutch, *The Meaning of Lives: Biography, Autobiography and the Spiritual Quest* (London: Cassell, 1997); Hugh Kerr and John Mulder, *Conversions: The Christian Experience* (Grand Rapids, Mich.: Eerdmans, 1983).

15. Linda Peterson, *Victorian Autobiography: The Tradition of Self-Interpretation* (New Haven, Conn.: Yale University Press, 1986), 36. See also Elaine J. Lawless, *Handmaidens of the Lord: Pentecostal Women Preachers and Tradition Religion* (Philadelphia: University of Pennsylvania Press, 1988), especially ch. 2.

16. William H. Myers, *God's Yes Was Louder Than My No: Rethinking the African American Call to Ministry* (Grand Rapids, Mich.: Eerdmans, 1994), 109, argues persuasively that the story and the narrative of a call are often different. That difference is not lying; it is hermeneutics. Carolyn Steedman, *Landscape for a Good Woman* (London: Virago Press, 1986), argues that "delineation of emotional and psychological selfhood has been made by and through the testimony of people in a central relationship to the dominant culture, that is to say by and through people who were not working class. . . . Superficially, it might be said that historians, failing to find evidence of most people's emotional or psycho-sexual existence, have simply assumed that there can't have been much there to find" (11–12). Steedman's point can be extended to spiritual and religious life; in order to do so, the sources must be read with attention to the theological and social context in which they were produced.

17. Colls, "Primitive Methodists," notes that oral performance was key to the Primitive Methodists: the "intonations, rhythms, dialects, anecdotes, addresses, prayers, the third dimension of music—which the historian can hardly know. It represents a buzz of words and music over our history, not audible through the written record. . . . In high language, Bible and hymnal raised the proceedings to the pitch of verse. Verse was the medium of monologue between Maker and made" (332). Colls's argument alerted me to the importance of oral performance in the Salvation Army.

18. These figures are drawn from Josef L. Altholz, *The Religious Press in Britain, 1760–1900* (New York: Greenwood Press, 1989), and Richard Altick, *The English Common Reader: A Social History of the Mass Reading Public, 1800–1910* (Chicago: University of Chicago Press, 1957). William Nicolson, *The Romance of the War Cry* (London: Salvationist Publishing, 1929), gives a circulation figure of seventeen thousand per week in 1879.

19. Richard Mudie-Smith, ed., *The Religious Life of London* (London: Hodder & Stoughton, 1904).

20. Murdoch, *Origins of the Salvation Army,* 120; McLeod, *Class and Religion,* 60, 89. McLeod states that 11.1 percent of attenders were at Salvation Army services in Scarborough, 7.4 percent in Hull, 6.8 percent in Barnsley, and 5.3 percent in Bristol.

21. Primitive Methodist Chapel, Tatham Street, Sunderland, Leaders' Meeting Minutes C/Su34/1/1, November 11, 1880, Tyne and Wear Archives Service, Newcastle-upon-Tyne.

22. Chase, *Tenant Friends,* 43.

23. Frank Hardy not only guided me through the complexities of nineteenth-century census returns and shared his valuable system for recording data but

joined in my search and found many of these Salvationists. I am most grateful for both his expertise and his enthusiasm.

24. See Patricia Malcolmson, *English Laundresses: A Social History, 1850–1930* (Urbana: University of Illinois Press, 1986).

25. George Lansbury, *My Life* (London: Constable, 1928), 28–29.

26. Elswick Local History Group, "May," in *Living and Working in Elswick* (Newcastle-upon-Tyne, 1984), 10. This kind of religious fluidity is suggested by Roberts, *A Woman's Place.*

27. Mark Noll, David Bebbington, and George Rawlyk, eds., *Evangelicalism: Comparative Studies of Popular Protestantism in North America, the British Isles and Beyond, 1700–1900* (New York: Oxford University Press, 1994), Introduction. For other perspectives on the Salvation Army's theology, see Murdoch, *Origins of the Salvation Army,* 65–70, and Horridge, *The Salvation Army,* 222–23.

28. William Booth, *Doctrines and Disciplines of the Salvation Army* (London: Salvation Army Headquarters, 1881), 12, 14, 38, 44, 49.

29. Ibid., 62.

30. Ibid., 77, 80, 81.

31. WC, 23 May 1885, 1.

32. Timothy L. Smith, "Holiness and Radicalism in Nineteenth Century America," in *Sanctification and Liberation,* ed. Theodore Runyon (Nashville, Tenn.: Abingdon Press, 1981), 118.

33. Anderson, "Women Preachers in Mid-Victorian Britain," 477.

34. Robertson, "The Salvation Army," 100.

35. Bebbington, *Evangelicalism in Modern Britain,* 166.

36. Ibid., 172–77.

37. On the status of head of household, see Geoffrey Crossick, *An Artisan Elite in Victorian Society: Kentish London, 1840–1880* (London: Croom Helm, 1978).

38. Ellen Ross, *Love and Toil: Motherhood in Outcast London* (New York: Oxford University Press, 1993), 44.

39. Charles Booth, *Life and Labour,* 1st ser., vol. 1, 50, quoted in Ross, *Love and Toil,* 22.

40. Ross, *Love and Toil,* 43, and A. E. Dingle, "Drink and the Working-Class Standard of Living, 1870–1914," *Economic History Review* 25, no. 4 (November 1972): 608–22.

41. Ross, *Love and Toil,* 34 and 44.

42. Davies, *Leisure, Gender and Poverty,* 61.

43. WC, 10 November 1881, 1.

44. WC, 30 March 1882, 2.

45. Geo. R., *The Salvation Navvy,* 26.

46. Elliot J. Gorn, *The Manly Art: Bare-Knuckle Prize Fighting in America* (Ithaca, N.Y.: Cornell University Press, 1986), analyzes pugilism in the United States in these terms. Paul Willis, *Learning to Labour* (Westmead, Farnborough, Hants: Saxon House, 1977), analyzes the link between masculinity and physical labor in contemporary Britain in a way that also informs this interpretation.

47. Charles Fry Papers, SAHC, "The Autobiography of Charles William Fry," manuscript, n.d.

48. WC, 17 March 1881, 3.

49. WC, 4 December 1880, 1.

50. *Daily Telegraph* (London), 3 February 1882, 5.

51. WC, 27 January 1881, 2.

52. *Lancashire Nancy: A Miracle Story of Today* (London: Salvationist Publishing, n.d.).

53. Capt. Albert Hadden, *Life and Death of Fish Pollie Late a Soldier in Leed II Corps, of the Salvation Army. Who Died Nov. 10th, 1885; and an Account of Her Funeral* (Leeds: Jas. Stafford, n.d.), 1.

54. WC, 10 October 1887, 5.

55. WC, 20 February 1884, 2.

56. WC, 27 March 1886, 4.

57. Bynum, "Women's Stories, Women's Symbols: A Critique of Victor Turner's Theory of Liminality," in *Fragmentation and Redemption*, 27–52, identifies a similar pattern in the vitas of medieval women. This similarity is suggestive of a broader culture of gender and Christianity in European societies.

58. Billy McLeod Papers, SAHC, poster, early 1880s?

59. See Davies, *Leisure, Gender and Poverty*, 71, for oral histories of Nancy Cunningham.

60. Valenze, *Prophetic Sons and Daughters*, 36.

61. Richard Free, *Seven Years' Hard* (New York: Dutton, 1905), 41, 43.

62. Loane, *An Englishman's Castle*, 3. See also Margaret Loane, *The Queen's Poor* (London: Edward Arnold, 1905), ch. 2, on working-class religion.

63. WC, 21 September 1882, 1.

64. WC, 26 October 1882, 2.

65. M. Greenwood et al., "Deaths by Violence, 1837–1937," *Journal of the Royal Statistical Society* 104, pt. 2 (1941): 146–71.

66. WC, 9 October 1880, 4.

67. WC, 3 March 1881, 1.

68. WC, 23 June 1881, 1.

69. WC, 26 October 1882, 2.

70. *Daily Telegraph* (London), 3 February 1882, 3.

71. WC, 3 March 1881, 2.

72. WC, 20 October 1881, 1.

73. WC, 9 March 1882, 2.

74. Elizabeth Churchill Papers, SAHC, "My Life Story" (manuscript autobiography), n.d.

75. WC, 3 November 1881, 1.

76. WC, 23 February 1882, 1.

77. WC, 14 February 1880, 2.

78. WC, 20 January 1881, 1.

79. WC, 3 February 1881, 1.

80. WC, 4 August 1881, 1.

81. Brig. William Baugh, "Reminiscences of Early Day Fighting," *Officers' Review*, March 1935, 137–39.

82. WC, 10 March 1881, 3.

83. Peterson, *Victorian Autobiography*, 36.

84. On Methodists, see Valenze, *Prophetic Sons and Daughters,* esp. 28–30 and 198–200.

85. WC, 3 February 1881, 1.

86. WC, 2 June 1881, 1.

87. WC, 11 August 1881, 1.

88. WC, 9 February 1881, 1.

89. Charles Rich Papers, SAHC, Candidate's Personal Experience, April 13, 1891.

90. John Addie, "Reminiscences of Early Day Fighting," *Officers' Review,* November 1934, 511.

91. WC, 27 March 1886, 4.

92. WC, 3 March 1881, 1.

93. WC, 9 October 1880, 1.

94. WC, 6 November 1880, 1.

95. WC, 19 April 1887, 1.

96. WC, 2 October 1880, 1.

97. William Booth, comp., *Salvation Army Music* (London: Salvation Army, n.d.), no. 74.

98. Cornelius Smith, *The Life Story of Gipsy Cornelius Smith* (London: John Heywood, [1890]), 35.

99. Ibid., 41–42.

100. WC, 27 November 1880, 1.

101. WC, 16 March 1882, 1.

102. WC, 21 September 1882, 1.

103. Charles Fry Papers, SAHC, "The Autobiography of Charles William Fry," manuscript, n.d.

104. WC, 10 March 1881, 1.

105. WC, 20 February 1886, 1.

106. Charles Fry Papers, SAHC, "The Autobiography of Charles William Fry," manuscript, n.d.

107. WC, 3 February 1881, 1.

108. WC, 10 January 1880, 1.

109. WC, 29 December 1881, 1.

110. WC, 9 February 1882, 2.

111. Ann Taves, "Knowing through the Body: Dissociative Religious Experience in the African- and British-American Methodist Traditions," *Journal of Religion* 73, no. 2 (April 1993): 200–222.

112. CMM, May 1876, 111, and CMM, June 1874, 166.

113. See, for example, Harold Bloom, *The American Religion: The Emergence of the Post-Christian Nation* (New York: Simon & Schuster, 1992); Clarke Garrett, *Respectable Folly: Millenarians and the French Revolution in France and England* (Baltimore: Johns Hopkins University Press, 1975); Ronald Knox, *Enthusiasm: A Chapter in the History of Religion* (Oxford: Oxford University Press, 1950).

114. Michael Warner, "Tongues Untied: Memoirs of a Pentecostal Boyhood," *Voice Literary Supplement,* no. 112 (February 1993): 15.

115. Bramwell Booth, *Echoes and Memories* (London: Salvationist Publishing, 1925), 53.

116. WC, 27 March 1886, 5.

117. Mack, *Visionary Women*, argues that seventeenth-century Quakers believed being in the light allowed a speaker to essentially transcend gender. See also Caroline Walker Bynum, Steven Harrell, and Paula Richman, eds., "Introduction," *Gender and Religion: On the Complexity of Symbols* (Boston: Beacon Press, 1986), and Judith Hoch-Smith and Anita Spring, eds., *Women in Ritual and Symbolic Roles* (New York: Plenum, 1978).

118. WC, 30 March 1882, 1.

119. WC, 27 April 1880, 1.

120. WC, 17 March 1881, 10, and WC, 27 January 1881, 4.

4. SAVING SOULS

1. Ervine, *God's Soldier*, 1:349.

2. Elijah Cadman Papers, SAHC, George Scott Railton, letter to Elijah Cadman, July 14, 1876.

3. Elijah Cadman Papers, SAHC, Bramwell Booth, letter to Elijah Cadman, April 13, 1878.

4. *All the World*, December 1918, 538.

5. Adalaide Cox Papers, SAHC, Form of Application for Appointment as an Officer to the Salvation Army, February 1881.

6. Adalaide Cox, *Hotchpotch* (London: Salvationist Publishing, 1937).

7. ELE, January 1869, 62.

8. ELE, October 1868, 10.

9. D. W. Bebbington, "The City, the Countryside, and the Social Gospel in Late Victorian Nonconformity," in *The Church in Town and Countryside*, ed. Derek Baker (Oxford: Blackwell, 1979); Heasman, *Evangelicals in Action*; Lewis, *Lighten Their Darkness*.

10. On other mission movements, see, for example, a report on the London Cottage Mission: *Tower Hamlets Independent and General East End Advertiser*, 22 January 1876, 5; the missions in Hoxton and Shoreditch: *Tower Hamlets Independent and General East End Advertiser*, 15 April 1876, 3, and Richard Weaver, *Bethnal Green Times and East London Advertiser*, 10 April 1869, 4; street preachers: *Bethnal Green Times and East London Advertiser*, 22 February 1868, 3. The *Revival* published regular short articles on activities in East London throughout the 1860s. See, for example, 4 May 1865, 282; 7 June 1866, 328–29; 6 December 1866, 319; 2 September 1869, 4; 29 October 1868, 599–600; 28 March 1869, 9.

11. *Morning Advertiser*, 5 April 1869, 3.

12. *Revival*, 7 June 1866, 329. See also "Irregular Religious Agencies," *Nonconformist*, 10 April 1867, 289–90.

13. *Revival*, 4 February 1869, 9.

14. *Nonconformist*, 4 November 1868, 1077.

15. *Tower Hamlets Independent and General East End Advertiser*, 23 November 1867, 6.

16. Clive Field, "Methodism in London, 1850–1920: A Social and Sociological Study" (Ph.D. thesis, Oxford University, 1974), and Henry D. Rack, "The

Decline of the Class Meeting and the Problem of Church Membership in Nineteenth-Century Wesleyanism," *Proceedings of the Wesley Historical Society* 39, pt. 1 (February 1973): 12–21. McLeod, *Class and Religion,* x, indicates that 28.52 percent of Inner London residents attended regular worship services, and of those 13.2 percent attended the Church of England.

17. Croydon Elders' Meeting Minutes, the (East London) Christian Mission, SAHC, 1869–71. The only elders' meeting minutes that have survived are from Croydon and Shoreditch (1868–74).

18. Christian Mission Conference Minutes, SAHC, "Member," 1870, n.p.

19. Christian Mission Conference Minutes, SAHC, "Leaders," 1870.

20. Christian Mission Conference Minutes, SAHC, "Leaders," June 18, 1879, n.p.

21. Circuit Plan, the Christian Mission at Whitechapel, SAHC, 1870. The Whitechapel circuit plan is the only one to survive, but no evidence suggests that the other circuit plans were any different.

22. Letterbooks, the Christian Mission, SAHC, George Scott Railton, letter to Mr. J. Fidler, 1876?

23. Christian Mission Conference Minutes, SAHC, "Open Air Services," 1870.

24. ELE, October 1868, 4.

25. Sandall, *The History of the Salvation Army,* vol. 2, pt. 3.

26. The Salvation Army published several similar hymnbooks before 1890. See Gordon Avery, *Companion to the Song Book of the Salvation Army* (London: Salvationist Publishing, 1961).

27. George Scott Railton, *Captain Ted: Being the Life Story of Captain Edward Irons of the Salvation Army* (London: Salvation Army, 1889), 76.

28. Letterbooks, the Christian Mission, SAHC, George Scott Railton, letter to Miss A. Woods, January 17, 1876.

29. Rodney Smith, *Gipsy Smith: His Life and Work by Himself* (London: National Council of Evangelical Free Churches, 1902), 95.

30. Ibid., 86–87.

31. Ibid., 96.

32. Ibid.

33. Rosina Davies, *The Story of My Life* (Llandyssul: Gomerian Press, 1942), 51.

34. Ervine, *God's Soldier,* 1:359–60.

35. Ibid., 1:457.

36. Alfred Tutte Papers, SAHC, typescript diary, 5.

37. *Brigadier William Bennett: The Black Prince* (London: Salvation Army, 1930), 12.

38. Booth, *Echoes,* 53.

39. Christian Mission Conference Minutes, SAHC, 1870, n.p. On the work of women in the American Salvation Army, see Taiz, "Hallelujah Lasses in the Battle for Souls," 84–105.

40. Croydon Elders' Meeting Minutes, SAHC, 1869–71; Circuit Plan, the Christian Mission at Whitechapel, SAHC, 1870.

41. CMM, July 1875, 193.

42. Manuscript Census, Public Records Office, London, 1871, RG 10, 566, f. 44.

43. Manuscript Census, Public Records Office, London, 1871, RG 10, 485, f. 76, schedule 6.

44. Manuscript Census, Public Records Office, London, 1871, RG 10, 520, 32 Oxford St.

45. WC, 19 April 1890, 2.

46. Prochaska, "A Mother's Country," 381.

47. Ibid., 385.

48. Martha Vicinus, *Independent Women: Work and Community for Single Women, 1850–1920* (Chicago: University of Chicago Press, 1985), ch. 2.

49. The *Revival,* 28 January 1869, 781, named as preachers Miss Robinson, Miss Octavia Jary, Miss MacFarlane, Mrs. Baxter, Miss Wilson, Mrs. Dening (lately Miss G. Hooper), and on 6 April 1865, 215, it reported on the services led by Mrs. Thistlewaite.

50. *Missing Link,* November 1866, 1.

51. Elizabeth Nightingale, ed., *Mrs. Collier of Birmingham, a Biblewoman's Story: Being the Autobiography of Mrs. Collier,* 2d ed. (London: T .Woolmer, 1885).

52. Heasman, *Evangelicals in Action;* F. K. Prochaska, *Women and Philanthropy in Nineteenth-Century England* (Oxford: Clarendon Press, 1980); Prochaska, "Body and Soul," 336–48; Prochaska, "A Mother's Country"; Judith R. Walkowitz, *City of Dreadful Delight* (Chicago: University of Chicago Press, 1992), 54.

53. Friendly societies were voluntary benefit organizations that provided members with, for example, money for funerals.

54. Joanna Bornat, "Lost Leaders: Women, Trade Unionism, and the Case of the General Union of Textile Workers, 1875–1914," in *Unequal Opportunities,* ed. Angela John (Oxford: Blackwell, 1986); Anna Clark, *The Struggle for the Breeches: Gender and the Making of the British Working Class* (Berkeley: University of California Press, 1995); Judy Lown, *Women and Industrialization: Gender and Work in Nineteenth Century England* (Cambridge: Polity Press, 1990); Sonya Rose, *Limited Livelihoods: Gender and Class in Nineteenth Century England* (Berkeley: University of California Press, 1992); Deborah Thom, "The Bundle of Sticks: Women, Trade Unionists and Collective Organization before 1918," *Nice Girls and Rude Girls: Women Workers in World War I* (London: Tauris, 1998).

55. Quoted in Bornat, "Lost Leaders," 209.

56. Ibid., 213. See also Ellen F. Mappen, "Strategists for Change: Social Feminist Approaches to the Problems of Women's Work," in *Unequal Opportunities,* ed. Angela John (Oxford: Blackwell, 1986), and Thom, *Nice Girls and Rude Girls.*

57. Hannah Mitchell, *The Hard Way Up: The Autobiography of Hannah Mitchell* (London: Faber, 1968); Jill Liddington and Jill Norris, *One Hand Tied behind Us: The Rise of the Women's Suffrage Movement* (London: Virago, 1978); Margaret Llewelyn Davis, ed., *Life as We Have Known It* (New York: Norton, 1974).

58. ELE, June 1869, 137.

59. Ibid., 142.

60. Ibid.

61. CMM, February 1871, 25.

62. ELE, December 1868, 47.

63. Quoted in Sandall, *The History of the Salvation Army*, 1:237.

64. Booth, *Female Ministry*, 20.

65. Christian Mission Conference Minutes, SAHC, June 1875.

66. [George Scott Railton], *Commissioner Dowdle: The Saved Railway Guard* (London: Salvation Army Publishing, 1901, 1912; reprint, London: Salvationist Publishing, 1930), 56.

67. WC, 2 March 1882, 1.

68. Capt. Pearson, "Blood and Fire," WC, 4 September 1880, 3.

69. Railton, *Twenty-One Years' Salvation Army*, 105.

70. To *open a town*, a term used by the Christian Mission and Salvation Army, meant to establish a first mission station or corps in a town.

71. For biographical information on Pamela Shepard, see Charles Preece, *Woman of the Valley: The Story of Mother Shepard* (Port Talbot, West Glamorgan: New Life Publications, 1988), and Sandall, *The History of the Salvation Army*, 2:12; for Sarah Sayers, see Manuscript Census, Public Records Office, London, 1871, RG 10, 413, f. 24, and Circuit Plans, the Christian Mission at Whitechapel, SAHC, 1870 and 1872.

72. Preece, *Woman of the Valley*, 85–88, and Sandall, *The History of the Salvation Army*, 2:112. This is a reference to the hymn "There is a fountain filled with blood, drawn from Immanuel's veins, where sinners come and wash away all their guilty stains."

73. Preece, *Woman of the Valley*, 113.

74. *Salvationist*, 12 December 1879, 37.

75. W. T. Stead Papers, Churchill College, Cambridge, William Booth, letter to W. T. Stead, July 19, 1879. Clapham was twenty-two years old at the time. See her biography in WC, 30 December 1880, 1.

76. CMM, December 1878, 317.

77. Manuscript Census, Public Records Office, London, 1881, RG 11, 312, ff. 107–8, and RG 11, 296, f. 21. This information was kindly provided by Gordon Taylor, the Salvation Army Heritage Centre, London.

78. *A Way to the World: Being the Annual Report and Statement of Accounts of the International Training Homes of the Salvation Army, 1885* (London: Salvation Army Book Depot, n.d.), 7. See also Emma Booth and Ballington Booth, *The Training Barracks or Our London Homes* (London: Salvation Army Bookstores, [1883]); *Through the Homes at Clapton* (London: Salvation Army, n.d.); *Men's Training Home: General Rules and Regulations* (London: Salvation Army, [1883]).

79. WC, 21 February 1885, 1, and 26 February 1887, 13.

80. Elizabeth Churchill Papers, SAHC, "My Life Story" (manuscript autobiography), n.d., 16.

81. WC, 10 December 1884, 3.

82. Elizabeth Churchill Papers, SAHC, "My Life Story" (manuscript autobiography), n.d., 17–18.

83. Ibid., 20, 20–21, 45, 52.

84. WC, 18 July 1889, 3.

85. WC, 8 March 1890, 9.

86. Catherine Booth Papers, SAHC, letter to Polly Ashton, February 24, 1890.

87. Letterbooks, the Christian Mission, SAHC, George Scott Railton, letter to G. Thursfield, Esq., August 3, 1876. See also Letterbooks, the Christian Mission, SAHC, William Booth letter to "A Sister," June 15, 1876, where he offers a salary of 14 shillings a week.

88. Letterbooks, the Christian Mission, SAHC, George Scott Railton, letter to F. Thursfield, May 23, 1867, and to Miss Woodcock, January 22, 1876.

89. Elijah Cadman Papers, SAHC, G. S. Railton, letter to Elijah Cadman, July 14, 1876. For Salvation Army wages, see "The Salvation Army," *Contemporary Review,* 42 (1882): 181; Jane Lewis, *Women in England, 1870–1950* (Bloomington: Indiana University Press, 1984), 8; A. L. Bowley, *Wages and Incomes in the United Kingdom since 1860* (Cambridge: Cambridge University Press, 1900), 60. Ross, *Love and Toil,* found that in "Britain as a whole, in 1886 and twenty years later as well, a quarter of employed adult workmen earned under a pound a week," and women's wages would have been substantially lower (45). On teachers' wages, see Copelman, *London's Women Teachers,* 75. On domestic servants' wages, see F. K. Prochaska, "Female Philanthropy and Domestic Service in Victorian England," *Bulletin of the Institute of Historical Research* 54 (1981): 80–82.

90. *Pall Mall Gazette,* 2 May 1884, 3.

91. Census information from *News of the World,* 14 September 1884, 2. Information on Salvation Army women from *Pall Mall Gazette,* 2 May 1884, 3.

92. WC, 11 January 1890, 12.

93. WC, 27 March 1880, 4. See also Sandall, *The History of the Salvation Army,* 2:44.

94. WC, 19 March 1887, 13.

95. Bonnie Smith, *Changing Lives: Women in European History since 1700* (Lexington, Mass.: Heath, 1989), 325.

96. CMM, April 1876, 84.

97. Dorothy E. Graham, "Chosen by God: The Female Itinerants of Early Primitive Methodism" (Ph.D. thesis, University of Birmingham, 1986), found some evidence that might suggest that women itinerants on rare occasions did give communion.

98. WC, 13 August 1880, 1.

99. *Record,* 8 February 1882, 2.

100. Over one hundred years later, in the year following the introduction of the ordination of women in the Anglican Church, a woman priest offered communion to a man who declined the wafer and bit her hand, drawing blood, while other women priests in England have had congregations simply refuse to come forward to take communion. Robert McClory, "Women of the Cloth," *Reader* 23, no. 45 (August 12, 1994): 14–18.

101. David Williams, Vicar of Llanelly, letter to the *Guardian,* 16 August 1882. The Salvation Army had a strict teetotal stance, so it was probably not actual wine that was used. See also "The Salvation Army," *Church Quarterly Review* 14, no. 27 (April 1882): 124–25, for a discussion of this issue, which pre-

sented one of the more important and serious divisions between the Church and the Salvation Army.

102. Catherine Booth, quoted in Sandall, *The History of the Salvation Army,* 2:130. Similarly, baptism was rejected. The Salvation Army did not believe that the sprinkling of water could have any effect on the state of an infant's soul. See Sandall, *The History of the Salvation Army,* 2:130–33.

103. William Booth corresponded with Dr. Benson, then bishop of Truro and later archbishop of Canterbury, on this subject. See Ervine, *God's Soldier,* 1:468–71.

104. Norman Vance, *The Sinews of the Spirit: The Ideal of Christian Manliness in Victorian Literature and Religious Thought* (Cambridge: Cambridge University Press, 1985).

105. On Anglo-Catholicism and the working class, see Reed, "Ritualism Rampant in East London," 375–404.

106. Muscular Christianity was one prominent attempt to make Christianity "manly." See Vance, *Sinews of the Spirit*; Michael Rosenthal, *The Character Factory: Baden-Powell and the Origins of the Boy Scout Movement* (New York: Pantheon Books, 1986); John Springhall, "Building Character in the British Boy: The Attempt to Extend Christian Manliness to Working-Class Adolescents, 1880–1914," in *Manliness and Morality: Middle-Class Masculinity in Britain and America,* ed. J. A. Mangan and James Walvin (Manchester: Manchester University Press, 1987).

107. McLeod, *Piety and Poverty,* esp. ch. 7. From a detailed study of both written and oral history sources, McLeod concludes that a greater proportion of women attended church than men, although the ratio varied considerably in different regions. Clive Field, "Adam and Eve: Gender in the English Free Church Constituency," *Journal of Ecclesiastical History* 44, no. 1 (January 1993): 65, found in the Baptist and Congregational membership lists he examined that two-thirds of the members were women.

108. CMM, March 1874, 71.

109. Bailey, *Leisure and Class;* Ellen Ross, "Fierce Questions and Taunts: Married Life in Working-Class London, 1870–1914," in *Metropolis London: Histories and Representations since 1800,* ed. David Feldman and Gareth Stedman Jones (London: Routledge, 1989), 219–44; Ellen Ross, "Survival Networks: Women's Neighbourhood Sharing in London before World War One," *History Workshop Journal,* no. 5 (spring 1983): 4–27; Stedman Jones, "Working-Class Culture and Working-Class Politics," 460–507.

110. WC, 6 February 1884, 1.

111. WC, 10 November 1881, 1, and ELE, November 1868, 29.

112. CMM, September 1874, 245.

113. WC, 27 January 1881, 4.

114. Quoted in CMM, October 1871, 159.

115. James Winter, *London's Teeming Streets,* esp. ch. 8.

116. CMM, August 1876, 189.

117. ELE, November 1868, 29.

118. WC, 24 March 1881, 4.

119. Charles Fry Papers, SAHC, Fred Fry, letter to Col. F. G. Hawkes, February 20, 1928.

120. Trevor Herbert, ed., "Nineteenth-Century Brass Bands: The Making of a Movement," *Bands: The Brass Band Movement in the Nineteenth and Twentieth Centuries* (Buckingham: Open University Press, 1991), 47, and Hugh Cunningham, *The Volunteer Force: A Social and Political History, 1859–1908* (London: Croom Helm, 1975).

121. "Obadiah Walked behind the Drum," written and composed by Harry Castling, sung by Miss Rose Fletcher (from the private collection of Max Tyler). Another song in the same vein is "The Preacher and the Pin," *Frank Coyle's Songbook* (n.p., 1896), n.p.

122. CMM, February and March 1874.

123. WC, 3 February 1881, 4.

124. Ross, *Love and Toil*, esp. ch. 3.

125. A *Daily News* survey of women as a percentage of those aged fifteen and over at 1902–3 services in Inner London indicated that women constituted 56.3 percent of the congregations at Salvation Army services compared with 65.67 percent at Anglican services, 56.97 percent at Wesleyan services, and 51.59 percent at Primitive Methodist services. Reported in McLeod, *Class and Religion*, 308. These figures are useful but limited because a Sunday service would not necessarily be the most important service to attend and different corps may well have had a different balance between women and men. But they do seem to suggest that the Army did not appeal overwhelming to men or to women.

126. CMM, July 1878, 167.

127. The General, *Orders and Regulations*, 55.

128. WC, 12 October 1882, 2.

129. "Not Really," words by Harry Nicholls, music by Ferdinand Wallerstein. *Era* commented that "there is plenty of applause for the savvy Sisters Cuthbert who made fun of those peripatetic, perambulating howling missionaries constituting what is called the Salvation Army" (October 27, 1881). I am grateful to Michael Diamond for a copy of this song and the comment from *Era*.

130. Brunell University Library, London, Elizabeth Rignall, "All So Long Ago," manuscript autobiography, n.p. Many thanks to Joy Dixon for providing me with a copy of this document. Ross, *Love and Toil*, suggests that this man might well have been the only one in all London who cooked for his family (89).

131. *Lloyds*, 6 May 1883, 6.

132. SAHC, Articles of War.

133. CMM, October 1875, 264.

134. WC, 20 February 1884, 4.

135. Ross, *Love and Toil*, 84.

136. Ibid., 85.

137. *Yorkshire Gazette*, 11 May 1889, 6, and E. P. Thompson, "The Sale of Wives," *Customs in Common* (London: Penguin Books, 1991), 404–66. I am grateful to the late E. P. Thompson for giving me a copy of this newspaper article.

138. Thompson, *Customs in Common*, 455, 459.

139. SAHC, Disposition of Forces, typescript, 1883.

140. Others do not explain why they left. For example, Davies, *The Story of My Life*, does not explain her break with the Army.

141. Smith, *Gipsy Smith*, 136.

142. Redstone, *An Ex-Captain's Experience*, 78.

143. Douglas Beven, *Startling Revelations: Eight Years Experience in the Salvation Army* (Liverpool, 1906).

144. Marechale [Catherine] Booth, "Why We Are Persecuted," in Redstone, *An Ex-Captain's Experience*, 78–81.

145. Booth, William, comp., *Salvation Army Songs* (New York: Salvation Army, 1925), Hymn 252.

5. AUTHORITY AND TRANSGRESSION

1. Walkowitz, *City of Dreadful Delight*, 41.

2. Valenze, *Prophetic Sons and Daughters*, especially chapter 2.

3. Barbara Taylor, *Eve and the New Jerusalem: Socialism and Feminism in the Nineteenth Century* (London: Virago, 1983).

4. Valenze, *Prophetic Sons and Daughters*, 35.

5. Elizabeth Flint, *Hot Bread and Chips* (London: Museum Press, 1963), 35.

6. Elizabeth Flint, *Kipper Stew* (London: Museum Press, 1964), 42.

7. Flint, *Hot Bread*, ch. 13.

8. Peter Bailey, "The Musical Comedy and the Rhetoric of the Girl, 1892–1914," *Popular Culture and Performance in the Victorian City* (Cambridge: Cambridge University Press, 1998), 183.

9. Davies, *Leisure, Gender and Poverty*; Francoise Barret-Ducrocq, *Love in the Time of Victoria* (London: Verso, 1991); Walkowitz, *City of Dreadful Delight*. J. S. Bratton, ed., "Jenny Hill: Sex and Sexism in the Victorian Music Hall," *Music Hall: Performance and Style* (Milton Keynes: Open University Press, 1986), argues that the music-hall performer Jenny Hill used stereotypical working-class figures in her routines in ways that both evoked and reworked the most conventional ideas about working-class femininity and class relations. Her reading of Hill has informed my reading of Salvationist women, who were active at the same time and were from the same class as Hill. On women and spectacle, see Lisa Tickner, *The Spectacle of Women: Imagery of the Suffrage Campaign, 1907–1914* (Chicago: University of Chicago Press, 1988).

10. Ellen Ross, "'Not the Sort That Would Sit on the Doorstep': Respectability in Pre-World War One London Neighborhoods," *International Labor and Working-Class History*, no. 27 (spring 1985): 37–59.

11. *Borough of Marylebone Mercury*, 26 June 1880, 3; *Indicator*, 29 May 1880, 3, and 3 July 1880, 2; Metropolitan Police Papers, Public Records Office, London, Special Division Report, April 13, 1880, PRO MEPO 2/168. See also Booth-Tucker, *The Life of Catherine Booth*, 1:214–16.

12. William Booth Papers, SAHC, Bramwell Booth, letter to William Booth, March 10, 1893.

13. WC, 5 August 1885, 1.

14. Karen L. King, "Afterword: Voices of the Spirit," in *Women Preachers and Prophets through Two Millennia of Christianity*, ed. Beverly Mayne Kienzle and Pamela J. Walker (Berkeley: University of California Press, 1998), esp. 336.

15. Alain Corbin, "Commercial Sexuality in Nineteenth Century France: A System of Images and Representations," in *The Making of the Modern Body*, ed.

Catherine Gallagher and Thomas W. Laqueur (Berkeley: University of California Press, 1987), 209–19, and Judith R. Walkowitz, *Prostitution and Victorian Society: Women, Class and the State* (Cambridge: Cambridge University Press, 1980).

16. Dr. G. Richelot, cited in Lynda Nead, *Myths of Sexuality: Representations of Women in Victorian Britain* (Oxford: Blackwell, 1988), 121.

17. *Daily News,* 17 June 1879, 5.

18. Benson's ambiguous feelings about the Army are evident in his diary, where he recorded his attraction to their fervor but his discomfort with the emotional services. E. M. Benson Papers, Trinity College, Cambridge University, Manuscript Diary, May 12, June 9, June 17, June 19, and June 21, 1882.

19. Stuart Mews, "The General and the Bishops: Alternative Responses to Dechristianization," in *Later Victorian Britain, 1867–1900,* ed. T. R. Gourvish and Alan O'Day (London: Macmillan Education, 1988), 223.

20. This debate was covered by the *Guardian:* 5 July 1882, 924, 937; 12 July 1882, 973; 19 July 1882, 996–97, 1003–4; 26 July 1882, 1034–35; 2 August 1882, 1067–70; 9 August 1882, 1099, 1100; 16 August 1882, 1134; 30 August 1882, 1196; 6 September 1882, 1215; 13 September 1882, 1258–59; 7 February 1883, 213; 28 February 1883, 305; 7 March 1883, 349.

21. See letter to the editor from "clericus," *Guardian,* 5 April 1882, 495, and WC, 27 July 1882, 2.

22. *Guardian,* 5 July 1882, 939.

23. *Saturday Review,* 19 August 1882, 243.

24. *Chronicle of Convocation,* Upper House, April 1883, 10–21, and *Times,* 11 April 1883, 5.

25. *Daily Telegraph,* 23 April 1883, 3.

26. Sandall, *The History of the Salvation Army,* 2:199.

27. Mews, "The General and the Bishops," 223. The bishop of Oxford, at the July 1883 session of the Convocation, reported that 449 stations had been investigated with "only twenty instances of immorality known." He apologized for his earlier statement and said that he was "sorry that any words used by me should have been taken to be in support of those who interfere with the Salvation Army proceedings by riotous methods." But he also cautioned that the Army should examine its methods and take great care with young people. *Chronicle of Convocation,* Upper House, 3 July 1883, 125–27.

28. Horridge, *The Salvation Army,* 237, n. 88, quotes a letter from William Booth to the corps captains about this incident. Horridge provides no information about the letter, stating merely that it is from some "previously unpublished letters and papers, copies in the author's possession." Without a citation for the archive that holds this letter or the date when it was written, it is difficult to place it in its proper context.

29. E. M. Benson Papers, Lambeth Palace Library, London, Manuscript Survey Reports, April 1883, vol. 7, ff. 98–147. The corps that reported were Aberdare, Basingstoke, Forfar, Tunbridge Wells, Chatham, Chippington, Kingswood, Lancaster, Spennymoor, Winsford, Boston, Bristol, Bridlington Quay, Hull, Leeds, Cheltenham, Welling on Tyne, Alveston, Bisbeck, Portsmouth, and one illegible. I do not know whether the Army surveyed only these corps or only these

corps responded, or whether these were in some way representative. If the other nearly three hundred corps had fewer illegitimate births, surely the Army would have included those corps to strengthen its case. It seems equally implausible that these were their best corps.

30. E. M. Benson Papers, Lambeth Palace Library, London, Captain Savage, letter to Bramwell Booth, April 1883, vol. 7, f. 132.

31. E. M. Benson Papers, Lambeth Palace Library, London, Captain Taylor, letter to Bramwell Booth, April 30, 1883, vol. 7, f. 142.

32. E. M. Benson Papers, Lambeth Palace Library, London, typescript letter, vol. 7, f. 147.

33. Bishop of Oxford, *Chronicle of Convocation*, 3 July 1883, 126.

34. John R. Gillis, *For Better, for Worse: British Marriage, 1600–the Present* (Oxford: Oxford University Press, 1985), 127–28, 237–38. See also Barret-Ducrocq, *Love in the Time of Victoria*, and Clark, *The Struggle for the Breeches*.

35. See, for example, *Lloyds*, 2 September 1883, 5, and WC, 22 September 1881, 4.

36. On these events, see Walkowitz, *City of Dreadful Delight;* Deborah Gorham, "The 'Maiden Tribute of Modern Babylon' Reexamined: Child Prostitution and the Idea of Childhood in Late-Victorian England," *Victorian Studies* 21, no. 3 (spring 1978); Michael Pearson, *The Age of Consent* (Newton Abbott, Devon: David and Charles, 1972); Alison Plowden, *The Case of Eliza Armstrong: A Child Bought for £5* (London: BBC, 1974).

37. WC, 23 January 1886, 1.

38. Jenty Fairbank, *Booth's Boots: Social Service Beginnings in the Salvation Army* (London: Salvation Army Publishing, 1983), 20–21.

39. Ann Rowell Higginbotham, "The Unmarried Mother and Her Child in Victorian London, 1834–1914" (Ph.D. diss., Indiana University, 1985), 108.

40. National Vigilance Association, *Report of the Executive Committee*, presented at the Annual Meeting, November 16, 1886 (London, 1887), lists as members of the governing council the archbishop of Dublin, the bishop of Durham, R. C. Morgan, several MPs, Dr. Elizabeth Blackwell, Mrs. Fawcett, Miss Ellice Hopkins, Bramwell and Florence Booth, and many others.

41. An MP who took a leading role in the passage of the Criminal Law Amendment Act.

42. "Buy Me Some Almond Rock," written and composed by Joseph Tabrar. A copy was kindly provided by Michael Diamond.

43. Samuel Charlesworth, *Sensational Religion as Resorted to in the System Called the "Salvation Army" in Its Influence upon the Young and in Its Effects upon the Duties and Claims of Home Life* (privately printed, [1885]), Preface.

44. Leonore Davidoff and Catherine Hall, *Family Fortunes: Men and Women of the English Middle Class, 1780–1850* (Chicago: University of Chicago Press, 1987), 146–47. See also Christine L. Krueger, *The Reader's Repentance: Women Preachers, Women Writers and Nineteenth Century Social Discourse* (Chicago: University of Chicago Press, 1992).

45. Samuel Charlesworth, *Memorials of a Blessed Life* (London: Seeley, Jackson and Halliday, 1882), 17–18.

46. Ibid., 33, 54.

47. Benson, Manuscript Diary, June 9, 1882, cited in Mews, "The General and the Bishops," 222.

48. Charlesworth, *Sensational Religion*, 6.

49. Quoted in ibid., 10.

50. Maud C. Booth, *Beneath Two Flags* (London and New York: Funk & Wagnalls, 1889), vi, vii, 44.

51. Charlesworth, *Sensational Religion*, 12.

52. Carolyn Scott, *The Heavenly Witch: The Story of the Marechale* (London: Hamish Hamilton, 1981), is the most recent biography of her.

53. Charlesworth, *Sensational Religion*, 30–34.

54. Ibid., 35.

55. Nettie Wallis, *A Brief Account of the Lord's Dealings with One of His Handmaidens in France and Switzerland, 1883* (London: Salvation Army, 1883), 8.

56. James Strahan, *The Marechale* (London: Hodder & Stoughton, 1913), 80–81.

57. Ibid., 82. See also Frances E. Willard, "La Marechale," *Review of the Churches,* 15 February 1894, 289.

58. Charlesworth, *Sensational Religion*, 28, 16.

59. Ervine, *God's Soldier.*

60. Josephine Butler, *The Salvation Army in Switzerland* (London: Dyer Brothers, 1883); Miss Catherine Booth, *French Notes: Being a Letter from Miss Booth Describing Some Cases of Conversion and the Work and Prospects of the Salvation Army in France* (London: Salvation Army, [1884]); Colonel Clibborn, *Arrest, Imprisonment, Trial and Acquittal of Miss Booth and Comrades* (London: Salvation Army, n.d.).

61. Quoted in Charlesworth, *Sensational Religion*, 71.

62. Ibid., 110.

63. Booth, *Beneath*, 76.

64. Ibid., 80.

65. Ibid., 247.

66. Wallis, *A Brief Account*, 6–8.

67. Charlesworth, *Sensational Religion*, 116.

68. WC, 4 September 1886, 4.

69. Charlesworth, *Sensational Religion*, Preface.

70. McKinley, *Marching to Glory,* 95. The advertisement appeared in *Munsey's Magazine,* June 1896, 57.

71. Copelman, *London's Women Teachers;* Deborah Epstein Nord, *Walking the Victorian Streets: Women, Representation and the City* (Ithaca, N.Y.: Cornell University Press, 1995); Vicinus, *Independent Women.* Taiz, "Hallelujah Lasses in the Battle for Souls," considers similar dynamics in the U.S. Salvation Army.

72. Copelman, *London's Women Teachers,* 26, also 8–9.

73. David Rubenstein, *Before the Suffragettes: Women's Emancipation in the 1890s* (New York: St. Martin's Press, and Brighton, Sussex: Harvester Press, 1986), argues that working-class women, "exploited by their husbands, their employers, by society at large," were in "no position to rebel against social in-

justice." Walkowitz, *City of Dreadful Delight,* argues that this class divide was not as unbridgeable as Rubenstein and others have suggested, and she includes the Hallelujah Lasses among those working-class "entrants to the public sphere" (73). My evidence strongly supports Walkowitz's argument, and research into other kinds of organizations, beyond the strictly political, may reveal other ways working-class women engaged with the ideas and practices of feminism. Another perspective on the relationship between religon and feminism is found in Kathryn Gleadle, *The Early Feminists: Radical Unitarians and the Emergence of the Women's Rights Movement, 1831–1851* (New York: St. Martin's Press, 1995).

74. Davies, *The Story of My Life,* 25–26.

75. Ibid., 29.

76. Ibid., 58.

77. Mrs. Colonel Carpenter, "Notable Staff Officers: Martha Chippendale,". *Staff Officer,* July 1926, 333.

78. Ellen Pash attended Girton College, Cambridge, and received her degree in 1878; Girton College, *The Girton College Register, 1869–1946* (Cambridge: Privately Printed for Girton College, 1946). She is mentioned several times in Maynard's diary for 1875, including a description of her as a participant in a game of charades where she was "capital, so ridiculous" and as a guest at a fancy dress party. Constance Maynard Papers, Queen Mary and Westfield College Archives, University of London, manuscript diary, November 28, 1875, 141, 144.

79. Constance Maynard Papers, Queen Mary and Westfield College Archives, University of London, manuscript diary, vol. 1, 163–64, 194.

80. George K. Behlmer, *Friends of the Family: The English Home and Its Guardians, 1850–1940* (Stanford, Calif.: Stanford University Press, 1998), ch. 6.

81. Fairbank, *Booth's Boots,* 51–53. Fairbank notes that of the 366 cases dealt with in 1898–99, only 10 resulted in adoption, while 100 men were forced to support their children. Perhaps the Army decided this child should be adopted because her father was, presumably, in Italy and could not be forced to support her.

82. Constance Maynard Papers, Queen Mary and Westfield College Archives, University of London, manuscript diary, vol. 1, 157.

83. Ibid., 159–60.

84. Ibid., 196.

85. Ibid., 223.

86. "Est-ce que *elle* sera la? Elle est mon amie. Je l'aime. Elle m'a donné beaucoup de choses, une poupée, un petit cheval et beaucoup de autres choses." Ibid., 222.

87. Ibid., 223.

88. "Moi, je ne sais pas, mais je crois qu'elle a perdue quelque chose de très précieuse. Elle est beaucoup pleurée." Ibid., 228.

89. Ibid., vol. 2, 8.

90. Ibid., 18.

91. Ibid., 91.

92. Ibid., 73.

93. Ibid., vol. 3, 181. On Barnardo, see Seth Koven, "Dr Barnardo's 'Artistic Fictions': Photography, Sexuality and the Ragged Child in Victorian London," *Radical History Review* 69 (1997): 6–45.

94. Constance Maynard Papers, Queen Mary and Westfield College Archives, University of London, manuscript diary, vol. 3, 19.

95. Ibid., vol. 2, 91.

96. Ibid., vol. 4, 9.

97. Ibid., 10.

98. Gillis, *For Better, for Worse;* Higginbotham, "The Unmarried Mother"; Lucy Bland, *Banishing the Beast: English Feminism and Sexual Morality, 1885–1914* (New York: Penguin Books, 1995).

99. Maynard arranged that she would not go first to 259 Mare Street, as was usual for "fallen women."

100. Quoted in Higginbotham, "The Unmarried Mother," 106–7. See also Fairbank, *Booth's Boots,* 12–18.

101. Fairbank, *Booth's Boots,* 29, and Higginbotham, "The Unmarried Mother," 107–8.

102. Higginbotham, "The Unmarried Mother," 108–22, and Louise A. Jackson, "'Singing Birds as Well as Soap Suds': The Salvation Army's Work with Sexually Abused Girls in Edwardian England," *Gender and History* 12, no. 1 (2000): 107–26.

103. Higginbotham, "The Unmarried Mother," 121–22.

104. Madge Unsworth, *Maiden Tribute: A Study in Voluntary Social Service* (London: Salvationist Publishing, 1949), chs. 1 and 4.

105. Fairbank, *Booth's Boots,* ch. 2.

106. Ann Rowell Higginbotham, "Respectable Sinner: Salvation Army Rescue Work with Unmarried Mothers, 1884–1914," in *Religion in the Lives of English Women, 1760–1930,* ed. Gail Malmgreen (Bloomington: Indiana University Press, 1986), 217. See also Cox, *Hotchpotch;* Ervine, *God's Soldier,* 1:589; Fairbank, *Booth's Boots,* chs. 2 and 3.

107. Constance Maynard Papers, Queen Mary and Westfield College Archives, University of London, manuscript diary, vol. 4, 35.

108. Ibid.

109. Ibid., 12–13.

110. Ibid., 33–34.

111. Major Bennett, letter to Maynard, transcribed in ibid., 48–49.

112. Major Bennett, letter to Maynard, March 19, 1897, transcribed in ibid., 53.

113. Ibid., 54.

114. Ibid., 55–56.

115. Ibid., 57–58.

116. Ibid., 60.

117. Ibid., 68.

118. Michael Mason, *The Making of Victorian Sexuality* (Oxford: Oxford University Press, 1994), 205–15.

119. Barbara Robinson, "Bodily Compassion: Values and Identity Formation in the Salvation Army, 1880–1900" (Ph.D. thesis, University of Ottawa,

1999), 137. I am grateful to Dr. Robinson for allowing me to read and quote from her thesis.

120. *Memorandum of Guidance to Commanding and Local Officers* (St. Albans: Salvation Army, 1903), quoted in ibid., 137.

121. Constance Maynard Papers, Queen Mary and Westfield College Archives, University of London, manuscript diary, vol. 4, 97.

122. Ibid., 99.

123. Ibid., 125, 119.

124. Ibid., vol. 5, 27, 29, 33, 39.

125. Ibid., 47.

126. Ibid., 53, 62.

127. Ibid., 65–66.

128. Ibid., 68.

129. Ibid., 77.

130. Ibid., 86.

131. Ibid., 148.

132. Ibid., 149.

133. Ibid., 116 and 151.

134. Reported in C. B. Frith, *Constance Louisa Maynard: Mistress of Westfield College* (London: Allen and Unwin, 1949), 246.

135. In the *War Cry,* 7 July 1881, Catherine Booth wrote, "Oh! how I see the emptiness and vanity of everything compared with the salvation of the soul. What does it matter if a man dies in the workhouse? If he dies on a doorstep covered with wounds, like Lazarus—what does it matter if his soul is saved?" Quoted in Inglis, *Churches and the Working Classes,* 176.

136. Walkowitz, *City of Dreadful Delight,* esp. chs. 2 and 3.

137. On Josephine Butler, see Walkowitz, *Prostitution and Victorian Society.*

138. *Christian,* 26 November 1885, 9. Butler's pamphlet and this magazine were published by Morgan and Chase, longtime friends of the Army.

139. Martha Vicinus, "Helpless and Unfriended: Nineteenth Century Domestic Melodrama," *New Literary History* 13, no. 1 (1981): 127–43; Nina Auerbach, The *Woman and the Demon: The Life of a Victorian Myth* (Cambridge, Mass.: Harvard University Press, 1982); Anna Clark, "The Politics of Seduction in English Popular Culture, 1748–1848," in *The Progress of Romance: The Politics of Popular Fiction,* ed. Jean Radford (London: Routledge & Kegan Paul, 1986), 47–70.

140. Josephine Butler, *Rebecca Jarrett* (London: Morgan and Scott, n.d.), 6.

141. Ibid., 6–7.

142. Ibid., 7, 12.

143. Ibid.

144. Amanda Sebestyen, "Two Women from Two Worlds," *Spare Rib* 155 (June 1985): 21–24.

145. Rebecca Jarrett Papers, SAHC, handwritten autobiography. I have retained all the spelling and punctuation in the original.

146. Warwick Wroth, *Cremorne and Later London Gardens* (London: Elliott Stock, 1907), 10.

147. Rebecca Jarrett Papers, SAHC, typescript autobiography, 1.

148. Ibid., 2, 3.

149. Ibid., 4.

150. William Acton, *Prostitution* (1870), quoted in Nead, *Myths of Sexuality*, 175.

151. Rebecca Jarrett Papers, SAHC, typescript autobiography, 6, 7, 8.

152. Ibid., 9.

153. Ibid., 12, 15.

154. Ibid., 18, 12.

155. Central Criminal Court, *Sessions Papers,* Public Records Office, London, Rebecca Jarrett, testimony, 1885, 985.

156. Rebecca Jarrett Papers, SAHC, typescript autobiography, 16.

157. Sir Charles Webster, quoted in Walkowitz, *City of Dreadful Delight,* 111.

158. Rebecca Jarrett Papers, SAHC, typescript autobiography, 37.

159. Florence Soper Booth Papers, SAHC, manuscript diary, January 14, 1885.

160. Ibid., August 30, 1885.

161. Ibid., September 2, 1885.

162. Central Criminal Court, *Sessions Papers,* Public Records Office, London, Rebecca Jarrett, testimony, 1885, 994.

163. This explanation is given by Josephine Butler in her biography.

164. Walkowitz, *City of Dreadful Delight,* ch. 3, esp. 116–17.

165. Central Criminal Court, *Sessions Papers,* Public Records Office, London, testimony, 1895, 924, quoted in Walkowitz, *City of Dreadful Delight,* 108.

166. Florence Soper Booth Papers, SAHC, manuscript diary, October 13, 1886, and March 11, 1887.

167. Her obituary was printed in the *War Cry,* 10 March 1928, 6.

168. Koven, "Dr Barnardo's 'Artistic Fictions,'" 13.

169. Walkowitz, *Prostitution and Victorian Society,* 211.

170. Jacqueline R. deVries, "Transforming the Pulpit: Preaching and Prophecy in the British Women's Suffrage Movement," in *Women Preachers and Prophets through Two Millennia of Christianity,* ed. Beverly Mayne and Pamela J. Walker (Berkeley: University of California Press, 1998), 321.

171. Ray Strachey, *The Cause: A Short History of the Women's Movement in Britain* (London: G. Bell, 1928; reprint, London: Virago, 1978), 216.

6. ROBBING THE DEVIL OF HIS CHOICE TUNES

1. "Other Arrangements," written and composed by Harry Nicolls, sung by Herbert Campbell, 1884?, from the collection of Michael Diamond.

2. *Punch,* 12 July 1890, 12.

3. Booth, *How to Reach,* 5. Keating, "Fact and Fiction," 585–602, argues that the East End was first widely perceived as a social problem only in the 1880s. The Christian Mission/Salvation Army argued that it was a particular, and dangerous, problem from the late 1860s.

4. McLeod, *Piety and Poverty,* ch. 2.

5. Booth, *How to Reach,* 6.

6. WC, 12 January 1884, 1.

7. WC, 26 April 1884, 1.

8. Booth, *Salvation Army Songs,* Hymn 222, 156.

9. CMM, July 1871, 102.

10. "Physiognomy," WC, 16 January 1886, 1.

11. CMM, July 1876, 145.

12. Nye, "The Bio-medical Origins," 661. See also Jones, *Outcast London,* ch. 16, and Stallybrass and White, *The Politics and Poetics,* ch. 3.

13. ELE, November 1868, 25.

14. Rule, "Methodism, Popular Beliefs and Village Culture," 48–70, and Trinder, *The Industrial Revolution,* 292–93. See also Colls, *The Pitman of the Northern Coalfield.*

15. Quoted in Hugh Cunningham, *Leisure in the Industrial Revolution* (London: Croom Helm, 1980), 149.

16. Bailey, *Leisure and Class*; Bailey, *Popular Culture*; Burnett, *A Social History of Housing*; Cunningham, *Leisure*; Daunton, "Public Place and Private Space"; Daunton, *House and Home in the Victorian City*; David Feldman and Gareth Stedman Jones, eds., *Metropolis London: Histories and Representations since 1800* (London: Routledge, 1989); John K. Walton, "Residential Amenity, Respectable Morality and the Rise of the Entertainment Industry: The Case of Blackpool, 1860–1914," *Literature and History* 1 (March 1975): 62–78.

17. Cunningham, *Leisure,* 166–71; Bailey, *Leisure and Class,* 148–52; A. E. Wilson, *East End Entertainment* (London: Arthur Barker, 1954). On the business aspects, see Summerfield, "The Effingham Arms and the Empire," 209–40.

18. Wilson, *East End Entertainment,* 83, 131.

19. Bailey, *Leisure and Class*; Davies, *Leisure, Gender and Poverty*; Harrison, *Drink*; Brian Harrison, "Pubs," in *The Victorian City: Images and Realities,* ed. H. J. Dyos and Michael Wolff (London: Routledge & Kegan Paul, 1973), 162; Ross McKibbin, "Working-Class Gambling in Britain, 1880–1939," *Past and Present,* no. 82 (February 1979): 147–78; Douglas Reid, "Beasts and Brutes: Popular Blood Sports c. 1760–1860," in *Sport and the Working Class in Modern Britain,* ed. Richard Holt (Manchester: Manchester University Press, 1990), 12–28; Stan Shipley, "Boxing," in *Sport in Britain,* ed. Tony Mason (Cambridge: Cambridge University Press, 1989).

20. Robert K. Roberts, *The Classic Slum* (Manchester: Manchester University Press, 1971; reprint, Harmondsworth, Middlesex: Penguin Books, 1973), 49–50, quoted in Davies, *Leisure, Gender and Poverty,* 34.

21. Cunningham, *Leisure,* 179.

22. McLeod, *Piety and Poverty,* 155.

23. Cox, *The English Churches in a Secular Society,* 88. Cox reports that the *Daily Telegraph* predicted a series of volumes by Brown with such titles as "Is Seven Hours of Sleep Satanic?," "The Sinfulness of a Country Walk," and "Lawn Tennis a Short Cut to Perdition."

24. Boyd Hilton, "The Role of Providence in Evangelical Social Thought," in *History, Society and the Churches,* ed. Derek Beales and Geoffrey Best (Cambridge: Cambridge University Press, 1985), 223.

25. WC, 13 April 1882, 1.; WC, 14 October 1882, 1; *Officer,* January 1893, 25.

26. See, for example, S. O. Addy, "Derbyshire Folklore," in *Memorials of*

Old Derbyshire, ed. Charles Cox (London: Bemrose and Sons, 1907); [Joseph Barker], *The History and Confessions of a Man* (London: Wortley, 1846); Jeremy Seabrook, *The Unprivileged* (Harmondsworth, Middlesex: Penguin Books, 1973). This point is also elaborated on by Patrick Joyce, *Visions of the People: Industrial England and the Question of Class, 1848–1914* (Cambridge: Cambridge University Press, 1991), ch. 6, and Sarah C. Williams, "The Language of Belief: An Alternative Agenda for the Study of Victorian Working-Class Religion," *Journal of Victorian Culture* 1, no. 2 (1996): 303–17.

27. *News of the World*, 26 January 1879, 5. The fact that this testimony was reported in a newspaper suggests that these beliefs, while not uncommon, were nevertheless considered worthy of comment.

28. William Lovett, *The Life and Struggles of William Lovett* (New York: Garland, 1984), 14.

29. John Wesley, *Journal*, ed. N. Church, 8 vols. (1906–16), entry for May 25, 1768, cited in Owen Davies, "Methodism, the Clergy and the Popular Belief in Witchcraft and Magic," *History* 82, no. 26 (April 1997): 255.

30. [Barker], *The History and Confessions*, 16. See also John Wilson, *Memories of a Labour Leader* (London: T. Fisher Unwin, 1910), 63.

31. Reginald Nettel, "Folk Elements in Nineteenth-Century Puritanism," *Folklore*, 80 (winter 1969): 284.

32. Rule, "Methodism, Popular Beliefs and Village Culture," 64; James Obelkevich, *Religion and Rural Society: South Lindsey, 1825–1875* (Oxford: Clarendon Press, 1976), ch. 6; Trinder, *The Industrial Revolution*, 292, also makes a related argument on this point.

33. J.F.C. Harrison, *The Second Coming: Popular Millenarianism, 1780–1850* (New Brunswick, N.J.: Rutgers University Press, and London: Routledge & Kegan Paul, 1979), 87.

34. Clark, *The Struggle for the Breeches;* Taylor, *Eve and the New Jerusalem;* Taylor, "Religion, Radicalism and Fantasy"; Thompson, *The Making of the English Working Class;* Thompson, *Witness against the Beast.*

35. Williams, "The Language of Belief," 311.

36. CMM, April 1871, 58.

37. CMM, February 1874, 49.

38. WC, 10 January 1880, 3.

39. WC, 7 October 1882, 1.

40. Quoted in Davies, *Leisure, Gender and Poverty*, 115. See also Jerry White, *Rothschild Buildings: Life in an East End Tenement Block, 1887–1920* (London: Routledge & Kegan Paul, 1980), and Jerry White, *The Worst Street in North London: Campbell Bunk Islington, between the Wars* (London: Routledge & Kegan Paul, 1986).

41. Ross, *Love and Toil*, 84.

42. "Marching," written and composed by Harry Castling, sung by Charles Gardener (London: Francis, Day and Hunter, n.d.), from the collection of Max Tyler.

43. Cunningham, *The Volunteer Force*, 71.

44. Michael Anton Budd, *The Sculpture Machine: Physical Culture and Body Politics in the Age of Empire* (New York: New York University Press, 1997), 15.

45. Hugh Cunningham, "Jingoism in 1877–1878," *Victorian Studies* 14, no. 5 (June 1971): 429–53.

46. Budd, *The Sculpture Machine,* esp. ch. 1.

47. Ervine, *God's Soldier,* 1:428.

48. *Salvationist,* February 1879, 33.

49. The *Field Officer* series on "Popular Songs to Popular Airs" offered this song, sung to the tune of "I'll Be Your Sweetheart" (February 1906, 57).

50. *Local Officer,* April 1900, 349.

51. Reported in Budd, *The Sculpture Machine,* 64. See also an article by Captain Thomas McCallum, *Vim* 1, no. 6 (15 May 1903); I am grateful to Michael Budd for drawing my attention to this article.

52. *Local Officer,* April 1900, 348.

53. Budd, *The Sculpture Machine;* Bruce Haley, *The Healthy Body and Victorian Culture* (Cambridge, Mass.: Harvard University Press, 1978); Ronald Numbers and Rennie Schoepflin, "Ministries of Healing: Mary Baker Eddy, Ellen G. White and the Religion of Health," in *Women and Health in America,* ed. Judith Walzer Leavitt (Madison: University of Wisconsin Press, 1984), 377–89; Ross, *Love and Toil,* ch. 2; James C. Whorton, *Crusaders for Fitness: The History of American Health Reformers* (Princeton, N.J.: Princeton University Press, 1982).

54. For a full discussion of Salvation Army health reform, see Robinson, "Bodily Compassion."

55. Free, *Seven Years' Hard,* 40.

56. John Eldred, *I Love the Brooks* (London: Skeffington, 1955), 47.

57. Ross, "Survival Networks," 10.

58. See Cox, *The English Churches in a Secular Society,* ch. 3; Harrison, "For Church, Queen and Family," 107–38; Brian Harrison, "Religion and Recreation in Nineteenth Century England," *Past and Present* 38 (December 1967): 98–125; Parsons, "A Question of Meaning," 63–87.

59. Cox, *The English Churches in a Secular Society.*

60. See, for example, Open Air Mission Society, *Occasional Papers* (London: Open Air Mission Society, 1855–57). See also Carwardine, *Transatlantic Revivalism;* Lewis, *Lighten Their Darkness;* Winter, *London's Teeming Streets.*

61. CMM, August 1874, 219.

62. Free, *Seven Years' Hard,* xiv, 16–17, 37.

63. CMM, January 1874, 8.

64. CMM, December 1870, 184.

65. ELE, November 1869, 209.

66. Douglas Reid, "Popular Theatre in Victorian Birmingham," in *Performance and Politics in Popular Drama,* ed. David Bradbury et al. (Cambridge: Cambridge University Press, 1980), 65–90.

67. *East London Observer,* 15 April 1871, 4.

68. Naomi Jacob, *Our Marie* (London: Hutchinson, 1936), 52.

69. Eagle and Grecian File, SAHC, "Purchase of the Eagle, Grecian Theater and Dancing Grounds."

70. WC, 27 September 1882, 2.

71. WC, 4 November 1882, 1.

72. Quoted in Begbie, *The Life of General William Booth*, 2:10.

73. WC, 27 September 1882, 1.

74. SAHC, poster, 1886.

75. *East London Observer*, 19 August 1882, 6.

76. Sandall, *The History of the Salvation Army*, 2:217–20, suggests that the premises were given up in 1898, but the circumstances are not entirely clear. According to Stedman Jones, "Working-Class Culture and Working-Class Politics," the Army's attempt to close down the Eagle was ultimately unsuccessful (495). But given that the Army held the premises for sixteen years and garnered a huge amount of publicity, it could also be seen as a rather successful endeavor.

77. *East London Observer*, 19 August 1882, 6; *Lloyds*, 13 August 1882, 7, and 17 September 1882, 12; WC, January 1884, 3.

78. CMM, August 1877, 202.

79. SAHC, poster, n.d., probably early 1880s.

80. A. C. Tait Papers, Lambeth Palace Library, London, Salvation Army poster, n.d., probably 1882, vol. 285, f. 55.

81. WC, 2 February 1884, 2, and WC, 7 September 1882, 3.

82. WC, 27 April 1882, 2.

83. Ervine, *God's Soldier*, 1:360.

84. WC, 11 January 1890, 2.

85. From the *Northern Echo*, quoted in the *Christian*, 29 May 1879, 14. The writer suggested that such a curiosity was not confined to revivalist services frequented by the working class. The Salvation Army continued to use novelty to attract potential converts. It was the first religious organization to make its own films and to embrace film as a means to attract an audience to its meetings. See Dean Rapp, "The British Salvation Army," 157–88.

86. Bailey, *Music Hall*, xviii.

87. Charles Fry Papers, SAHC, Fred Fry, letter to Lt. Col. F. G. Hawkes, February 20, 1929; Sandall, *The History of the Salvation Army*, 2:117–19; Herbert, "Nineteenth Century Bands," *Bands*.

88. Ira D. Sanky, *My Life and the Story of the Gospel Hymns* (New York: Sunday School Times, 1907; reprint, London: AMS Press, 1974), 74. Interestingly, the phrase *singing the gospel* was coined when Moody and Sanky were invited to Sunderland by the Rev. A. A. Rees, who had denounced Phoebe Palmer and occasioned the publication of Catherine Booth's first pamphlet. Rees produced a poster that announced Sanky would sing the gospel, and that phrase was taken up and used to describe this style. Their work drew on the nineteenth-century African American song tradition, and it in turn influenced the work of twentieth-century African American gospel singers. See Michael W. Harris, *The Rise of Gospel Blues: The Music of Thomas A. Dorsey in the Urban Church* (New York: Oxford University Press, 1992).

89. Booth, *Salvation Army Music*, Hymn 5.

90. Quoted in Bailey, "Champagne Charlie: Performance and Ideology in the Music Hall Swell Song," *Popular Culture*, 110–11.

91. Ibid., 101.

92. Ibid., 112.

93. The song was published in the 1882 Christmas edition of the *War Cry*.

94. The Rev. J. Frome Wilkinson, letter to the *Guardian,* 7 February 1883, 213.

95. *Lloyds,* 7 June 1885, 7.

96. WC, 30 July 1887, 4, 6. See WC, 20 July 1889, 3–11, for similar descriptions of exotic attractions.

97. WC, 31 March 1888, 8.

98. WC, 21 April 1888, 9.

99. Ibid. See also Booth-Tucker, *The Life of Catherine Booth,* 2:534–35.

100. WC, 21 April 1888, 9.

101. Robert W. Jones, "The Sight of Creatures Strange to Our Clime: London Zoo and the Consumption of the Exotic," *Journal of Victorian Culture* 2, no. 1 (spring 1997): 1–26, makes a persuasive argument about the London zoo and the culture of empire. It is possible to suggest that the Army was constructing something not wholly different from a zoo of foreign converts.

102. Nina Auerbach, *Ellen Terry: Player in Her Time* (New York: Norton, 1987), 8.

103. See especially Katherine Ludwig Jansen, "Maria Magdalena: Apostolorum Apostola," Beverly Mayne Kienzle, "The Prostitute Preacher: Patterns of Polemic against Medieval Waldensian Women Preachers," and Karen L. King, "Afterword: Voices of the Spirit," all in *Women Preachers and Prophets through Two Millennia of Christianity,* ed. Beverly Mayne Kienzle and Pamela J. Walker (Berkeley: University of California Press, 1998).

104. The poster was criticized by the *Christian,* 10 August 1882, 18. The term *Hallelujah Lass* was invented, according to William Booth, by "great rough men," and he was "rather shocked" when he first heard it. WC, 13 August 1880, 1.

105. WC, 9 October 1886.

106. *Borough of Marylebone Mercury,* 26 June 1880, 3; *Indicator,* 29 May 1880, 3, and 3 July 1880, 2; Metropolitan Police Papers, Public Records Office, London, Special Division Report, April 13, 1880, PRO MEPO 2/168. See also Booth-Tucker, *The Life of Catherine Booth,* 1:214–16.

107. WC, 10 April 1880, 1.

108. "Happy Eliza and Converted Jane," written and composed by Will Oliver; from the Raymond Mander and Joe Mitchenson Theater Collection, Beckenham Kent. I am grateful to the directors of this collection for sending me a photocopy of this song.

109. Bailey, "The Victorian Barmaid as Cultural Prototype," *Popular Culture,* 151–74.

110. "Sister 'Ria," words by A. J. Mills and music by Arthur Lennard, private collection of Max Tyler.

111. Margaret Lonsdale, "Platform Women," *Nineteenth Century,* November 1884, 409–15, expressed a fear of the "unpleasant consequences" of women speaking in public. See also Anderson, "Women Preachers in Mid-Victorian Britain."

112. Quoted in Walkowitz, *City of Dreadful Delight,* 74.

113. Elijah Cadman Papers, SAHC, Bramwell Booth, letter to Elijah Cadman, December 10, 1879.

114. CMM, July 1874, 181.

115. WC, 3 February 1883, 1.

116. Louis Billington, "Revivalism and Popular Religion," in *In Search of Victorian Values: Aspects of Nineteenth Century Thought and Society,* ed. Eric M. Sigsworth (Manchester: Manchester University Press, 1988), 147–61, and Valenze, *Prophetic Sons and Daughters.*

117. "Symposium: How to Evangelise the Masses," *Primitive Methodist Quarterly Review,* January 1883, 142, and April 1883, 319.

118. WC, 13 January 1883, 4.

119. WC, 7 February 1880, 1.

120. WC, 7 January 1888, 5.

121. *Lloyds,* 19 February 1882, 7.

122. *Lloyds,* 2 April 1882, 7.

123. *Lloyds,* 14 February 1886, 4.

124. The Grecian was exempted from the rate, but the remainder of the premises was to be taxed. The Plymouth court rejected the Army's defense that it should not be taxed because money was taken at the door. At Worcester the poor rate was applied to Salvation Army buildings because refreshments were sold on the premises and admission was charged. *Lloyds,* 28 January 1883, 2, and 6 July 1884, 12.

125. Quoted in Stedman Jones, "Working-Class Culture and Working-Class Politics," 491.

126. Victor E. Neuburg, *Chapbooks: Guide to Reference Material on English, Scottish and American Chapbook Literature of the Eighteenth and Nineteenth Centuries,* 2d ed. (London: Woborn Press, 1972), 1–6.

127. Printed in Charles Hindley, ed., *Curiosities of Street Literature* (London: Reeves and Turner, 1871), 32–33.

128. William Corbridge, *The Up Line to Heaven and the Down Line to Hell,* 7th ed. (London: Salvation Army Headquarters, n.d.). This pamphlet was published by the Salvation Army, but the references to the Christian Mission and the Rev. William Booth suggest it was written prior to 1878.

129. Ibid., 5–6.

130. Hindley, *Curiosities of Street Literature,* 32.

131. Corbridge, *The Up Line to Heaven,* 12–13.

132. More included laboring people among her characters, but the language and narrative style were in sharp contrast to those of the working-class literature of her period. Hannah More, *The Works of Hannah More* (New York: Harper and Brothers, 1835), vol. 1.

133. [George Scott Railton], *The Salvation Paper Mill* (London: Salvation Army Bookstores, n.d.), 2.

134. Ibid., 6–7.

135. There were other pamphlets in this style, notably William Corbridge, *Salvation Mine: Down to Death! Up to Glory!* (London: Salvation Army, 1881). The *War Cry* also published small articles that used these same techniques.

136. See, for example, *East London Observer,* 17 March 1877, 5.

137. Budd, *The Sculpture Machine;* W. Hamish Fraser, *The Coming of the Mass Market, 1850–1914* (Hamden, Conn.: Archon, and London: Macmillan, 1981); Thomas Richards, *The Commodity Culture of Victorian England* (Stanford, Calif.: Stanford University Press, 1990).

138. CMM, September 1874, 240, and February 1877, 39–40.

139. Ross, *Love and Toil,* 41, 189–90.

140. WC, 2 November 1882, 1.

141. WC, 4 January 1890, 12.

142. CMM, June 1877, 164.

143. CMM, October 1875, 264.

144. WC, 2 August 1890, 3.

145. Ross, *Love and Toil,* ch. 2.

146. WC, 17 August 1888, 16.

147. WC, 25 February 1885, 4.

148. Harry Stout, *Divine Dramatist,* 68, quoted in R. Laurence Moore, *Selling God: American Religion in the Marketplace of Culture* (New York: Oxford University Press, 1994), 42. See also Susan Curtis, *A Consuming Faith: The Social Gospel and Modern American Culture* (Baltimore: Johns Hopkins University Press, 1991).

149. *Pall Mall Gazette,* 29 January 1884, 10. I am grateful to Judith Walkowitz for this citation.

7. DISORDERLY CHAMPIONS OF ORDER

1. The discussion among clergymen was reported closely in the *Guardian.* See also Mews, "The General and the Bishops," 209–28.

2. Andrew Mearns, *The Bitter Cry of Outcast London,* edited and with an introduction by Anthony Wohl (1883; reprint, New York: Humanities Press, 1970), 56.

3. See Stedman Jones, *Outcast London,* 281. See also Paul Thompson, *Socialists, Liberals and Labour: The Struggle for London* (London: Routledge & Kegan Paul, 1967).

4. Mayne, *The Imagined Slum,* 130, 137. See also White, *Rothschild Buildings,* and Winter, *London's Teeming Streets, 1830–1914* (London: Routledge, 1993).

5. Carwardine, *Transatlantic Revivalism;* Heasman, *Evangelicals in Action;* Kent, *Holding the Fort;* Prochaska, *Women and Philanthropy.*

6. Booth, *Life and Labour of the People in London,* 270, quoted in Heasman, *Evangelicals in Action,* 30.

7. Behlmer, *Friends of the Family,* 34.

8. Jane Lewis, *The Voluntary Sector, the State and Social Work in Britain: The Charity Organisation Society/Family Welfare Association since 1869* (London: Edward Elgar, 1995); Charles Loch Mowat, *The Charity Organisation Society, 1869–1913* (London: Methuen, 1961); Standish Meacham, *Toynbee Hall and Social Reform, 1880–1914* (New Haven, Conn.: Yale University Press, 1987); Canon S. A. Barnett and Mrs. S. A. Barnett, *Practicable Socialism* (London: Longman, Green, 1915).

9. Heasman, *Evangelicals in Action,* and Prochaska, *Women and Philanthropy.*

10. *Nonconformist,* 10 April 1867, 10.

11. *Bethnal Green Times,* 22 February 1868, 3. See also *Bethnal Green Times,* 29 February 1866, 2, 18 April 1868, 3, 13 June 1868, 3; *East London Observer,*

31 July 1869, 2, 1 January 1870, 6, 12 April 1872, 6; *Morning Advertiser,* 5 April 1869, 3; *Tower Hamlets Independent,* 23 November 1867, 6, 1 May 1875, 5.

12. Stallybrass and White, *The Politics and Poetics,* ch. 3.

13. Booth, *How to Reach,* 5–6.

14. *East London Observer,* 17 March 1877, 5.

15. *Sensation or Salvation?* (London: Printed and Published for the Author by Civil Service Printing and Publishing, [1882]), 3.

16. A Layman, *Sensationalism: A Broadsider into Moody and Sankyism; a Skirmish with the Salvation Army and a Side Thrust at Shakers, Bible Thumpers, Jumpers, Latter Day Saints and Other "Peculiar People"* (London: John Heywood, [1884]), 12.

17. J. W. Hooper, letter to the *Guardian,* 12 April 1882, 514.

18. *The Temperance Movement and the Salvation Army* (London: Strangeways and Sons, 1882), 16–17.

19. Cobbe was active in workhouse philanthropy, the antivivisection movement, and efforts to promote the Matrimonial Causes Act of 1878, which gave separation orders to women with violent spouses.

20. Frances Power Cobbe, "The Last Revival," *Contemporary Review* 52 (August 1882): 188.

21. Albert Muspratt, *The Salvation Army: Is It a Benefit to the Cause of Religion? The Negative as Delivered before the Ripon Mechanics Institute Debating Society February 12, 1884* (Ripon: William Harrison, 1884), 7, and John Price, *The Salvation Army Tested by Their Works* (Chester: Minshull and Hughes, 1882), 4.

22. Catherine Booth criticized the idea that the soul always remained partially sinful. She asked, if the doctrine of "two natures" is true, "what becomes of the 'old, wicked soul' of man at death? If it is immortal, it cannot die. If it forever remains unclean, it cannot enter heaven. If is not redeemed, or washed in the blood, it must go to hell. So that a real believer according to [this] school, will have one soul in heaven and another in hell!" Quoted in Booth-Tucker, *The Life of Catherine Booth,* 1:606.

23. CMM, August 1877, 202.

24. Price, *The Salvation Army,* 12.

25. *Saturday Review,* 26 June 1886, 873.

26. On the question of ritualism, William Booth wrote, "The masses want to see a change in the home furniture, not in the furniture of the church;—in the vestments of the wife and children, not of the priest." CMM, November 1873, 164–65.

27. Reed, "Ritualism Rampant in East London."

28. Sandall, *The History of the Salvation Army,* 2:130–33.

29. *The Salvation Army (So-Called): A Friendly Exposure of Its Unscriptural Pretensions and Proceedings by a Christian Minister* (London, [1880]), 7. See also *Sensation or Salvation?; The Temperance Movement and the Salvation Army;* Cardinal Manning, "The Salvation Army," *Contemporary Review* 52 (September 1882); Muspratt, *The Salvation Army.*

30. Rev. Wyndham Heathcote, *My Salvation Army Experience* ([1892]; reprint, London: Marshall Brothers, 1927), 74.

31. *The Temperance Movement and the Salvation Army,* 15.

32. Price, *The Salvation Army,* 10.

33. O.W.L.A., *Some Reasons Why I Do Not Sympathise with the Salvation Army* (London: John F. Shaw, n.d.), 17, 20.

34. A Layman, *Sensationalism,* 13.

35. Charles B. Waller, *The Salvation Army: How Should the Thoughtful Christian Judge This Movement* (London: Kegan Paul and Trench, 1882), 7–8.

36. Benjamin Wills Newton, *An Address Respecting the Methods of the Salvation Army* (London: Houlston and Sons, 1882), 6.

37. *Saturday Review,* 6 October 1883, 432.

38. J. H. Cynds, quoted in An Investigator, *Behind the Scenes with the Salvation Army,* 2d ed. (London: 8, Salisbury Court, Fleet St., [1882]), 11.

39. Harrison, *The Second Coming,* 170–71; Phyllis Mack, "Gender and Spirituality in Early English Quakerism," in *Witnesses for Change: Quaker Women over Three Centuries,* ed. Elisabeth Potts Brown and Susan Mosher Stuard (New Brunswick, N.J.: Rutgers University Press, 1989), 31–63; Marjorie Proctor-Smith, *Women in Shaker Community and Worship* (Lewiston, N.Y.: Mellen Press, 1985).

40. Muspratt, *The Salvation Army,* 9.

41. O.W. L. A., *Some Reasons,* 9.

42. Price, *The Salvation Army,* 21.

43. Muspratt, *The Salvation Army,* 14.

44. Hodges, *General Booth,* 17.

45. *Punch,* 27 October 1883, 21.

46. Price, *The Salvation Army,* 15.

47. *The New Papacy: Behind the Scenes at the Salvation Army by an Ex-Staff Officer* (Toronto: Albert Britnell, 1889), 15.

48. Hodges, *General Booth,* 19.

49. The author imagined an old England that was entirely Protestant.

50. *Pope Booth: The Salvation Army A.D. 1950* (London: Sully and Ford, n.d.), 10.

51. *The New Papacy,* 3.

52. Ibid., 9.

53. Cobbe, "The Last Revival," 189.

54. Reverend Cunningham Geike, "Introduction," in Redstone, *An Ex-Captain's Experience,* ix.

55. Quoted in E. R. Norman, *Anti-Catholicism in Victorian England* (London: Allen and Unwin, 1968), 19.

56. SAHC, Articles of War.

57. Norman, *Anti-Catholicism in Victorian England;* D. G. Paz, *Popular Anti-Catholicism in Mid-Victorian England* (Stanford, Calif.: Stanford University Press, 1992); Joan Smith, "Class, Skill and Sectarianism in Glasgow and Liverpool, 1880–1914," in *Class, Power and Social Structure in British Nineteenth Century Towns,* ed. R. J. Morris (Leicester: Leicester University Press, 1986), 157–15; Frank H. Wallis, *Popular Anti-Catholicism in Mid-Victorian Britain* (Lewiston, N.Y.: Mellon Press, 1993).

58. Geike, "Introduction," in Redstone, *An Ex-Captain's Experience,* ix. See also A Layman, *Sensationalism,* 11, and *The New Papacy,* 16.

59. *En'tracte*, 7 October 1882, reproduced in Ervine, *God's Soldier*, 1:545; *Punch*, 26 March 1892, 154.

60. These associations were not limited to his critics. William Booth's biographer suggests that his mother, Mary Moss Booth, was "of Jewish origin" as "her wonderfully handsome face corroborates." Begbie, *The Life of General William Booth*, 1:16. Catherine occasionally commented on William's "Jewish" features in her early correspondence. It would seem that his physical appearance was typical of "Jewishness" in the eyes of his contemporaries. Alan Lee, "Some Aspects of the Working-Class Response to Jews in Britain, 1880–1914," in *Hosts, Immigrants and Minorities*, ed. Kenneth Kamm (London: St. Martin's Press, 1980), 107–33.

61. Quoted in *Sensation or Salvation?*, 13.

62. Geo R., *The Salvation Navvy*, 20.

63. CMM, June 1869, 141.

64. CMM, January 1877, 18.

65. CMM, May 1876, 116.

66. WC, 16 November 1882, 2.

67. *Christian*, 22 April 1880, 11.

68. CMM, January 1877, 19.

69. CMM, May 1871, 76.

70. WC, 7 May 1884, 2.

71. CMM, March 1869, 93.

72. WC, 6 March 1880, 2.

73. Horridge, *The Salvation Army*, includes several case studies of opposition to the Army; they contain much detailed and valuable information about reaction to the Army in particular communities. His analysis, however, does not engage with the debates about working-class politics, and it is based on limited sources. For example, he uses one local newspaper's coverage to claim that the publicans of Honiton saw their trade diminish as the Army grew stronger (203). I would regard this claim to carry more rhetorical than literal meaning.

74. CMM, March 1871, 44.

75. CMM, February 1877, 46.

76. *Salvationist*, March 1879, 65.

77. CMM, December 1872, 186.

78. WC, 28 October 1882, 4.

79. Captain Barrett Papers, Persecution File, SAHC, Manuscript Diary.

80. Alfred Tutte Papers, Persecution File, SAHC, Typescript Diary, September 13, 1887.

81. WC, 20 June 1885, 4.

82. *Lloyds*, 14 June 1885, 4.

83. WC, 8 July 1885, 2.

84. WC, 12 October 1888.

85. See, for example, *Fun*, 20 September 1882; *Moonshine*, 14 May 1881, 16 December 1882, 309, 2 July 1881, 4; *Punch*, 15 July 1882, 22, 12 August 1882, 82, 27 October 1883, 26, 27 October 1883, 22.

86. Andrew Davies, "Youth Gangs, Masculinity and Violence in Late Victorian Manchester and Salford," *Journal of Social History* 32, no. 2 (winter 1998): 350.

87. CMM, March 1869, 90–91.

88. "Our Neighbourhood," written and composed by Harry Castling, from the collection of Michael Diamond.

89. Stedman Jones, "Working-Class Culture and Working-Class Politics," 471.

90. Bailey, "Salvation Army Riots," 239.

91. CMM, October 1872, 153.

92. There is a considerable literature on this tradition and its persistence in the later nineteenth century. See, for example, Eugenio Biagini and Alastair Reid, eds., *Currents of Radicalism* (Cambridge: Cambridge University Press, 1991); James Epstein, "Understanding the Cap of Liberty: Symbolic Practice and Social Conflict in Early Nineteenth Century England," *Past and Present* 122 (1989): 75–118; Joyce, *Visions of the People;* Jon Lawrence, "Popular Radicalism and Socialist Revival in Britain," *Journal of British Studies* 31 (April 1992): 163–86; James Vernon, *Politics and the People: A Study in English Political Culture, c.1815–1867* (Cambridge: Cambridge University Press, 1993); Eileen Yeo, "Christianity in Chartist Struggle, 1838–1842," *Past and Present,* no. 91 (May 1981): 109–39.

93. Sandall, *The History of the Salvation Army,* 2:195.

94. Bailey, "Salvation Army Riots," 232.

95. See Roy, *"Go Out Quickly";* Stevenson, *Historical Sketch of the Christian Community.*

96. *Lloyds,* 11 March 1883, 6.

97. WC, 7 March 1981, 5. These facts were remembered by her daughter.

98. WC, 8 January 1887, 6.

99. Respectability is a complicated notion. See Ross, "'Not the Sort That Would Sit on the Doorstep,'" 37–59.

100. It is impossible to know who wrote this publication, but some historians, including Victor Bailey and Glenn Horridge, have argued that it was most probably produced by the same groups who organized rowdy anti-Army street events, and I concur with that assessment.

101. *Skeleton* (Honiton), 16 December 1882, 2.

102. Ibid., 2 and 3.

103. Bailey, "Salvation Army Riots," 239, and Sandall, *The History of the Salvation Army,* 2:170–73.

104. CMM, October 1874, 274.

105. Home Office Papers, Public Records Office, London, PRO HO 45/A2886/13, quoted in Bailey, "Salvation Army Riots," 239. See also Eastbourne Clippings File, SAHC, *Eastbourne Gazette,* January 6, 1892.

106. The *Christian,* January 6, 1881, stated that the publicans were responsible for the opposition to the Salvation Army, "who, like the silversmiths of the ancient story, could not help seeing that the hope of their unholy gains was going, if not already gone" (13).

107. Theodore Koditschek, *Class Formation and Urban Industrial Society: Bradford, 1750–1850* (Cambridge: Cambridge University Press, 1990), 285.

108. *Times,* 5 May 1888, 7, and 10 May 1888, 6.

109. *Times,* 7 May 1888, 16; 10 May 1888, 3; 12 May 1888, 18. The leading match manufacturers, Bryant and May, also wrote to the *Times* to say that Adamson's statements were false; *Times,* 10 May 1888, 6.

110. *Torquay Directory and South Devon Journal,* 4 July 1888, 3.

111. WC, 12 May 1888.

112. *Daily Telegraph,* 31 October 1881, 2.

113. See Home Office Papers, Public Records Office, London, PRO HO 144/481/X32743/107 and HO 45/9965/X18313/31.

114. James Walvin, *Beside the Seaside,* 76. See also *Applegate's New Guide to Eastbourne and Its Neighbourhood* (Eastbourne: S. Applegate, [1871]).

115. Eastbourne Watch Committee, Meeting Minutes, East Sussex Record Office, Petition to the Chief of Police, April 24, 1891, DE/A6/1. See also Eastbourne Borough Council, Meeting Minutes, East Sussex Record Office, 1891, DE/A4/2.

116. Eastbourne Watch Committee, Meeting Minutes, East Sussex Record Office, June 19, 1891, DE/A6/1.

117. Eastbourne Clippings File, SAHC, *Eastbourne Gazette,* August 19, 1891.

118. Ibid., March 16, 1892.

119. Ibid., September 30, 1891.

120. Eastbourne Watch Committee, Meeting Minutes, East Sussex Record Office, January 3, 1892, DA/A6/1.

121. From a selection of the reports in *Lloyds,* the *Eastbourne Gazette,* the *Torquay Directory and South Devon Journal,* and the *Torquay Times and South Devon Advertiser* (1882–93), the occupations of the "Skeletons" were as follows: 1 costermonger, 2 flower hawkers, 16 laborers, 1 postman, 1 furniture dealer, 3 cabmen, 2 sailors, 3 bricklayers, 1 blacksmith, 1 tailor, 1 grocer's assistant, 1 luggage porter, 1 looking-glass-frame maker, 1 dealer, 1 stableman, 1 japanner, 1 wheelwright, 1 fisherman, 1 auctioneer, 1 ironworker, 1 lacemaker, 1 bargeman, 1 porter, 1 tailor's assistant, and 1 "elderly woman." The attacked Salvationists who were not full-time officers listed their occupations as follows: the men comprised 2 hairdressers, 1 gardener, 1 blacksmith, 1 waiter, 1 clerk, 2 laborers, 1 printer, 1 photographer's assistant; the women comprised 1 laundress and 1 dressmaker.

122. Davies, "Youth Gangs, Masculinity and Violence," 350, 351.

123. The evidence suggests that few women were involved in the attacks on Salvationists. The majority of scuttlers were working-class men in unskilled or semiskilled occupations, but some women were involved in street fighting. See Davies, "Youth Gangs, Masculinity and Violence," and Andrew Davies, "These Viragoes Are No Less Cruel Than the Lads: Young Women, Gangs and Violence in Late Victorian Manchester and Salford," *British Journal of Criminology* 39, no. 1 (1999): 72–89.

124. The occupations of those who signed the petitions were found in *Pike's Eastbourne Blue Book* (n.p., 1894–95).

125. See also Asa Briggs, "The Salvation Army in Sussex 1883–1892," in *Studies in Sussex Church History,* ed. M. J. Kitch (London: Leopard's Head Press, 1981), 189–208, and Glenn K. Horridge, "Invading Manchester: Responses to the Salvation Army, 1878–1900," *Manchester Region History Review* 6 (1992): 16–29.

126. *Times,* 7 September 1891, 10; 11 September 1891, 10; 14 September 1819, 9.

127. Rohan MacWilliam, "Radicalism and Popular Culture: The Tichbourne Case and the Politics of 'Fair Play,' 1867–1886," in *Currents of Radicalism*, ed. Eugenio Biagini and Alastair Reid (Cambridge: Cambridge University Press, 1991), 44–64. The Tichbourne case involved a man allegedly deprived of an inheritance. It received widespread publicity and sparked working-class protests.

128. T. Ashby Wood, *Man Made Bye Laws Examined from the Standpoint of Christian Ethics* (Tunbridge Wells: A. K. Baldwin, n.d.), 1.

129. WC, 12 April 1890, 9.

130. John Roberts, *The Battle of Torquay and One Months Experience in Devon County Jail* (n.p., n.d.).

131. McLeod, "Introduction," *European Religion in the Age of Great Cities*, 24.

132. See Bailey, "Salvation Army Riots"; McLeod, *Class and Religion*; Parsons, "A Question of Meaning," 63–87.

133. Thomas Wright, *Our New Masters* (London: Strahan, 1873), quoted in John Kent, "Feelings and Festivals: An Interpretation of Some Working-Class Religious Attitudes," in *The Victorian City: Images and Realities*, vol. 2, ed. H. J. Dyos and Michael Wolff (London: Routledge & Kegan Paul, 1973), 859.

POSTSCRIPT

1. *Bible Christian Magazine* 69 (November 1890), 710.

2. Ervine, *God's Soldier*, 2:759–64.

3. Herbert Booth Papers, SAHC, and Ford C. Ottman, *Herbert Booth: A Biography* (New York: Doubleday, Doran, 1928), 212.

4. Catherine Booth-Clibborn Papers, SAHC, and Scott, *The Heavenly Witch*.

5. Emma Booth-Tucker Papers, SAHC; Harry Williams, *Booth-Tucker: William Booth's First Gentleman* (London: Hodder & Stoughton, 1980); author's interview with Muriel Booth-Tucker (youngest daughter of Emma Booth-Tucker), London, March 1989.

6. Ervine, *God's Soldier*, 2:753, 1000.

7. A group of senior officers declared General Bramwell Booth unfit, removed him from office, and altered the Deed Poll to establish a system to elect the general. General Edward Higgins served from 1929 to 1934.

8. Ervine, *God's Soldier*, 2:815–1027; Wiggins, *The History of the Salvation Army*, vol. 5; and Coutts, *The History of the Salvation Army*, vol. 6. Garry Alligan, *Four Bonnets to Golgotha* (London: MacDonald, 1961), offers an unorthodox and not particularly well-documented discussion of the disputes among the Booth siblings.

9. William Booth, *In Darkest England and the Way Out* (London: Salvation Army Publishers, 1890; reprint, Monclair, N.J.: Paterson Smith, 1975), 11–12.

10. Ibid., 36.

11. Bailey, "In Darkest England and the Way Out," 151. The connections between religion and socialism are explored by Stephen Yeo, "A New Life: The Religion of Socialism in Britain, 1883–1896," *History Workshop Journal* 4 (autumn 1977): 5–56, and Logie Barrow, "Socialism in Eternity: The Ideology of

Plebeian Spiritualists, 1853–1913," *History Workshop Journal* 9 (spring 1980): 37–69.

12. See Bailey, "In Darkest England and the Way Out," 151–52; Inglis, *Churches and the Working Classes,* 195; Stedman Jones, *Outcast London,* 304, 308–11; Mearns, *The Bitter Cry;* George Sims, *How the Poor Live and Horrible London,* ed. F. M. Leventhal (London: Chatto & Windus, 1889; reprint, New York: Garland, 1984).

13. Herman Ausubel, "General Booth's Scheme of Social Salvation," *American Historical Review* 56, no. 3 (April 1951): 519–25.

14. WC, 30 May 1885, 1.

15. WC, 3 November 1888, 1.

16. WC, 26 February 1887, 7.

17. WC, 27 February 1886, 9.

18. Murdoch, *Origins of the Salvation Army,* argues the Darkest England scheme was a "new departure" for the Salvation Army. "As its evangelistic program stagnated in the 1880s, social salvation replaced evangelism as the army's mission" (147). I do not agree that its evangelism had stagnated, and the continuities with its earlier work are strong. Fairbank, *Booth's Boots,* in response to those "still labouring under the popular fallacy that all Salvation Army social work stemmed from the 1890 scheme," points out that only three of the ten social services did not begin before 1890 (131).

19. *All the World,* 1 (1885): 212, quoted in Higginbotham, "The Unmarried Mother," 106–7. See also Fairbank, *Booth's Boots,* 12–18.

20. Fairbank, *Booth's Boots,* 20–21.

21. WC, 10 November 1884, 2. See also WC, 10 December 1884, 3.

22. Bailey, "In Darkest England and the Way Out," 160, and General Frederick Coutts, *Bread for My Neighbour: The Social Influence of William Booth* (London: Hodder & Stoughton, 1978), 111.

23. Other cheap food depots were established in 1886 and 1887. WC, 21 January 1888, 1; Sandall, *The History of the Salvation Army,* 3:67–71; Fairbank, *Booth's Boots,* ch. 8.

24. Ben Tillett, *Memories and Reflections* (London: John Long, 1931), quoted in Bailey, "In Darkest England and the Way Out," 146.

25. WC, 25 December 1889, 3; Bailey, "In Darkest England and the Way Out," 144–46; Coutts, *Bread for My Neighbour,* 13; Fairbank, *Booth's Boots,* 8. Another perspective on the Salvation Army and the labor movement is found in Lynne Marks, "The Knights of Labour and the Salvation Army: Religion and Working-Class Culture in Ontario, 1882–1890," *Labour/Le Travail* 28 (fall 1991): 89–127.

26. Bailey, "In Darkest England and the Way Out," 141.

27. E. P. Thompson, "Blood, Fire and Unction," *New Society* 5, no. 128 (1965): 25.

28. Bailey, "In Darkest England and the Way Out," 156. Henry Hyndman, leader of the Social Democratic Federation and *Commonweal,* did not support the scheme; Bailey, "In Darkest England and the Way Out," 156–58.

29. Ibid., 158. See also Marks, "The Knights of Labour and the Salvation Army," 89–127.

30. Many have asserted that W. T. Stead actually wrote it. See, for example, Inglis, *Churches and the Working Classes*. But Stead denied it (see Fairbank, *Booth's Boots*, 136), and the book certainly resembles much else Booth wrote.

31. See Ausubel, "General Booth's Scheme."

32. Fairbank, *Booth's Boots*, 142–43.

33. Ervine, *God's Soldier*, 2:728–29, and Bailey, "In Darkest England and the Way Out," 160–62.

34. Rider Haggard, *Regeneration: Being an Account of the Social Work of the Salvation Army in Great Britain* (London: Longman, Green, 1910), and Sidney Webb and Beatrice Webb, *The Prevention of Destitution* (London: Longman, Green, 1911).

35. Bailey, "In Darkest England and the Way Out," 163–71.

36. Ervine, *God's Soldier*, 2:786, 790.

37. Ibid., 2:698.

38. Historians have debated the whole notion of secularization at great length. See, for example, Bruce, *Religion and Modernization*, and Williams, "The Language of Belief," 303–17. See also Robertson, "The Salvation Army," 49–105.

39. deVries, "Transforming the Pulpit," 319. See also Brian Heeney, *The Women's Movement in the Church of England, 1850–1930* (Oxford: Clarendon Press, 1988).

40. Daniel Mark Epstein, *Sister Aimee: The Life of Aimee Semple McPherson* (New York: Harcourt Brace Jovanovich, 1993). Taiz, "Applying the Devil's Works in a Holy Cause," 195–223, examines the dynamics of the Salvation Army's use of popular culture in the United States.

41. Harvey Cox, *Fire from Heaven: Pentacostalism, Spirituality and the Reshaping of Religion in the Twenty-First Century* (Reading, Mass.: Addison-Wesley, 1995).

Bibliography

MANUSCRIPT SOURCES

PERSONAL PAPERS

British Library, London. Catherine Mumford and William Booth Papers.

Brunell University Library, London. Elizabeth Rignall, "All So Long Ago," manuscript autobiography.

Churchill College, Cambridge University. W. T. Stead Papers.

Lambeth Palace Library, London. E. M. Benson Papers. R. T. Davidson Papers. A. C. Tait Papers.

Methodist Archives and Research Centre at the John Rylands University Library, Manchester. William Booth Papers. William Cooke Papers.

Queen Mary and Westfield College Archives, University of London. Constance Maynard Papers.

Salvation Army Heritage Centre, London. Agar Family Papers. Captain Barrett Papers. Ballington Booth Papers. Bramwell Booth Papers. Catherine Mumford Booth Papers. Florence Soper Booth Papers. Herbert Booth Papers. William Booth Papers. Catherine Booth-Clibborn Papers. Lucy Booth-Hellberg Papers. Emma Booth-Tucker Papers. Alfred Braine Papers. F. Brooks Papers. Elijah Cadman Papers. Elizabeth Churchill Papers. Adalaide Cox Papers. Frederick Coxhead Papers. Francis Crossley Papers. William Crow Papers. Mildred Duff Papers. George Ewens Papers. Onslow Ewens Papers. Charles Fry Papers. Henry Hodder Papers. Horatio Hodges Papers. Rebecca Jarrett Papers. James Jermy Papers. George Jollifee Papers. Susan Jones Papers. Letitia E. Kent Papers. Theodore Kitching Papers. Charles Knott Papers. Alexandria Lee Papers. Kate Lee Papers. Billy McLeod Papers. John Murfitt Papers. Florence Newland Papers. Mary Mabel Poole Papers. George Scott Railton Papers. Caroline Reynolds Papers. Charles Rich Papers. William Ridsdel Papers. John Rowe Papers. Charles Sowten Papers. Frederick Taylor Papers. Alfred Tutte Papers. Kate Watts Papers.

Trinity College, Cambridge University. E. M. Benson Papers.

OTHER MANUSCRIPT SOURCES

East Sussex Record Office. Eastbourne Borough Council, Meeting Minutes, 1891, DE/A4/2. Eastbourne Watch Committee, Meeting Minutes, 1890–92, DE/A6/1.
Methodist Archives and Research Centre at the John Rylands University Library, Manchester. Annual Committee Report Book of the Methodist New Connexion, 1855–1862. *Methodist New Connexion Conference Journal,* 1855–1861.
Public Records Office, London. Central Criminal Court, *Sessions Papers,* 1885. Home Office Papers, HO 45, 144, and 145. Manuscript Census, 1871 and 1881. Metropolitan Police Papers, MEPO 2.
Salvation Army Heritage Centre, London. Articles of War. Christian Mission Conference Minutes, 1870–71, 1873–78.Christian Mission Minutes, 1868–74. Circuit Plans, the Christian Mission at Whitechapel, 1870 and 1872. Croydon Elders' Meeting Minutes, the (East London) Christian Mission, 1869–71. Letterbooks, the Christian Mission, 1875–78. Shoreditch Elders Meetings, the (East London) Christian Mission, 1868–1874.
Somerset House, London. William Booth, Will.
Tyne and Wear Archives Service, Newcastle-upon-Tyne. Bethesda Methodist New Connexion, Leaders Meeting Minutes, Chapel, Gateshead, 1858–1860, TWAS 2095/11/2. Gateshead Society Members' Class Register, 2095/18. Primitive Methodist Chapel, Tatham Street, Sunderland, Leaders' Meeting Minutes C/Su34/1/1.

PUBLISHED PRIMARY SOURCES

SALVATION ARMY PERIODICALS

All the World, 1885–
Christian Mission Magazine, 1870–78
East London Evangelist, 1868–69
Local Officer, 1897–1906
Officer, 1893–
Salvationist, 1879
War Cry, 1879–

OTHER PERIODICALS CONSULTED

Place of publication is London unless otherwise noted in title or in parentheses.

Bethnal Green Times and East London Advertiser
Bible Christian Magazine
The Book and Its Mission
Borough of Marylebone Mercury
Christian
Daily News
Daily Telegraph
East London Leader
East London Observer

Eastbourne Gazette
Eastbourne Scorpion
Eastern Post and City Chronicle
Fun
Gateshead Observer
Guardian
Hackney Express
Hackney Times
Indicator
Lloyds
London City Mission Magazine
Methodist New Connexion Magazine (Manchester)
Missing Link, or Bible Women in the Homes of the London Poor
Moonshine
Morning Advertiser
Munsey's Magazine (New York)
Newcastle Weekly Chronicle
News of the World
Nonconformist
Northern Daily Express (Darlington and Newcastle)
Pall Mall Gazette
Penny Illustrated Paper
Primitive Methodist Quarterly Review and Christian Ambassador
Punch
Record
Revival. Name changed in 1870 to *Christian*.
Reynolds Newspaper
Saturday Review
Shoreditch Advertiser
Skeleton (Honiton)
South Durham and Cleveland Mercury
Sunderland Daily Echo
Sunderland Daily Post
Times
Torquay Directory and South Devon Journal
Torquay Times and South Devon Advertiser
Tower Hamlets Independent and General East End Advertiser
*Vim: An Illustrated Monthly Magazine Promoting Health and Vigour of Body
    and Mind*
Wesleyan Methodist Magazine
Wesleyan Times
Women's Penny Paper

ARTICLES

Addie, John. "Reminiscences of Early Day Fighting." *Officers' Review*, November 1934, 511–15.

Baugh, Brig. William. "Reminiscences of Early Day Fighting." *Officers' Review,*
    March 1935, 137–39.
Brown, Antoinette. "Exegesis of 1 Corinthians XIV: 34–35 and 1 Timothy II:
    11–12." *Oberlin Quarterly Review,* January 1849, 358–73.
Butler, Josephine. "Catherine Booth." *Contemporary Review* 58 (November
    1890): 639–54.
Carpenter, Mrs. Colonel. "Notable Staff Officers: Martha Chippendale." *Staff
    Officer,* July 1926, 331–40.
Cobbe, Frances Power. "The Last Revival." *Contemporary Review* 52 (August
    1882): 182–89.
"Darkest England." *Church Quarterly Review* 32, no. 63 (April 1891): 223–47.
Foote, Rev. C. C. "Women's Rights and Duties." *Oberlin Quarterly Review,* Jan-
    uary 1849, 381–408.
"The Glorified Spinster." *MacMillans Magazine* 58 (September 1888): 371–76.
Hollins, John. "The Salvation Army: A Note of Warning." *Contemporary Re-
    view* 74 (September 1898): 436–45.
"An Hour with the Salvation Army." *Indicator,* 30 October 1880, 3.
"Irregular Religious Agencies." *Nonconformist,* 10 April 1867, 289–90.
Lewis, M. A. "The Salvation Army." *MacMillans Magazine* 46 (September
    1882): 403–16.
Lonsdale, Margaret. "Platform Women." *Nineteenth Century,* November 1884,
    409–15.
Manning, Cardinal. "The Salvation Army." *Contemporary Review* 52 (Septem-
    ber 1882): 335–42.
Pearson, Capt. "Blood and Fire." *War Cry,* 4 September 1880, 3.
"Popular Songs to Popular Airs." *Field Officer,* February 1906, 57.
"The Salvation Army." *Church Quarterly Review* 14, no. 27 (April 1882): 107–34.
"The Salvation Army." *Contemporary Review* 42 (1882).
"Selling a Wife for One Shilling." *Yorkshire Gazette,* 11 May 1889, 6.
"Symposium: How to Evangelise the Masses." *Primitive Methodist Quarterly
    Review,* January 1883 and April 1883.
"Two Girls of the Period." *MacMillans Magazine* 19 (February 1869): 331–39.
Willard, Frances E. "La Marechale." *Review of the Churches* 15 (February 1894):
    286–90.

ARCHIVAL SOURCES

Salvation Army Heritage Center, London. Eagle and Grecian File. Eastbourne
    Clippings File.

AUTOBIOGRAPHIES AND BIOGRAPHIES

Acorn, George. *One of the Multitude.* London: William Heinemann, 1911.
[Barker, Joseph]. *The History and Confessions of a Man.* London: Wortley, 1846.
Barnes, Cyril J. *You Can't Stop Lawrance! Harriet Lawrance.* London: Salva-
    tion Army Publishers, 1953.

Begbie, Harold. *The Life of General William Booth, the Founder of the Salvation Army.* 2 vols. (New York: Macmillan, 1920).

Booth, Bramwell. *Echoes and Memories.* London: Salvationist Publishing, 1925.

Booth, Catherine Bramwell. *Catherine Booth: The Story of Her Loves.* London: Hodder & Stoughton, 1970.

Booth-Tucker, Frederick St-George de Latour. *The Life of Catherine Booth: The Mother of the Salvation Army.* 2 vols. New York: Fleming H. Revell, 1892.

Brigadier William Bennett: The Black Prince. London: Salvation Army, 1930.

Bullard, Henry. *A Missionary's Memories.* London: Salvationist Publishing, 1946.

Butler, Josephine. *Rebecca Jarrett.* London: Morgan and Scott, n.d.

Carpenter, Minnie L. *The Angel Adjunct of "Broken Earthware": Life Sketch of Staff-Capt. Kate Lee (1872–1920).* London: Hodder & Stoughton, n.d.

Champress, E. I. *Frank Smith: Pioneer and Modern Mystic.* London: Whitefriars Press, n.d.

Chappell, Jennie. *Women Who Have Worked and Won: The Life Story of Mrs. Spurgeon, Mrs. Booth-Tucker, F. R. Havergal and Ramabai.* London: S. W. Partridge, [1904].

Claughton, Lillian M. *Charles H. Jeffries: From "Skeleton" to Salvationist Leader.* London: Salvationist Publishing, 1946.

Cox, Adalaide. *Hotchpotch.* London: Salvationist Publishing, 1937.

Davies, Lieut. Commissioner Emma. *Sure of Her Call: Betty Thorne.* London: Salvationist Publishing, 1952.

Davies, Rosina. *The Story of My Life.* Llandyssul: Gomerian Press, 1942.

Douglas, Eileen, and Mildred Duff. *Commissioner Railton.* London: Salvation Army, n.d.

Eldred, John. *I Love the Brooks.* London: Skeffington, 1955.

Elswick Local History Group. *Living and Working in Elswick.* Newcastle-upon-Tyne, 1984.

Ervine, St. John. *God's Soldier: General William Booth.* 2 vols. London: Heinemann, 1934.

Everett, James. *The Midshipman and the Minister; the Quarter Deck and the Pulpit.* London: Hamilton, Adams, 1867.

Flint, Elizabeth. *Hot Bread and Chips.* London: Museum Press, 1963.

———. *Kipper Stew.* London: Museum Press, 1964.

Flockhart, Robert. *The Street Preacher: Being the Autobiography of Robert Flockhart.* Edinburgh: Adam and Charles Black, 1858.

Free, Richard. *Seven Years' Hard.* New York: Dutton, 1905.

Gauntlett, S. Carvosso. *John Murfitt: From Miner to Major.* London: Salvationist Publishing, 1944.

Gellatley, James. *Twice Saved by a Song: Hannah Starling* [Hallelujah Nancy]. London: Salvationist Publishing, 1947.

Grant, Clara. *From Me to We: Forty Years on Bow Common.* London: Fern Street Settlement, n.d.

Hadden, Capt. Albert. *Life and Death of Fish Pollie Late a Soldier in Leed II Corps, of the Salvation Army. Who Died Nov. 10th, 1885; and an Account of Her Funeral.* Leeds: Jas. Strafford, n.d.

Hatcher, Matilda. *Catherine Hine: "Teacher" of Chinatown.* London: Salvationist Publishing, 1943.

Hoggart, Richard. *The Uses of Literacy.* Oxford: Oxford University Press, 1970.

Holloway, Henry. *A Voice from the Convict Cell: or Life and Conversion of Henry Holloway.* London: Simkin, Marshall, [1877].

Hope, Noel. *Mildred Duff: A Surrendered Life.* London: Salvationist Publishing, 1933.

Jack Stoker: Drunkard and Soul-Saver. London: Salvationist Publishing, 1930.

Johnson, Jane. *The Life of Jane Johnson: The Champion Drunkard of the World (Captured by the Salvation Army) as Related by Herself.* Leeds: Pinder and Bowes, n.d.

Lancashire Nancy: A Miracle Story of Today. London: Salvation Army Publishing, n.d.

Lansbury, George. *My Life.* London: Constable, 1928.

The Life Story of Rosie Bannister (Mrs. Eastwood): A Modern Miracle. Burnley: S. Fielden, n.d.

Lovett, William. *The Life and Struggles of William Lovett.* New York: Garland, 1984.

Morgan, R. C. *The Life of Richard Weaver.* London: Morgan and Scott, n.d.

Nightingale, Elizabeth, ed. *Mrs. Collier of Birmingham, a Biblewoman's Story: Being the Autobiography of Mrs. Collier,* 2d ed. London: T. Woolmer, 1885.

Ottman, Ford C. *Herbert Booth: A Biography.* New York: Doubleday, Doran, 1928.

Preece, Charles. *Woman of the Valley: The Story of Mother Shepard.* Port Talbot, West Glamorgan: New Life Publications, 1988.

R., Geo. *The Salvation Navvy: Being an Account of the Life, Death and Victories of Captain John Allen of the Salvation Army.* London: Salvation Army, 1880.

Railton, George Scott. *Captain Ted: Being the Life Story of Captain Edward Irons of the Salvation Army.* London: Salvation Army, 1889.

————. *Commissioner Dowdle: The Saved Railway Guard.* London: Salvation Army Publishing, 1901, 1912. Reprint, London: Salvationist Publishing, 1930.

Roberts, Robert K. *The Classic Slum.* Manchester: Manchester University Press, 1971. Reprint, Harmondsworth, Middlesex: Penguin Books, 1973.

Sanky, Ira D. *My Life and the Story of the Gospel Hymns.* New York: Sunday School Times, 1907. Reprint, London: AMS Press, 1974.

Scott, Carolyn. *The Heavenly Witch: The Story of the Marechale.* London: Hamish Hamilton, 1981.

Seabrook, Jeremy. *The Unprivileged.* Harmondsworth, Middlesex: Penguin Books, 1973.

Smith, Cornelius. *The Life Story of Gipsy Cornelius Smith.* London: John Heywood, [1890].

Smith, Rodney. *Gipsy Smith: His Life and Work by Himself.* London: National Council of the Evangelical Free Churches, 1902.

Stead, W. T. *Life of Mrs. Booth: The Founder of the Salvation Army.* New York: Fleming H. Revell, 1900.

Strahan, James. *The Marechale.* London: Hodder & Stoughton, 1913.

Taylor, Gladys M. *So Sure of Herself! Nancy (Dickeybird) Cunningham*. London: Salvationist Publishing, 1944.

Taylor, Gordon. *In the Strength of the King: A Short History of the Hodgeson Family*. London, 1984.

Thompson, Tierl, ed. *Dear Girl: The Diaries and Letters of Two Working Women, 1897–1917*. London: Women's Press, 1987.

Tillett, Ben. *Memories and Reflections*. London: John Long, 1931.

Truelove, Elizabeth. *His Love Is Worth It All: Memories of Nellie Truelove*. St. Albans: Salvation Army, Campfield Press, 1905.

Walford, John. *Memoirs of the Life and Labours of the Late Venerable Hugh Bourne*. 2 vols. London: T. King, 1855–56.

Williams, Harry. *Booth-Tucker: William Booth's First Gentleman*. London: Hodder & Stoughton, 1980.

Willis, Frederick. *101, Jubilee Road, a Book of London Yesteryears*. London: Phoenix House, 1948.

Wilson, John. *Memories of a Labour Leader*. London: T. Fisher Unwin, 1910.

Woodward, Kathleen. *Jipping Street: Childhood in a London Slum*. London: Harper and Bros., 1928.

Wright, Thomas. *Our New Masters*. London: Strahan, 1873.

BOOKS AND PAMPHLETS

The American Revival and Individual Agency: An Address to Christians in England by a Canadian. London: Alexander Heylin, 1859.

A Appeal to Truth, or Revival Facts by a Wesleyan Layman. London: A. Hall, Virtue, 1854.

Ashton, John. *Modern Street Ballads*. London: Chatto & Windus, 1888.

Atkinson, Rev. J. A. *The Salvation Army and the Church*. London: John Heywood, 1882.

Babylon: or the Pall Mall Gazette and the Salvation Army on the Corruption, Cruelties and Crime of London. London: Salvation Army, 1885.

Baggaly, Rev. William. *A Digest of the Minutes of the Institutions, Polity, Doctrines, Ordinances, and Literature of the Methodist New Connexion*. London: Methodist New Connexion Bookroom, 1862.

Bairstow, J. O. *Sensational Religion in Past Times and Present Day*. London: Elliot Stock, 1890.

Barry, M. L. *Hard Realities*. London: John and Robert Maxwell, [1884].

Beven, Douglas. *Startling Revelations: Eight Years Experience in the Salvation Army*. Liverpool, 1906.

Booth, Catherine. *Female Ministry: Women's Right to Preach the Gospel*. London: Morgan and Chase, 1870. Reprint, London: Salvation Army Publishing, 1975.

———. *Female Teaching: or, the Rev. A. A. Rees versus Mrs. Palmer, Being a Reply to a Pamphlet by the Above Gentleman on the Sunderland Revival*, 2d ed. London: George J. Stevenson, 1861.

———, Mrs. *Female Ministry or Women's Right to Preach the Gospel*. London: Morgan and Chase, [1870].

————. *Holiness: Being an Address Delivered in St. James Hall, Piccadilly, London.* London: Salvation Army, n.d.

————. *Mrs. Booth on Recent Criticisms of the Salvation Army. Being An Address Delivered in St. James's Hall, London on Monday July 17, 1882.* London: 101, Queen Victoria Street, n.d.

————. *The Salvation Army in Relation to the Church and State.* London: Salvation Army, 1883.

Booth, Miss Catherine. *French Notes: Being a Letter from Miss Booth Describing Some Cases of Conversion and the Work and Prospects of the Salvation Army in France.* London: Salvation Army, [1884].

Booth, Emma M., and Ballington Booth. *The Training Barracks or Our London Homes.* London: Salvation Army Bookstores, [1883].

Booth, Herbert. *Called Out! And What Comes of It.* London: Salvation Army, [1887].

Booth, Maud C. *Beneath Two Flags.* London and New York: Funk & Wagnalls, 1889.

Booth, Mrs. Bramwell. *Mothers and the Empire and Other Addresses.* London: Salvation Army Book Department, 1914.

Booth, William. *Doctrines and Disciplines of the Salvation Army.* London: Salvation Army Headquarters, 1881.

————. *The Doctrines of the Salvation Army.* London: Salvation Army, 1891.

————. *How To Reach the Masses with Gospel.* London: Morgan, Chase and Scott, [1872].

————. *In Darkest England and the Way Out.* London: Salvation Army Publishers, 1890. Reprint, Montclair, N.J.: Paterson Smith, 1975.

————. *Report of the Christian Mission, October 1867.* London, 1867.

————, comp. *Revival Music for Evangelistic Services, Open Air Meetings and the Home Circle.* London: S. W. Partridge, 1876.

————. *Rules of the Christian Mission.* London, n.d.

————, comp. *Salvation Army Music.* London: Salvation Army, n.d.

————, comp. *Salvation Army Songs.* New York: Salvation Army, 1925.

————. *A Talk with Mr. Gladstone.* London: Salvation Army, 1897.

Booth, William, and G. S. Railton. *Behind the Pigeon Shop.* London: S. W. Partridge, [1868].

Butler, Josephine. *The Salvation Army in Switzerland.* London: Dyer Brothers, 1883.

Carter, William B. *The Case Tested: Being an Inquiry into the Character and Labours of the Rev. James Caughey and the Action of the Wesleyan Conference Thereon.* London: Wittaker, 1847.

Caughey, Rev. James. *Showers of Blessing from Clouds of Mercy; Selected from the Journal Writings of the Rev. James Caughey.* Boston: J. P. Magee, 1857.

Chadwick, Samuel. *Doings of Despotism: Being a Report of the Quarterly Meeting of the Wesleyan Reformers of the Cleckheaton Circuit.* Batley: Jas. Fearnsides, 1859.

Charlesworth, Maria Louisa. *Ministering Children.* London: Ward, Lock, 1899.

Charlesworth, Samuel. *Memorials of a Blessed Life.* London: Seeley, Jackson and Halliday, 1882.

————. *Sensational Religion as Resorted to in the System Called the "Salvation Army" in Its Influence upon the Young and in Its Effects upon the Duties and Claims of Home Life*. Privately printed, [1885].

Chase, Ellen. *Tenant Friends in Old Deptford*. London: Williams and Norgate, 1929.

Clibborn, Colonel. *Arrest, Imprisonment, Trial and Acquittal of Miss Booth and Comrades*. London: Salvation Army, n.d.

Corbridge, William. *Battle Array: The Ruination and Salvation Armies in Six Parts*. London: Salvation Army Bookstores, n.d.

————. *Salvation Mine: Down to Death! Up to Glory!* London: Salvation Army, 1881.

————. *The Up Line to Heaven and the Down Line to Hell*. 7th ed. London: Salvation Army Headquarters, n.d.

Dale, R. W. *General Booth's Scheme*. Birmingham: Cornish Brothers, 1890.

Dwyer, Philip. *General Booth's "Submerged Tenth."* London: Swan Sonnenschein, 1891.

Facts Are Stubborn Things: An Illustration of Conference Methodism in the Bacup Circuit. N.p.: Printed for the General Wesleyan Reform Committee, n.d.

A Faithful Verbatim Reprint of the "Fly Sheets," by a Wesleyan Minister Who Is Not Yet Expelled. Birmingham: William Cornish, 1849.

A Few Facts about Wesleyan Conference Expulsions. Hastings: W. Ransom, n.d.

Finney, Charles G. *Lectures on Revivals of Religion*. New York: Leavitt, Lord, 1835.

Fishbourne, Admiral. *A Calm Plea for the Enlargement of Salvation Army Work*. London: Elliot Stoke, [1882].

Fisher, Pearl. *The Harvest of the City and the Workers of Today*. London: John F. Shaw, 1884.

Frank Coyle's Songbook. N.p., 1896.

Freeman, Flora L. *Polly: A Study of Girl Life*. London: A. R. Mowbray, 1904.

————. *Religious and Social Work amongst Girls*. London: Skeffington and Sons, 1901.

Gasparin, la Comtess Agenor de. *Read and Judge the (So-Called) Salvation Army*. Translated by E.O.B. London: Griffith and Farran, 1883.

————. *A Simple Request to Mr. Booth*. Translated by E.O.B. London: Griffith and Farran, 1883.

The General. *Orders and Regulations for Field Officers*. London: Salvation Army, 1886.

General's Methodist Resignation. Manchester: New Papacy Company, [1887].

A Good Shepard or What a Salvation Army Captain Should Be; Being a Shepard's Letter to General Booth. London: Salvation Army Bookstores, [1884].

Green, Walford, and John Hugh Morgan. *Methodist Revival Missions: A Small Handbook*. London: Wesleyan Conference Office, 1876.

Hancock, Rev. Thomas. *Salvation by Mammon: Two Sermons on Mr. Booth's Scheme*. London: Office of the Church Reformer, 1891.

Harris, Constance. *The Uses of Leisure in Bethnal Green*. London: Lindsay Press, 1927.

Heathcote, Rev. Wyndham. *My Salvation Army Experience*. [1892]. Reprint, London: Marshall Brothers, 1927.

Hindley, Charles, ed. *Curiosities of Street Literature*. London: Reeves and Turner, 1871.

Hodges, S. H. *General Booth: "The Family" and the Salvation Army, Showing Its Rise, Progress, and Moral and Spiritual Decline*. Manchester: Printed and Published by the Author, 1890.

In Perils in the City. Published under the direction of the Working Girls Clubs. London: Headley Bros., 1909.

An Investigator. *Behind the Scenes with the Salvation Army*. 2d ed. London: 8, Salisbury Court, Fleet St., [1882].

James, John Angell. *Revival of Religion: Its Principles, Necessity and Effects*. London: John Snow, 1859.

Jannaway, F. G. *The Salvation Army and the Bible*. Birmingham: Robert Roberts, 1889.

Jarbo, Rev. Dr. *A Letter to Mrs. Palmer in Reference to Women Speaking in Public*. Northshields: Philipson and Hare, 1859.

Jesus Altogether Lovely or a Letter to Some Single Women in Methodist Society. Bristol, 1766.

A Layman. *Sensationalism: A Broadsider into Moody and Sankyism; a Skirmish with the Salvation Army and a Side Thrust at Shakers, Bible Thumpers, Jumpers, Latter Day Saints and Other "Peculiar People."* London: John Heywood, [1884].

Lee, Luther. *Women's Right to Preach the Gospel: A Sermon Preached at the Ordination of Rev. Miss Antoinette L. Brown*. Syracuse, N.Y.: Published by the Author, 1853.

A Letter to William Booth, the "General" of the So-Called Salvation Army. London, 1879.

Lightfoot, J. B. *Primary Charge: Two Addresses Delivered to the Clergy of the Diocese of Durham in December 1882*. London: Macmillan, n.d.

Loane, Margaret. *An Englishman's Castle*. London: Edward Arnold, 1909.

———. *The Next Street but One*. London: Edward Arnold, 1907.

———. *The Queen's Poor*. London: Edward Arnold, 1905.

MacGlennon's Authorised Edition. N.p., 1888.

MacGlennon's Authorised Edition. N.p., 1896.

MacGlennon's Star Song-Book. N.p., 1888.

Mearns, Andrew. *The Bitter Cry of Outcast London*. Edited and with an introduction by Anthony Wohl. 1883. Reprint, New York: Humanities Press, 1970.

Men's Training Home: General Rules and Regulations. London: Salvation Army, [1883].

Methodist New Connexion. *Minutes of the Annual Conference of the Methodist New Connexion*. London: Methodist New Connexion Book Room, 1858, 1859, 1860, and 1861.

More, Hannah. *The Works of Hannah More*. Vol. 1. New York: Harper and Brothers, 1835.

Muspratt, Albert. *The Salvation Army: Is It a Benefit to the Cause of Religion? The Negative as Delivered before the Ripon Mechanics Institute Debating Society February 12, 1884*. Ripon: William Harrison, 1884.

The New Papacy: Behind the Scenes at the Salvation Army by an Ex-Staff Officer. Toronto: Albert Britnell, 1889.

Newton, Benjamin Wills. *An Address Respecting the Methods of the Salvation Army.* London: Houlston and Sons, 1882.

Open Air Mission Society. *Occasional Papers.* London: Open Air Mission Society, 1855–57.

O.W.L.A. *Some Reasons Why I Do Not Sympathize with the Salvation Army.* London: John F. Shaw, n.d.

Palmer, Phoebe. *Four Years in the Old World.* New York: Foster, Palmer Jr., 1867.

———. *The Promise of the Father; or a Neglected Spirituality of the Last Days.* Boston: Henry V. Deglan, 1859.

Pope Booth: The Salvation Army A.D. 1950. London: Sully and Ford, n.d.

Pratt, Charles T. *The "Salvation Army": A Sermon.* London: I. W. Davis, 1892.

Price, John. *The Salvation Army Tested by Their Works.* Chester: Minshull and Hughes, 1882.

Radcliffe, Alexander. *The Salvation Army: Its Jewish Origins, Methods and Tyranny.* Glasgow: A. Radcliffe, 1945.

Railton, George Scott. *Madame Jeanne de la Mothe Guyon.* London: Salvation Army Publishing, 1881.

———. *The Salvation Paper Mill.* London: Salvation Army Bookstores, n.d.

———. *Twenty-One Years' Salvation Army.* London: Salvation Army, 1889.

Redstone, J.J.R. *An Ex-Captain's Experience of the Salvation Army.* London: Christian Commonwealth Publishing, [1888].

Rees, Arthur Augustus. *Reasons for Not Co-operating in the Alleged "Sunderland Revivals."* Sunderland: Wm. Henry Hills, 1859.

Roberts, John. *The Battle of Torquay and One Months Experience in Devon County Jail.* N.p., n.d.

Roberts, W. Hazlitt. *General Booth's Scheme and the Municipal Alternative.* London: Simpkin, Marshall, Hamilton, Adams, 1891.

Roberts, William. *A Review of the "Doctrine and Discipline of the Salvation Army."* Madras: S. Ruthna Chettiar, 1889.

Ropper, Rev. W. H. *General Booth, and the Salvation Army.* London: Simpkin, Marshall, Hamilton, Kent, 1892.

Ross, Adalaide. *Manual for Workers of the East London Association for the Care of Friendless Girls.* London: Hatchards, n.d.

Roy, Rob. *"Go Out Quickly" into the Streets and Lanes of the City.* London: Open Air Mission Society, 1855.

Salvation Army. *All about the Salvation Army.* London: Salvation Army, 1883.

———. *The Darkest England Social Scheme: A Brief Review of the First Year's Work.* London: Salvation Army, 1891.

———. *International Music Drills: Healthy Home Exercises with Deep Breathing.* London: Salvation Army, 1909.

———. *The Salvation Army Songbook.* London: Salvation Army, 1930.

———. *Wounded in the Warfare of Life: Being a Report of the Annual Meeting of the Women's Social Work of the Salvation Army.* London: Salvation Army, 1900.

The Salvation Army (So-Called): A Friendly Exposure of Its Unscriptural Pretensions and Proceedings by a Christian Minister. London, [1880].

Sensation or Salvation? London: Printed and Published for the Author by Civil Service Printing and Publishing, [1882].

Sims, George. *How the Poor Live and Horrible London.* Edited by F. M. Leventhal. London: Chatto & Windus, 1889. Reprint, New York: Garland, 1984.

Sims, George, and F. A. McKinzie. *Sketches of the Salvation Army Social Work.* London: Salvation Army, 1906.

Socialism and the Temperance Societies: A Teaching Delivered in London, February 20, 1883 with Some Additional Remarks on the So-Called Salvation Army. London: Thomas Bosworth, 1883.

Stevenson, George J. *Historical Sketch of the Christian Community, A.D. 1818–1826 by One of Their Members.* London: George J. Stevenson, 1868.

Swift, Elizabeth Reeves. *Drum Taps.* London: 8 & 9 Paternoster Square, n.d.

The Temperance Movement and the Salvation Army. London: Strangeways and Sons, 1882.

Through the Homes at Clapton. London: Salvation Army, n.d.

Truth. *Sleeping Christianity: An Answer to "Behind the Scenes with the Salvation Army."* London: Printed and Published for the Author by Civil Service Printing and Publishing, n.d.

The Truth about the Armstrong Case and the Salvation Army. London: Salvation Army, n.d.

Waller, Charles B. *The Salvation Army: How Should the Thoughtful Christian Judge This Movement.* London: Kegan Paul and Trench, 1882.

Wallis, Nettie. *A Brief Account of the Lord's Dealings with One of His Handmaidens in France and Switzerland, 1883.* London: Salvation Army, 1883.

A Way to the World: Being the Annual Report and Statement of Accounts of the International Training Homes of the Salvation Army, 1885. London: Salvation Army Book Depot, n.d.

Wesley, John. *A Plain Account of Christian Perfection.* Bristol: William Pine, 1770.

White, Arnold, Francis Peek, and Farrar, the Venerable Archdeacon. *The Truth about the Salvation Army.* London: Simpkin, Marshall, Hamilton, Kent, 1892.

Wood, T. Ashby. *Man-Made Bye Laws Examined from the Standpoint of Christian Ethics.* Tunbridge Wells: A. K. Baldwin, n.d.

Wright, Thomas. *Our New Masters.* London: Strahan, 1873.

Wroth, Warwick. *Cremorne and Later London Gardens.* London: Elliot Stock, 1907.

Young, Rev. Robert. *North of England Revivals: The Prophesying of Women.* Newcastle-upon-Tyne, 1859.

FICTION

Law, John. *In Darkest London: Captain Lobe.* With an Introduction by William Booth. London: William Reeves, [1890].

SECONDARY SOURCES

Addy, S. O. "Derbyshire Folklore." In *Memorials of Old Derbyshire,* edited by Rev. J. Cox. London: Bemrose and Sons, 1907.

Alligan, Garry. *Four Bonnets to Golgotha*. London: MacDonald, 1961.

Altholz, Josef L. *The Religious Press in Britain, 1760–1900*. New York: Greenwood Press, 1989.

Altick, Richard. *The English Common Reader: A Social History of the Mass Reading Public, 1800–1910*. Chicago: University of Chicago Press, 1957.

Anderson, Olive. "The Growth of Christian Militarism in Mid-Victorian Britain". *English Historical Review* 86, no. 338 (January 1971): 64–72.

———. "Women Preachers in Mid-Victorian Britain: Some Reflections on Feminism, Popular Religion and Social Change." *Historical Journal* 12, no. 3 (1969): 467–85.

Andrews, William L., ed. *Sisters of the Spirit: Three Black Women's Autobiographies of the Nineteenth Century*. Bloomington: Indiana University Press, 1986.

Applegate's New Guide to Eastbourne and Its Neighbourhood. Eastbourne: S. Applegate, [1871].

Auerbach, Nina. *Ellen Terry: Player in Her Time*. New York: Norton, 1987.

———. *The Woman and the Demon: The Life of a Victorian Myth*. Cambridge, Mass.: Harvard University Press, 1982.

Ausubel, Herman. "General Booth's Scheme of Social Salvation." *American Historical Review* 56, no. 3 (April 1951): 519–25.

Avery, Gordon. *Companion to the Song Book of the Salvation Army*. London: Salvationist Publishing, 1961.

Bailey, Peter. *Leisure and Class in Victorian England, 1830–1885*. London: Routledge & Kegan Paul, 1978.

———, ed. *[Music Hall]: The Business of Pleasure*. Milton Keynes: Open University Press, 1986.

———. *Popular Culture and Performance in the Victorian City*. Cambridge: Cambridge University Press, 1998.

Bailey, Victor. "In Darkest England and the Way Out: The Salvation Army, Social Reform and the Labour Movement, 1885–1910." *International Review of Social History* 29 (1984): 134–71.

———. "Salvation Army Riots, the 'Skeleton Army' and Legal Authority in the Provincial Town." In *Social Control in Nineteenth-Century Britain*, edited by A. P. Donajgrodzki. London: Croom Helm, 1977.

Ball, Gillian. "Practical Religion: A Study of the Salvation Army's Social Services for Women." Ph.D. thesis, University of Leicester, 1987.

Banks, Olive. *Becoming a Feminist: The Social Origins of the "First Wave" Feminism*. Athens: University of Georgia Press, 1986.

Banton, Micheal. *Anthropological Approaches to the Study of Religion*. London: Tavistock, 1966.

Barnett, Canon S. A., and Mrs. S. A. Barnett. *Practicable Socialism*. London: Longman, Green, 1915.

Barnhart, Joe E., and Mary Ann Barnhart. *The New Birth: A Naturalistic View of Religious Conversion*. Macon, Ga.: Mercer University Press, 1981.

Barret-Ducrocq, Francoise. *Love in the Time of Victoria*. London: Verso, 1991.

Barrow, Logie. *Independent Spirits: Spiritualism and English Plebeians, 1850–1910*. London: Routledge & Kegan Paul, 1986.

———. "Socialism in Eternity: The Ideology of Plebeian Spiritualists, 1853–1913." *History Workshop Journal*, 9 (spring 1980): 37–69.

Bebbington, D. W. "The City, the Countryside, and the Social Gospel in Late Victorian Nonconformity." In *The Church in Town and Countryside*, edited by Derek Baker. Studies in Church History, vol. 16. Oxford: Blackwell, 1979.

———. *Evangelicalism in Modern Britain: A History from the 1730s to the 1980s*. London: Allen Unwin, 1989.

Beckford, James A. "Accounting for Conversion." *British Journal of Sociology* 29, no. 2 (June 1978): 249–62.

Behlmer, George K. *Friends of the Family: The English Home and Its Guardians, 1850–1940*. Stanford, Calif.: Stanford University Press, 1998.

Benson, John, ed. *The Working Class in England, 1875–1914*. London: Croom Helm, 1985.

Biagini, Eugenio, and Alastair Reid, eds. *Currents of Radicalism*. Cambridge: Cambridge University Press, 1991.

Billington, Louis. "Revivalism and Popular Culture." In *In Search of Victorian Values: Aspects of Nineteenth Century Thought and Society*, edited by Eric M. Sigsworth. Manchester: Manchester University Press, 1988.

Bland, Lucy. *Banishing the Beast: English Feminism and Sexual Morality, 1885–1914*. New York: Penguin Books, 1995.

Blauvelt, Nancy Tomhave. "Women and Revivalism." In *Women and Religion in America*, edited by Rosemary Radford Reuther and Rosemary Skinner Keller. San Francisco: Harper & Row, 1981.

Bloom, Harold. *The American Religion: The Emergence of the Post-Christian Nation*. New York: Simon & Schuster, 1992.

Booth, Charles. *Life and Labour of the People in London*. 7 vols. Religious Influences, 3rd ser. 1903. Reprint, London: AMS Press, 1970.

Bornat, Joanna. "Lost Leaders: Women, Trade Unionism, and the Case of the General Union of Textile Workers, 1875–1914." In *Unequal Opportunities*, edited by Angela John. Oxford: Blackwell, 1986.

Bowley, A. L. *Wages and Incomes in the United Kingdom since 1860*. Cambridge: Cambridge University Press, 1900.

Bradby, David, Louis James, and Bernard Sharratt, eds. *Performance and Politics in Popular Drama*. Cambridge: Cambridge University Press, 1980.

Bradley, Ian. "Blowing for the Lord." *History Today* 27, no. 3 (1977): 190–95.

———. *The Call to Seriousness*. London: Cape, 1976.

Bratton, J. S., ed. *Music Hall: Performance and Style*. Milton Keynes: Open University Press, 1986.

Braude, Ann. *Radical Spirits: Spiritualism and Women's Rights in Nineteenth Century America*. Boston: Beacon Press, 1989.

Brereton, Virginia Lieson. *From Sin to Salvation: Stories of Women's Conversions 1800 to the Present*. Bloomington: Indiana University Press, 1991.

Briggs, Asa. "The Salvation Army in Sussex, 1883–1892." In *Studies in Sussex Church History*, edited by M. J. Kitch. London: Leopard's Head Press, 1981.

Brown, Callum. "The Mechanism of Religious Growth in Urban Societies: British Cities since the Eighteenth Century." In *European Religion in the Age of Great Cities, 1830–1930*, edited by Hugh McLeod. London: Routledge, 1995.

Bruce, Steve. *Religion and Modernization: Sociologists and Historians Debate the Secularization Thesis*. Oxford: Clarendon Press, 1992.

Buchanan, Constance H. *Choosing to Lead: Women and the Crisis of American Values*. Boston: Beacon Press, 1996.

Budd, Michael Anton. *The Sculpture Machine: Physical Culture and Body Politics in the Age of Empire*. New York: New York University Press, 1997.

Burnett, John. *A Social History of Housing, 1815–1985*. 2d ed. London: Methuen, 1986.

Bynum, Caroline Walker. *Fragmentation and Redemption: Essays on Gender and the Human Body in Medieval Religion*. New York: Zone Books, 1991.

Bynum, Caroline Walker, Steven Harrill, and Paula Richman, eds. *Gender and Religion: On the Complexity of Symbols*. Boston: Beacon Press, 1986.

Campbell, Debra. "Hannah Whitall Smith: Theology of the Mother-Hearted God." *Signs* 15, no. 1 (winter 1989): 79–101.

Carwardine, Richard. *Transatlantic Revivalism: Popular Evangelicalism in Britain and America, 1790–1865*. London: Greenwood Press, 1978.

Chambers, George F. *Eastbourne Memories of the Victorian Period, 1845–1901*. Eastbourne: V. T. Sunfield, 1910.

Church, Leslie. *More about the Early Methodist People*. London: Edworth Press, 1949.

Clark, Anna. "The Politics of Seduction in English Popular Culture, 1748–1848." In *The Progress of Romance: The Politics of Popular Fiction*, edited by Jean Radford. London: Routledge & Kegan Paul, 1986.

———. "The Rhetoric of Chartist Domesticity: Gender, Language and Class in the 1830s and 1840s." *Journal of British Studies* 31, no. 1 (January 1992): 62–88.

———. *The Struggle for the Breeches: Gender and the Making of the British Working Class*. Berkeley: University of California Press, 1995.

Clarke, Adam. *Adam Clarke's Commentary on the Old Testament*. London: Joseph Butterworth and Son, 1825.

Cohen, Charles Lloyd. *God's Caress: The Psychology of the Puritan Religious Experience*. New York: Oxford University Press, 1986.

Collier, Richard. *The General Next to God*. London: Collins, 1965.

Colls, Robert. *The Collier's Rant*. London: Croom Helm, 1977.

———. *The Pitman of the Northern Coalfield: Work, Culture and Protest, 1790–1850*. Manchester: Manchester University Press, 1987.

———. "Primitive Methodists in the Northern Coalfields." In *Disciplines of Faith*, edited by Jim Obelkevich, Lyndal Roper, and Raphael Samuel. London: Routledge & Kegan Paul, 1986.

Copelman, Dina. *London's Women Teachers: Gender, Class and Feminism, 1870–1930*. London: Routledge, 1996.

———. "A New Comradeship between Men and Women: Family, Marriage, and London's Women Teachers, 1870–1914." In *Labour and Love: Women's Experience of Home and Family, 1850–1940*, edited by Jane Lewis. Oxford: Oxford University Press, 1986.

Corbin, Alain. "Commercial Sexuality in Nineteenth Century France: A System of Images and Representations." In *The Making of the Modern Body*, edited by Catherine Gallagher and Thomas W. Laqueur. Berkeley: University of California Press, 1987.

Coutts, General Frederick. *Bread for My Neighbour: The Social Influence of William Booth*. London: Hodder & Stoughton, 1978.

———. *The History of the Salvation Army*. Vol. 6. 1973. Reprint, London: Salvation Army, 1979.

Cox, Jeffrey. *The English Churches in a Secular Society: Lambeth, 1870–1930*. Oxford: Oxford University Press, 1982.

Cox, Harvey. *Fire from Heaven: Pentecostalism, Spirituality and the Reshaping of Religion in the Twenty-First Century*. Reading, Mass.: Addison-Wesley, 1995.

Crossick, Geoffrey. *An Artisan Elite in Victorian Society: Kentish London, 1840–1880*. London: Croom Helm, 1978.

Cuming, G. D., and D. Baker, eds. *Popular Belief and Practice*. Vol. 8 of *Studies in Church History*. Cambridge: Cambridge University Press, 1972.

Cunningham, Hugh. "Jingoism in 1877–1878." *Victorian Studies* 14, no. 5 (June 1971): 429–53.

———. *Leisure in the Industrial Revolution*. London: Croom Helm, 1980.

———. *The Volunteer Force: A Social and Political History, 1859–1908*. London: Croom Helm, 1975.

Curtis, Susan. *A Consuming Faith: The Social Gospel and Modern American Culture*. Baltimore: Johns Hopkins University Press, 1991.

Daunton, M. J. *House and Home in the Victorian City: Working-Class Housing, 1850–1914*. Baltimore: Arnold, 1983.

———. "Public Place and Private Space: The Victorian City and the Working-Class Household." In *The Pursuit of Urban History*, edited by Derek Fraser and Anthony Sutcliffe. London: Arnold, 1983.

Davidoff, Leonore, and Catherine Hall. *Family Fortunes: Men and Women of the English Middle Class, 1780–1850*. Chicago: University of Chicago Press, 1987.

Davies, Andrew. *Leisure, Gender and Poverty: Working-Class Culture in Salford and Manchester, 1900–1939*. Buckingham: Open University Press, 1992.

———. "These Viragoes Are No Less Cruel Than the Lads: Young Women, Gangs and Violence in Late Victorian Manchester and Salford." *British Journal of Criminology* 39, no. 1 (1999): 72–89.

———. "Youth Gangs, Masculinity and Violence in Late Victorian Manchester and Salford." *Journal of Social History* 32, no. 2 (winter 1998): 349–69.

Davies, Owen. "Methodism, the Clergy and the Popular Belief in Witchcraft and Magic." *History* 82, no. 26 (April 1997): 252–65.

Davis, Jennifer. "Jennings Buildings and the Royal Borough: The Construction of the Underclass in Mid-Victorian England." In *Metropolis London: Histories and Representations since 1800*, edited by David Feldman and Gareth Stedman Jones. London: Routledge, 1989.

Davis, Margaret Llewelyn, ed. *Life as We Have Known It*. New York: Norton, 1974.

Davis, Natalie Zemon. "Some Tasks and Themes in the Study of Popular Religion." In *The Pursuit of Holiness in Late Medieval and Renaissance Religion*, edited by Charles Trinkhaus with Heiko Oberman. Leiden: E. J. Brill, 1974.

Davis, Rupert. *Methodism.* Harmondsworth, Middlesex: Penguin Books, 1963.

Dayton, Donald W. *Discovering an Evangelical Heritage.* New York: Harper & Row, 1976.

———, ed. *Holiness Tracts Defending the Ministry of Women.* New York: Garland, 1985.

deVries, Jacqueline R. "Transforming the Pulpit: Preaching and Prophecy in the British Women's Suffrage Movement." In *Women Preachers and Prophets through Two Millennia of Christianity,* edited by Beverly Mayne and Pamela J. Walker. Berkeley: University of California Press, 1998.

Dingle, A. E. "Drink and the Working-Class Standard of Living, 1870–1914." *Economic History Review* 25, no. 4 (November 1972): 608–22.

Dunn, Samuel. *Christian Theology by Adam Clarke with a Life of the Author.* London: Thomas Tegg and Son, 1835.

Dyos, H. J. *Exploring the Urban Past: Essays in Urban History.* Cambridge: Cambridge University Press, 1982.

Epstein, Daniel Mark. *Sister Aimee: The Life of Aimee Semple McPherson.* New York: Harcourt Brace Jovanovich, 1993.

Epstein, James. "Understanding the Cap of Liberty: Symbolic Practice and Social Conflict in Early Nineteenth Century England." *Past and Present* 122 (1989): 75–118.

Fairbank, Jenty. *Booth's Boots: Social Service Beginnings in the Salvation Army.* London: Salvation Army Publishing, 1983.

Feldman, David, and Gareth Stedman Jones, eds. *Metropolis London: Histories and Representations since 1800.* London: Routledge, 1989.

Field, Clive. "Adam and Eve: Gender in the English Free Church Constituency." *Journal of Ecclesiastical History* 44, no. 1 (January 1993): 63–79.

——— "Methodism in London, 1850 1920: A Social and Sociological Study." Ph.D. thesis, Oxford University, 1974.

Fraser, W. Hamish. *The Coming of the Mass Market, 1850–1914.* Hamden, Conn.: Archon, and London: Macmillan, 1981.

Fredricksen, Paula. "Paul and Augustine: Conversion Narratives, Orthodox Traditions and the Retrospective Self." *Journal of Theological Studies* 37, no. 1 (1986): 3–34.

Frith, C. B. *Constance Louisa Maynard: Mistress of Westfield College.* London: Allen and Unwin, 1949.

Gagnier, Regina. *Subjectivities: A History of Self-Representation in Britain, 1832–1920.* Oxford: Oxford University Press, 1991.

Galbraith, Gretchen. *Reading Lives: Reconstructing Childhood, Books, and Schools in Britain, 1870–1920.* London: Macmillan, 1997.

Gardner, Viv, and Susan Rutherford, eds. *The New Woman and Her Sisters: Feminism and Theatre, 1850–1914.* London: Harvester Wheatsheaf, 1992.

Garrett, Clarke. *Respectable Folly: Millenarians and the French Revolution in France and England.* Baltimore: Johns Hopkins University Press, 1975.

Garside, Peter. "London and the Home Counties." In *The Cambridge Social History of Britain,* edited by F.M.L. Thompson. Cambridge: Cambridge University Press, 1990.

Gilbert, A. D. *Religion and Society in Industrial England: Church, Chapel and Social Change*. New York: Longman, 1976.

Gilkes, Cheryl Townsend. "The Politics of 'Silence': Dual-Sex Political Systems and Women's Traditions of Conflict in African-American Religion." In *African-American Christianity: Essays in History*, edited by Paul E. Johnson. Berkeley: University of California Press, 1994.

———. "Together and in Harness: Women's Traditions in the Sanctified Church." *Signs* 10, no. 41 (1985): 678–99.

Gillespie, V. Bailey. *The Dynamics of Religious Conversion*. Birmingham, Ala.: Religious Education Press, 1991.

Gillis, John R. *For Better, for Worse: British Marriage, 1600–the Present*. Oxford: Oxford University Press, 1985.

Gilroy, Paul. *The Black Atlantic: Modernity and Double Consciousness*. Cambridge, Mass.: Harvard University Press, 1993.

Girton College. *The Girton College Register, 1869–1946*. Cambridge: Privately Printed for Girton College, 1946.

Gleadle, Kathryn. *The Early Feminists: Radical Unitarians and the Emergence of the Women's Rights Movement, 1831–1851*. New York: St. Martin's Press, 1995.

Gorham, Deborah. "The 'Maiden Tribute of Modern Babylon' Reexamined: Child Prostitution and the Idea of Childhood in Late-Victorian England." *Victorian Studies* 21, no. 3 (spring 1978): 353–79.

———. *The Victorian Girl and the Feminine Ideal*. Bloomington: Indiana University Press, 1982.

Gorn, Elliott J. *The Manly Art: Bare-Knuckle Prize Fighting in America*. Ithaca, N.Y.: Cornell University Press, 1986.

Gosden, P.H.J.H. *The Friendly Society in England, 1815–1875*. New York: Kelley, 1967.

Graham, Dorothy E. "Chosen by God: The Female Itinerants of Early Primitive Methodism." Ph.D. thesis, University of Birmingham, 1986.

Green, Roger J. *Catherine Booth: A Biography of the Cofounder of the Salvation Army*. Grand Rapids, Mich.: Baker, 1996.

Greenwood, M., W. J. Martin, and W. T. Russell. "Deaths by Violence, 1837–1937." *Journal of the Royal Statistical Society* 104, pt. 2 (1941): 146–71.

Greven, Philip. *The Protestant Temperament: Patterns of Child-Rearing, Religious Experience, and Self in Early America*. New York: Knopf, 1977.

Haggard, Rider. *Regeneration: Being an Account of the Social Work of the Salvation Army in Great Britain*. London: Longman, Green, 1910.

Halevy, Elie. *History of the English People in the Nineteenth Century*. 5 vols. 1913. Reprint, London: Ernest Benn, 1960.

Haley, Bruce. *The Healthy Body and Victorian Culture*. Cambridge, Mass.: Harvard University Press, 1978.

Hardesty, Nancy. *Women Called to Witness: Evangelical Feminism in the Nineteenth Century*. Nashville, Tenn.: Abingdon Press, 1984.

Harding, Susan. "Convicted by the Holy Spirit: The Rhetoric of Fundamental Baptist Conversion." *American Ethnologist* 14, no. 1 (February 1987): 167–81.

Hardman, Keith J. *Charles Grandison Finney.* Syracuse, N.Y.: Syracuse University Press, 1987.

Harris, Michael W. *The Rise of Gospel Blues: The Music Of Thomas A. Dorsey in the Urban Church.* New York: Oxford University Press, 1992.

Harrison, Brian. *Drink and the Victorians.* Pittsburgh: University of Pittsburgh Press, 1971.

———. "For Church, Queen and Family: The Girls Friendly Society, 1874–1920." *Past and Present,* no. 61 (November 1973): 107–38.

———. "Pubs." In *The Victorian City: Images and Realities,* edited by H. J. Dyos and Michael Wolff. London: Routledge & Kegan Paul, 1973.

———. "Religion and Recreation in Nineteenth Century England." *Past and Present* 38 (December 1967): 98–125.

———. "State Intervention and Moral Reform." *Pressure from Without in Early Victorian England,* edited by Patricia Hollis. New York: St. Martin's Press, 1974.

Harrison, J.F.C. *The Second Coming: Popular Millenarianism, 1750–1850.* New Brunswick, N.J.: Rutgers University Press, and London: Routledge & Kegan Paul, 1979.

Heasman, Kathleen. *Evangelicals in Action: An Appraisal of Their Social Work in the Victorian Era.* London: Geoffrey Bles, 1962.

Heeney, Brian. *The Women's Movement in the Church of England, 1850–1930.* Oxford: Clarendon Press, 1988.

Herbert, Trevor, ed. *Bands: The Brass Band Movement in the Nineteenth and Twentieth Centuries.* Buckingham: Open University Press, 1991.

Higginbotham, Ann Rowell. "Respectable Sinner: Salvation Army Rescue Work with Unmarried Mothers, 1884–1914." In *Religion in the Lives of English Women, 1760–1930,* edited by Gail Malmgreen. Bloomington: Indiana University Press, 1986.

———. "The Unmarried Mother and Her Child in Victorian London, 1834–1914." Ph.D. diss., Indiana University, 1985.

Higginbotham, Evelyn Brooks. *Righteous Discontent: The Women's Movement in the Black Baptist Church, 1880–1920.* Cambridge: Harvard University Press, 1993.

Hilton, Boyd. "The Role of Providence in Evangelical Social Thought." In *History, Society and the Churches,* edited by Derek Beales and Geoffrey Best. Cambridge: Cambridge University Press, 1985.

Hobsbawm, E. J. *Primitive Rebels.* New York: Norton, 1959.

———. *Workers.* New York: Pantheon Books, 1984.

Hobsbawm, E. J., and George Rude. *Captain Swing.* Harmondsworth, Middlesex: Penguin Books, 1973.

Hoch-Smith, Judith, and Anita Spring, eds. *Women in Ritual and Symbolic Roles.* New York: Plenum, 1978.

Holt, Richard, ed. *Sport and the Working Class in Modern Britain.* Manchester: Manchester University Press, 1990.

Hopkins, James K. *A Woman to Deliver Her People: Joanna Southcott and English Millenarianism in an Age of Revolution.* Austin: University of Texas Press, 1982.

Horridge, Glenn K. "Invading Manchester: Responses to the Salvation Army, 1878–1900." *Manchester Region History Review* 6 (1992): 16–29.

———. *The Salvation Army, Origins and Early Days: 1865–1900*. Godalming: Ammonite Books, 1993.

Howe, Daniel Walker. "The Decline of Calvinism: An Approach to Its Study." *Comparative Studies in Society and History* 13, no. 3 (June 1972): 306–27.

Hughes, Richard, ed. *The American Quest for the Primitive Church*. Urbana: University of Illinois Press, 1988.

Humez, Jean. "'My Spirit Eye': Some Functions of Visionary Experience in the Lives of Five Black Women Preachers, 1810–1880." In *Women and the Structure of Society*, edited by Barbara Harris and JoAnn McNamara. Durham, N.C.: Duke University Press, 1984.

Humphries, Stephen. *Hooligans or Rebels? An Oral History of Working-Class Childhood and Youth, 1889–1939*. Oxford: Basil Blackwell, 1981.

Hutch, Richard H. *The Meaning of Lives: Biography, Autobiography and the Spiritual Quest*. London: Cassell, 1997.

Inglis, K. S. *Churches and the Working Classes in Victorian England*. London: Routledge & Kegan Paul, 1963.

Jackson, Louise A. "'Singing Birds as Well as Soap Suds': The Salvation Army's Work with Sexually Abused Girls in Edwardian England." *Gender and History* 12, no. 1 (2000): 107–26.

Jacob, Naomi. *Our Marie*. London: Hutchinson, 1936.

Jansen, Katherine Ludwig. "Maria Magdalena: Apostolorum Apostola." In *Women Preachers and Prophets through Two Millennia of Christianity*, edited by Beverly Mayne Kienzle and Pamela J. Walker. Berkeley: University of California Press, 1998.

John, Angela, ed. *Unequal Opportunities*. Oxford: Blackwell, 1986.

Johnson, Dale. "The Methodist Quest for an Educated Ministry." *Church History* 51, no. 3 (September 1982): 304–20.

———, ed. *Women in English Religion*. Lewiston, N.Y.: Mellen Press, 1983.

Johnson, Paul E., ed. *African-American Christianity: Essays in History*. Berkeley: University of California Press, 1994.

Jones, Robert W. "The Sight of Creatures Strange to Our Clime: London Zoo and the Consumption of the Exotic." *Journal of Victorian Culture* 2, no. 1 (spring 1997): 1–26.

Jones, W. H. *History of the Wesleyan Reform Union*. London: Epworth Press, 1952.

Joyce, Patrick. *Visions of the People: Industrial England and the Question of Class, 1848–1914*. Cambridge: Cambridge University Press, 1991.

Juster, Susan, and Lisa MacFarlane. *A Mighty Baptism: Race, Gender and the Creation of American Protestantism*. Ithaca, N.Y.: Cornell University Press, 1996.

Keating, P. J. "Fact and Fiction in the East End." In *The Victorian City: Images and Realities*, vol. 2, edited by H. J. Dyos and Michael Wolff. London: Routledge & Kegan Paul, 1973.

Kelley, Robin D. G. *Race Rebels: Culture, Politics and the Black Working Class*. New York: Free Press, 1994.

Kent, John. "Feelings and Festivals: An Interpretation of Some Working-Class Re-

ligious Attitudes." In *The Victorian City: Images and Realities*, vol. 2, edited by H. J. Dyos and Michael Wolff. London: Routledge & Kegan Paul, 1973.
———. *Holding the Fort: Studies in Victorian Revivalism*. London: Epworth Press, 1978.

Kerr, Hugh, and John Mulder. *Conversions: The Christian Experience*. Grand Rapids, Mich.: Eerdmans, 1983.

Kew, Clifford W. *Catherine Booth: Her Continuing Relevance*. London: Salvation Army, 1990.

Kienzle, Beverly Mayne. "The Prostitute Preacher: Patterns of Polemic against Medieval Waldensian Women Preachers." In *Women Preachers and Prophets through Two Millennia of Christianity*, edited by Beverly Mayne Kienzle and Pamela J. Walker. Berkeley: University of California Press, 1998.

King, Karen L. "Afterword: Voices of the Spirit." In *Women Preachers and Prophets through Two Millennia of Christianity*, edited by Beverly Mayne Kienzle and Pamela J. Walker. Berkeley: University of California Press, 1998.

Knox, Ronald. *Enthusiasm: A Chapter in the History of Religion*. Oxford: Oxford University Press, 1950.

Koditschek, Theodore. *Class Formation and Urban Industrial Society: Bradford, 1750–1850*. Cambridge: Cambridge University Press, 1990.

Koven, Seth. "Dr Barnardo's 'Artistic Fictions': Photography, Sexuality and the Ragged Child in Victorian London." *Radical History Review* 69 (1997): 6–45.

Krueger, Christine L. *The Reader's Repentance: Women Preachers, Women Writers and Nineteenth Century Social Discourse*. Chicago: University of Chicago Press, 1992.

Kselman, Thomas, ed. *Belief in History*. Notre Dame, Ind.: University of Notre Dame Press, 1991.

Lambert, Frank. *"Pedlar in Divinity": George Whitefield and the TransAtlantic Revivals, 1737–1770*. Princeton, N.J.: Princeton University Press, 1994.

Laqueur, Thomas W. *Religion and Respectability: Sunday Schools and Working Class Culture*. New Haven, Conn.: Yale University Press, 1976.

Lauer, Laura. "Women in British Nonconformity, ca. 1880–1920: With Special Reference to the Society of Friends, Baptist Union and Salvation Army." Ph.D. thesis, Oxford University, 1998.

Lawless, Elaine J. *Handmaidens of the Lord: Pentecostal Women Preachers and Tradition Religion*. Philadelphia: University of Pennsylvania Press, 1988.

Lawrence, Jon. "Popular Radicalism and Socialist Revival in Britain." *Journal of British Studies* 31 (April 1992): 163–86.

Lee, Alan. "Some Aspects of the Working-Class Response to Jews in Britain, 1880–1914." In *Hosts, Immigrants and Minorities*, edited by Kenneth Kamm. London: St. Martin's Press, 1980.

Lees, Lynn. *Exiles of Erin: Irish Migrants in Victorian London*. Ithaca, N.Y.: Cornell University Press, 1979.

Levine, Lawrence. *Black Culture, Black Consciousness: Afro-American Folk Thought from Slavery to Freedom*. New York: Oxford University Press, 1977.

Lewis, Donald. *Lighten Their Darkness: The Evangelical Mission to Working-Class London, 1828–1860*. London: Greenwood Press, 1986.

Lewis, Jane. *The Voluntary Sector, the State and Social Work in Britain: The Char-*

ity Organisation Society/Family Welfare Association since 1869. London: Edward Elgar, 1995.

———. *Women in England, 1870–1950*. Bloomington: Indiana University Press, 1984.

Lewis, Sarah. *Women's Mission*. 10th ed. London: John W. Parker, 1842.

Liddington, Jill, and Jill Norris. *One Hand Tied Behind Us: The Rise of the Women's Suffrage Movement*. London: Virago, 1978.

L.N.R. [Mrs. Ellen Raynard]. *The Book and Its Story: A Narrative for the Young on the Occasion of the Jubilee of the British and Foreign Bible Society*. London: Samuel Bagster and Sons, 1853.

Loveland, Anne C. "Domesticity and Religion in the Antebellum Period: The Career of Phoebe Palmer." *Historian* 39 (1977): 455–71.

Lown, Judy. *Women and Industrialization: Gender and Work in Nineteenth Century England*. Cambridge: Polity Press, 1990.

Luker, David. "Revivalism in Theory and Practice: The Case of Cornish Methodism." *Journal of Ecclesiastical History* 37, no. 3 (October 1986): 603–19.

Mack, Phyllis. "Gender and Spirituality in Early English Quakerism." In *Witnesses for Change: Quaker Women over Three Centuries*, edited by Elisabeth Potts Brown and Susan Mosher Stuard. New Brunswick, N.J.: Rutgers University Press, 1989.

———. *Visionary Women: Ecstatic Prophecy in Seventeenth-Century England*. Berkeley: University of California Press, 1992.

MacWilliam, Rohan. "Radicalism and Popular Culture: The Tichbourne Case and the Politics of 'Fair Play,' 1867–1886." In *Currents of Radicalism,* edited by Eugenio Biagini and Alastair Reid. Cambridge: Cambridge University Press, 1991.

Malcolmson, Patricia. *English Laundresses: A Social History, 1850–1930*. Urbana: University of Illinois Press, 1986.

Malmgreen, Gail. *Religion in the Lives of English Women, 1760–1930*. Bloomington: University of Indiana Press, 1986.

Mappen, Ellen F. "Strategists for Change: Social Feminist Approaches to the Problems of Women's Work." In *Unequal Opportunities,* edited by Angela John. Oxford: Blackwell, 1986.

Marks, Lynne. "The Knights of Labour and the Salvation Army: Religion and Working-Class Culture in Ontario, 1882–1890." *Labour/Le Travail* 28 (fall 1991): 89–127.

Martin, David. *The Religious and the Secular*. New York: Schocken Books, 1969.

Mason, Michael. *The Making of Victorian Sexuality*. Oxford: Oxford University Press, 1994.

Mason, Tony, ed. *Sport in Britain*. Cambridge: Cambridge University Press, 1989.

Mayne, Alan. *The Imagined Slum: Newspaper Representation in Three Cities, 1870–1914*. Leicester: Leicester University Press, 1993.

McClelland, Keith. "Time to Work, Time to Live: Some Aspects of Work and the Reformation of Class in Britain, 1850–1880." In *The Historical Meanings of Work,* edited by Patrick Joyce. Cambridge: Cambridge University Press, 1987.

McClory, Robert. "Women of the Cloth." *Reader* 23, no. 45 (August 12, 1994): 14–18.

McCord, Norman. *Northeast England: The Region's Development, 1760–1960.* London: Batsford, 1979.

McKibbin, Ross. "Working-Class Gambling in Britain, 1880–1939." *Past and Present,* no. 82 (February 1979): 147–78.

McKinley, Edward H. *Marching to Glory: The History of the Salvation Army in the United States, 1880–1992.* Grand Rapids, Mich.: Eerdmans, 1995.

McLeod, Hugh. *Class and Religion in the Late Victorian City.* London: Croom Helm, 1974.

———, ed. *European Religion in the Age of Great Cities, 1830–1930.* London: Routledge, 1995.

———. "New Perspectives on Victorian Working-Class Religion: The Oral Evidence." *Oral History* 14, no. 1 (1986): 31–49.

———. *Piety and Poverty: Working-Class Religion in Berlin, London and New York, 1870–1914.* New York: Holmes & Meier, 1996.

———. *Religion and the Working Class in Nineteenth Century Britain.* London: Macmillan, 1984.

McLoughlin, William G. *Modern Revivalism: Charles Grandison Finney to Billy Graham.* New York: Ronald Press, 1959.

Meacham, Standish. *Toynbee Hall and Social Reform, 1880–1914.* New Haven, Conn.: Yale University Press, 1987.

Mews, Stuart. "The General and the Bishops: Alternative Responses to Dechristianization." In *Later Victorian Britain, 1867–1900,* edited by T. R. Gourvish and Alan O'Day. London: Macmillan Education, 1988.

Milburn, G. E. *Church and Chapel in Sunderland, 1780–1914.* Occasional Paper 4, Department of Geography and History, Sunderland Polytechnic, 1988.

———. "Tensions in Primitive Methodism in the Eighteen Seventies." *Proceedings of the Wesley Historical Society* 40, pts. 4 and 5 (February and June 1976): 93–101.

Miller, Lyn. "Chastening: Susan Warner's Theology of Pleasure in *Wide, Wide World.*" Unpublished paper, Divinity School, Harvard University, 1993.

Mitchell, Hannah. *The Hard Way Up: The Autobiography of Hannah Mitchell.* London: Faber, 1968.

Moore, R. Laurence. *Selling God: American Religion in the Marketplace of Culture.* New York: Oxford University Press, 1994.

Mowat, Charles Loch. *The Charity Organisation Society, 1869–1913.* London: Methuen, 1961.

Moyles, R. G. *A Bibliography of Salvation Army Literature in English, 1865–1987.* Lewiston, N.Y.: Mellon Press, 1988.

Mudie-Smith, Richard, ed. *The Religious Life of London.* London: Hodder & Stoughton, 19

Murdoch, Norman. "Evangelical Sources of Salvation Army Doctrine." *Evangelical Quarterly* 59, no. 3 (July 1987): 235–44.

———. "Female Ministry in the Thought and Work of Catherine Booth." *Church History* 53 (September 1984): 348–62.

———. *Origins of the Salvation Army.* Knoxville: University of Tennessee Press, 1994.

————. "The Salvation Army: An Anglo-American Revivalist Social Mission."
    Ph.D. diss., University of Cincinnati, 1985.
Murphy, Howard R. "The Ethical Revolt against Christian Orthodoxy in Early
    Victorian England." *American Historical Review* 60, no. 4 (July 1955):
    800–817.
Myers, William H. *God's Yes Was Louder Than My No: Rethinking the African
    American Call to Ministry.* Grand Rapids, Mich.: Eerdmans, 1994.
Mynot, Edward. "Frank Crossely—Saint or Sinner?" *Manchester Region His-
    tory Review* 11 (1997): 52–59.
Nead, Lynda. *Myths of Sexuality: Representations of Women in Victorian
    Britain.* Oxford: Blackwell, 1988.
Nettel, Reginald. "Folk Elements in Nineteenth-Century Puritanism." *Folklore*
    80 (winter 1969): 272–85.
Neuburg, Victor E. *Chapbooks: Guide to Reference Material on English, Scot-
    tish and American Chapbook Literature of the Eighteenth and Nineteenth
    Centuries.* 2d ed. London: Woborn Press, 1972.
Nicolson, William. *The Romance of the War Cry.* London: Salvationist Pub-
    lishing, 1929.
Noll, Mark, David Bebbington, and George Rawlyk, eds. *Evangelicalism:
    Comparative Studies of Popular Protestantism in North America, the Brit-
    ish Isles and Beyond, 1700–1900.* New York: Oxford University Press,
    1994.
Nord, Deborah Epstein. *Walking the Victorian Streets: Women, Representation
    and the City.* Ithaca, N.Y.: Cornell University Press, 1995.
Norman, E. R. *Anti-Catholicism in Victorian England.* London: Allen and Un-
    win, 1968.
Norton, Mary Beth. "My Resting Reaping Times: Sarah Osborn's Defense of
    Her Unfeminine Activities, 1767." *Signs* 2, no. 2 (1976): 515–29.
Numbers, Ronald, and Rennie Schoepflin. "Ministries of Healing: Mary Baker
    Eddy, Ellen G. White and the Religion of Health." In *Women and Health in
    America,* edited by Judith Walzer Leavitt. Madison: University of Wisconsin
    Press, 1984.
Nye, Robert. "The Bio-medical Origins of Urban Sociology." *Journal of Con-
    temporary History* 20, no. 4 (October 1985): 659–75.
Obelkevich, James. *Religion and Rural Society: South Lindsey, 1825–1875.* Ox-
    ford: Clarendon Press, 1976.
Obelkevich, Jim, Lyndal Roper, and Raphael Samuel, eds. *Disciplines of Faith.*
    London: Routledge & Kegan Paul, 1986.
Outler, Albert C., ed. *John Wesley.* New York: Oxford University Press, 1964.
Owen, Alex. *The Darkened Room: Women, Power and Spiritualism in Late Vic-
    torian England.* London: Virago Press, 1989.
Parkin, Christine. "A Woman's Place: Catherine Booth and Female Ministry."
    In *Catherine Booth: Her Continuing Relevance,* edited by Clifford W. Kew.
    London: Salvation Army, 1990.
Parsons, Gerald. "A Question of Meaning: Religion and Working-Class Life."
    In *Religion in Victorian Britain,* vol. 2, edited by Gerald Parsons. Manches-
    ter: Manchester University Press, 1988.

Paz, D. G. *Popular Anti-Catholicism in Mid-Victorian England*. Stanford, Calif.: Stanford University Press, 1992.

Pearson, Michael. *The Age of Consent*. Newton Abbott, Devon: David and Charles, 1972.

Peterson, Linda. *Victorian Autobiography: The Tradition of Self-Interpretation*. New Haven, Conn.: Yale University Press, 1986.

Philips, Mrs. *A Dictionary of Employments Open to Women*. London: Women's Institute, 1898.

Pike's Eastbourne Blue Book. N.p., 1894–95.

Plowden, Alison. *The Case of Eliza Armstrong: A Child Bought for £5*. London: BBC, 1974.

Prochaska, F. K. "Body and Soul: Bible Nurses and the Poor in Victorian London." *Historical Research* 60, no. 143 (October 1987): 336–48.

———. "Female Philanthropy and Domestic Service in Victorian England." *Bulletin of the Institute of Historical Research* 54 (1981): 80–82.

———. "A Mother's Country: Mothers' Meetings and Family Welfare in Britain, 1850–1950." *History* 74, no. 242 (October 1989): 379–99.

———. *Women and Philanthropy in Nineteenth-Century England*. Oxford: Clarendon Press, 1980.

Proctor, Tammy. "(Uni)forming Youth: Girl Guides and Boy Scouts in Britain, 1908–1939." *History Workshop Journal* 45 (1998): 103–34.

Proctor-Smith, Marjorie. *Women in Shaker Community and Worship*. Lewiston, N.Y.: Mellen Press, 1985.

Rack, Henry D. "The Decline of the Class Meeting and the Problem of Church Membership in Nineteenth-Century Wesleyanism." *Proceedings of the Wesley Historical Society* 39, pt. 1 (February 1973): 12–20.

Rapp, Dean. "The British Salvation Army, the Early Film Industry and Urban Working-Class Adolescents, 1897–1918." *Twentieth Century British History* 7, no. 2 (1996): 157–88.

Raser, Harold E. *Phoebe Palmer: Her Life and Thought*. Lewiston, N.Y.: Mellen Press, 1987.

Reed, John Shelton. "Ritualism Rampant in East London: Anglo-Catholicism and the Urban Poor." *Victorian Studies* 31, no. 3 (spring 1983): 375–404.

Reid, Douglas. "Beasts and Brutes: Popular Blood Sports c. 1760–1860." In *Sport and the Working Class in Modern Britain,* edited by Richard Holt. Manchester: Manchester University Press, 1990.

———. "Popular Theatre in Victorian Birmingham." In *Performance and Politics in Popular Drama,* edited by David Bradbury, Louis James, and Bernard Sharratt. Cambridge: Cambridge University Press, 1980.

Rhemick, John Rossario. "The Theology of a Movement: The Salvation Army in Its Formative Years." Ph.D. diss., Northwestern University, 1984.

Richards, Thomas. *The Commodity Culture of Victorian England*. Stanford, Calif.: Stanford University Press, 1990.

Rivers, Isabel. "'Strangers and Pilgrims': Sources and Patterns of Methodist Narrative." In *Augustan Worlds*. Leicester: Leicester University Press, 1978.

Roberts, Elizabeth. *A Woman's Place: An Oral History of Working-Class Women, 1890–1940*. Oxford: Basil Blackwell, 1984.

Robertson, Roland. "The Salvation Army: The Persistence of Sectarianism." In *Patterns of Sectarianism: Organisation and Ideology in Social and Religious Movements,* edited by Bryan R. Wilson. London: Heinemann, 1967.

Robinson, Barbara. "Bodily Compassion: Values and Identity Formation in the Salvation Army, 1880–1900." Ph.D. thesis, University of Ottawa, 1999.

Roper, Lyndal. *Holy Household: Women and Morals in Reformation Augsburg.* Oxford: Clarendon Press, 1989.

Roper, Michael, and John Tosh, eds. *Manful Assertions.* London: Routledge, 1991.

Rose, E. A. "The Methodist New Connexion, 1797–1907." *Proceedings of the Wesley Historical Society* 48 (October 1990): 241–53.

Rose, Millicent. *The East End of London.* London: Cresset Press, 1951.

Rose, Sonya. *Limited Livelihoods: Gender and Class in Nineteenth Century England.* Berkeley: University of California Press, 1992.

Rosell, Garth M. "Charles G. Finney: His Place in the Stream." In *The Evangelical Tradition in America,* edited by Leonard Sweet. Nashville, Tenn.: Mercer University Press, 1984.

Rosenthal, Michael. *The Character Factory: Baden-Powell and the Origins of the Boy Scout Movement.* New York: Pantheon Books, 1986.

Ross, Ellen. "Fierce Questions and Taunts: Married Life in Working-Class London, 1870–1914." In *Metropolis London: Histories and Representations since 1800,* edited by David Feldman and Gareth Stedman Jones. London: Routledge, 1989.

———. *Love and Toil: Motherhood in Outcast London.* New York: Oxford University Press, 1993.

———. "'Not the Sort That Would Sit on the Doorstep': Respectability in Pre-World War I London Neighbourhoods." *International Labor and Working-Class History,* no. 27 (spring 1985): 37–59.

———. "Survival Networks: Women's Neighbourhood Sharing in London before World War One." *History Workshop Journal,* no. 5 (spring 1983): 4–27.

Rubenstein, David. *Before the Suffragettes: Women's Emancipation in the 1890s.* New York: St. Martin's Press, and Brighton, Sussex: Harvester Press, 1986.

Rule, John. "Methodism, Popular Beliefs and Village Culture in Cornwall, 1800–1850." In *Popular Culture and Custom in Nineteenth Century England,* edited by Robert Storch. London: Croom Helm, 1982.

Runyon, Theodore, ed. *Sanctification and Liberation: Liberation Theologies in Light of the Wesleyan Tradition.* Nashville, Tenn.: Abingdon Press, 1981.

Ryan, Mary P. *The Cradle of the Middle Class: The Family in Oneida County New York, 1790–1865.* New York: Cambridge University Press, 1981.

———. "A Women's Awakening: Evangelical Religion and the Families of Utica, New York, 1800–1840." In *Women in American Religion,* edited by Janet Wilson James. Philadelphia: University of Pennsylvania Press, 1980.

Sandall, Robert. *The History of the Salvation Army.* Vols. 1–3. 1947, 1950, 1955. Reprint, London: Salvation Army, 1979.

Scott, James. *Domination and the Art of Resistance.* New Haven, Conn.: Yale University Press, 1990.

Scott, Patrick. "Victorian Religious Periodicals: Fragments That Remain." In *The*

Materials, Sources and Methods of Ecclesiastical History, edited by Derek Baker. Oxford: Basil Blackwell, 1975.

Sebestyen, Amanda. "Two Women from Two Worlds." *Spare Rib* 155 (June 1985): 21–24.

Senelick, Laurence. *British Music Hall, 1840–1923.* Hamden, Conn.: Archon Books, 1981.

Shipley, Stan. "Boxing." In *Sport in Britain,* edited by Tony Mason. Cambridge: Cambridge University Press, 1989.

Smedley's Bath Book. Manchester and London: John Heywood, 1916.

Smith, Bonnie. *Changing Lives: Women in European History since 1700.* Lexington, Mass.: Heath, 1989.

Smith, Joan. "Class, Skill and Sectarianism in Glasgow and Liverpool, 1880–1914." In *Class, Power and Social Structure in British Nineteenth Century Towns,* edited by R. J. Morris. Leicester: Leicester University Press, 1986.

Smith, Timothy L. "Holiness and Radicalism in Nineteenth Century America." In *Sanctification and Liberation,* edited by Theodore Runyon. Nashville, Tenn.: Abingdon Press, 1981.

Sobel, Mechal. *Trabelin' On: The Slave Journey to an Afro-Baptist Faith.* Princeton, N.J.: Princeton University Press, 1988.

Springhall, John. "Building Character in the British Boy: The Attempt to Extend Christian Manliness to Working-Class Adolescents, 1880–1914." In *Manliness and Morality: Middle-Class Masculinity in Britain and America,* edited by J. A. Mangan and James Walvin. Manchester: Manchester University Press, 1987.

Stallybrass, Peter, and Allon White. *The Politics and Poetics of Transgression.* London: Methuen, 1986.

Stedman Jones, Gareth. *Outcast London: A Study in the Relationship between the Classes in Victorian Society.* Oxford: Clarendon Press, 1971.

———. "Working-Class Culture and Working-Class Politics in London, 1870–1914: Notes on the Remaking of a Working Class." *Journal of Social History* 7, no. 4 (summer 1974): 460–507.

Steedman, Carolyn. *Landscape for a Good Woman.* London: Virago Press, 1986.

Stignant, P. "Wesleyan Methodism and Working Class Radicalism in the North, 1792–1821." *Northern History* 6 (1971): 98–116.

Storch, Robert D. "The Policeman as Domestic Missionary: Urban Discipline and Popular Culture in Northern England, 1850–1880." *Journal of Social History* 9, no. 4 (June 1976): 481–509.

Strachey, Ray. *The Cause: A Short History of the Women's Movement in Britain.* London: G. Bell, 1928. Reprint, London: Virago, 1978.

Strang, Jillian. "Reclaim London: Salvation Army Rescue Missions, 1865–1895." Paper presented at the North American Conference on British Studies, 1998.

Summerfield, Penelope. "The Effingham Arms and the Empire: Deliberate Selection in the Evolution of Music Hall in London." In *Popular Culture and Class Conflict, 1590–1914,* edited by Eileen Yeo and Stephen Yeo. Sussex: Harvester Press, 1981.

Symondson, Anthony, ed. *The Victorian Crisis of Faith.* London: SPCK, 1970.

Taiz, Lillian. "Applying the Devil's Works in a Holy Cause: Working-Class Popular Culture and the Salvation Army in the United States, 1879–1900." *Religion and American Culture* 7, no. 2 (1997): 195–223.

———. "Hallelujah Lasses in the Battle for Souls: Working- and Middle-Class Women in the Salvation Army in the United States, 1872–1896." *Journal of Women's History* 9, no. 2 (1997): 84–105.

Taves, Ann. "Knowing through the Body: Dissociative Religious Experiences in the African- and British-American Methodist Traditions." *Journal of Religion* 73, no. 2 (April 1993): 200–222.

Taylor, Barbara. *Eve and the New Jerusalem: Socialism and Feminism in the Nineteenth Century.* London: Virago, 1983.

———. "Religion, Radicalism and Fantasy." *History Workshop Journal* 39 (1995): 102–12.

Thom, Deborah. *Nice Girls and Rude Girls: Women Workers in World War I.* London: Tauris, 1998.

Thomas, Hilah F., and Rosemary Skinner Keller, eds. *Women in New Worlds.* Nashville, Tenn.: Abingdon Press, 1981.

Thompson, E. P. "Blood, Fire and Unction." *New Society* 5, no. 128 (1965): 25–26.

———. *Customs in Common.* London: Penguin Books, 1991.

———. *The Making of the English Working Class.* London: Penguin Books, 1968.

———. *Witness against the Beast: William Blake and the Moral Law.* Cambridge: Cambridge University Press, 1993.

Thompson, Paul. *Socialists, Liberals and Labour: The Struggle for London.* London: Routledge & Kegan Paul, 1967.

Tickner, Lisa. *The Spectacle of Women: Imagery of the Suffrage Campaign, 1907–1914.* Chicago: University of Chicago Press, 1988.

Tolen, Rachel J. "Colonizing and Transforming the Criminal Tribesmen: The Salvation Army in British India." *American Ethnologist* 18, no. 1 (February 1991): 106–25.

Trinder, Barrie. *The Industrial Revolution in Shropshire.* London: Phillimore, 1973.

Ullman, Chana. *The Transformed Self: The Psychology of Religious Conversion.* New York: Plenum, 1989.

Unsworth, Madge. *Maiden Tribute: A Study in Voluntary Social Service.* London: Salvationist Publishing, 1949.

Valenze, Deborah. *Prophetic Sons and Daughters: Female Preaching and Popular Religion in Industrial England.* Princeton, N.J.: Princeton University Press, 1985.

Vance, Norman. *The Sinews of the Spirit: The Ideal of Christian Manliness in Victorian Literature and Religious Thought.* Cambridge: Cambridge University Press, 1985.

Vernon, James. *Politics and the People: A Study in English Political Culture, c.1815–1867.* Cambridge: Cambridge University Press, 1993.

Vicinus, Martha. "Helpless and Unfriended: Nineteenth Century Domestic Melodrama." *New Literary History* 13, no. 1 (1981): 127–43.

———. *Independent Women: Work and Community for Single Women, 1850–1920.* Chicago: University of Chicago Press, 1985.

Vincent, David. *Bread, Knowledge and Freedom: A Study of Nineteenth-Century Working-Class Autobiography.* London: Europa, 1981.

Walker, Pamela J. "Pulling the Devil's Kingdom Down: Gender and Popular Culture in the Salvation Army, 1865–1890." Ph.D. diss., Rutgers University, 1992.

Walkowitz, Judith R. *City of Dreadful Delight.* Chicago: University of Chicago Press, 1992.

———. *Prostitution and Victorian Society: Women, Class and the State.* Cambridge: Cambridge University Press, 1980.

Wallis, Frank H. *Popular Anti-Catholicism in Mid-Victorian Britain.* Lewiston, N.Y.: Mellon Press, 1993.

Walsh, John. "Methodism and the Common People." In *People's History and Socialist Theory,* edited by Raphael Samuel. London: Routledge & Kegan Paul, 1981.

———. "Methodism and the Mob." In *Popular Belief and Practice,* vol. 8 in *Studies in Church History,* edited by G. J. Cumming and Derek Baker. Cambridge: Cambridge University Press, 1972.

Walton, John K. *The English Seaside Resort: A Social History, 1750–1914.* New York: St. Martin's Press, 1983.

———. "Residential Amenity, Respectable Morality and the Rise of the Entertainment Industry: The Case of Blackpool, 1860–1914." *Literature and History* 1 (March 1975): 62–78.

Walvin, James. *Beside the Seaside.* London: Allen Lane, 1978.

Ward, Christine. "The Social Sources of the Salvation Army, 1865–1890." M. Phil. thesis, Bedford College, University of London, 1970.

Warner, Michael. "Tongues Untied: Memoirs of a Pentecostal Boyhood." *Voice Literary Supplement,* no. 112 (February 1993): 13–15.

Webb, Sidney, and Beatrice Webb. *The Prevention of Destitution.* London: Longman, Green, 1911.

Weightman, Gavin, and Steve Humphries. *The Making of Modern London: 1815–1914.* London: Sidgwick and Jackson, 1983.

Weisner, Merry. "Women's Defense of Their Public Role." In *Women in the Middle Ages and Renaissance,* edited by Mary Beth Rose. Syracuse, N.Y.: Syracuse University Press, 1985.

White, Charles Edward. *The Beauty of Holiness: Phoebe Palmer as Theologian, Revivalist, Feminist and Humanitarian.* Grand Rapids, Mich.: Francis Asbury Press, 1986.

White, Jerry. *Rothschild Buildings: Life in an East End Tenement Block, 1887–1920.* London: Routledge & Kegan Paul, 1980.

———. *The Worst Street in North London: Campbell Bunk Islington, between the Wars.* London: Routledge & Kegan Paul, 1986.

Whorton, James C. *Crusaders for Fitness: The History of American Health Reformers.* Princeton, N.J.: Princeton University Press, 1982.

Wiggins, Arch. *The History of the Salvation Army.* Vols. 4–5. 1964, 1968. Reprint, London: Salvation Army, 1979.

Williams, Sarah C. "The Language of Belief: An Alternative Agenda for the Study of Victorian Working-Class Religion." *Journal of Victorian Culture* 1, no. 2 (1996): 303–17.

————. *Religious Belief and Popular Culture in Southwark, c. 1880–1939*. Oxford: Oxford University Press, 1999.

————. "Urban Popular Culture and the Rites of Passage." In *European Religion in the Age of Great Cities, 1830–1930*, edited by Hugh McLeod. London: Routledge, 1995.

Willis, Paul. *Learning to Labour*. Westmead, Farnborough, Hants: Saxon House, 1977.

Wilson, A. E. *East End Entertainment*. London: Arthur Barker, 1954.

Wilson, Bryan R., ed. *Patterns of Sectarianism: Organisation and Ideology in Social and Religious Movements*. London: Heinemann, 1967.

————. *Religion in Sociological Perspective*. Oxford: Oxford University Press, 1982.

Winston, Diane. *Red Hot and Righteous: The Urban Religion of the Salvation Army* (Cambridge, Mass.: Harvard University Press, 1999).

Winter, James. *London's Teeming Streets, 1830–1914*. London: Routledge, 1993.

Wroth, Warwick. *Cremore and Later London Gardens*. London: Elliot Stock, 1907.

Yeo, Eileen. "Christianity in Chartist Struggle, 1838–1842." *Past and Present*, no. 91 (May 1981): 109–39.

Yeo, Stephen. "A New Life: The Religion of Socialism in Britain, 1883–1896." *History Workshop Journal* 4 (autumn 1977): 5–56.

Zikmund, Barbara Brown. "The Struggle for the Right to Preach." In *Women and Religion in America*, edited by Rosemary Radford Reuther and Rosemary Skinner Keller. San Francisco: Harper & Row, 1981.

Text:	10/13 Sabon
Display:	Sabon
Composition:	Integrated Composition Systems
Printing and binding:	Friesens